A Dictionary of Alchemica

This dictionary documents the rich store-house of alchemical symbolism from the early centuries AD to the late twentieth century, making it available for the use of historians of literary culture, philosophy, science and the visual arts, as well as for those readers with an interest in alchemy and hermeticism. The emphasis is on literary and intellectual references to alchemy in the Western tradition, written in or translated into English. The dictionary focuses most closely on works current in the sixteenth and seventeenth centuries when alchemy flourished, captivating the minds of some of the greatest figures of the day, from Sir Walter Raleigh to Isaac Newton. Each entry includes a definition of the symbol, giving the literal (physical) and figurative (spiritual) meanings, an example of the symbol used in alchemical writing, and a quotation from a literary source. Writers cited range from Shakespeare, Milton and Donne to Vladimir Nabokov and P. G. Wodehouse. Drawing from the unique holdings of the Ferguson Collection at the University of Glasgow, the dictionary offers a representative selection of fifty visual images (graphic woodcuts, copperplate engravings, or hand-painted emblems), some of which have not been reproduced since they first appeared.

LYNDY ABRAHAM is a Research Fellow in the School of English, University of New South Wales. Her books include *Marvell and Alchemy*, and a critical edition of Arthur Dee's *Fasciculus chemicus*. She has published numerous journal articles on the subject of alchemy, specializing in Renaissance studies.

Illustrations from the Ferguson Collection of alchemical books and manuscripts, University of Glasgow Library

A Dictionary of Alchemical Imagery

Lyndy Abraham

CAMBRIDGE
UNIVERSITY PRESS

PUBLISHED BY THE PRESS SYNDICATE OF THE UNIVERSITY OF CAMBRIDGE
The Pitt Building, Trumpington Street, Cambridge, United Kingdom

CAMBRIDGE UNIVERSITY PRESS
The Edinburgh Building, Cambridge CB2 2RU, UK
40 West 20th Street, New York, NY 10011–4211, USA
10 Stamford Road, Oakleigh, VIC 3166, Australia
Ruiz de Alarcón 13, 28014 Madrid, Spain
Dock House, The Waterfront, Cape Town 8001, South Africa

http://www.cambridge.org

First published 1998
Reprinted 2000
First paperback edition 2001

Printed in the United Kingdom at the University Press, Cambridge

Typeset in Lexicon 8.5/12pt (*from the Enschedé Font Foundry*), in QuarkXPress™   [SE]

A catalogue record for this book is available from the British Library

Library of Congress cataloguing in publication data
Abraham, Lyndy.
A dictionary of alchemical imagery / Lyndy Abraham.
     p.   cm.
Includes bibliographical references and index.
ISBN 0 521 63185 8 (hardback)
ISBN 0 521 00000 9 (paperback)
1. Alchemy in literature.   2. Symbolism in literature.
3. European literature–History and criticism.   4. Alchemy–
Dictionaries.   I. Title.
PN56.A44A27   1998
809'.9337–dc21   98-4544   CIP

ISBN 0 521 63185 8 hardback
ISBN 0 521 00000 9 paperback

To Michael Wilding

Contents

Figures

Figures 3, 19, 31 and 39 are reproduced by kind permission of the British Library; figures 7 and 36 by kind permission of the Bodleian Library Oxford; figure 15 by kind permission of the Universitätsbibliothek, Basel; and figure 46 by kind permission of the Bibliotheca Medicea-Laurenziana, Florence.

All other illustrations are taken from books and manuscripts in the Ferguson Collection, Department of Special Collections, University of Glasgow, whose permission is gratefully acknowledged by author and publisher.

Acknowledgements

I am most grateful to the librarians of Special Collections, University of Glasgow, for their expertise and for their generosity in allowing me to use the Ferguson collection of alchemical books and manuscripts as the basis for this book. I would especially like to thank David Weston at Special Collections for his help. I am also grateful to the staffs of the following libraries: the Bodleian Library, Oxford, the British Library, Öffentliche Bibliothek der Universität Basel, Bibliotheca Medicea-Laurenziana, Florence, Fisher Library, University of Sydney, University of New South Wales Library, and the Henry E. Huntington Library, San Marino.

I would like to thank the Australian Research Council for the post-doctoral fellowship which enabled me to do the research for this book. I would also like to thank the School of English at the University of New South Wales, who generously gave me the position of Research Associate to complete the book.

I am grateful to the following people for their help and support: Alison Adams, Christine Alexander, Peter Alexander, Michael Bath, Peter Becky, June Billingham, Mary Chan, Warren Chernaik, Paul Chipchase, Doris and Alf Commins, R. M. Cummings, H. Neville Davies, Allen Debus, Josie Dixon, Wim van Dongen, Lyn and Stephen Edwards, Mark Erickson, Jennifer Gribble, Jenny Harris, the late Joan Hodgson, Kaye Gartner, Achsah Guibbory, Stanton J. Linden, Philip Martin, Adam McLean, Jean-Pierre Mialon, Sabine Mödersheim, Jennifer Nevile, David Norbrook, Brigitta Olubas, Ross Penman, Stephen Rawles, Gay Robinson, Susan Sirc, Nigel Smith, Elizabeth Watson, Shirley Webster, David Weston, Michael Wilding, and Sunny Wilding.

Abbreviations

The abbreviations listed below have been used to refer to frequently occurring books cited throughout the text. A full Bibliography at the end of the Dictionary (pp. 222–38 below) gives details of all books used. Parenthetical page references at the end of a quotation in the Dictionary refer to the source of the quotation which is mentioned at that point by author and title or by title alone if there is no known author. An asterisk beside a word in the text indicates that this word has its own separate entry.

AA	*Artis auriferae quam chemiam vocant*
AC	Saint Thomas Aquinas (attributed), *Aurora consurgens*
AE	Johann Mylius, *The Alchemical Engravings of Mylius*
AF	Michael Maier, *Atalanta fugiens*
ALA	John Read, *The Alchemist in Life, Literature and Art*
AP	Robert M. Schuler, *Alchemical Poetry 1575–1700*
Archidoxis	*Paracelsus his Archidoxis: comprised in ten books*
AS	C. G. Jung, *Alchemical Studies*
Ashm.	Ashmole
BB	Sir George Ripley, *The Bosome Book of Sir George Ripley*
BL	British Library
Bod	Bodleian Library
CC	*Collectanea chymica*
DSP	St Dunstan, *Dunstan of the Stone of the Philosophers* in *Philosophia maturata*
embl.	emblem
EP	Allen G. Debus, *The English Paracelsians*
FC	Arthur Dee, *Fasciculus chemicus* (all page references to this work are to Ashmole's translation of 1650)
FT	*Five Treatises of the Philosophers' Stone*
GU	Glasgow University Library
HE	Nicolas Flamel, *His Exposition of the Hieroglyphicall Figures*
HM	*Hermetic Museum*
JA	Raphael Patai, *The Jewish Alchemists*
Janus	Betty Jo Teeter Dobbs, *The Janus Faces of Genius: The Role of Alchemy in Newton's Thought*
MC	C. G. Jung, *Mysterium coniunctionis*
MP	William Salmon, *Medicina Practica*
OED	*Oxford English Dictionary*
PA	C. G. Jung, *Psychology and Alchemy*
pl.	plate
PS	*Paracelsus: Selected Writings*

PW   *The Hermetic and Alchemical Writings of Aureolus Philippus Theophrastus Bombastus of Hohenheim, called Paracelsus*

RR   Eirenaeus Philalethes, *Ripley Reviv'd: or an Exposition upon Sir George Ripley's Hermetico-Poetical Works*

SB   Artephius, *The Secret Book of Artephius*

TAC   John Read, *Through Alchemy to Chemistry*

TCB   Elias Ashmole (ed.), *Theatrum chemicum Britannicum*

TGH   Robert Fludd, 'Truth's Golden Harrow'

VW(R)   *The Works of Thomas Vaughan*, edited by Alan Rudrum

VW(W)   *The Works of Thomas Vaughan*, edited by A. E. Waite

ZC   *Zoroaster's Cave*, in Raphael Iconius Eglinus, *An Easie Introduction to the Philosophers Magical Gold*

Introduction

The origins of alchemy in Western culture can be traced back to the world of Alexandria and Hellenistic Egypt around 300 BC, when Greek science was flourishing. In Alexandria at this time, the art of alchemy developed in both Graeco-Egyptian and Hebraic cultures. The Arabs became interested in alchemy when they took Alexandria from the Byzantine Empire, and Islamic alchemical practice became well established by AD 750. It was not until the twelfth century that the art of alchemy began to influence European culture, spreading there from the Arabs in Spain and Southern Italy. Pope John XXII's papal bull of 1317 condemned the practice of alchemy, forcing it to retreat underground. By the late sixteenth and early seventeenth centuries, however, it had become an intellectually respectable, if controversial, discipline, and the great passion of the age. At this time alchemy was considered to be a significant scientific and philosophical thought system which provided a mode of perceiving substances, processes, relationships, and the cosmos itself. In its various manifestations – as the inquiry into chemical substances, the search for the new 'chymicall' medicines, the scientific observation of the processes of nature, as an esoteric philosophy and cosmology, and as an exploration of the act of creation itself – alchemy flourished in sixteenth- and seventeenth-century Europe. Alchemical theory was a dynamic force in the various influences which came together to form an intelligent explanation of the world.

Some of the most famous names of the day in England pursued the art of alchemy – Sir Philip Sidney and Sir Edward Dyer, Sidney's sister Mary Herbert, Countess of Pembroke, Sir Walter Raleigh and his half-brother Adrian Gilbert, Henry Percy, ninth Earl of Northumberland, the mathematician Thomas Harriot, Edward Kelly and Dr John Dee, George Villiers, second Duke of Buckingham, Anne, Viscountess Conway, Samuel Hartlib, Isaac Newton, and King Charles II. The rising physicians of the day were the Paracelsian alchemists, and the revolutionary new chemical medicines, which began to replace traditional Galenic herbal practice, were introduced into the pharmacopoeia in the late sixteenth and early seventeenth centuries in England by these pioneering 'chymists'. It is becoming increasingly clear that Hermetic and alchemical thought deeply influenced Elizabethan and Jacobean culture, and that writers of the stature of Shakespeare, Jonson, Donne, Marvell, Cleveland, Milton and Dryden drew on the rich source of alchemical imagery for their writing. The satiric reference to alchemy in the work of such writers as Thomas Nashe, Ben Jonson and John Donne is well known. But alchemical metaphor was used to express deep philosophical and spiritual truths as frequently as it was used as a subject for satire and comedy. When, in 'Resurrection Imperfect', Donne wrote of the crucified Christ as 'all gold when he lay down' but 'All tincture' when he rose, capable of transmuting 'leaden and iron wills to good', he was using alchemical terms to express a deep spiritual vision of the transforming power of Christ's love. And when, in *Paradise Lost,* Milton wrote of the 'arch-chemic sun' whose fields and rivers 'Breathe forth elixir pure' and run 'potable gold' (3.606–9), it is a living, working, spiritual alchemy that is referred to, a spiritual alchemy in contrast to the material alchemy which 'here below / Philosophers in vain so long have sought' (3.595–612). Alchemy provided a vibrant model for denoting physical, psychological, spiritual and cosmological concepts, and the writers of this era naturally drew on its rich symbolism for their art.

The impact of alchemical concepts and imagery on culture has not been confined to late Renaissance Europe. From King Lear's 'Ripeness is all' to the young golfer in P. G. Wodehouse, seeking the secret of the game 'like an alchemist on the track of the Philosopher's Stone', alchemy has provided abundant material for the creative imagination. As alchemy separated itself into a materialist chemistry and an esoteric spiritual discipline in the eighteenth century, what had been a more or less unified 'art' divided into two strands. The materialist chemical project continued, and alchemy's heritage is still present in terms like 'alcohol' and 'bain-Marie', as well as in the discovery of such substances as nitric acid, hydrochloric acid, ammonia, sugar of lead and some compounds of antimony. Nevertheless, the esoteric, spiritual component of alchemy kept on, and has continued to provide a major source of material for research in the field of psychology by such thinkers as Herbert Silberer, Carl Jung and Marie-Louise von Franz in the twentieth century, and for writers and visual artists from Dryden, Pope, Goethe, Joseph Wright of Derby and Browning, through to the nineteenth-century Symbolists, Victor Hugo, Marcus Clarke, W. B. Yeats, August Strindberg, Antonin Artaud, Max Ernst, Paul Klee, Laurence Durrell, Ted Hughes, Vladimir Nabokov, Marguerite Yourcenar and Jackson Pollock.

In alchemical treatises from the Middle Ages until the end of the seventeenth century, including tracts by Isaac Newton, alchemical ideas were expressed in coded language, in emblem, symbol and enigma. Martin Ruland states in his *Lexicon alchemiae* (1612), that the alchemists 'discourse in enigmas, metaphors, allegories, tables, similitudes, and each Philosopher adapts them after his own manner' (381). One reason for this practice was the desire of the adept to hide alchemical truth from the 'ungodly, foolish, slouthful and unthankefull hypocrites' (R. Bostocke, in EP, 62). Thus the expression of ideas was made deliberately obscure. The alchemists openly stated that they were using an enigmatic mode of discourse. Geber wrote: 'Wheresoever we have spoken plainly, there we have spoken nothing, but where we have used riddles and figures, there we have hidden the truth' (McLean, *Rosary*, 47). Ben Jonson's *The Alchemist* parodies such alchemical discourse. Subtle answers Surly's contemptuous question, 'What else are all your termes, / Whereon no one o' your writers grees with other?':

> *Was not all knowledge*
> *Of the* Egyptians *writ in mystick symbols?*
> *Speake not the* Scriptures, *oft in* parables?

Are not the choisest fables of the Poets,
That were the fountaines, and the first springs of wisdome,
Wrapt in perplexed allegories?   (2.3.202–7)

The use of symbolic language by the alchemists was also due to the fact that the material and metaphorical worlds were as yet undivided. From the earliest treatises, alchemy had been as concerned with the metaphysical as with the physical. The spiritual component of Alexandrine and Islamic alchemy entered the European West as an integral part of that science. The alchemist's aim was to explore the inner workings of nature, and this meant delving into the very secret of God's creation. Zosimos of Panopolis (third–fourth century AD) wrote in the sequel to *The First Book of the Final Reckoning* that 'the proper, authentic, and natural tinctures' were to be obtained by 'plunging into meditation' (JA, 55). Alchemical symbols expressed the philosophical properties residing in matter as well as the outer form of that chemical matter. Such a philosophical experience of matter existed beyond the scope of the rational mind, and could only be adequately expressed in symbol, emblem, paradox and allegory. Later scientists and philosophers were to see the alchemical vision of correspondences and the idea of the continuum of spirit and matter as a blurring of the boundaries. Carl Jung wrote that 'The alchemy of the classical epoch (from antiquity to about the middle of the seventeenth century), was, in essence, chemical research work into which there entered, by way of projection, an admixture of unconscious psychic material' (PA, 476). It may be argued, however, that such writers as Gerhard Dorn, Heinrich Khunrath, Robert Fludd, Thomas Vaughan, John Donne and John Milton were consciously aware of expressing purely spiritual truths in alchemical symbolism. The Renaissance world view of dynamic correspondences between substances, objects and states of mind was not necessarily the result of unconscious projection, but a valid perception of an inner, subtle connection existing between things.

Certainly alchemical symbols are ambiguous, multi-dimensional and flexible, with a tendency towards eluding any attempt to define them once and for all. The 'pelican', for example, refers to a form of circulating still, but is, in other contexts, a symbol for the red elixir, or for the stage in the opus known as the 'multiplication'. The 'king' can symbolize common gold, the raw matter of the Stone, 'our sulphur' or the red stone. The definition of the alchemical king undergoes changes in meaning as the substances he symbolizes undergo transformation. In like manner the name of the alchemical vessel changes according to the particular 'chymical' changes that are occurring within it. During the dissolution, death and putrefaction of the Stone's matter, the vessel is variously known as the coffin, grave, prison, den, ship or bath, but during the generation of the philosopher's stone from the conjunction of 'male' sulphur and 'female' argent vive, the vessel is referred to as the bed, nest, egg, womb, globe or garden in which the roses bloom. Mercurius, symbol of the magical transforming substance in alchemy, changes shape and name during the many different phases through which it passes in the process of the opus. This paradoxical substance plays the role of both agent and patient, male and female principle, dissolver and coagulator, duplicitous and faithful servant, poison and elixir. Some of the symbols for Mercurius are the dragon, serpent, mermaid, whore, virgin, wife or white woman, flower, hermaphrodite, fleeing hart, tears, rain, sweat, dew, sea, river, fountain, bee, Cupid, lion, priest, and philosophical tree. The changing imagery aptly expresses the instability of the substance represented. The multiplicity of images used to symbolize one substance or vessel may be seen as an attempt to convey the fluid, changing, transforming nature of reality.

The philosopher's stone, which was seen as an embodiment *par excellence* of all that is unchanging, eternal, and unified, was also known by a multiplicity of names. *The Epistle of John Pontanus* (1624) stated: 'The Philosophers Stone ... hath many names' (240). It was even considered a mark of originality to create a new symbol for the Stone. Some of the names ocurring in the alchemical texts are: elixir, tincture, rose, lily, red lion, medicine, tree, fountain, ruby, red king, sun, son, daughter, homunculus, orphan, bird, phoenix. Such a state of affairs might provoke a rationalist to exclaim as Surly does in Jonson's *The Alchemist*: 'What else are all your termes, / Whereon no one o' your writers grees with other?' (2.3.182–3). In his study *Speaking Pictures: English Emblem Books and Renaissance Culture* Michael Bath addresses the problem of using a multiplicity of names to symbolize one concept. Discussing emblematics and Henry Hawkin's *Partheneia Sacra* (1633), Bath writes that it may seem problematical that the Blessed Virgin is variously presented as a nightingale, palm tree, pearl, dove, phoenix, swan, ship, rose, lily, dew, star, moon, rainbow, mountain and bee: 'The answer, I want to argue, is not simply that this is allegorical opportunism of a kind which was to eventually expose emblematics to the Enlightenment's charges of arbitrary ingenuity; it is rather a consequence of taking the mutable variety of the created world as a source of symbols for immutable and unitary truths. Far from being opportunistic or arbitrary, the instabilities of this representation are those of the inherited epistemology on which it is based' (243). Alchemical writing, like that of the emblem tradition to which it is closely linked, is a writing which delights in the variety of the created world, while simultaneously recognizing the world as a manifestation of God's unity. The author of *Zoroaster's Cave* stresses the idea of unity in multiplicity in alchemical theory: 'Although the wise men have varied names, and perplext their sayings, yet they allwayes would have us think that of One Thing, one Disposition, one Way. The wise men know this one thing, and, that it is one, they have often proved' (66).

Twentieth-century readers have tended to be perplexed by the alchemists' practice of using a multiplicity of images to represent a single concept, by their use of the same name for different substances, and by their apparent disagreement regarding both the quantities of material needed and the exact sequence of the stages of the opus. This confusion is partly the result of our unfamiliarity with the emblematic mode of perceiving and communicating information, a mode which was current in European thought from the Middle Ages until the late seventeenth century. The emblematic mode aside, certain alchemists of this period were nevertheless aware that contradictory information in the treatises could present a problem. Arthur Dee wrote in *Fasciculus chemicus* (1631) that he thought it worth his labour to 'reconcile … the appearing contradiction' between George Ripley's instruction that the alchemist take equal parts of earth and water and John Dastin's view that the water should exceed the earth nine times (FC, 92–3). He pointed out that if one knows enough about alchemy the surface disagreements are easily solved. In Corollary 8 of the *Fasciculus* he wrote that 'to the unexperienced Reader … contradiction may appear between *Raimund* and *Ripley*' on the subject of fermentation. Raimund affirmed two ferments, one sun (gold), the other moon (silver), while Ripley added a third, the green lion, also called 'Laton'. But what, asked Dee, is Laton if it is not immature gold and silver? Therefore the contradiction is solved.

Fortunately most alchemical writers seem to be in accord on the principal points and processes of the opus, if not on all the detail. By understanding these general principles, it is possible for the twentieth-century reader to interpret the individual symbol. The image of the moon, for example, may signify common silver, 'our argent vive', the white queen, the albedo or the white elixir. If the context in which it occurs is understood, the symbol can be decoded.

Probably the first 'encyclopaedia' concerned with alchemy in the West was a twenty-eight-volume work by Zosimos of Panopolis and his sister Eusebeia around 300 AD. There have been a number of alchemical dictionaries, both published and in manuscript, from the sixteenth century onwards, including Gerhard Dorn's *Dictionarium Theophrasti Paracelsi* (1584), Simon Forman's unpublished two-volume alchemical lexicon and his 'Principles of Philosophi, Gathered' (1597), Martin Ruland's *Lexicon alchemiae* (1612), *A Chymicall Dictionary* (1650) (an abbreviated translation of Dorn), William Johnson's *Lexicon Chymicum* (1652) (based on Dorn, but extended), Isaac Newton's unpublished 'Index chemicus' (1680s), William Salmon's *Dictionaire Hermetique* (1695), A. J. Pernety's *Dictionnaire Mytho-Hermetique* (1758), A. E. Waite's 'Short Lexicon of Alchemy' (1894), Albert Poisson's *Théories et Symboles des Alchimistes* (1891) and, most recently, Mark Haeffner's *A Dictionary of Alchemy* (1991).

The concern of this present dictionary is with documenting the rich store-house of alchemical symbolism, making it available for the use of historians of literary culture, philosophy, science and the visual arts, as well as for the informed general reader with an interest in alchemy and Hermeticism. It focuses on the intellectual and literary references of alchemy – alchemical imagery as reflected in literature, the visual arts and in the writings of the alchemists themselves. The corpus of alchemical writing is vast, and includes Arabic, Chinese, English, French, German, Greek, Indian, Italian, Korean, Latin, Spanish and Slavic texts. Jack Lindsay's *The Origins of Alchemy in Graeco-Roman Egypt* (1970) systematically examines the early alchemical Greek texts. The Arabic tradition has been researched by E. J. Holmyard in *Alchemy* (60–104), and the Indian medieval tradition explored by David Gordon White in *The*

Alchemical Body: Siddha Traditions in Medieval India (1996). C. G. Jung has studied the work of the German alchemists in *Psychology and Alchemy* (1968), *Alchemical Studies* (1967) and *Mysterium Coniunctionis* (1963). Joseph Needham has made a substantial contribution to our understanding of alchemy in the Eastern tradition, while J. C. Cooper has recently added to this work with his publication, *Chinese Alchemy*. For a detailed list of studies on the different alchemical traditions, see Alan Pritchard, *Alchemy: A Bibliography of English-Language Writings* (1980), 135–279.

The earlier alchemical texts come from the period before the concept of individual authorship became widespread. Even when authorship is known, the dates and biographical details of many of the alchemists remain uncertain. Many texts are anonymous; many were written pseudonymously and transmitted through manuscript copies over the centuries. To complicate matters further, alchemical treatises were frequently ascribed to such authorities and famous figures as Isis, Cleopatra, Moses, Hermes, Plato, Theophrastus, Aristotle, Arnald of Villanova, Geber, Roger Bacon, St Thomas Aquinas and Raymond Lull, though these treatises are not now generally believed to have been written by these figures. Many texts draw on and recycle the work of previous tracts – for example, the *Turba philosophorum* (tenth-century Islamic), the *Rosarium philosophorum* (1550), and Johann Mylius's *Philosophia reformata* (1622). Arthur Dee's *Fasciculus chemicus* draws on no fewer than thirty earlier works.

This dictionary is designed for twentieth-century readers of English, and in selecting from the vast corpus of alchemical writings I have chosen primarily to cite those works in the Western tradition translated into English or written in English. I have focused on works current in the sixteenth and seventeenth centuries, when alchemy flourished and the publication of alchemical books in Britain was at its height, peaking in the 1650s and 1660s. This period saw the publication of works of the earlier alchemists that had previously circulated only in manuscript, as well as new contemporary materials. These are arguably the main texts which influenced the poets and dramatists of the period. Of course they were able to draw on the major continental Latin compilations such as *Artis Auriferae* (1593), *Musaeum Hermeticum* (1678) and the *Theatrum chemicum* (1602–61), texts which are the basis of Jung's monumental alchemical studies. In J. W. Binns's *Intellectual Culture in Elizabethan and Jacobean England: The Latin Writings of the Age* (1990), the English Renaissance neo-Latin culture is explored.

The foremost seventeenth-century collection of English alchemical texts is Elias Ashmole's *Theatrum chemicum Britannicum* (1652). Works cited in the dictionary from this collection by Ashmole are: *John Gower Concerning the Philosopher's Stone*, the translation of the *Secreta secretorum* by John Lydgate, *Dastin's Dreame* by John Dastin, *Bloomefield's Blossoms* by William Bloomfield, the anonymous *Liber patris sapientiae*, *The Hunting of the Greene Lyon* by Abraham Andrewes, *The Ordinall of Alchemy* begun in 1477 by Thomas Norton, *The Breviary of naturall philosophy* written in 1557 by Thomas Charnock, *The Magistery* by William Backhouse, *Verses belonging to an Emblematicall Scrowle* and *The Vision of Sr. George Ripley* by Ripley.

Other works cited in the dictionary include *The Mirror of Alchimy*, attributed to Roger Bacon, first published in English in 1597; 'Tractatus ... de Lapide Philosophorum', attributed to St Dunstan; *The Compound of Alchemy* by Sir George Ripley, dedicated to Edward IV; *Tractatus duo egregii, de Lapide Philosophorum, una cum Theatro Astronomiae Terrestri* by Edward Kelly; 'A Treatise Touching the Philosopher's Stone' by Edward Cradock; 'Of the Division of the Chaos' and 'Compositor huius libri ad lectorem' by Simon Forman; 'Benjamin Lock, His Picklock to Riply his Castle'; *Alchymiae complementum* by the great-grandson of Thomas Norton, Samuel Norton; 'A Light in Darkness' by Thomas Tymme; and *Fasciculus chemicus* (1629) by Arthur Dee. Dee's book is a collection of quotations from earlier alchemists and alchemical texts including Aristotle, Morienus, Senior, Avicenna, Albertus Magnus, Geber, Raymond Lull, Bernard Trevisan, Basil Valentine, Arnald of Villanova, 'Clangor buccinae', 'Ludus puerorum', 'Rosinus ad Saratantem', 'Semita semitae', and 'Consilium coniugii'. I have also drawn on the 'Sententiae notabilis', 'Praxis' and a commentary on the *Emerald Tables* manuscript treatises by Isaac Newton, who wrote more than two million unpublished words on alchemy.

On occasion I have drawn more widely from the alchemical corpus. I have used material from the early Greek alchemists, Zosimos of Panopolis, Ostanes (a legendary Egyptian priest), Morienus, Maria Prophetissa and Archelaos, as well as the Arabic alchemists, Khalid or Calid, Abu'L-Qasim, and Artephius, whose identity is obscure but is thought to be twelfth-century Arabic. I have also used the work of Italian, French, Catalan, Dutch, German, Swiss, Czech and Polish alchemists, including Petrus Bonus, Giovanni Baptista della Porta, Laurentius Ventura, Lacinius, Bernard Trevisan, Giovanni Baptista Agnelli, Nicolas Flamel, Jean de la Fontaine, Denis Zachaire, pseudo-Jean de Meun, Lambsprinke, Nicaise Le Fevre, Arnald of Villanova, Raymond Lull, Theobald de Hoghelande, Basil Valentine, Paracelsus, Gerhard Dorn, Martin Ruland and many others.

Since this dictionary is designed for a wide-ranging general readership (as well as for the scholar) I have not burdened the text with Greek, Arabic or Latin quotations, and have used the standard available English translations. However, as some translations, particularly those of A. E. Waite, tend to be rather free, it is suggested that for scholarly purposes the reader consult the originals.

Each entry in the dictionary includes a definition of the symbol, an example of the symbol used in alchemical writing and, where possible, a quotation from a literary source. Both an exoteric/physical and an esoteric/philosophical perspective are provided. In attempting to define a symbol, I have indicated where there are a number of different meanings, depending on context, and also where there is agreement or difference amongst alchemical authors. Quotations from the alchemical authors have been included, not only to give support to the definition, but also to give a sense of the content and characteristic rhythms of alchemical language as it is expressed in the treatises available in the sixteenth and seventeenth centuries. Literary quotations from Chaucer to

Nabokov demonstrate the impact of alchemical thought on the literary imagination through the centuries. They provide an indication of the extent of alchemical reference in literature, and offer guidance towards the elucidation and interpretation of literary texts that have, in the absence of alchemical decoding, proved obscure. The citations from such modern writers as Wodehouse, Nabokov, Durrell, Clarke, Hughes, Amis, Yourcenar and Wilding show that the idea of alchemy persists in the popular imagination.

Examples of visual emblems and symbols are also included since, for the Renaissance, chemical, philosophical and spiritual truths were as readily expressed by visual emblems as by verbal formulation. Alchemical treatises were often, though not always, accompanied by graphic woodcuts, copperplate engravings, or hand-painted emblems of the startling images representing the key stages of the opus. Some tracts – for example, the 'Coronatio naturae' and the *Mutus Liber* – are composed entirely of visual material. The visual component was an integral part of the alchemical work. This dictionary reproduces a representative selection of visual emblems from alchemical treatises, some of which have not been reproduced since their first appearance. Jacques van Lennep's *Alchimie* (Brussels, 1985) is a major source of alchemical visual images and any serious student will want to consult this invaluable collection of over a thousand emblems. In selecting the fifty illustrations for the present dictionary I have chosen to represent the classical alchemical emblems, but I have also made a point of including twenty emblems not reproduced in van Lennep. Drawing on the unique holdings of the Ferguson collection at the University of Glasgow for all but eight of the illustrations, I have been able to include not only different versions of manuscript emblems represented in van Lennep, but also emblems from series not represented at all in that collection.

Each entry has been made sufficiently complete and independent of the others, with detailed cross-referencing. Entries on the key concepts – the prima materia, the chemical wedding, the philosopher's stone, Mercurius, and the stages known as the nigredo, albedo and rubedo – provide basic information about the main ideas of the alchemical opus for those unfamiliar with alchemical theory.

A Dictionary of Alchemical Imagery

A

ablution the stage in the circulation of the matter of the *philosopher's stone in the *alembic when the blackness of the *nigredo is washed and purified into the whiteness of the *albedo. *Zoroaster's Cave* says of the Stone or metal: 'when [the body] begins to change from black they call it Ablution' (72), and 'by how much the Stone has more of Ablution, so much the more Intense is the whitenesse' (77). The same treatise related the four main processes of the opus, including ablution, to the *four elements: 'Solution turns the Stone into its Materia prima, that is into Water: Ablution into Ayre: Conjunction into Fire: Fixion into Earth Spiritual and Tingent' (73). The ablution or purification is also known as the mundification. Calid wrote: 'Thou art moreover to understand that Decoction, contrition, cribation [*sic*], mundification, and ablution, with sweet waters is very necessary to this secret mastery' (*Booke of the Secrets*, 38).

The alchemists believed that in order for a metal to be transmuted it first had to be 'killed' or dissolved into its *prima materia, the original stuff of creation, and cleansed of its impurities. When the old 'body' of the metal or matter of the Stone has been dissolved and lies putrefying at the bottom of the alembic, the 'soul' is released and the 'spirit' rises as a volatile vapour to the top of the vessel, where it condenses and descends as rain, *dew, or *tears from *heaven onto the dead body below. John Dryden refers to this alchemical rain in *Annus Mirabilis*: 'Yet judg'd like vapours that from Limbecks rise, / It would in richer showers descend again' (lines 49–52). This rain or dew signifies the *mercurial water or secret *fire which cleanses the putrefied body of its corruption and makes it ready to be reunited with the soul (or the already united soul/spirit entity). The soul then re-animates the new body and resurrects it. The eighth emblem of *The Rosary of the Philosophers* shows the mercurial water as rain or dew descending onto the dead bodies lying in a *coffin below and cleansing them of their impurities (fig. 1). The ablution is equivalent to the metaphysical purification of sins by baptism. Alchemical emblems of the ablution show women *laundering dirty linen in streams or tubs (the mercurial waters) and then putting them out to dry in the meadow (see fig. 37). This process is also symbolized by the figure of *Naaman the leper being washed in the waters of the Jordan (*AF*, embl. 13), by the washing of the stains from *Latona's face (*AF*, embl. 11), and by the *king washed by dew in his sweat bath (*AF*, embl. 28). The term occurs in an alchemical context in John Donne's *Sermons*. He wrote of David: 'Therefore he saw that he needed not only a liquefaction, a melting into tears, not only an ablution and a transmutation, those he had by his purging and this washing ... but he needed fixionem and establishment' (in Mazzeo, *Renaissance ... Studies*, 75). See **laundering**.

PHILOSOPHORVM.

ABLVTIO VEL
Mundificatio.

1 The ablution

abortion a name given to the the opus when it has failed to come to completion. The generation of the *philosopher's stone from the *chemical wedding of *Sol and *Luna (form and matter) was frequently compared to the birth of a child or chick. If the alchemist attempted to hasten the process of the opus alchymicum or made an error, the work could fail to come to fruition. The birth of the *philosophical child was thus aborted. In the epigram to emblem 1 of *Atalanta fugiens*, Michael Maier expressed the hope that the 'unborn child' of the alchemist may be born 'under a lucky star' and 'not as a useless abortion' (55). *The Sophic Hydrolith* warns, 'If thou strivest unduly to shorten the time thou wilt produce an abortion' (HM, 1:84). In 'Paradox. That Fruition destroyes Love', Henry King plays on the idea of the 'still' birth of the Stone when speaking of post-coital disillusionment: 'After Fruition once, what is Desire / But ashes kept warm by a dying fire? / This is (if any) the Philosopher's Stone / Which still miscarries at Projection' (lines 73–6).

abyss the ancient chaos or formless primordial matter, or the alchemists' *prima materia which was a piece of the original *chaos. In his 'Index chemicus' (Keynes MS 30, f. 58), Isaac Newton listed 'abyss', along with 'hyle' and 'chaos', as one of the names of the prima materia (Westfall, 'Index', 180). The *Arcanum* states that through the dissolution of the old metal or body into the prima materia the alchemist brought back 'the whole into its ancient Chaos and dark abyss' (208). Guillaume Salmon's *Dictionaire Hermetique* states that the chaos signifies the matter of the Stone when it has become black and putrefied at the *nigredo. *The Abyss* provides the title for Marguerite Yourcenar's novel about the life of an imaginary Renaissance philosopher-alchemist, Zeno.

Adam   the *prima materia, *Mercurius; the first adept and natural philosopher, according to alchemical tradition. The secret of the *philosopher's stone was said to have been divinely revealed to Adam and then taken from paradise into the world and handed down to the holy Patriarchs. Elias Ashmole wrote that Adam 'before his *Fall*, was so absolute a *Philosopher*, that he fully understood the true and pure knowledge of *Nature* (which is no other then what we call *Naturall Magick*) in the highest degree of Perfection' (TCB, 445). (See **doctrine of signatures**.) In Ben Jonson's *The Alchemist* Sir Epicure Mammon claims to have an alchemical treatise written by Adam: 'I'll show you a booke, where MOSES, and his sister, / And SALOMON haue written, of the art; / I, and a treatise penn'd by ADAM' (2. 1. 81–3). Paracelsus attributes Adam's longevity to the fact that he was 'so learned and wise a Phisition, and knew all things that were in Nature her self' (*Arch.*, 114).

In the context of the opus alchymicum Adam is a synonym for the prima materia, the substance from which it was believed the universe and all the things in it were created. The name 'Adam' was thought to have been derived from the Hebrew *adom*, meaning 'red earth', and thus the prima materia is sometimes referred to as the *red earth. This materia is also referred to as the aqua permanens, the 'sperm' (sometimes *'menstruum') of the world, and 'our Mercury' (philosophical mercury as opposed to common mercury). John Dee referred in his *Monas hieroglyphica* to 'that most famous Mercury of the philosophers, the microcosm and Adam' (165). 'Mercurius' is the name given to the secret transforming substance which transmutes itself from the prima materia into the ultimate goal of the opus, the philosopher's stone. Thus Adam is potentially the 'new' Adam, Christ or the philosophic man (see **furnace**). The Hermetic tradition held that Adam was hermaphroditic before the Fall. In alchemy Mercurius personifies the Adamic *hermaphrodite because, as prima materia, he contains both the male and female seeds of metals (*sulphur and *argent vive). The hermaphrodite also represents the entity which consists of the union of the male and female seeds, *Sol and *Luna, at the *chemical wedding. The necessity for the chemical wedding (or coniunctio) was based on the idea that after the Fall man lost his original, undivided Adamic state and had to strive to reconcile and unite the conflicting halves of his self to regain his integrated nature (symbolized by the union of male and female).

adrop   (from the Arab *usrubb*, lead), the ore from which *philosophical mercury was said to be extracted; philosophical mercury. In *The Compound of Alchymie*, Sir George Ripley equates 'our *Magnesia*, our *Adrop*' with the sister and brother that are '*Agent* and *Pacyent* / *Sulphure* and *Mercury*' in the alchemical coniunctio (TCB, 135) (see chemical wedding). *Zoroaster's Cave* cites Arnoldus and Saturninus: 'Our Stone is called Adrop, that is Saturn', and 'The Stone is called Adrop, that is Saturnus; because, as Saturn is the chiefest of the Planets; so our mercuriall Saturnine Stone, is the highest and most precious of Stones' (65, 64).

Aeson Jason's old, sick father who was rejuvenated by Medea. He is synonymous with the aged, diseased *king (or metal) who is killed in order to
be transmuted, rejuvenated and resurrected. Aeson signifies the death
and *putrefaction of the matter in the alchemical vessel at the *nigredo.
The dead matter may then be purified, revived and transformed into the
white stone and the red stone. John Dastin wrote in his alchemical poem
'Dastin's Dreame': 'Old *Aeson* was made young by *Medea*, / With her
drinks and with her potions, / Soe must your Brother [the King] of pure
Volunta / Dye and be young through his operation' (TCB, 264). The
alchemist Toutguerres in Bassett Jones's 'Lithochymicus' recounts the
tale of an old Italian who 'did comaund me to revive *Medea's* art uppon
Duke *Aeson's* age, / By practice uppon him' (AP, 262). In François
Rabelais's *Pantagruel*, Pantagruel and his company arrive at the
'Kingdom of the Quintessence' where they are shown the rejuvenating
action of the alchemical quintessence upon the aged and decrepit. 'This
is the true Fountain of Youth' by which means the old suddenly become
young, as happened 'to Aeson by Medea's art, and to Jason likewise'
(651).

air one of the four elements, the mastery of which brings the brotherhood
of all life. Volatile spirits in alchemy are often referred to as 'airy'.
Michael Sendivogius described this element: 'The Aire is an entire
Element, most worthy of the three in its quality, without, light and
invisible, but within, heavy, visible, and fixed, it is hot and moist, and
tempered with fire ... It is volatile but may be fixed, and when it is fixed
it makes every body penetrable' (*New Light of Alchymie*, 95). See **elements,
Mercurius, volatile, wind.**

alabaster a symbol of the *white stone of the philosophers attained at the *albedo.
Edward Kelly wrote: 'As the Mercury becomes white, our white Sulphur
becomes incombustible, containing the poison, whose whiteness is like
the whiteness of alabaster' (*Two excellent Treatises*, 142). See **albedo,
white stone.**

albedo the pure, white stage in the opus, also known as the albificatio. The
albedo occurs after the blackened matter, the putrefied body of the
metal or matter for the Stone, lying dead at the bottom of the alembic,
has been washed to whiteness by the mercurial waters or fire (see *ablution). Artephius said of the mercurial water: 'This aqua vitae, or water of
life, being rightly ordered and disposed with the body, it whitens it, and
converts or changes it into its white colour' (SB, 14). Ripley wrote of the
blackened matter: 'Sone after by blacknes thou shalt espy / That they
draw fast to putrefying, / Whych thou shalt after many colers bryng, /
To perfyt Whytenes' (TCB, 149). During the circulation, the matter of the
Stone passes from the black *nigredo (the death) through the rainbow
colours of the cauda pavonis (*peacock's tail) through to the white
albedo where the many colours are integrated into a perfect white. *The
Sophic Hydrolith* stated that after the 'peacock's tail' the matter turns
'a dazzling white' (HM, 1: 83).

When the matter reaches the albedo it has become pure and spotless. This whitening of the Stone's body by the *mercurial waters is sometimes called the 'albification'. Chaucer's Canon's Yeoman tells of 'our fourneys eek of calcinacioun, / And of watres albificacioun' (*Canon's Yeoman's Tale*, lines 804–5). At this stage the body of the Stone (the *white foliated earth) smells fragrant and has attained to a spiritual state where it is no longer subject to sin or decay. The body has been whitened and spiritualized (i.e. the fixed is volatilized) and the soul has been prepared to receive illumination from the spirit. This is the stage at which the alchemist achieves the white stone and white elixir which has the power to transmute all imperfect metals to silver. The albedo is symbolized by all things pure, white or silver, some of which are: *Luna (the white *queen), the *moon (because the matter has attained the perfect state of receptivity, ready to be imprinted by form), *Diana, the *virgin, *dove, *snow, *swan, *white rose, *white lily, *alabaster, *marble, paradise (the *Elysian fields), *salt, *ash, silver and *white foliated earth. Edward Kelly wrote that the 'tincture or elixir' which 'melts, tinges and coagulates ... imperfect metals into pure silver' is 'called the Virgin's milk, the everlasting water, and water of life, because it is as brilliant as white marble; it is also called the white Queen' (*Two excellent Treatises*, 142). And Philalethes wrote of the albedo: 'when by continuance of decoction the colour changeth to white, they call it their Swan, their Dove, their white stone of Paradise, their white Gold, their Alabaster, their Smoak, and in a word whatever is white they do call it by' (*RR*, 178). The clear moonlight of the albedo leads the adept out of the black night of the soul (the *nigredo) into the dawning of consciousness, heralding the advent of full consciousness symbolized by the midday *sun at the final red stage of the opus, the *rubedo. Thus Benjamin Lock wrote: 'Before thy matter be perfectly congelate / Into rosynes, gloriously albificate' ('His Picklock', f. 32v).

albification see **albedo**.

alembic, limbeck a vessel with a beaked cup or head, the upper part of a still used for distilling. The beak of the alembic carries vaporous substances to a receiver, in which they are then condensed. The alembic was invented by Kleopatra, its name coming from the Arabic *al-anbiq*, which in turn is from the Greek *ambix*, meaning cup, beaker, and still-head. Ramon Lull's *Testamentum* states that the matter for the Stone should be placed 'in the *Balneo* for the space of six days, in a Glasse very well sealed; after that open the vessell, and setting the Alembicke on again, with a most gentle fire distill the humidity' (*FC*, 18). Calid wrote of the equipment needed by the alchemist: 'As for the instruments, they are two in number. One is a *Cucurbit*, with his *Alembick*' (*Booke of the Secrets*, 34). In *Macbeth* Shakespeare uses 'limbeck' in its sense as the upper part of the still conveying vapours to the receiver. Lady Macbeth plans to get Duncan's guards so drunk that 'memory, the warder of the brain, / Shall be a fume, and the receipt of reason / A limbeck only' (1.7.66–8). John Dryden likewise wrote of the alembic in its distilling role in an 'Apostrophe to the Royal Society': 'O truly royal! who behold the law /

And rule of beings in your maker's mind, / And thence, like limbecs, rich ideas draw / To fit the levelled use of human kind' (*Annus Mirabilis*, lines 661–4). Other names for the alembic are *head, *helm, and helmet. The 'imperfect creatures' of alchemy's 'Art', who appear as a second anti-masque group in Ben Jonson's *Mercurie Vindicated*, wear 'helmes of lymbecks on their heads' (lines 183–4).

In alchemy, the term is also applied to the generic circular vessel, the vas rotundum, in which the alchemist carries out all the operations of the opus. Roger Bacon wrote: 'which vessel must be round, with a small necke, made of glass or some earth representing the nature or close knitting togither of glasse: the mouth whereof must be signed or sealed with a covering of the same matter, or with lute' (*Mirror*, 12) (see lute). The treatises stress that although the vessel is known by many names there is but one vessel in which the work of transmutation is accomplished. Roger Bacon wrote: 'in one vessel the whole mastery is performed' (*Mirror*, 10). Some of the names of the vessel are: pot, vessel, body, *prison, *grave or coffin, chest, box, barrel, *ark, *ship, chariot, trough, *well, *bath, pocket, sack, oven, kettle, *womb, *egg, *oval, sphere, globe, *bed, *pelican, *stork, cormorant, goose, pumpkin, *nest, *den, *house, glass-house, glass, citadel, *fort, *castle, treasure-house, *garden, *temple and *city. The name of the vessel changes according to the particular chemical operation in process. During the blackness of the *putrefactio when the chemically united *lovers (*sulphur and *argent vive) are killed and buried in order to generate the philosopher's stone, the vessel was represented as a grave, coffin or prison. John Donne employed this idea in 'A Nocturnal upon S. Lucy's Day': 'I, by love's limbeck, am the grave / Of all that's nothing' (lines 21–2). At the *chemical wedding the vessel is represented as the conjugal bed in which the lovers unite (fig. 3), and at the stage where the alchemist has attained the red and white elixirs or stone, the vessel is spoken of as the garden in which bloom *roses red and white, or the *philosophical tree with its *flowers of sun and moon (see fig. 17).

The alchemists sometimes identify the secret transforming water (*Mercurius) as their secret vessel. Philalethes enigmatically wrote: 'When we speak of our vessel and our fire, we mean by both expressions, our water; nor is our furnace anything diverse or distinct from our water. There is then, one vessel, one furnace, one fire, and all these make up one water' (*HM*, 2:263). The mercurial water is paradoxically referred to as the contents of the container and the container itself. In the metaphysically oriented treatises it is made clear that man is the vessel in which the transformation takes place and from which the transformative substance issues. The vessel is viewed as a little universe in which the adept attempts to duplicate God's creation in miniature. Morienus wrote of the Stone: 'Truly this matter is that created by God which is firmly captive within yourself, inseparable from you wherever you be' (*Testament*, 27).

aludel   a pear-shaped bottle used as a condensing receiver during the sublimation process. The name comes from the Arabic *al-uthal*. It is also one of the names of the philosophical vessel or *egg in which the entire opus alchymicum is accomplished. Calid wrote of the utensils needed by the alchemist: 'As for the instruments, they are two in number. One is a *Cucurbit*, with his *Alembick*: the other is *Aludel*, that is well made' (*Booke of the Secrets*, 34). Subtle in Ben Jonson's *The Alchemist* addresses Face: 'Looke well to the register, / And let your heat, still, lessen by degrees, / To the *Aludels*' (2.3.33–5).

amalgam, amalgamation   originally, a soft mass formed especially by the combination (of gold etc.) with mercury (OED). In an appendix to 'Lithochymicus' Bassett Jones defined amalgamation as 'a particular operation for the calcina- tion of mineralls. It is perform'd by vertue of quick silver incorporating itself with the minerall, soe reduceing the composition into a soft and pliable consistencie' (AP, 353). In *The Canon's Yeoman's Tale*, Chaucer writes of the 'amalgaming and calcening / Of quik-silver, y-clept Mercurie crude' (lines 771–2). Jean de la Fontaine stated that 'If a body and Soule be impure / Thou shalt not make Amalgame sure' (AP, 94).

amber   a synonym for gold. Amber was known among the ancients and the philosophers as a very precious substance and there was a close associa- tion between gold (Sol) and amber in alchemical thought. It was known principally as three things: as a golden exudation of certain trees (poplar, alder, pine and fir); as an alloy of gold and silver; and as a synonym for gold. Ruland wrote that its composition as an alloy was one part silver to five parts gold (*Lexicon*, 122). To some alchemists the amber alloy was known as *Laton or Latona, the mother of *Apollo (sun-gold) and *Diana (moon-silver) (see AF embl. 11). As the exuded, hardened gum of trees, amber is associated with alchemical Sol or gold. The *philoso- pher's stone is frequently depicted as a tree (see **philosophical tree**). Mylius wrote of the 'philosophical stone, from which branches multiply into infinity' (in AS, 319). The congealed sap of the philosophical tree is seen as part of the tree's 'fruit', and this *fruit is silver and gold. Flamel wrote: 'the *living* fruit (the real silver and gold), we must seek on the tree' (HM, 1: 144). The alchemists saw amber, the golden, coagulated sap, as a potent image for the gold which issued from their growing metallic tree. The idea of amber gold or vegetable gold occurs in Crashaw's 'The Weeper': 'Not the soft Gold which / Steales from the Amber-weeping Tree' (80), and in Milton's description of the tree of life in *Paradise Lost*: 'And all amid them stood the tree of life, / High eminent, blooming ambrosial fruit / Of vegetable gold' (4.218–20).

amorous birds of prey   see **bird.**

androgyne   see **hermaphrodite**

angels   the volatile or spiritualized matter of the *Stone during *sublimation. The alchemical texts always depict volatile substances as winged (see **volatile**). Nicholas Flamel wrote in *His Exposition*: 'The natures then are here transmuted into *Angels*, that is to say, are made *spiritual* and most subtle, so are they now the true *tinctures*' (123). (See also **castle, bird.**) 'Angel' is also the name of an English gold coin of the late sixteenth and early seventeenth century, so named because of its device depicting the archangel Michael slaying the dragon (OED). In John Lyly's *Gallathea*, Peter says of the alchemist: 'He can make of thy cap gold, and by multiplication of one grote, three old Angels' (2.3.38–9).

antimony a silvery metalloid chemical element of which stibnite is the main ore. John Read glosses it as 'strictly, metallic antimony; but alchemically, stibnite (native antimony sulphide)' (TAC, 194). Basil Valentine's *Triumphant Chariot of Antimony* (1660) was the text responsible for the antimony craze in the seventeenth century. According to Newton's 'Clavis', Dobbs writes, when the ore of antimony was reduced using iron, it could be purified to such an extent that it would crystallize in a star-like pattern and was thus known as the 'star of antimony' (*Foundations*, 199). Sir George Ripley used antimony or sericon to prepare the alchemical substance known as the green lion (BB, 101), an experiment repeated by Edward Kelly on 8 February 1588 at Trebon (Dee, *Diary*, 26). In alchemy, antimony or the *black earth is one of the names given to the arcane substance at the black stage of the work (the *nigredo) and is depicted in alchemical emblems as the grey wolf and sometimes the griffon. *The Golden Tract* indicates that the name antimony is used metaphorically 'on account of the brilliant blackness which it assumes after solution' (HM, 1: 23). In *Poly-Olbion* Michael Drayton depicted a mountain in the Derbyshire Peak District as an alchemist producing antimony: 'For shee a *Chimist* was, and Nature's secrets knew / And from amongst the *Lead*, she *Antimony* drew' (*Works*, 4:531. lines 386–7).

Apollo the son of *Latona and Jupiter, twin brother of *Diana. Apollo is a symbol for the red tincture, *Sol, *gold, the *sun and the *red 'sun' stage of the opus which succeeds the white lunar stage. In 'Lithochymicus' Bassett Jones writes that the lunar stage must 'be advaunced to th' state divine / Of great *Apollo*' (AP, 296). Isaac Newton wrote in his commentary on the *Emerald Table* of Hermes Trismegistus: 'and the earth is the nurse, Latona washed and cleansed, whom the Egyptians assuredly had for the nurse of Diana and Apollo, that is, the white and red tinctures' (Dobbs, *Janus*, 276). Apollo represents the hot, dry, active, masculine principle of the opus which the alchemist must unite with his sister, Diana, the cold, moist, receptive female principle. This process is depicted as an incestuous *chemical wedding or union from which the *philosopher's stone is conceived and born. See **incest.**

apples see **Atalanta, Hesperides, fruit.**

aqua ardens (Latin, burning water) *Mercurius, the universal solvent of the wise, the 'mother' of the *Stone, the first mercury in the opus alchymicum which mortifies bodies, breaking them down and dissolving them into their *prima materia. In *Ripley Reviv'd* Philalethes wrote: 'This water they call sometimes, *Aqua ardens,* sometimes *Acetum Acerrimum*, but most commonly they call it their *Mercury*' (3). This use of the term probably came from treatises by Ramon Lull where *aqua ardens*, the spirit of wine, was treated as an impure form of the universal quintessence (Moran, *The Alchemical World of the German Court*, 78).

aqua divina   see **Mercurius.**

aqua fortis   (Latin, strong water) nitric acid, originally referring to any powerful solvent. In alchemy it is another name for *Mercurius as the universal solvent which can dissolve any metal into its *prima materia (see **aqua ardens**).

aqua nostra   see **Mercurius.**

aqua permanens   see **Mercurius.**

aqua regia, regis   (Latin, royal water) a concentrated mixture of nitric acid (aqua fortis) and hydrochloric acid, able to dissolve gold. In *De natura acidorum,* Isaac Newton wrote of the reduction of gold or other bodies into the *prima materia for transmutation: 'Mercury can pass, and so can Aqua Regia, through the pores that lie between particles of last order, but not others' (in Dobbs, *Foundations*, 218). In Ben Jonson's *The Alchemist* Subtle quizzes Face on his knowledge of repeated distillation: 'What's *Cohobation?*' and Face answers ''Tis the powring on / Your *Aqua Regis*, and then drawing him off' (2.5.26–7).

aqua vitae   (Latin, water of life) alcoholic spirits, especially of the first distillation; ardent spirits; distilled wine. It is also a name for the catalyst or agent of the opus, philosophical mercury known as *Mercurius, and the *quintessence. Colson's *Philosophia maturata* states: 'first calcine, then putrefie, and dissolve, and fix often with our *Aqua vitae*; wash and dry, and make a Marriage between the Body and Spirit' (34). Artephius likewise identifies aqua vitae with the beneficent *'dew of grace' which washes and whitens the blackened body of the Stone after *putrefaction, leading to the *albedo: 'This aqua vitae, or water of life, being rightly ordered and disposed with the body, it whitens it, and converts or changes it into its white colour' (*SB*, 14) (see **Mercurius**). Synonyms for aqua vitae are *bath, balneum (or balmy), moist fire, *dunghill, *horse-belly, blood of the *green lion, philosophic mercury. The *Philosophia maturata* says of philosophic mercury: 'This is our Fire always equally burning in one measure within the Glass, and not without: This is our Dung-hill, our Aqua vitae, our Balmy, our horse-belly, working and producing many wonders in the most secret Work of Nature' (32). Calid equated aqua vitae with the alchemical quintessence: 'This is the true *Aqua Vitae* of the Philosophers; the true Spirit so many have fought for, and which has been desired of all Wise Men, which is called the *Essence, Quintessence, Spirit*' (*Booke of the Secrets*, 125).

arbor inversa   see **philosophical tree.**

arbor philosophica   see **philosophical tree.**

argent vive   or quicksilver, also known as mercury, the cold, moist, receptive, female
*seed of metals which must be united with the hot, dry, active masculine
seed known as *sulphur in order to create the philosopher's stone.
Sulphur has the power to fix and coagulate the volatile spirit while
argent vive or mercury has the power to dissolve fixed matter. Nicolas
Flamel explained that 'all metals have been formed out of sulphur and
quicksilver, which are the seeds of all metals, the one representing the
male, and the other the female principle. These two varieties of seed are,
of course, composed of elementary substances; the sulphur, or male
seed, being nothing but fire and air . . . while the quicksilver, or female
seed is nothing but earth and water' (HM, 1: 42). Calid equated sulphur
with the 'form' and argent vive with the 'matter' of metals: 'all Metals
are compounded of Mercury and Sulphur, Matter and Form; Mercury is
the Matter, and Sulphur is the Form' (*Booke of the Secrets*, 126). Argent vive
is symbolized by the serpent or dragon, as Mammon points out in
Jonson's *The Alchemist*: 'our *argent vive*, the Dragon' (2.1.95). See **gold
and silver.**

Argus, Argus-eyes   a symbol for the rainbow-coloured stage in the opus known as the
*peacock's tail (see Bassett Jones in AP, 294). In Greek myth, the hundred
eyes of Argus were transferred to the tail of the peacock by Hera.
Mammon in Jonson's *The Alchemist* lists 'Argus eyes' as one of the
'abstract riddles of our *stone*' (2.1.102–4). The multi-coloured stage of the
peacock's tail occurs after the black *nigredo, where the dead bodies of
the 'lovers' (male *sulphur and female *argent vive) are putrefied,
preparing the way for the white stage or *albedo, where the blackened
bodies have been cleansed and purified. See **jackdaw, Mercurius.**

ark   the name of the alchemists' secret vessel while the matter of the Stone is
undergoing the dissolution and *putrefaction at the *nigredo, leading
to the generation of the philosophical chick or stone. In both biblical
and alchemical symbolism the waters of the *flood were paradoxically
destructive and regenerative. The old outmoded race was drowned
while the new race was generated from the ark on the waters. Since the
ark contained the new race of beings which were to repopulate the
world, it was seen by the alchemists as a matrix of generation. In
Jonson's masque *Mercurie Vindicated from the Alchemists at Court*, Mercury
refers to the alchemists' 'great act of generation, nay almost creation',
equating their vessel with the ark of Deucalion: 'For in yonder vessels
which you see in their laboratorie they have enclosed *Materials*, to
produce men, beyond the deedes of *Deucalion*, or *Prometheus* (of which,
one, they say, had the *Philosophers* stone, and threw it over his shoulder,
the other the fire, and lost it)' (lines, 133–9). Arthur Dee named a later
version of his *Fasciculus chemicus* (1631) the 'Arca arcanorum' (the ark or
vessel of secrets), playing on the words 'ark' and 'arcane' and implying

that the secret can be found within the book as vessel. The ark as alchemical vessel is illustrated in Goossen van Vreeswijk, *De Goude Leeuw* (Amsterdam, 1675). See also **Noah, flood**.

Armenian bitch   see **dog and bitch**.

art and nature   Alchemy was considered to be an art. Edward Kelly opens his *Theatre of Terrestrial Astronomy*: 'Many books have been written on the art of Alchemy' (113), and Arthur Dee refers to 'the art of Chymistry', 'this Divine Art', in the preface 'To the Students in Chymistry' of his *Fasciculus chemicus*. 'Art' features in the title of numerous tracts, such as Gratianus's *Book of the Art of Alchemy*, the *Artis auriferae quam chemiam vocant* (Basel, 1593) and the *Ars chemica* (Strasbourg, 1566).

Man has long used the concept of a division between art and nature as a mode of perceiving and analysing the world, and as a way of defining his own role in the cosmos. During the seventeenth century, the ancient philosophical debate of art versus nature was employed in expounding not only such subjects as education, gardening and cosmetics, but was also used in scientifc discourse. Alchemy was viewed as an 'art' that could perfect 'nature'. Gold was thought to grow within the earth like a great tree, formed out of sulphur and argent vive, but this process took nature thousands of years to perform. The alchemists claimed that they could grow gold above ground in a much shorter time by using their art – the artificial means employed in the laboratory. In the general debate, art and nature were often seen as antithetical, with one or other of the two taking precedence depending on the situation or on individual opinion. In other contexts art and nature were perceived as complementary, with each serving the other to advantage. It is in this latter capacity that the alchemists consistently viewed the relationship of art and nature in the production of the *philosopher's stone, though there are variations on this view. In some instances the emphasis is on the alchemist as the 'perfecter' of nature's 'imperfections'. Paracelsus stated that nature does not produce anything that is perfect in itself and that it is man's role to bring things to perfection (*PS*, 92–3). In other instances, the emphasis is on the alchemist as nature's servant, a view illustrated by Dr Allslagen's statement in Bassett Jones's 'Lithochymicus': 'th' Artist beinge noe more / Then Nature's servant' (*AP*, 242). Whatever the emphasis, the alchemical texts make it clear that the alchemist could in no way be ignorant of the workings of nature and attain the goal of the opus. The epigram to emblem 42 in Maier's *Atalanta fugiens* states: 'Nature be your guide; follow her with your art willingly, closely' (*AF* 94). In the seventeenth-century texts, the alchemist is advised to co-operate with nature, using its processes and structures as a creation blueprint for the opus. The first treatise of Trismosin's *Splendor Solis* says: 'Here nature serves Art with Matter, and Art serves Nature with suitable instruments and method convenient for Nature to produce such new forms; and although the before mentioned Stone can only be brought to its proper form by Art, yet the Form is from Nature' (18). Roger Bacon wrote of the construction of the alchemical furnace in which metals were to be engendered: 'If therefore wee intend to immitate nature, we must needes have such a furnace like unto the Mountaines, not in greatnesse, but in continuall heate, so that the fire put in, when it ascendeth, may find no vent' (*Mirror*, 11–12).

The alchemist who fails to acknowledge the key role played by nature risks failure. He is invariably rebuked by nature, as in Jean de Meun's 'The Alchimyst's Answere to Nature', a verse monologue consisting of Nature's diatribe against alchemists who fail to imitate her processes (*AP*, 129). Chastened by Nature's harangue, the alchemist replies: 'Therefore, deere *Madam*, I conclude / Henceforth my Workes shall more allude / And heedful bee unto your Love, / Traceing your Stepps for evermore . . . And all this Art more certeinly / Comes to us from you' (*AP*, 192). The alchemist as smoky persecutor of nature became a stock figure in both alchemical and literary texts, including Michael Sendivogius's *Dialogus Mercurii, Alchymistae et Naturae* (1607) and Ben Jonson's masque, *Mercurie Vindicated from the Alchemists at Court* (1616). Thomas Nashe makes a jokey reference to the alchemist in this role in the second preface to *Strange Newes*, where he denounces his literary detractors: 'What ever they be that thus persecute Art (as the Alcumists are said to persecute Nature) I would wish them to abate the edge of their wit' (*Works*, 1:261). Metaphysically, the adept must use the 'art' of meditation to become aware of and thus acknowledge the lower nature, 'natural' man, in order to transmute and integrate this aspect to become the illumined, philosophical man or man of 'art'. See **opus contra naturam**.

asafoetida see **green lion**.

ash that which remains after the *calcination (conversion to a fine white powder through heat) of the base metal; the philosophical earth which remains in the bottom of the vessel when the volatile matter of the Stone ascends into the *alembic. Ash is the incorruptible substance left in the alembic after the matter of the Stone has been subjected to the purgatorial *fire. The ash can no longer be set on fire, and is, psychologically speaking, free from the turmoil of the passions. It is a synonym for the white stage of the opus, the *albedo, when the dead, blackened body or bodies (of united *sulphur and *argent vive) have been whitened and purified by the refining fire (i.e. the *mercurial water). *Zoroaster's Cave* says: 'Our Black Materia dealbated is called the Terra Foliata, Ashes of Ashes, ferment of ferments and white Sulphur enduring the fire' (63). In Andreae's *The Chymical Wedding* the body of the beheaded *philosophical bird is burnt to ashes (160) which are then used as the purified matter for the bodies of the king and queen who will be resurrected: 'But this was our work, we were to *moisten* the Ashes with our fore-prepared *Water* till they became altogether like a very thin Dough . . . then we cast it thus hot as it was into two *little* forms or moulds' (199). The ash or purified body of the Stone which has ascended in the vessel during sublimation is also referred to as the alchemical *snow, the white *dust, the *white foliated earth and *Bird of Hermes. Ramon Lull called this substance the 'white foliated earth', the 'sought for Good', 'the Salt of Nature' and 'the

Ashes of Ashes' (in FC, 71). *The Rosary of the Philosophers*, on the other hand, applied the name 'Ashes of Ashes' to the dross or dregs that are separated from the ascending pure white dust, itself referred to as 'ashes': 'The Dust ascending higher from the Dregs, is Ashes, Honoured, Sublimed, Extracted from the Ashes, but that which remains below is Ashes of Ashes, inferiour, vilified, condemned Ashes, a dreg and like drosse' (in FC, 72). Ashes are also used by the alchemist as a form of gentle heat for the alembic (see **assation**). Artephius spoke of the hermetically sealed vessel buried in ashes which give a 'most sweet and gentle heat' (SB, 35). Ripley equated the ashes of Hermes' tree with the *crow's head, symbol of the blackness of the *nigredo, the stage before the albedo (TCB, 134). Peter, the alchemist's servant in John Lyly's *Gallathea*, lists 'ashes' as one of the alchemists' key substances: 'our Mettles, Saltpeeter, Vitrioll, Sal tartar ... Vnsleked lyme, Chalke, Ashes' (2.3.22–5).

assa foetida, asafoetida   see **green lion**.

assation   the act of roasting or baking the matter of the Stone in a glass vessel over *ashes. Arthur Dee records that in the preparation of the Stone the spirits should often be 'reiterated by Contrition and Assation with their Body, untill thou see these things which thou desirest in it' (FC, 35).

astronomy (earthly)   Alchemy was known as the terrestrial or inferior astronomy. In a dedicatory letter to Gerard Mercator in his *Propedeumatic Aphorisms* (London, 1558), John Dee referred to his hieroglyphic monad as 'the *insignia* of *astronomia inferior* [i.e. alchemy]' (Josten, 'A translation of John Dee's *Monas Hieroglyphica*, 86). Edward Kelly wrote to Sir Edward Dyer: 'Yea, honorable sir, you know very well, what delight we took together, when from the metals simply calcined into powder after the usual manner, distilling the liquor so prepared with the same we converted appropriate bodies (as our astronomy inferior teaches) into mercury their first matter' (Bod. Ashm. MS 1420). Kelly named one of his treatises *The Theatre of Terrestrial Astronomy* (*Two excellent Treatises*, 113–47). In the Renaissance world view of correspondences, alchemy was seen as the science of metals in the earth, which was the counterpart to heavenly astronomy. The seven main metals – mercury, tin, iron, copper, lead, silver and gold – were known by the names of the seven planets, Mercury, Jupiter, Mars, Venus, Saturn, Moon and Sun. In the theory of correspondences, set down in the 'As above, so below' law of Hermes' *Emerald Table*, everything that existed in heaven was said to be reflected in earth. Thus gold, for example, was the equivalent of the sun in the realm of the metals, and silver the equivalent of the moon.

Atalanta   the fugitive, elusive mercurial water which is the alchemists' transforming arcanum (see **Mercurius**). In his race against the fleet Atalanta, Hippomenes cunningly threw golden apples in front of her in order to distract her and slow her pace. The alchemists used this myth to symbolize the fixation of fugitive mercury (Atalanta) by the coagulating power of *sulphur (the golden apples). One of the most famous alchemical emblem books of the seventeenth century, Michael Maier's *Atalanta fugiens* (1617), illustrates the myth of Atalanta in its frontispiece.

athanor the furnace in which the egg-shaped vessel is placed in a sandbath over a fire; named from the Arabic *al-tannur* (the furnace). The athanor is shaped like a small domed *tower which provides a constant heat with charcoal. Philalethes wrote that the alembic is set 'in a Philosophical Athanor ... the doores being firmly shut up' (RR, 12). Subtle in Jonson's *The Alchemist* informs Mammon that he has obtained the salt of mercury by 'reverberating in *Athanor*' (2.3.66). See **furnace**, **tower**.

augmentation see **multiplication**.

auripigmentum orpiment (arsenic trisulphide); also a name for the *red stone. See **coral**.

aurum potabile drinkable gold or medicine, a name for the *philosopher's stone (or *medicine), the pure love essence which fills the grail cup of the adept (see **gold** and **silver**). Colson's *Philosophia maturata* refers to 'a thick Oyl, which we call potable Gold, a curing and preserving Elixir of Life, and of Metals' (70) and gives a recipe for it: 'Ferment one part of the white earth with the oyl of *Lune*, that is, with white water, and the other part with the oyl of *Sol*, that is, with the red water; and so by greater heat and digestion, it shall be converted into a most red powder, like Dragon's blood. This powder being joyned with a part of our *Mercury*, and circulated, is called *Aurum Potabile* which transmuteth *Mercury* and all imperfect mettals into most perfect *Sol*' (37). St Dunstan wrote that 'this *Aurum Potabile*, Elixir of life and of Mettals, is the highest Medicine next unto the universal, and being taken in appropriated vehicles, Cureth all Disease, without causing any paines at all' (DSP, 92). Robert Fludd described 'the Phisitians truest aurum potabile' in divine or metaphysical alchemy as 'wisdom' and 'the glittering seed of true and simple philosophicall and Theologicall Light' (TGH, 125).

Aurum potabile was the subject of a debate in the early seventeenth century. Matthew Gwinne's anti-Paracelsian medical treatise, *In assertorum chymicae, sed verae medicinae desertorum Fra. Anthonium* (London, 1611), attacked Francis Anthony's theory on potable gold. Anthony's famous recipe was published in *The Apologie, or defence of a Verity Heretofor Published Concerning a medicine called Aurum Potabile* (London, 1616). In 1632 Francis Anthony's son, John, sent Tsar Mikhael Romanov of Russia a gift of aurum potabile. In Ben Jonson's *Volpone*, Mosca's eulogy on material gold mocks the alchemical idea of the aurum potabile: 'Yea mary, sir! / This [material gold] is true physick, this your sacred medicine. / No talke of opiates to this great elixir', to which Corbaccio answers: ''Tis *aurum palpable*, if not *potabile*' (1.4.71–3). See **gold and silver**.

autumn the season in which the opus alchymicum is accomplished, brought to fruition. This is the time when the *arbor philosophica bears its fruit of *gold and silver, *sun and moon (see Salmon, *Dictionaire Hermetique*, 15). See **harvest**. The leaves of the tree, like ripening corn, turn to gold.

Avis Hermetis   see **Bird of Hermes**.

azoth, azot, azoch   *Mercurius, named from the Arabic *al-zauq*; the first matter of metals; philosophical mercury; the mercurial water or solvent which cleanses the spots from the unclean matter of the Stone known during this phase as *Latona's face. In Paracelsus, azoth is the universal *medicine which can cure the disease of all metals and of man. *Zoroaster's Cave* explained that '*Azot* is a fift Essence, a body of itself Subsistent, differing from all the Elements and all the Elementals both in Matter and Form, Nature and Virtue, having nothing of the Corruptible: and it is called a fift Essence because it is extracted from four, and has no Elemental motion, as other Elementals bodyes, Tinging and purifying metallic bodyes by its Colour, and keeping from Corruption all other Bodyes that are joyn'd with it' (65).

azure   The mercurial water and alchemical *quintessence are frequently described as being sky blue or azure. Paracelsus introduced the symbol of the sapphire from the Cabbala into alchemy, where it came to signify the arcane substance. Thomas Vaughan described the tincture as having the colour of 'a certain inexpressible *Azure* like the *Body* of *Heaven* in a *clear Day*'. He called the Stone 'an *azure Heaven*'. Elswhere Vaughan wrote that the water of the sages was a '*deep Blew Tincture*' (VW(R), 488, 463, 332). To clothe in an azure shirt or garment means to make *projection of the tincture on molten metal in order to convert it into silver or gold.

B

bain-marie   a water bath or double boiler used for *separation, said to have been invented by Maria Prophetissa, the famous Graeco-Egyptian alchemist of the third century who also discovered hydrochloric acid. The 'balneum Mariae' (or 'Marienbad' in German) consists of a double vessel, the outer one of which is filled with water while the inner one holds the material to be heated moderately (Patai, 'Maria', 179). The *Chymicall Dictionary* defines the '*Balneum Mariae*, or *Maris*' as 'a furnace for distillation containing water, in which being warm Chymicall vessels are put for putrefaction of the matter which they contain, as also for their separation, and for the performing the operations of that kind of moist ascensions'. Nicaise Le Fevre referred to the use of this bath in the directions for preparing the pearls of Sir Walter Raleigh's 'Great Cordial': 'dissolve the Pearls with a *Menstruum* ... [then dissolve] again in equal parts of Cinnamon and Rose-water, which must be drawn off again in Mary's Bath' (*Discourse*, 70). In Jonson's *The Alchemist* Subtle informs Mammon that 'tinct F.' is 'come ouer the *helme* too, / I thanke my Maker, in S. MARIES *bath*, / And shewes *lac Virginis*' (2.3.61). See **bath**.

balm, balsam, balsome   According to Paracelsus, balm is an all-healing, animating life-principle both internal and external to man, which preserves bodies from disease, decay and putrefaction. It is to this balsamum vitae that John Donne referred in 'To the Countess of Bedford': 'In everything there naturally grows / A balsamum to keep it fresh, and new, / If 'twere not injured by extrinsic blows; / Your birth and beauty are this balm in you' (lines 21–4). The balsam is the same as the *fifth element or quintessence which is a pure, incorruptible substance made by unifying the four elements of the body of the Stone, a process which precedes the final production of the philosopher's stone. Balm is a panacea, a medicine able to transform the perishable into the imperishable, the impure into the pure, and is frequently identified with the final goal of the opus. As in Christianity, where the blood of Christ is seen as the healing balm of all afflictions, disease and original sin, so the alchemists give the name of 'our balm' to the miraculous *philosopher's stone or *elixir, the panacea for all sickness and infirmity in man and metals. Paracelsus wrote of 'the preparation of the Stone or Balsam' which has the power to cure all disease (PW, 96). *The Book of Lambspring* described a universal body 'from which flows forth a glorious Balm / With all its miraculous virtues' (HM, 1: 287). Philalethes likewise referred to 'this blessed Tincture, which expelleth all Poyson, though it self were a deadly Poyson before the Preparation, yet after it is the Balsam of Nature, expelling all Diseases' (RR 24). In 'Fuscara, or the Bee Errant', John Cleveland jokily equated the fair Fuscara's shed blood with the all-healing balm, when she is stung by the *poison of the bee, whose 'suckets are moyst *Alchimie*': 'For as in Gummy trees there's found / A salve to issue at the wound / Of this her breach the like was true / Hence trickled out a balsome too' (lines 65–8). Jean-Jacques Rousseau wrote of his beloved Madame Warens: 'So, though she knew some elements of philosophy and physics, she did not fail to pick up her father's taste for experimental medicine and alchemy; she manufactured elixirs, tinctures, balsams, and magic potions' (*Confessions*, 56–7).

balmy   the same as balneum. See **bath**.

balneum   see **bath**.

balneum mariae   see **bain-marie**.

baptism   see **ablution**.

basilisk   a fabulous reptile supposedly hatched by a serpent from a cock's egg, and thought to be able to kill any living thing by casting one of its eyes upon it. Also known as the cockatrice, it was a symbol of the alchemical *elixir which could transmute base metal into gold. Topsell wrote in his *Historie of Foure-Footed Beastes* that Hermes 'maketh mention of a Bazeliske ingendered in dung, whereby he meaneth the Elixir of Life, wherewithall the *Alchemistes* convert metalls' (128). Ripley referred to 'Our *Baselysk*, otherwyse our *Cokatryse*, / Our great *Elixir*, most of pryse'

(*TCB*, 127). He explained that the elixir is compared to the basilisk because it can kill the base metal upon which it is projected and tinge it to silver or gold in an instant. Bassett Jones wrote of the elixir or Stone: 'cast / Him uppon *Sol* or *Lune*, whome if full fast / With Basiliskish eies he powders, then / it is a signe the Cock hath trodd the Henn' ('Lithochymicus', in *AP*, 269).

bath (balneum) the mercurial waters of dissolution and purification, and the name of the alchemical warming bath of sand, water or ashes during this cleansing process. These mercurial waters are the secret, inner, invisible fire which dissolves and kills, cleanses and resurrects the matter of the Stone in the vessel. Colson's *Philosophia maturata* says of 'our *Mercury*' or the bath (identifying it with the dunghill and horse-belly): 'This is our Fire always equally burning in one measure within the Glass, and not without: This is our Dung-hill, our Aqua vitae, our Balmy, our Horse-belly, working and producing many wonders in the most secret Work of Nature ... a Fire hot and moist, most sharp, a Water-carrying Fire in its belly; otherwise it could not have power to dissolve Bodies into their first Matter' (32) and, 'Whosoever therefore keeps not this our heat, our fire, our balnium, our invisible and most temperate flame, and of one regiment, and continually burning in the quality and measure within our Glasse ... shall labour in vain, and shall never attain this Science' (19).

In certain versions of the *chemical wedding the solar *king (the hot, dry, active masculine seed of metals, *sulphur) and the lunar *queen (the cold, moist, receptive feminine seed of metals, *argent vive) bathe in order to be cleansed of their impurities before uniting (fig. 2). The bodies of the united lovers are then placed in a bath of *sea water over a moderate fire so that they will be dissolved, putrefied and regenerated in order to conceive the *philosophical child (see McLean, *Rosary*, embl.

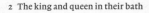

2 The king and queen in their bath

5). The sea water symbolizes the *prima materia, the mercurial waters or *sperm of the philosophers from which all things were thought to be generated. Artephius wrote of the king and queen bathing in a fountain of living water: 'Our water then is the most beautiful, lovely, and clear fountain, prepared only for the king, and queen, whom it knows very well, and they it ... and they abide therein for two or three days, to wit, two to three months, to wash themselves therewith, whereby they are made young again and beautiful. And because Sol and Luna have their original from this water their mother it is necessary therefore that they enter into it again, to wit, their mother's womb, that they may be regenerated or born again' (SB, 38). In other versions the entombed father and son are putrefied in a hot bath, or the diseased, melancholic king is placed (sometimes dismembered) in a *fountain, spring or sweat bath where he is cleansed of his black bile through undergoing distillation, and rises purified and rejuvenated (see **sweat**). An anonymous treatise writes of the Stone's matter in its bath: 'seeth him in his own Water and afterwards fry him in his own Grease; and then wash him till all his grease and his Water be dried up all' (GU Ferguson MS 238, f. 3r). A jokey version of this occurs in Shakespeare's *The Merry Wives of Windsor* where the 'gross' and 'unclean' Falstaff is tricked into escaping from a jealous husband by being shut up in a 'buck-basket' (laundry basket). Falstaff recounts the experience: 'To be stopped in, like a strong distillation, with stinking clothes that fretted in their own grease ... think of that – that am as subject to heat as butter, a man of continual dissolution and thaw ... And in the height of this bath, when I was more than half stewed in grease like a Dutch dish, to be thrown into the Thames and cooled, glowing-hot, in that surge, like a horseshoe' (3.5.81–112).

The bath, submersion, drowning and baptism are synonymous, and symbolize the breaking down and cleansing of the old outmoded state of being, leading to the birth of the rejuvenated, illumined man. The infant Stone or chick, born from the union of *king and *queen, was also placed in a bath of mercurial water which he usually consumed by drinking. Christian Rosenkreutz in Andreae's *The Chymical Wedding* relates that 'a Bath was prepared for our Bird ... Now it was at first cool when the Bird was set into it. He was mightily well pleased with it, drinking of it, and pleasantly sporting in it' (157). John Dastin wrote of the infant Stone: 'It is meet the King rest in a sweet Bath, till by little and little he hath drunk the Trinity of his Nourisher' (in FC, 100). See imbibation. Arthur Dee instructed the alchemist to place the infant Stone in a 'Glassen Lodge' and then 'placed and reposed in a Bath, and being lulled asleep his limbs dissolve and melt with sweat, which by the help of Art and Nature, and due governance, shall resume their former shape, renued [sic], and their strength so multiplied that now he desires kingly food, with which nourishment in a short space he will become a king, stronger than a king, and so stout in Battell, that he alone being a most powerfull Conqueror, will obtain victory against ten thousand Enemies' (FC, 109–10). Subtle in Jonson's *The Alchemist* refers to this bathing process when he says of the Stone, 'lute him well; / And leave him closed in *balneo*' (2.3.40–1). See **bain-marie**.

3 The bed as vessel

beak the spout of a retort or still through which the rising vapour from the vessel descends into the receiver to condense. In his *Archidoxis* Paracelsus wrote of distilling 'by an Alembick of three quils or beaks' (35). The alchemical vessels are often called by the names of such birds as *pelican, *stork and *goose, and 'beak' is an extension of this imagery. The beak of the alembic was also known as the stag's horn and the *crow's beak.

bed the name given to the alchemical vessel during the coniunctio or union of male (*sulphur) and female (*argent vive or mercury); the *prima materia. The bed is the place where the *chemical wedding of *Sol (red) and *Luna (white) is consummated, and the matrix in which the philosophical Stone is conceived and born (fig. 3). Rosinus said of these substances, 'they wedded themselves in their bed that is, mingled in their vessel' (in AC, 227). An anonymous treatise says: 'take a Red Man and a White Woman and Wed them together, and let them go to Chamber both, and look that the Door and Windows be fast barred . . . for if she may go out nowhere she will come to him again and lye with him on bed and then she shall conceive and beare a Son' (GU Ferguson MS 238, f. 2v). Benjamin Lock wrote: 'Then make coniunctio of the whyt oyle and red / And put them in a glass where they may lye together / The Chamber must be faire wher they ly in bed' ('Picklock', f. 33v). The alchemist was advised to construct this vessel in accordance with the *'square and circle' principle. The 'square and circle' symbolizes the birth of the

Stone (the circle) from the square of the four *elements. In Ripley's *Cantilena* the gestation of the *philosophical child (Stone) in the pregnant mother's womb causes a transformation not only in the shape of the mother but also in the shape of the bed in which she lies – the square bed is transformed into a sphere: 'The Mother's Bed which erst stood in a Square / Is shortly after made Orbicular' (lines 108–9). (See also **alembic**). The bed is also a name for the prima materia which contains the male and female seeds of metals. *The Hunting of the Greene Lyon* describes the lion as the 'bed' or matrix from which the 'sun' (male seed) and 'moon' (female seed) are born: 'The *Lyon* ys the Preist [*sic*], the *Sun* and *Moon* the wed, / Yet they were both borne in the *Lyons* Bedd' (TCB, 280) ('the wed' reads 'to wed' in MS Wellcome 436).

bee synonymous with the *mercurial serpent. In seventeenth-century bestiaries bees were classified as winged snakes. Bees, snakes and dragons were all classified in the same category (see Topsell). Herrick's poem 'The Wounded Cupid' has the young god complaining that 'A winged Snake has bitten me, / Which Country People call a Bee', to which his mother, Venus, replies, 'Come, tel me then, how great's the smart / Of those, thou woundest with thy Dart' (*Works*, 50). The bee/snake is also frequently identified with Cupid, as in Herrick's 'The Showre of Blossomes': 'Love turn'd himself into a Bee, / And with his Javelin wounded me; / From which mishap this use I make, / Where most Sweets are, there lyes a Snake' (*Works*, 283). In this context it is easy to see how the alchemists came to use both the bee and Cupid as an image of the mercurial serpent, the universal solvent which is said to 'poison' and kill metals (i.e. dissolve them into the *prima materia from which the *philosopher's stone is made). The sting of the bee and the dart of Cupid both signify the secret fire, the mercurial solvent which destroys the old metal or outmoded state of being. Bassett Jones's 'Lithochymicus' discourses on the many methods chosen by alchemists to make the philosopher's stone: 'A third, disdayning much that thus theyr king/ Should poyson'de bee by *Basiludra's* [Mercurius's] sting' (AP, 232). 'Mercurie', in Sir George Ripley's *Cantilena,* appears before the *queen bearing 'the Dart of passion' and a cup of his deadly poison (verse 17). In John Cleveland's 'Fuscara or the Bee Errant' the bee, whose 'suckets are moyst *Alchymie*', plays both alchemist and mercurial bee. He mints the green of 'the Garden into Gold' in the 'refining' still of his body (lines 1–4) and he stings Fuscara's wrist so that her '*Argent* skin with *or* so stream'd' (line 35). See **honey**.

beheading the decapitation or dismemberment of the *bird, *lion, *serpent, *dragon, *tree, man or *king signifies the dissolution, putrefaction and division of the body, the matter in the alembic, at the black *nigredo, the first step in the opus. This stage, which is a time of sacrifice and lament, is sometimes referred to as the caput mortuum or caput corvi (see **crow**, **raven**). *The Six Keys of Eudoxus* clearly equated the dissolution of the matter with the beheading and death of the bird: 'the wise Artist ought to dissolve the body with the spirit: he must cut off the Raven's head' (in Regardie, *Philosopher's Stone*, 105). The crow or raven's head is a well known name for the black stage or nigredo. The *Hermetis Trismegisti tractatus aureus* advised the alchemist to 'Take this Volatile Bird' and 'cut off its Head with a fiery sword' (Salmon, *Medicina Practica*, 279). This means that the volatile (flying) matter in the alembic has to be fixed (made non-volatile) and that the heating and digestion of the matter are to be continued until the black colour is transformed into the white of the *albedo. Nicolas Flamel wrote in his *Exposition*: 'Take away the head of this blacke man, cut off the head of the Crow, that is to say, whiten our blacke' (*HE*, 98). The protagonist in Andreae's *The Chymical Wedding* likewise must witness the beheading of both the *philosophical bird (159) and the beheading of the *king and his entourage who are clothed in black garments: 'Finally, there stept in a very *cole-black* tall Man, who has in his hand a sharp Ax. Now after the old King had been first brought to the Seat, his *Head* was instantly whipt off, and wrapped up in a black cloth' (123). The mercurial *blood or water of life is collected in a golden bowl and used to resurrect the dead bodies. The beheading of the king on his knees (symbolizing the raw matter) is illustrated in the 'Buch von Vunderverken' (GU Ferguson MS 4) (see fig. 4). The decapitation of the serpent is synonymous with the beheading of the bird. Flamel wrote: 'Take the viper ... cut off his head etc, that is to say, Take away from him his blacknesse' (*HE*, 99).

Variants of the beheading are the dismemberment of the king's body, the felled or truncated *tree (see fig. 47), the cutting off of the lion's paws, the chopping or tearing off of Mercurius's wings or feet (see **Hermes' seal**) and the clipping of the bird's wings (see *AF*, embl. 43). Dr Allslagen in Bassett Jones's 'Lithochymicus' states that the mark 'of perfect dissolution is / When that the bodie thus disjoynted lies, / By loveinge poysonous draughts in attome-wise' (*AP*, 249). Vaughan wrote in *Aula Lucis*: 'Separate the *Eagle* from the *Green-Lyon,* then clip her *wings*' (*VW* (R), 463). The last sonnet of Sir Philip Sidney's *Astrophil and Stella* included this image in a context which is alchemical: in the 'dark

4 The beheading

furnace', sorrow 'Melts down his lead into my boiling breast' and 'Most rude despair, my daily unbidden guest, / Clips straight my wings, straight wraps me in his night / And makes me then bow down my head and say: / "Ah, what doth Phoebus' gold that wretch avail / Whom iron doors do keep from use of day?" ' (*Selected Poems*, 188). Metaphysically, the decapitation represents the freeing of the soul from the prison of the body so that through detatchment it can gain the ability to discriminate between the merely natural man, bound by his thoughts, opinions and desires, and the illumined, philosophical man, freed from these illusions (the 'blackness'). But this understanding necessarily entails sacrifice and suffering, the death of the old outmoded state of being. See **melancholia**. (For the cutting off the feet of mercury, see **Mercurius**.)

bellows an instrument for producing a blast of air to fan and increase the fire in the alchemical furnace or *athanor. The bellows blower must stay alert and awake during this task because if the the fire goes out the magnum opus is ruined. Toutguerres in Bassett Jones's 'Lithochymicus' states that the opus will come to nothing 'unlesse [during the projection] with bellowes you mayntayne your flame / Uppon your metall on a Coppell plac'd' (*AP*, 281). The bellows blower is described in Book 2 of Edmund Spenser's *The Faerie Queene*: 'One with great bellowes gathered filling aire, / And with forst wind the fewell did inflame' (2.7.36). Alchemists who made excessive use of the bellows were known as *puffers. Face, the puffer in Ben Jonson's *The Alchemist*, assures Mammon: 'I haue blowne, sir, / Hard for your worship: throwne by many a coale, / When 'twas not beech; weigh'd those I put in, iust, / I keepe your heat, still euen.' (2.2.21–4). Bishop John Thornborough (1551–1641), who maintained a life-long interest in alchemy, had the alchemical motto 'Dum Spiro, Spero' (while I blow, I hope) inscribed on the north side of his alabaster tomb in Worcester cathedral. In Victor Hugo's *Notre-Dame de Paris*, the bellows in Claude Frollo's alchemist's cell are inscribed with a similar motto: 'Spira, spera' (361). The bellows are one of the best known insignia of the alchemist. In François Rabelais's *Pantagruel* (1532), one of the books that Pantagruel finds in the Library of St Victor is named *The Bellows of the Alchemists* (190). And in 'Le Club des haschischins', Théophile Gautier recounts a vision of 'alchemists whose heads were shaped like bellows, and limbs twisted into alembics' (*Romans et contes*, 483).

bind the fixation or coagulation of the volatile spirit, the same as 'nailing' and 'tying'. Loosing and binding means to dissolve and coagulate the matter in the alembic (see **solve et coagula**). One of the alchemist's tasks was to capture the elusive spirit *Mercurius and close him up in the vessel and tame him. It is to this binding of Mercurius that Milton referred in *Paradise Lost*: 'by their powerful art they bind / Volatile Hermes, and call up unbound / In various shapes old Proteus from the sea, / Drained through a limbeck to his native form' (3.602–5). During the process of the opus, Mercurius, the dissolving element, paradoxically becomes a binding element. He is the gum or *glue, the mediating

5 Raining birds

soul which binds the spirit and body, the male and female principles, at the *chemical wedding from which the *philosopher's stone is born (see **Mercurius**).

bird Birds of all kinds appear in alchemical texts. The birth of the philosopher's stone from the union of the male and female substances at the *chemical wedding is frequently compared to the birth of a bird or chick from the philosopher's *egg or vessel (see **Bird of Hermes**). Some of the vessels in which the opus is carried out are named after birds: the *pelican (or *goose or gander), the *cormorant and the *stork. The pelican is also a symbol of the stage known as the *multiplicatio, where the quality and quantity of the Stone are augmented by a repeated process of *solve et coagula (dissolution and coagulation). The four main stages of the opus are likewise symbolized by birds: the black *nigredo by the *crow or *raven, the multi-coloured or rainbow stage by the argus, *peacock or peacock's tail, the white *albedo by the *swan or *dove, and the red *rubedo by the *phoenix. Paracelsus described this succession of colours and stages: 'This black substance is the bird which flies by night without wings, which ... [is] changed into the blackness of a crow's head. Then it assumes the tail of a peacock, and subsequently, acquires the wings of a swan. Lastly it takes the highest red colour' (PW, 104–5). In Jonson's *The Alchemist* Face assures Mammon that he has put the matter in the alembic through the 'seueral colours ... the *crow*, / The *peacocks taile*, the *plumed swan*' (2.2.26–7). Michael Maier's *Atalanta fugiens* uses the raven as an image for the nigredo at the beginning of the opus and the *vulture for a symbol of the consummation of the opus.

In other contexts birds, *rain and *dew are closely associated. Within the alembic the *mercurial spirit goes through its repeated cycle of circulations, *distillations and *sublimations. Freed from the prison of

Duæ aves sunt nobiles & magni pretii,
Corpus & Spiritus, alter alterum consumit.
OCTAVA FIGURA.

Corpus iterum ponatur pro digestione in fimum equinum vel
balneum, superfuso suo aere vel Spiritu à Corpore olim subtracto. Corpus
factum est pro operationem album, Spiritus verò rubeus arte. Entium o-
pus tendit ad perfectionem, præparaturq́; sic Lapis Philosophorum.
C 3   Nunc

6 Amorous birds of prey

matter (the body), the spirit rises as a volatile vapour to the top of the
vessel where it condenses and descends as showers of rain, tears or dew
from heaven onto the dead, blackened bodies below, cleansing and
whitening them (see **ablution**). *A Chymicall Dictionary* (1650) defines the
Hermetic bird as 'the Mercury of Philosophers, which ascends, and then
descends for nourishment'. All volatile substances, vapours, fumes,
spirits or souls, which rise to the top of the alembic and fall as rain, are
symbolized by flying birds (fig. 5). Sir George Ripley wrote: 'Therefore
thy Water out of the Erth thou draw, / And make the soul therwyth for
to assend; / Then downe agayne into the Erth hyt throw, / That they oft
tymes so assend and dessend', which 'Waters some men call / . . . Byrds'
(*TCB*, 152).

Another dramatic image encountered in the alchemical texts is that
of the 'amorous birds of prey' who simultaneously copulate with and
devour one another in a cannibalistic merging. This image symbolizes
the paradoxical process of solve et coagula (dissolve and coagulate)
which the alchemist must continually reiterate throughout the opus in
order to purify the matter of the Stone in the alembic. The 'solve' is the
separation or death, the 'coagula' is the union which occurs at the
*chemical wedding of male (*sulphur) and female (*argent vive or
mercury). The antagonism and destruction of the amorous birds paradoxically brings about the interpenetration, mixing and union of substances and qualities at this union (fig. 6). The epigram to the eighth
emblem of *The Book of Lambspring* reads: 'Here are Two Birds, great and
strong – the body and spirit; one devours the other' (*HM*, 1:291). These
birds are variously represented by *ravens, vultures, and *hen and cock.

The 'amorous birds of prey' occur in an alchemical context in Andrew Marvell's 'To his Coy Mistress' which urges male and female to unite: 'Now let us sport us while we may; / And now, like am'rous birds of prey, / Rather at once our Time devour' (lines 37–9). A variant of this motif is that of the winged bird who devours the wingless bird, signifying the simultaneous dissolution of the fixed matter (wingless bird) by the volatile spirit (winged bird), and the fixation (by the wingless bird) of the volatile substance (the winged bird). The act of ingestion in alchemy, as in the purely Christian mysteries, is an emblem of the union of the consumer with the consumed. It is an image of sacrifice which leads to integration. Other hieroglyphs of this process are the *uroboros, the serpent which swallows its own tail and unites in a perfect circle, the *Bird of Hermes which eats its own wings, and that of *Saturn who ingests the mercurial *child. See **Argus, feathers**.

Bird of Hermes   philosophical mercury (*Mercurius) at various stages of the opus. The Bird of Hermes symbolizes the mercurial vapours as they ascend in the alembic during *distillation and *sublimation, and descend as celestial *rain or *dew, washing the black earth (the dead bodies) below (see **ablution**). Calid wrote that during the *calcination, when the matter in the vessel has been heated for a week in the *sand-bath, 'the Volatile ascends into the Alembeck which we call *Avis Hermetis*' (*Booke of the Secrets*, 119). The Bird of Hermes is the name of the philosophical bird or chick born from the vessel of the philosopher's *egg. The birth of the *philosopher's stone from the union of male and female substances at the *chemical wedding is frequently compared to the birth of a bird. Philalethes wrote: 'Join heaven to earth [male and female] . . . and you will see in the middle of the firmament the bird of Hermes' (HM, 2:263). The birth of this bird during the sublimation of the matter is described by Aristotle: 'Therefore burn it with a dry Fire, that it may bring forth a Son, and keep him warily lest he fly away into smoke; and this is that which the Philosopher saith in his *Turba*. Whiten the earth, and Sublime it quickly with Fire, untill the Spirit which thou shalt finde in it goe forth of it, and it is called *Hermes Bird*; for that which ascends higher is efficacious purity but that which fals to the bottome, is drosse and corruption' (in FC, 70). Aristotle identified the Hermes Bird with the *white foliated earth, the *quintessence. The hatching of the bird is described in Andreae's *The Chymical Wedding*: 'Our Egg being now ready was taken out; but it needed no cracking, for the *Bird* that was in it soon freed himself' (155). During the process known as the *cibation, the newly born bird is nourished with *'milk' (mercurial water) and placed in a sweat bath where he loses all his feathers and is thus tamed.

Another version of the cibation is represented in the *Emblematicall Scrowles* attributed to Sir George Ripley, where the Bird of Hermes consumes its own feathers under the sweating heat of a flaming sun (fig. 7). The title of the verse accompanying the emblem reads: 'The Bird of Hermes is my name, Eating my wings to make me tame'. The taming of the elusive mercurial bird is a key task in the work of maturing the philosopher's stone. Mercurius must be captured and tamed so that he

7 The Bird of Hermes eating her wings

becomes the alchemist's willing servant, a force controlled and directed rather than one which is overwhelming and out of control. Paracelsus wrote: 'Verily by the dissolution of that same natural mixtion our Mercury is tamed or subjected' (*Aurora*, 48). In Ben Jonson's *Mercurie Vindicated from the Alchemists at Court*, Vulcan says of the taming of Mercurius: 'Begin your charme, sound musique, circle him in, and take him: If he will not obey, bind him' (lines 112–13). The image from the Ripley *Scrowles* of the sacred bird eating its own wings signifies both the dissolution of that which is fixed and the fixation of the volatile aspect of the Stone's matter. It is synonymous with the process symbolized by the *beheading of the bird. The *blood of the bird is a name for the miraculous healing *elixir of the alchemists. Nicolas Flamel wrote of the birth of the philosopher's stone: 'there will come out a chicken, that will deliver you with its blood from all diseases, and feed you with its flesh and clothe you with its feathers, and shelter you from the cold' (*HM*, 1: 146).

bitch   see **dog and bitch**.

black, blackness   the colour which signifies the onset of the *nigredo, the dissolution or death and *putrefaction of the old form or body of the metal (or the Stone's matter) at the beginning of the opus. Nicolas Flamel stated that at the time of the nigredo, which is 'the black of the blackest black', the 'Matter is dissolved, is corrupted, groweth black' (HE, 75, 73). Philalethes likewise wrote of the putrefaction that it is 'no other colour but black of the blackest' (RR, 17). In a letter to Robert Boyle dated 28 October 1658, Johann Morian described one of Samuel Hartlib's attempts to produce the philosopher's stone: 'All succeeded favorably, and [the material passed] through various inconstant colors, arriving then at perfect blackness' (in Newman, 'Prophecy', 108). Thomas Nashe makes a jokey reference to the alchemical 'black of the blackest' when denouncing his literary detractors in the second preface to *Strange Newes*: 'What ever they be that thus persecute Art (as the Alcumists are said to persecute Nature) I would wish them to abate the edge of their wit, and not grinde their colours so hard; having founde that which is blacke, let them not, with our forenamed Gold-falsifiers, seeke for a substance that is blacker than black' (*Works*, 1:261). According to alchemical theory, renewal or regeneration could only occur after the 'death' of the old form of the metal or outmoded state of being. Artephius pointed out that it is only by going through this black death and profound mortification that the body, separated from soul and spirit, can be purified of its corruption and whitened in preparation for its perfect union with the spirit or the united soul and spirit: 'Now as to colours, that which does not make black cannot make white, because blackness is the beginning of whiteness and a sign of putrefaction and alteration, and that the body is now penetrated and mortified' (SB, 36). The alchemists compared the matter of the Stone at this stage of the opus to all black things, some of which are: the *crow, the *raven, blacking, *coal, pitch, ebony, the black man, *Ethiopian or Moor, *eclipsed sun, night, *sable robe, *black shirt, black doublet. See **colours**.

black earth the matter of the Stone during *calcination or *putrefaction, at the death and dissolution of the old metal or outmoded state of being. The black earth or mud, frequently symbolized by dead bodies, lies in the bottom of the alembic waiting to be washed, purified and whitened by the descent of the celestial *dew (mercurial water) from the top of the alembic. Calid wrote that during calcination, when the volatile spirit rises to the top of the alembic, 'that which remains in the bottom of the Glass, is like Ashes or sifted earth, called, the Philosophers Earth' (*Booke of the Secrets*, 119). Once whitened, it can be sown with the *seed of gold, with the spirit, and united with it. (See **white foliated earth**.) The eighth plate of Salomon Trismosin's *Splendor Solis* shows the blackened *Ethiopian (the Stone's matter) emerging from a muddy stream to meet his *queen (the pure, whitened matter). The *red head of the Ethiopian and the red robe held out by the queen indicate that the whitened matter will ultimately be transformed into the *red stone at the culmination of the opus.

black king see **Ethiopian, king**.

black man see **Ethiopian**.

black shirt see **saturn**.

black stage see **black, blackness, nigredo**.

black sun see **sol niger, eclipse**.

blood a synonym for the transforming arcanum, *Mercurius, as both solvent and coagulator; the *philosopher's stone, the *red tincture or *elixir. *The Rosary of the Philosophers* says: 'No solution ought to be made without Blood, proper or appropriate, *viz.* the Water of Mercury, which is called the Water of the Dragon' (in *FC*, 25). The alchemical blood appears in various forms throughout the opus. It first occurs as the blood of death and sacrifice at the opening of the opus, when the old body of the metal (or outmoded state of being) is dissolved or killed in order to be renewed. The alchemical principle of death and putrefaction is based on the idea that nature could only be renewed after first dying away. The biblical metaphor of the grain of wheat which must first be buried before producing more grain, and the image of Christ's crucifixion and resurrection, are often cited by the alchemists. *The Sophic Hydrolith* said of Christ: '[his] power, strength, and purple tincture, changes us imperfect men and sinners in body and soul, and is marvellous medicine for all our diseases' (*HM*, 1:103).

The age-old idea of the shedding of blood from a pure being in order to cleanse the sins of the impure occurs frequently in the alchemical texts. Colson's *Philosophia maturata* says of the alchemical sacrifice: 'then the Body shall dye of Flux, shedding its blood, and putting on many Colours' (35). In *The Worke of John Dastin*, 'Mother Mercury', the *prima materia, conceives a pure child whose blood cures the sick and leprous brothers (the base metals which have not yet matured into silver or gold) (*TCB*, 261–3). Likewise in Nicolas Flamel's *Philosophical Summary*, the blood of the pure *bird hatched in the *egg of the alembic has the power to deliver man from all disease (*HM*, 1:146). Flamel's *Exposition* borrows the story of the sacrifice of the Innocents to symbolize this process. *Sol and *Luna are bathed and cleansed in vessels containing the blood of the sacrificed infants (*HE*, 14). The blood in this context represents the mercurial water which dissolves the matter of the Stone, then washes and transforms this matter at the *ablution. The mercurial blood of the *green lion is used (along with *virgin's milk) as a drink for nourishing the *philosophical stone or infant to help it grow to maturity. This stage of the work was known as the *cibation.

At the final stage of the work, known as the *rubedo, the image of blood symbolizes the precious *red elixir or purple tincture. The attainment of the red elixir (gold), after the white (silver), is sometimes compared to the dyeing or staining of white sheets with red blood (see **rubedo**). Paracelsus's *Aurora* called the purple tincture 'the blessed blood of Rosie colour' (19), and Basil Valentine wrote that 'this Tincture is the Rose of our Masters, of purple hue, called also red blood' (*HM*, 1:330). Laurentius Ventura wrote of the fixation of the Stone: 'For the Stone must be kept in the fire, till it cannot any more be changed from one nature to another, from one colour to another, but become like the

Reddest blood running like wax in the fire, and yet diminishing nothing at all' (in ZC, 81). The divine *tincture is thought to be capable of tingeing all metals to gold and of restoring man to perfect health and consciousness of God. The colour of the red tincture or Stone is sometimes compared to dragon's blood. A recipe for the tincture in Lancelot Colson's *Philosophia maturata* instructs the alchemist to 'increase the fire, till it [the matter for the Stone] be perfect yellow, and then again increase the fire, until it be red as Dragon's blood' (46).

blood of the green lion   see **green lion**.

blossom   see **flowers, lily, philosophical tree, rose**

blow   see **bellows, puffer**.

blue   see **azure**.

blush   the reddening of the purified, white matter of the Stone at the final stage of the opus, the *rubedo. In Ben Jonson's *The Alchemist*, Face assures Mammon that the rubedo (the red stage) is almost perfected, and Mammon asks, 'Blushes the *bolts-head* ?' (2.2.9). See **rubedo**.

body   see **philosopher's stone, nigredo, albedo, chemical wedding, earth**.

boil   To cook or boil means to bring the matter in the alembic to clear perfection over the fire. Michael Maier described the cooking as *"women's work': 'When you have obtained the white lead, then do women's work, that is to say: COOK' (AF, 176). The dictum 'Boyl, boyl and again boyl, and accompt not tedious our long decoction' is often cited in the alchemical texts (Klossowski, de Rola, *Alchemy*, 25). The raw matter to be 'boiled' is sometimes referred to as the fruit, as in the treatise 'Aristeus Pater', which says of the fire: 'So being enkindled, look thou dayly to it, / that it burn not, but boyl the golden Fruit' (lines 143–4, AP, 476). Artephius used the term 'boyling' to cover the process of 'solve et coagula', the continually reiterated process of the dissolution and coagulation which purifies the matter of the Stone (SB, 20). *The Only True Way* likewise stated that in order to be brought to purity and perfection the 'crude and raw' material had to be 'cooked or digested by the process of coction' (HM, 1:163). Coction is the refinement of matter through heat. Milton uses the coction/concoction metaphor in an alchemical context in *Paradise Lost* to describe the transformative process of digestion. Raphael sits down with Adam and Eve and proceeds to eat with 'keen despatch / Of real hunger, and concoctive heat / To transubstantiate; what redounds, transpires / Through spirits with ease; nor wonder; if by fire / Of sooty coal the empiric alchemist / Can turn, or holds it possible to turn / Metals of drossiest ore to perfect gold' (5.436–42).

bolt's-head, bolt-head   a long-necked, round-bottomed flask used in the distillation process. In an appendix to 'Lithochymicus', Bassett Jones defined the 'boult's head' as 'a globular flask with a long cylindrical neck used for distillation' (*AP*, 389). He also cites a recipe using the bolt's-head as a vessel: 'take the sprite of wine / Moste pure, and in a boult's head christalline / *Hermeticly* shutt up they place't in Ice' (*AP*, 284). In Jonson's *The Alchemist*, Face assures Subtle that he has taken the right ingredients 'and then married 'hem, / And put 'hem in a *Bolts-head*, nipp'd to *digestion*' (2.3.73–4).

brass   the same as laton (see **laton**).

bread   see **paste**.

bride and bridegroom   see **chemical wedding**.

bronze   a name for laton or the terrestrial body (see **laton**).

brother   see **incest**.

bud   see **flowers, green**.

bury   see **grave**.

C

Cadmus   see **oak**.

caduceus   the wand of *Mercury, with two intertwining serpents crossing each other to form three circles, symbolizing the circulation of the universal male and female energies, known in alchemy as *philosophical sulphur and *argent vive or *Sol and *Luna. The three circles represent the three main separations and unions of male and female during the opus alchymicum (see **chemical wedding**). In his 'Praxis', Isaac Newton wrote of the Caducean rod as the 'medium of joying their [the serpents'] tinctures'. 'The rod of Mercury reconciles the two serpents', he stated (Dobbs, *Janus*, 300). After much quarrel and strife, the snakes become entwined in perfect harmony. Metaphysically, the union of the snakes on the caduceus symbolizes 'the exact balance which must be maintained between the positive and negative life-streams, and between the two states of life, earth and heaven' (Hodgson, *Astrology*, 202). This magic rod thus has the power of reconciling the conflicting elements into harmony and raising the soul into the temple of wisdom. In the human body the stem of the wand symbolizes the spinal cord, the central axis of the human nervous system (Hodgson, *Astrology*, 36, 154). In the alchemical treatise, 'Hermetick Raptures', the caduceus is referred to as both 'the powerfull Hermetick wand' and the 'fam'd Caduceus' (lines 123, 137, *AP*, 579). Mercury, in Ben Jonson's *Mercurie Vindicated*, comically 'defends himself with his Caducaeus' against the persecutions of 'a troupe of threedbare Alchymists' (lines 115–16, 110–11). The alchemical caduceus is illustrated in 'Incipit tractatulus de phenice siue de lapide philosoph-ico' (fig. 3) and in one of the hieroglyphs in Nicolas Flamel's *Exposition* (see GU Ferguson MS17, f. 11). In other manuscripts of Flamel the number of circles made by the entwining serpents ranges from two (St Andrews) to four (Paris, Arsenal) (see van Lennep, *Alchimie*, 138).

calcination the conversion of a metal or mineral to powder or dust by the heat of the fire. This process reduces the metallic body (or soul of man) into its first matter and renders it porous so that it may more easily receive the influx of the divine *tincture or spirit. Colson's *Philosophia maturata* speaks of the calcination of the blackened matter of the Stone: the matter is 'our Crows Bill, far blacker then Pitch, which thou may'st set on fire, by putting a kindled Cole into it; so as [it] shall be calcined … into a most yellow Earth; But this Calcination sufficeth not for its perfect cleansing; put it therefore into a Reverberatory with a moderate heat, for eight dayes, and so many Nights following, increasing the heat and flame, till it be white as Snow' (33). George Herbert used the calcination metaphor when writing of Christ in 'Easter': 'That, as his death calcined thee to dust, / His life may make thee gold, and much more, just' (*Works*, 41). Goethe, who spent a great deal of his life exploring alchemy, used the same metaphor in a letter to E. T. Langer in 1769: 'I have suffered and am free again, this calcination was very profitable for my soul' (in Gray, *Goethe the Alchemist*, 24).

calx the product of *calcination, the powder, ashes or essence produced by roasting or burning a metal or mineral; the philosophical *earth, the body of the Stone. Geber wrote that during distillation 'The Calx or Body must be often imbibed, that thence it might be sublimed, and more yet purged then before' (in FC, 72).

caput corvi see **crow**, **raven**, **nigredo**, **beheading**.

caput mortuum colcothar, now refers to the brownish-red ferric oxide which remains in the retort after the distillation of sulphuric acid from iron sulphate. In alchemy the caput mortuum is a symbol of the initial stage of the opus, the black *nigredo, during which process the old form of the metal or matter for the Stone is 'killed', dissolved into the *prima materia or original stuff of creation. It can also specifically symbolize the dross or residue left at the bottom of the vessel during this stage. Nicaise Le Fevre referred to the caput mortuum in this sense when describing the process of making Sir Walter Raleigh's 'Great Cordial': nothing is left in the bottom of the retort 'after the last action of Fire, but that which may be called legitimately a mere *caput mortuum*, or dead earth' (*Discourse*, 65). See **nigredo** and **beheading**.

castle a name for the hermetically sealed vessel which not only keeps the con-tents within well defended from the invasion of outside influences or substances, but also stops the volatile contents from escaping (see fig. 46). A manuscript of Nicola d'Antonio degli Agli (1480) shows an emblem of an angel (the winged, volatile substance) besieged in the ramparts of a red castle (the fixing, coagulating agent) (in Klossowski de Rola, *Alchemy*, fig. 30). In Denis Zachaire's 'Practise of the Divine Work' (lines 138–40), the Prince (the raw material for the Stone) retires 'alone into the Castle, then / Into a round and secret little Den. / 'Twas round and little as a Hermit's cell' (*AP*, 439). Both castle and *den are names for the sealed vessel. By extension the turreted castle becomes a name for the philosopher's *furnace in which the vessel is placed (see **tower**). Dorn's *Congeries Paracelsicae* instructs the alchemist to break the coal for heating the furnace into pieces and 'fill up the turrets with these and kindle the fire at the doors beneath' (*PW*, 285). The castle is also a term for the impure matter in which the pure spirit or secret transforming arcanum is locked and from which it must be freed during the process of the opus. Ripley referred to his treatise, *A Compound of Alchymie,* as a 'castle' and also used this image to represent the opus alchymicum itself. He wrote at the end of chapter one: 'At the *fyrst Gate,* now art thou in, / Of the *Phylosophers Castle* … Proceed wysely that thou may wyne / In at mo Gates of that Castell, / Which Castle ys round as any Bell' (*TCB*, 134). The castle is the container which holds the arcanum, the secret of the *philosopher's stone and that container can be a book of alchemical secrets, the alembic or man himself. See **alembic**.

cauda pavonis   see **peacock's tail**.

cement, cementation   Cement is a tenacious substance used in the *distillation process; a paste placed on sheets of metal about to be heated in the furnace in order to examine their purity (see **glue**). Cementation is the process by which one solid is made to penetrate and combine with another at high temperature without *liquefaction taking place. Ruland's *Lexicon* defines 'Cimentare' as 'to unite' (105). In John Donne's 'The Extasie' the hands of the lovers are described as 'firmly cemented / With a fast balm, which thence did spring' (lines 5–6), just prior to experiencing the alchemical soul *separation. See **balm, glue**.

cervus fugitivus   the fleeing hart, one of the best known epithets of the alchemical *Mercurius, also known as the deer, fawn and stag. In *The Anatomie of Alchymie*, Thomas Lodge includes the flying hart as one of the major alchemical enigmas: 'First aske they where the flying Eagle dwels … Then of the Lyon greene, and flying hart' (*Works*, 3:69). The cervus fugitivus is a symbol of fleeting evanescence. One of *Mercurius's key qualities is his elusiveness, his fugitive nature. Face in Jonson's *The Alchemist* answers Subtle's question 'And what's your *Mercury*?' with 'A very fugitiue, he will be gone, sir' (2.5.31–2). In his role as the fleeing hart Mercurius serves as the messenger or soul which mediates between the spirit and the body, uniting them in the *chemical wedding. The deer/soul equivalent is common in seventeenth-century poetry and emblem collections. The image appears in an alchemical context in

The Book of Lambspring where the verse accompanying the third emblem says: 'The deer desires no other name / But that of the Soul' (*HM*, 1: 280). A variant of the cervus fugitivus is the servus fugitivus, the fleeing servant (see **red servant**). 'Cervus' and 'servus' are used interchangeably. In *A Revelation of the Secret Spirit...of Alchymie* Baptiste Lambye (Giovanni Agnelli) referred to 'Mercury or the fugitive slave' (60) and Bassett Jones names Mercurius 'the servaunt truant of the fate-ruleing hoast' ('Lithochymicus', in *AP*, 324). With a verbal play on cervus/servus, the hart and servant (or messenger) become one.

The dual nature of Mercurius is clearly expressed in the symbol of the cervus fugitivus. In one aspect he is a faithful ministering servant, while in the other he is volatile, elusive and evasive, even unfaithful and deceptive. The alchemist is repeatedly warned that he must capture unstable Mercurius and seal him tightly in the vessel. Vulcan exclaims in Ben Jonson's *Mercurie Vindicated from the Alchemists at Court*: 'Deare *Mercury*! Helpe He flies. He is 'scap'd. Precious golden *Mercury*, be fixt; be not so volatile' (lines 23–6). The elusive Mercurius must be captured and tamed so that he may become the adept's faithful servant (see **Bird of Hermes**). Andrew Marvell's quick 'silver' fawn in 'The Nymph Complaining' is a very embodiment of the dual cervus fugitivus, who is elusive and deceptive and at the same time a faithful servant. The fawn, who is wondrously 'fleet...on those little silver feet' (lines 63–4) and who is the gift from the 'counterfeit' Sylvio and 'might be / Perhaps as false or more false than he' (lines 48–9), is also the nymph's friendly ally: the faun 'did invite / Me to its game; it seemed to bless / Itself in me' (lines 43–4).

chameleon   a name for the alchemists' *chaos. An anonymous treatise compares the colour of the earth or matter for the Stone during the process of *rarefaction to the chameleon: 'At first it appeareth dry, then Moist and Viscous, then, coloured like the Chameleon, which if it be acted upon by the heat of a bath the Earth breaketh and sublimeth into a Water like gold, which is our so glorious mercury' (BL Sloane MS 3631, f. 7).

chaos   the formless, shapeless matter from which the world and the *philosopher's stone were thought to have been formed. The alchemist used the process of the macrocosmic creation of the world as the blueprint for the creation of the *philosopher's stone in microcosm. The alchemists have indicated that the raw material or massa confusa, with which they work, is the original chaos from which the world was created. They saw their *prima materia as a 'piece' of this chaos. Martin Ruland wrote in his *Lexicon of Alchemy* that the Hermetic chemists 'compared their work to the development of the primeval Chaos' (353). Edward Kelly wrote in his exposition on George Ripley's *The Compound of Alchymie*: 'Riplye compareth the Worke to the Chaos which Chaos containing all things without division, the Sun the Moone the Stars and Elements all as it weare cast up in a Ball of Earth which by the word of God were separated in six days and perfected, even so our Stone, which all the first must have' (BL Sloane MS 3631, f. 51). In his commentary on the *Emerald Table* of

Hermes Trismegistus (Keynes MS 28), Isaac Newton wrote: 'And just as all things were created from one Chaos by the design of one God, so in our art all things, that is the four elements, are born from this one thing, which is our Chaos, by the design of the Artifcer and the skillful adaption of things' (Dobbs, *Janus*, 276). In another work, the 'Index chemicus' (Keynes MS 30, f. 58), Newton listed 'chaos', along with 'dark abyss' and 'hyle', as one of the names of the prima materia (Westfall, 'Index', 180).

During the opus the alchemist must perform the primordial task of dividing or differentiating the undifferentiated chaos into the four elements, earth, air, fire and water. The opposing aspects of the elements (for instance, hot and cold, dry and moist) then have to be reconciled and united in a *coniunctio by using the qualities that each element has in common (for example, earth, which is cold and dry, shares with water, which is cold and moist, the quality of coldness). This union of opposing qualities is frequently represented by the emblem of the copulating lovers at the *chemical wedding. Once united, the elements become the *fifth element or *quintessence, the perfect 'little world' or microcosm in which all the elements are harmonized. The alchemists thought of God as the divine alchemist who created the harmonious, ordered universe through a process of chemical extraction, *separation, *sublimation, and *conjunction upon the original chaos. In an alchemical context in 'A Nocturnal upon S. Lucy's Day', John Donne compared the uniting lovers to the matter of the Stone which grows like 'two chaoses' (lines 24–5). These 'chaoses' are the alchemical raw material symbolized by the bodies of the dead lovers of the *chemical wedding whose separated souls float above them: 'often absences / Withdrew our souls, and made us carcasses' (lines 26–7).

chariot of Phaethon a name for the opus alchymicum, the opus circulatorium. The 'Chariot of Phaethon', wrote Ruland, is 'one of the designations which the Philosophers have given to the Grand Work' (*Lexicon*, 346). The *opus circulatorium is sometimes compared to a wheel (or wheels) of a chariot, as well as to the sun's 'circular' course through the heavens. In Ovid's account of the Heliades myth, Phaethon desires to drive the chariot of the sun through the heavens, against his father's advice. The inexperienced Phaethon loses control of the sun's chariot and is blasted to earth by a thunderbolt hurled by Jupiter, plunging into the river Eridanus to his death. At Phaethon's death, Phoebus (the sun) 'sits in gloomy mourning garb, shorn of his brightness, just as when he is darkened by eclipse' (Ovid, *Metamorphoses*, 1.87, lines 381–3). The blackening or *eclipse of the sun is an image used by the alchemists to denote the darkness of the *nigredo, the initial part of the work involving the death of the matter of the Stone. The night or blackness of the opus is that part of the circular course when the sun appears to be extinguished. The night symbolizes the 'solve' (or dissolution) as opposed to the day which symbolizes the 'coagula' (coagulation) in the reiterated cycle of *solve et coagula. The myth of Phaethon's death and the extinguishing of the sun came to be used as an image for the nigredo or mortification. In *The*

Golden Calf Helvetius wrote: 'The Sages have seen ... the moon kindled by Phaeton's conflagration ... Blessed, yea, thrice blessed is the man to whom Jehovah has revealed the method of preparing that Divine Salt by which the metallic or mineral body is corrupted, destroyed, and mortified' (*HM*, 2:227).

chemic, chymick an adjective and noun used regularly from the sixteenth to the eighteenth century to mean 'alchemical' and 'an alchemist'. Alexander Pope celebrated the happy man who gathers herbs and 'with chymic art exalts the mineral powers, / And draws the aromatic souls of flowers' ('Windsor Forest', lines 243–4). In 'The Cross' John Donne compared the power of spiritual crosses to the quintessence of a remedy made by chemical extraction: 'These for extracted chemic medicine serve, / And cure much better, and as well preserve' (lines 27–8). Andrew Marvell wrote of the sun's alchemical power to distil the earth in 'Eyes and Tears': 'So, the all-seeing Sun each day / Distills the World with Chymick Ray; / But finds the Essence only Showers, / Which straight in pity back he powers' (lines 21–4). In *Paradise Lost* Milton described the alchemical nature of the sun and its power to generate precious stones in the earth: 'What wonder then if fields and regions here / Breathe forth elixir pure, and rivers run / Potable gold, when with one virtuous touch / The archchemic sun ... Produces with terrestrial humour mixed / Here in the dark so many precious things' (3.606–11). For the chemical action of the sun penetrating the earth's crust, see **prima materia**.

chemical wedding one of the central images of the opus alchymicum and a crucial operation in the creation of the *philosopher's stone. The alchemists were ultimately concerned with the union of substances, the reconciliation of opposites. Through this 'marriage' of opposites the goal of the opus, the production of gold and its metaphysical equivalent, was obtained. The idea of the alchemical marriage is older than the corresponding mystical marriage of the Church Fathers, and is based on classical and preChristian tradition (*MC*, 467).

The opus alchymicum consists of a repeated cycle of dissolutions and coagulations of the matter of the Stone in the alembic. The old form of the metal or matter for the Stone is dissolved into the original stuff of creation, the *prima materia, and this materia is coagulated into a new, purer form. Each time the process of *solve et coagula is reiterated, the substance in the alembic becomes more and more purified. In certain instances this sequence of solve et coagula is referred to as the cycle of separatio and coniunctio. The coagulation or coniunctio is the triumphant moment of chemical combination where such opposite states and qualities as *sulphur and mercury, hot and cold, dry and moist, fixed and volatile, spirit and body, form and matter, active and receptive, and male and female are reconciled of their differences and united (see **peace and strife**). *Zoroaster's Cave* says: 'The Generation of Metalls and the Philosophers Stone is to conjoyn proper principles; videlicet Man with Woman, Active with Passive, Sulphur with Mercury, that so Generation may ensue Corruption' (70). This union is symbolized by the

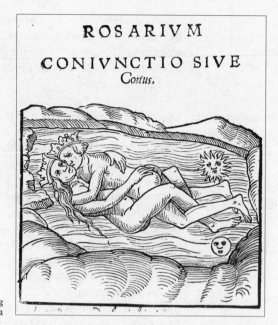

ROSARIVM

CONIVNCTIO SIVE
Coitus.

8 The red man and white woman coupling
in the mercurial sea

chemical wedding in the retort with the lovers frequently personified
by *Sol and *Luna, sun and moon. Edward Kelly wrote: 'In this art you
must wed the Sun and the Moon' (*Two excellent Treatises*, 37). The coniunctio is sometimes portrayed as an incestuous copulation between
brother and sister, or mother and son (see **incest**). The wedding does not
always take the form of a direct union, but occurs by means of a third
mediating principle, *Mercurius, the *prima materia or seminal matter
of both male and female. In this role Mercurius is known as the glue,
gum or priest who ties the knot at the wedding (see **glue, green lion**).
The copulation is sometimes depicted as occurring in *sea water, a
symbol for the mercurial prima materia (fig. 8).

Images both verbal and visual representing this union range from
the most primitive animal matings (*dog and bitch, *hen and cock,
*amorous birds of prey, winged and wingless *dragons or serpents) to
the union of human lovers, *red man and white woman (see fig. 8), and
ultimately to the royal wedding of Sol and Luna as *king and *queen
(fig. 9). The union occurs a number of times throughout the process of
the opus (as the solve et coagula is repeated), each time at a more refined
level. The nature of the image indicates the level of refinement attained:
hen and cock at the primitive beginning of the work, and king and
queen at the highly refined culmination of the work. From this union
of male and female, philosophical sulphur (fire and air) and argent vive
(earth and water), there arose the precious philosopher's stone, the
divine love essence which could transmute base metals into gold and
earthly man into the divine. For the union or reconciliation of the
elements, earth, air, fire and water see **conversion**.

Alchemy is based on the Hermetic view that man had become divided
within himself, separated into two sexes, at the fall in the garden of
Eden and could only regain his integral Adamic state when the oppos-

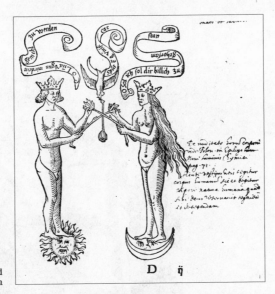

9 The chemical wedding of King Sol and
Queen Luna

ing forces within him were reconciled. The union of these universal
male and female forces produced that third substance or effect which
could heal not only the disease of the physical world but also the
affliction of the separated soul. Metaphysically, the chemical wedding is
the perfect union of creative will or power (male) with wisdom (female)
to produce pure love (the child, the Stone). The creation of this Stone
always involves some kind of sacrifice or death. Thus emblems of the
chemical wedding almost always include symbols of death which over-
shadow the coniunctio. The amorous birds of prey (see fig. 6) copulate
while devouring each other (see **bird**, **strife**). The sixth emblem of *The
Rosary of the Philosophers* shows the united lovers lying on a coffin
(McLean, *Rosary*, 39), while the lovers in the sixth emblem (second series)
of Mylius's *Philosophia reformata* are shown encased in a glass coffin with
Saturn and a skeleton with a scythe at either side (fig. 10). The death at
the wedding symbolizes the extinction of the earlier differentiated state
before union, and also powerfully conveys the alacrity with which the
festive moment of the coagula or wedding is transformed into the
lamentation of the solve or death. Many texts state that the solve and
coagula are simultaneous. Alchemical theory stated that generation
could not take place unless there had first been a death. In Christian
mysticism the same idea occurs with the parable of the grain of wheat
which must first die in the earth before it can bring forth fruit (John
12:24–5), a parable which the alchemists often cite. The philosopher's
stone cannot be generated until the lovers have died and their bodies
putrefied in the mercurial waters. Artephius wrote of the lovers: 'If
therefore these do not die, and be converted into water, they remain
alone, or as they were and without fruit; that if they die, and are resolved
in our water, they bring forth fruit, an hundred fold' (*SB*, 38). The bodies
of the lovers (the red man and white woman) lying dead in the grave
symbolize the death which frees the soul to be released and rise to the
top of the alembic. Some treatises indicate that the soul is then united in

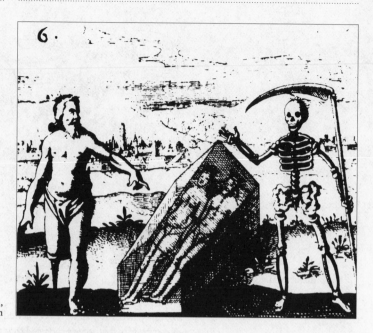

10 The lovers in the coffin, with Saturn, the scythe, and skeleton

a new wedding with the spirit while the blackened, putrefying bodies below are washed of their impurities and whitened (see **ablution**). The union of soul with spirit is frequently represented as the marriage of Sol and Luna. The next step is the union of the already joined soul and spirit with the purified body below, at which point the body is resurrected. This union is also frequently represented by the marriage of Sol and Luna. Some treatises say that the soul unites with the purified body by means and mediation of the spirit, some that spirit and body unite by means of the mediation of the soul. But whatever names are applied, a supreme union occurs, with the death and resurrection symbolizing the transmutation of matter. When the union of body and spirit takes place, the body is dissolved into spirit, while the spirit is simultaneously coagulated into form (i.e. body) so that the 'opposites' may be perfectly mingled. It is clear that the coniunctio is primarily a philosophical operation, namely, the union of form and matter. 'The Golden Rotation' states: 'nothing can be sayde to be perfect but by the coniunctio of the matter and form which coniunction bringeth new unity' (f. 24). Some alchemical philosophers, such as Gerhard Dorn, indicate that a further wedding may occur, involving the ultimate union of the resurrected body, soul and spirit with the 'unus mundi' or universal oneness (MC, 458).

At a metaphysical level, the aim of the separation of the soul from the body is to free it from its age-old attachment to the body so that it can transcend the turmoil and pull of the merely natural forces of matter. The separation of the soul is a kind of 'death' to the world. In its new state of equanimity the soul is able to become conscious of its own true nature and of the difference between natural and spiritual man. In the light of this knowledge the soul desires to unite with the spirit above and become illumined by it. The subsequent reunion of this spiritual awareness with the new, purified body means that knowledge gained in a state of higher consciousness can now be put into action, made manifest in the phenomenal world. At this point the male and female energies of the universe are united and balanced within the individual, bringing into being a whole or holy state (see **caduceus**). This idea occurs in John Donne's 'The Exstasy' where the united lovers' bodies lie below 'like sepulchral statues' while their 'souls, (which to advance their state, / Were gone out), hung 'twixt her, and me'. Freed from the bodies, the souls gain a new vantage point of consciousness: 'We then, who are this new soul, know, / Of what we are composed and made'. The newly aware souls then reunite with the bodies below: 'So must pure lovers' souls descend / T'affections, and to faculties ... To our bodies turn we then, that so / Weak men on love revealed may look; / Love's mysteries in souls do grow, / But yet the body is his book' (lines 18–72). Johann Andreae's influential alchemical treatise *The Chymical Wedding of Christian Rosenkreutz* (1616) in particular features the chemical wedding of the king and queen. Christian witnesses the wedding enacted in a comedy in the House of the Sun: 'In the last *Act* the Bride-groom appeared in such pomp as is not well to be believed, and I was amazed how it was brought to pass: The Bride met him in the like Solemnity. Whereupon all the people cried out *VIVAT SPONSUS, VIVAT SPONSA*. So that by this comedy they did with all congratulate our King and Queen in the most stately manner' (117–18). The concept of this alchemical process provides a key strand in the narrative of Lindsay Clarke's contemporary novel, *The Chemical Wedding* (1990).

chemist, chymist used regularly from the sixteenth to the eighteenth century to mean alchemist or *iatrochemist. Elias Ashmole wrote in his prolegomena to Arthur Dee's *Fasciculus chemicus* that the author has chosen to present only pertinent information, 'even as a skilful *Chymist*, who by *Spagyrical* operations, separates the *gross* and *earthy* from the more *fine* and *pure*'. John Dryden wrote in 'Absalom and Achitophel' that Zimri 'in the course of one revolving moon, / Was chemist, fiddler, stateman, and buffoon' (lines 529–30). (Zimri is based on George Villiers, Duke of Buckingham, who built a laboratory in order to find the philosopher's stone.) Alexander Pope wrote in his *Essay on Man*: 'Whate'er the passion, knowledge, fame or pelf, / Not one will change his neighbour with himself ... The starving chemist in his golden views / Supremely Blessed, the poet in his muse' (2.261–70).

child see **philosophical child**.

child's play see **ludus puerorum**.

children's games see **ludus puerorum, children's piss**.

children's piss a synonym for the *mercurial water or *prima materia at the stage of *putrefaction and blackness. *Mercurius as a pissing manikin is illustrated in *Cabala mineralis* (in PA, 238) and in Trismosin's *Splendor Solis* (pl.

3). The *Turba Philosophorum* advised the alchemist to prepare the *tincture 'with the urine of boys ... and decoct with a gentle fire, until the blackness altogether shall depart from it' (48–9). *The Glory of the World* observes that children's piss is a name for Mercurius as prima materia, the *seed or sperm of metals attained at the putrefaction: 'the urine of children ... is the seed and the first principle of metals. Without this seed there is no consummation of our Art' (*HM*, 1: 201). Sir George Ripley compared the interaction of the elements during the putrefaction to playing, pissing children: 'And when ther sherts be fylyd wyth pysse, / Then lat the Woman to wash be bound' (*TCB*, 149). The stage known as the *ablution follows the putrefaction and is symbolized by women laundering dirty shirts or linen (see laundering). Musgrove has argued that Robert Herrick's poem, 'Upon Sudds, a Laundresse', refers to this alchemical process: 'SUDDS Launders Bands in pisse; and starches them / Both with her Husband's, and her own tough fleame' (lines 1–4) (Musgrove, 'Herrick's alchemical vocabulary', 247). See also **urine**.

churchyard   see **grave**.

chymia   a name for the alchemist's vessel. Subtle enquires of Face in Jonson's *The Alchemist*: 'Ha' you set the oile of *Luna* in *kemia*?' (2.3.99). 'Chymia' is also a name for alchemy. *A Chymicall Dictionary* defines 'chymia' as 'the art of Separating pure from impure, and of making essences'. In the Hellenistic Egyptian tradition a connection was sometimes made between the name Ham (Cham) and the word 'chymia' (*JA*, 21). From this association the idea came about that alchemy was named after Ham, son of *Noah, who was thought to have kept the *philosopher's stone and the *Emerald Table* safe from the flood waters.

chymick   see **chemic**.

chymist   see **chemist**.

cibation   the nourishment of the *philosopher's stone born from the union of *Sol and *Luna at the *chemical wedding, also known as cohobation, *imbibation, and sometimes as *fermentation. *Zoroaster's Cave* states: 'Cibation is the Nutrition of our Materia Sicca with milk and meate, both moderately given' (74). The Stone needs to be nourished so that it will grow in size, strength and sweetness (see **multiplication**). Sir George Ripley wrote that '*Cibacion* ys callyd a fedyng of our Matter dry' (*TCB*, 169). The cibation of the Stone is frequently compared to the feeding of an infant (or baby bird) with milk and meat: 'fede thy Chyld ... wyth mylke and mete' (Ripley, in *TCB*, 147). The Stone in Andreae's *The Chymical Wedding* is portrayed as a baby bird hatched from the *egg (the philosophical vessel). The bird is fed with the *blood of the beheaded king and queen diluted with 'prepared water'. The food causes him to grow at great speed, turn 'black and wild', moult, and then grow new *snow-white feathers, by which stage he has become 'somewhat tamer' (Andreae, *Chymical Wedding*, 155) (see **Bird of Hermes; feathers**). This imagery symbolizes the process of *solve et coagula occurring during the augmentation of the quality and quantity of the Stone at the stage known as the *multiplication. Figure 83 of Daniel Stolcius's *Viridarium chimicum* shows the Stone being fed with white *virgin's milk and red blood (331). Isaac Newton cited Mundanus on the mercurial nourishment of the Stone: the 'white and red' is 'ye milk and bread wherewith ye infant or animal stone is fed and multiplied to perform miraculous effects' ('Sententiae', 71). In his 'Index chemicus' (Keynes MS 30, f. 23), Newton observed that the processes of cibation, fermentation and multiplication are synonymous: 'Cibation ... is the nutrition of the stone with milk and food i.e. with *terra alba foliata* and the soul of gold ... cibation, fermentation and multiplication are the same' (Westfall, 'Index', 179). See also **imbibation.**

cimentation   see **cementation.**

cinnabar   native mercury sulphide, the only important ore of mercury. In his *Lexicon of Alchemy*, Martin Ruland warns the alchemist that 'the term is applied by different authorities to very diverse substances' and that true cinnabar, also known by the name minium, 'was called by the ancients the Blood of the Dragon, a name it still retains'. Pure cinnabar, he continues, is 'red like Sandarac and red lead. It is found in the form of small lumps ... and when melted it makes quicksilver and sulphur' (102–3). Christoph Bergner, an eighteenth-century alchemist from Prague, wrote of making cinnabar artificially: 'At length, as is known, of sulphur and mercury the so called cinnabar is made ... Once I prepared cinnabar from 6 parts of mercury and 1 part of sulphur, but this was, when pulverized, only light red and by far not as beautifully red as that which was prepared from 3 parts of mercury and one part of sulphur' (in Karpenko, 'Christoph Bergner', 116–17). Cinnabar is used as a pigment known as vermilion. Ruland wrote: 'It was used by Venetian painters, because it is blood-coloured' (*Lexicon*, 102). In the final stages of the opus the Stone transforms into a rich blood red, sometimes compared to the vermilion of cinnabar or to the colour of the pomegranate. Edward Cradock wrote in 'A Treatise Touching the Philosopher's Stone': 'Like Cynobre or purple is the State / Of this our Stone, or like the Pomegranate' (lines 521–2, *AP*, 26).

circle   the symbol of perfection. The circle signifies the perfect, eternal spiritual realm in contrast to the square ,which signifies the earth, the corruptible world of illusion, the four elements, the four arms of the earthly cross (see **square and circle**). The circle with the dot in the centre symbolizes, at the macrocosmic level, the Creator, and at the microcosmic level, gold. The completed opus alchymicum is also symbolized by the circle. See **opus circulatorium.**

circular work   see **opus circulatorium.**

circulation of elements   see **opus circulatorium.**

circulatory an *alembic with a neck bent back, re-entering its lower part, used for the purpose of continuous *distillation. A recipe for the elixir in Colson's *Philosophia maturata* instructs the alchemist to 'put into a Circulatory, an ounce of the calx of the Egg-shells very well reverberated, and pour thereon of white or red *Mercury* to cover it' (54).

citrinitas the yellow stage of the opus alchymicum, following the white *albedo, symbolized by the golden flower, the golden rose. From the early Christian era the opus was divided into four main stages characterized by specific colours: (1) the *nigredo or black stage, (2) the albedo or white (silver) stage, (3) the citrinitas or yellow stage, and (4) the *rubedo or red (gold) stage. From around the fifteenth or sixteenth-century the three main colours and stages of the opus became black, white and red, and the citrinitas was generally, but not wholly, dropped from use. Benjamin Lock is an example of a sixteenth-century alchemist who continued to include the citrine stage: 'betweene whyte and red there is noe color but one, and that is citrine' ('Picklock', f. 5). Chaucer's Canon's Yeoman speaks of 'our silver citrinacioun' (line 816). See also **colours**.

city see **fort**.

cloud a name for the volatile vapour, the spirit, or *argent vive, which rises to the top of the alchemical vessel during *sublimation. Jodocus Greverius wrote that during the blackening of the Stone's matter 'there will rise from the Earth a certain humidity of Argent vive like a Cloud' (ZC, 71). Richardus Anglicus is cited in the same treatise: 'The fire ought to be very soft, till the Spirit be separated from the Body, ascending into black clouds above the body' (ZC, 70). During this stage, when the 'body' of the metal or Stone is killed and separated from its soul and spirit, a black cloud or shadow is said to be cast over the alchemist and his work. Thus the cloud is closely associated with the 'shadow' (see **sun and shadow**). However, the continuing heat of the philosophical *sun or alchemical fire soon disperses the philosophical clouds, as Samuel Norton indicates in the motto to an emblem from *Alchymiae Complementum et perfectio*: 'Oritur tenebrosas, Sol dispergere philosophorum nubes' (18) (see fig. 36). *Distillation follows sublimation and the clouds are transformed into the mercurial rain or *dew of grace which waters, washes and whitens the dead body (or earth) lying at the bottom of the vessel, making it ready to receive the 'seed' of gold (the soul which has previously been separated from it), leading to the conception and birth of the *philosopher's stone (see **ablution**). Greverius instructed the alchemist: 'Turne thy clouds into raine to water thy Earth, and make it fruitful. This Reduction of clouds into raine is called by some *Cauda Draconis*, The Dragon's Taile' (ZC, 72). See also 'white fume' in **green lion**.

coagulate see **solve et coagula**.

coal a symbol for the blackness of the nigredo, during which stage the dissolution and putrefaction of the metal or matter for the Stone takes place.

Lull is cited in *Zoroaster's Cave*: 'Blacknesse like that of the blackest Coal, is the Secret of True Dissolution' (71) (see **black**, **nigredo**).

cock and hen   the names given to *Sol and *Luna, the male and female aspects of matter, in the early stages of the opus alchymicum. In order to produce the *philosopher's stone the *chemical wedding of the seeds of metals, male *sulphur and female *argent vive, takes place several times and at varying levels of refinement throughout the opus. In the first primitive stages the union is presented as the quarrelling copulation of beasts and birds, such as hen and cock, while the later unions are represented by the copulation of human lovers, the marriage of the red man and white lady and, ultimately, the noble wedding of *king and *queen (Sol, sun, and Luna, moon). The motto to emblem 30 of Maier's *Atalanta fugiens* says: 'The sun needs the moon, like the cock needs the hen' (217) (fig. 11) (see **bird**). Dr Allslagen in Bassett Jones's 'Lithochymicus' uses the image to refer not just to the first in the series of chemical weddings but to that union in general: 'cast him [the Stone] upon *Sol* or *Lune*, whome if full fast / With Basiliskish eies he powders, then / It is a signe the Cock hath trodd the Henn' (AP, 269).

cockatrice   see **basilisk**.

11 Cock and hen

EMBLEMA XXX. *De secretis Naturæ.*
Sol indiget lunâ,ut gallus gallinâ.   129

EPIGRAMMA XXX.
O SOL, *solus agis nil.si non viribus adsim,*
Ut sine gallinâ est gallus inanis opę.
Auxiliúmque tuum præsens ego luna viciſſim
Postulo.gallinæ gallus ut expetitur.
Quæ natura simul conjungi flagitat,ille est
Mentis inops,vinclis qui religare velit.
                    R   AVI-

coction   see **boil**.

coffin   see **grave**.

cohobation   the repeated distillation of the matter for the Stone by returning the distillate to the liquid being distilled. This process is known as the *cibation or nourishment of the *infant Stone with its own *blood or mercurial water. In Ben Jonson's *The Alchemist* Face answers Subtle's question 'What's *Cohobation*?' with ''Tis the powring on / Your *Aqua Regis*, and then drawing him off' (2.5.26–7). See **cibation**, **imbibation**.

coition   see **chemical wedding**.

colours   One of the ways in which the alchemists divided the opus alchymicum into stages was by identifying the various colours through which the matter of the Stone passed in the alembic. Roger Bacon wrote: 'thou shalt knowe the certaine maner of working, by what manner and regiment, the Stone is often chaunged in decoction into diverse colours. Wherupon one saith, so many colours, so many names' (*Mirror*, 12). The young Swiss mathematician, Nicolas Fatio de Duillier, wrote to Isaac Newton in a letter dated 4 May 1693 that mercury and filings of gold sealed in an 'egg' and placed in a sand heat 'grow black and in a matter of seven days go through the coulours of the philosophers' (Dobbs, *Janus*, 172).

Up until the sixteenth century the opus was divided into four main stages represented by the four colours, black (*nigredo), white (*albedo), yellow (*citrinitas) and red (*rubedo). Artephius wrote of these colours: 'And as heat working upon that which is moist causeth or generates blackness, which is the prime or first colour; so always by decoction, more and more heat working upon that which is dry begets whiteness, which is the second colour; and then working upon that which is purely and perfectly dry it produceth citrinity and redness, thus much for colours' (*SB*, 37). *Carpenter's Worke* likewise says: 'For thou schalt see marveles grete, / Colures spring oute of the heate: / Fyrst Blakke and Whyte, and so Redde, / And after Setryne wythouten drede' (*TCB*, 276). The *Tractatus aureus* of Hermes Trismegistus enigmatically refers to the four main colours of the opus in the figure of a vulture who announces: 'I am the white of the black, and the red of the white and the yellow of the red, and I am very truthful' (in Salmon, *Medicina Practica*, 180). The succession of colours in Bernard Trevisan's 'Practice of the Philosophick Stone' is depicted by the several garments put on by the *king or raw matter for the Stone, during the opus. The first is 'the black silk Doublet', followed by 'the Shirt as white / As is the Snow', then the 'yellow vizard' and finally 'the Shirt that crimsons all the Spheres' (lines 175–95, *AP*, 454).

In the sixteenth and seventeenth centuries, the third stage known as the citrinitas tended to be dropped as an independent stage, and the three main colours became black, white and red. Dastin wrote in his *Visio*: 'The thing whose head is Red, feet White, and eyes Black, is the whole Mystery' (in *FC*, 11). And Trithemius stated that 'The Colours are

only Three, the others that come are called the middle Colours, that
vanish away: But the Black, White, and Red, are Eminent and Lasting
Scenes' (ZC, 80). In *Zoroaster's Cave* (1667), the citrine stage is still
included. The colours are linked to the four main alchemical processes
and to the *four elements: 'Dissolution begets blacknesse, Reduction
Whitenesse, Fixion Citrinity, Inceration Rednesse. Blackness is the
Earth, Whiteness the Water, Citrinity the Ayre, Rednesse the fire' (ZC,
73). Other colours are mentioned in the alchemical treatises. After the
blackness of the nigredo there appear many colours, like the colours of
the *rainbow, a stage which is known as the cauda pavonis or *peacock's
tail. This stage heralds the coming of the albedo where all the colours
merge into white. The colour blue or *azure occurs in alchemy as the
colour of the pure and incorruptible quintessence (or *fifth element),
the *dyeing tincture. Another prominent colour of the opus is *green,
which is associated with *Venus and the *green lion. The colour green
signifies that the matter in the alembic is still immature or unripe, in
the same way that unripe fruit is green. It also signifies the principle of
fertility and growth which is a crucial property of the transforming
arcanum (mercurial water) and the philosopher's stone itself. The
alchemists stated that only from 'green' gold (the living fertile seed)
could true gold be 'grown' (see **green lion**). For silver see **albedo**; see
also **gold, rubedo**.

columba   see **dove**.

conception   see **putrefaction**.

congelation   the conversion of a liquid to a solid state, also known as fixation, crystallization and freezing. Calid wrote: '*Fixation*, or *Congelation*, is the
making the flowing and volatile matter fixt, and able to endure the fire;
and this is the changing of the Spirit into a Body' (*Booke of the Secrets*, 118).
Congelation is the same as the coagulation or conjunction in the cycle of
*solve et coagula (dissolve and coagulate) where the 'body' of the Stone
is dissolved or made soft and the spirit is congealed or made hard.
Edward Kelly wrote: 'Consider that congelation is but Conjunction' (BL
Sloane MS 3631, f. 60). Calid wrote of the double operation of solve et
coagula: 'And this solution and congelation which wee have spoken of,
are the solution of the bodie, and the congelation of the spirite, and they
are two, yet have but one operation' (*Booke of the Secrets*, 31). The congelation is synonymous with the alchemical processes of fixing, freezing
and dyeing. It is the fixation of the volatile spirit, the hardening of that
which is soft, the bringing of the dissolved matter of the Stone in the
*alembic to the dry white stage so that it can be infused with form. Sir
George Ripley wrote that the congelation 'ys of soft thyngs Induracyon
of Colour whyte ... when the Matter ys made parfyt Whyte, / Then wyll
thy Spryte wyth the Body Congelyd be' (TCB, 161). Monachus, cited in
Zoroaster's Cave, saw congelation as the hardening, drying stage just
prior to the white stage: 'And when the philosophers saw their water
diminished, and their earth increased, they called it Ceration. Then,

when all became Earth, they called their Work Congelation; and when White, Calcination' (zc, 73). The congealed white mass of matter which appears at the albedo is sometimes referred to as the *pearls of the opus. Andrew Marvell's 'On a Drop of Dew' uses the metaphor of distillation and the cycle of dissolution and congelation to describe the changes occurring to the *dew-drop: 'Such did the Manna's sacred Dew destil; / White and intire, though congeal'd and chill. /Congeal'd on Earth: but does dissolving, run / Into the Glories of th' Almighty Sun' (lines 37–40). Musgrove has argued that Robert Herrick's 'The frozen zone: or *Julia* disdainfull' depicts an alchemical congelation so icy that it prevents the next stage, the feeding or *cibation of the Stone, from occurring: 'That's my *Julia's* breast; where dwels / Such destructive Ysicles; / As that the Congelation will / Me sooner starve, then those can kill' (lines 11–16) (Musgrove, 'Herrick's alchemical vocabulary', 255).

coniunctio   see **chemical wedding**.

consume   see **devour**.

contrition   the act of pounding, bruising or pulverizing. Arthur Dee refers to the *Consilium coniugii* on the preparation of the Stone's matter: the spirits must often be 'reiterated by Contrition and Assation with their Body, untill thou see these things which thou desirest in it' (FC, 35).

conversion   the transmutation of base metal into gold, of base man into divine man. Calid wrote of metals: 'Now according to *Avicen*, it is not possible to convert or transmute Metals, unless they be reduced to their First Matter; then by the help of Art they are transmuted into another Metal' (*Booke of the Secrets*, 122). The idea of 'converting' the contrary four elements into a state of union to form the *fifth element or *philosopher's stone is frequently met with in the alchemical treatises. Johannes Mylius wrote of the four elements: 'the first, second, third and fourth are all made one by converting the square into the circle' (AE, 71) (see **square and circle**). The process of converting the four elements into one 'circular' unity is synonymous with the union of opposites, male and female, spirit and body, at the *chemical wedding. Artephius wrote: 'By this means also is made mixtion and conjunction of body and spirit, which is called a conversion of contrary natures' (SB, 50). During this process the body is dissolved into spirit while the spirit is simultaneously coagulated into form, so that they may be perfectly mingled together in union. In alchemy the spiritual conversion of man was seen as analogous to the purification of metals. John Donne wrote in a sermon: 'God can work in all metals and transmute all metals: he can make . . . a superstitious Christian a sincere Christian: a Papist a Protestant' (*Sermons*, 4: 110). Mary Astell refers to spiritual, alchemical conversion in 'Awake my Lute': 'Who has the true Elixir, may impart / Pleasure to all he touches, and convert / The most unlikely greif to Happiness. / Vertue this true Elixir is' (lines 100–3, Greer, *Kissing the Rod*, 340).

cook   see **boil**.

cooks   see **Geber's cooks**.

copper   see **Venus**.

copulation   see **chemical wedding**.

coral   a synonym for the *red stone and *red tincture attained at the *rubedo, the final stage of the opus. Synesius referred to 'the bloody Stone, the purple, red Coral, the pretious Ruby, red Mercury, and the red Tincture' (*The True Book*, 175). *Zoroaster's Cave* likewise states: 'When [our matter] is Red, it's call'd Auripigment, Corall, Gold, Ferment, a Stone, a lucid Water of celestiall colour' (62–3). Michael Maier compared the *philosopher's stone to coral in the thirty-second emblem of *Atalanta fugiens*: 'The Philosopher's Stone may be compared ... with coral. For just as coral grows in water and gets its food out of the earth, in the same way the Philosopher's Stone grows out of the mercury water ... Just like coral, the Stone gets a red colour, when it becomes solidified ... and is then called tincture and has a colouring power' (AF, 227). As the 'tree' of the sea, coral is also adopted as a symbol of the *philosophical tree. Coral is listed as an ingredient in Nicaise Le Fevre's account of Sir Walter Raleigh's 'Great Cordial'. Le Fevre wrote of this ingredient: 'It is for certain in the Red Coral that a Solar Tincture is to be found, since that all the rare effects that it produces cannot be had else-where but from that Sulphur mineral and embryonated, which the Gold communicates to it in abundance, which renders it most worthy to be in our Great Remedy' (*Discourse*, 58).

Corascene dog and Armenian bitch   see **dog and bitch**.

cormorant   the vessel. See **worm**.

corn   see **grain, golden harvest**.

cornerstone   one of the central images of Christianity which has been given an alchemical interpretation. Christ the Cornerstone or filius macrocosmi was identified with the all-healing *philosopher's stone which could cast out all corruption and confer immortality. Basil Valentine wrote: 'I promised to communicate to you a knowledge of our Corner Stone, or Rock, of the process by which it is prepared, and of the substance from which it was already derived by those ancient Sages' (HM, 1:315).

corruption   see **putrefaction**.

cream   a symbol of the white stage or *albedo. Artephius wrote that when the bodies of the *wedded lovers are dissolved during the *black nigredo, the matter in the vessel is congealed and whitened. The volatile spirits are fixed and the 'soul of the two bodies swims above the water, like white cream' (SB, 36). In 'Herrick's alchemical vocabulary', Musgrove has argued that strawberries and cream is a name for the *red and white tinctures or elixirs and cites Robert Herrick's 'The Lilly in a Christal': 'You see how *Creame* but naked is; / Nor daunces in the eye / Without a Strawberrie: / Or some fine tincture, like to this' (lines 9–12).

creation   The process of producing the *philosopher's stone was viewed as a creation in microcosm, modelled on the blueprint of God's macrocosmic creation. In order to replicate the macrocosm on a microcosmic scale in the vessel the alchemist needed to understand the laws of nature and the secret of creation itself. Hortulanus wrote: 'Like as the world was created, so is our stone composed' (*Commentarie*, 25). Edward Kelly cited Rhasis: 'Our Stone is named after the creation of the world being three and yet one' (*Two excellent Treatises*, 45–6); and Thomas Norton stated that 'our *Stone* in generation / Is most like thing to Man's Creation' (TCB, 61). In this primordial task the alchemist had to deal with unformed matter. The *prima materia or first matter of the philosopher's stone was frequently symbolized by the *abyss or *chaos of God's creation. Figure 3 of *Janitor pansophus* depicts the creation of the Stone with scenes illustrating verses from Genesis (HM, 2:306). The alchemists not only viewed their creation as a duplication of God's creation, but they also perceived God's creation as an alchemical process, describing it as a divine chemical separation in the krater of the universe. Thomas Tymme cast God as the great alchemist whose spirit moved upon the waters and by 'Halchymicall Extraction, Separation, Sublimation, and coniunction, so ordered and conioyned' the 'Chaos' (EP, 88). In *Theophila* Edward Benlowes writes of the love of God as an alchemical force: 'In *Chymick Art* Thou my *Elixir* be; / Convert to *Gold* the worthless *Dross* in me' (8.66.139). In the same poem Theophila addresses the son of God: '*Though nought but* dross I *in* my self *can spie*, / *Yet melted with* THY beaming EYE, / *My* Refuse *turns to* Gold, *by mystick* Alchymie' (4.79.62).

crocodile   the mercurial *serpent or transforming arcanum in its initial chthonic aspect during the dark, destructive opening of the opus alchymicum. Like the *bee, the crocodile was classified as a serpent in the bestiaries of the sixteenth and seventeenth centuries. The amphibious nature of the crocodile made it an apt symbol for the dual-natured *Mercurius. When Lepidus in Shakespeare's *Antony and Cleopatra* says, 'Your serpent of Egypt is bred of your mud by the operation of your sun; so is your crocodile' (2.7.26–7), he is referring to the generation of gold in the earth, and the generation of the mercurial serpent through the heat of the secret *fire or 'sun'. With the phrase 'operation of your sun' Lepidus also alludes to the final law of the alchemical *Emerald Table*: 'That which I had to say about the operation of the Sun is completed'.

cross   an ancient symbol which is used in alchemy to represent the fixation of the volatile spirit. One of Nicolas Flamel's hieroglyphs displays the serpent nailed to a wooden cross, symbolizing the completion of the opus (*HE*, 7). Abraham Eleazar wrote of this hieroglyph in *Uraltes Chymisches Werck* (the treatise on which Flamel is said to have based his book): 'Therefore know that if you can fasten the serpent Python to this cross with a golden nail, you will lack nothing in wisdom' (*JA*, 246). In the text of Abraham Eleazar the *mercurial serpent symbolizing the fixation of the volatile spirit says: 'I must be fixed to this black cross' (in *MC*, 50). The nailing to the cross is a type of dismemberment and is related to the *division of the undifferentiated *prima materia into the differentiated four elements. John Dee's *Hieroglyphic Monad* stated that the cross is composed of four lines which unite at a central point. The four lines represent the four elements which, at their point of union, form the magical *fifth element. Thus the cross contains within it not only the symbol of the dismemberment or sacrifice of the old body or outmoded state, but also the image of the creation of a new state of unity. The alchemists saw the death of their matter in the alembic as analogous to the crucifixion of Christ on the cross. One of their most often stated ideas is that regeneration and resurrection of the matter of the Stone can only come about through an initial stage of death and corruption.

crosslet *crucible. Peter, in John Lyly's *Gallathea,* complains bitterly of his lot with his master, the alchemist: 'What a life do I lead with my master! Nothing but blowing of bellows, beating of spirits, and scraping of crosslets' (2.2.8–9).

crow, crow's head, crow's bill a symbol of the *putrefaction and *black nigredo which is the first stage of the opus alchymicum. The old body of the metal or matter for the Stone is dissolved and putrefied into the first matter of *creation, the *prima materia, so that it may be regenerated and cast into a new form. The *Hermetis Trismegisti Tractatus Aureus* said of this initial stage of death and dissolution in the work: 'The First is the *Corvus*, the Crow or Raven, which from its blackness is said to be the beginning of the Art' (bk. 2, 235). In his *Aurora*, Paracelsus wrote that when the matter has been placed in the gentle heat of the secret fire it passes through corruption and grows black: 'This operation they call putrefaction, and the blackness they name the head of the Crow' (55). Thomas Charnock likewise wrote of the putrefaction: 'The Crowes head began to appeare as black as Jett' (*TCB*, 296). In *Zoroaster's Cave* the matter produced during this stage is identified with the name of the process: 'When the matter has stood for the space of forty dayes in a moderate heat, there will begin to appear above, a blacknesse like to pitch, which is the *Caput Corvi* of the Philosophers, and the wise men's Mercury' (80). According to Ripley the terms 'crows head' and 'crows bill' are synonymous: 'The hede of the Crow that tokyn call we, / And sum men call hyt the Crows byll' (*TCB*, 134) (see **ashes**). In *A Fig for Momus* Thomas Lodge listed the crow's head amongst other alchemical enigmas: 'Then of the crowes-head, tell they waighty things' (*Works*, 3: 69). When Face in Jonson's *The Alchemist* says that the matter of the Stone has become 'ground black', Mammon enquires of him, 'That's your *crowes-head*?' and Subtle replies, 'No, 'tis not perfect, would it were the *crow*' (2.3.67–8).

crown   see **king, royal**.

crow's beak   the neck of the *alembic. Arthur Dee cites Laurence Ventura on distilla-tion: 'the vapour of the Matter ascends and then it descends again by the Crows beak, that is, the Neck of the vessell of the Alembick' (FC, 34). See **beak**. Another name for the crow's beak is the 'stag's horn'.

crucible   a melting-pot for metals or a vessel for collecting molten metal at the bottom of a furnace during the refining process. The crucible has a narrow base which widens into a triangular or round bowl. Michael Drayton wrote of the false alchemist in 'The Moone-Calfe' that he would 'shew you in a Crusible, or Glasse: / Some rare extraction' (*Works*, 3:190, lines 912–13). The projection of the philosopher's stone (or powder) on the molten base metal usually takes place in the crucible because it can withstand great heat. The *Clangor buccinae* advised the alchemist on transmuting tin into silver: 'If thou would'st make Projection upon Jupiter, melt it in a Crucible, and put to one pound of Jupiter one ounce of pure Luna, and melt them together; then cast on it thy White Tincture' (ZC, 85). The alchemical assay or trial of gold also took place in the crucible. Lucy Hastings used the term as a generic name for the alchemical vessel in a poem written on the fly-leaf of a copy of *Lachrymae Musarum*. The subject of the poem is the death of her son, Henry Lord Hastings: 'His soul is he, which when his Dear / Redeemer had refin'd to a height / Of purity, and Solid Weight; / No longer would he Let it Stay, / With in this Crucible of Clay' (lines 7–11, in Greer, *Kissing the Rod*, 9–10). Henry More wrote publicly to the Hermeticist Thomas Vaughan in 1651: 'Put thy Soul into a crysiple, O pragmatic chemist and set it on that fire that will excoct and purge out thy drosse, and then judge of Platonisme' (*Second Lash*, 208). Ted Hughes employs the term in 'The Risen' in a transformation metaphor: 'On his lens / Each atom engraves with a diamond. / In the wind-fondled crucible of his splen-dour / The dirt becomes God' (lines 19–22).

crucifixion   see **cross**.

crystal, crystallization   Crystal is a name for the *philosopher's stone or *elixir at both the white stage, or *albedo, and the red stage, or *rubedo. In 'The Mistery of Alchymists' Sir George Ripley wrote of the white stone: 'His first Vertue is White and pure, / as any Christall shining cleere, / Of White tincture then be you sure' (TCB, 382). Benjamin Lock likewise compared the white stone to pure crystal: 'let the matter being fermented be set in drye fyer of ashes, and in the fyer let the ferment be continued tyll the matter wyll congeale no more, but stand in the fyer liquid and molten as wax having the color of burnished silver or moste pure christall. And then is yt the perfecte Elixir whyte: able to turne arg: vive into medicine and all imperfect bodys of the myne into most fine silver' ('Picklock', f. 21). The crystallization in alchemy also refers to the final *congelation of the matter in the alembic, the final fixation of a state which before was flowing, mutable, volatile, into a state of immutability and permanence. In this process pure spirit is materialized, brought into a perfect incarnation (see **fixation**, **vitrification**).

cucurbite a glass vessel or retort shaped like a gourd or pumpkin, forming the lower part of the distilling apparatus. The cucurbite is also a generic name for the philosophical *egg, the 'one' vessel in which the opus is accomplished. *Zoroaster's Cave* says: 'Our vessel is a Glasse, firmly shut, round bellied, of a neck strict and long, half a foot, or thereabout. This vessel is called an Egge or Sublimatory, a Sphear, a sepulcher, a Cucurbit' (79). The *coniunctio or coupling of the two waters, the *red man (*sulphur) and *white woman (*argent vive), takes place in this vessel. Arnold of Villanova wrote: 'Take of the red Water and White as much of the one as of the other ... and put them together in a Cucurbite, made of Glasse, strong and thick, having a Mouth like an Urinall, afterward the whole Water will be Citrine, even soon enough, and so will the true Elixer be perfected in respect of both *viz.* perfect Impregnation, and true Coition' (in *FC*, 90). John Sawtre recommended 'a Cucurbit or Gourd with a limbeck round above and beneath' as the vessel in which to conduct the opus alchymicum (*FT*, 28). Cucurbite can sometimes be the name for the oven or *athanor of the philosophers (see Salmon's *Dictionaire Hermetique*, 37). In John Lyly's play *Gallathea*, the alchemist's servant includes the cucurbite amongst the list of his master's necessary instruments: 'Then our instruments, Croslets, Subliuatories, Cucurbits, Limbecks, Decensors, Violes, manuall and murall, for enbibing' (2.3.18–20).

cupel a small shallow porous cup usually made of bone-ash, and used in assaying gold or silver with lead (*OED*). Toutguerres in Bassett Jones's 'Lithochymicus' recounts his master's method of carrying out projection 'wi' th' rubie medcin to sweet taste / Exalted ... To tourne full twenty partes of silver mine / Uppon the Coppell into Gould most fine' (*AP*, 280).

Cupid the secret fire, the burning water, Mercurius. In a treatise on the mercurial activating agent, Isaac Newton called it 'Mercury's caducean rod ... the winged dragon, a water, a moist fire, our Cupid' ('Praxis', in Dobbs, *Janus*, 40). Cupid's dart of passion, like all *weaponry in alchemy, signifies the secret fire, the deathly active dissolvent which kills metals and reduces them into their *prima materia. Jung writes of Mercurius–Cupid: 'Mercurius is the archer who, chemically, dissolves the gold, and morally, pierces the soul with the dart of passion' (in *MC*, 304). Christian Rosencreutz in *The Chymical Wedding* is pricked with a dart by Cupid after having stumbled upon the naked Venus (56). This incident is presented as a necessary step in Christian's initiation into the mysteries of the opus. Robert Fludd used Cupid as a symbol for the pure love essence released by the Stone or elixir: 'this Elixir is the true temple of wisdome, the impregnable castell of Cupid that powerfull god of love' (*TGH*, 108).

D

decapitation   see **beheading**.

decoction   the preparation of an ore, a mineral, or the philosopher's stone by heat. Also the extraction of the essence of a substance through boiling in water. Artephius described the process of decoction as causing the advent of the three major stages and *colours in the opus: 'And as heat working upon that which is moist causeth or generates blackness, which is the prime or first colour; so always by decoction, more and more heat working upon that which is dry, begets whiteness, which is the second colour; and then working upon that which is purely and perfectly dry, it produceth citrinity and redness' (SB, 37). Martin Luther refers to decoction in *Table Talk*: 'The science of alchymy I like very well, and indeed, 'tis the philosophy of the ancients. I like it not only for the profits it brings in melting metals, in decocting, preparing, extracting and distilling herbs, roots; I like it also for the sake of the allegory and secret signification, which is exceedingly fine, touching the resurrection of the dead at the last day' (326). See **liquefaction**.

deer   one of the best known epithets for *Mercurius, also known as the hart, fawn and stag. The fleeing deer or hart symbolizes Mercurius in his role as the intermediary soul which unites the body and spirit of the Stone (see **cervus fugitivus**). The deer is illustrated in Trismosin's *Splendor Solis* (plates 2, 8), in Ripley's 'Emblematicall Scrowle' (Bod. Ashm. Rolls 53, A. 1530, first two sheets), and in emblem 3 of *The Book of Lambspring,* whose motto declares: 'The deer desires no other name / But that of the Soul' (HM, 1:280). The images of the deer, hart and stag are used in other contexts in alchemical writing. Toutguerres in Bassett Jones's 'Lithochymicus' observes concerning the colour of the 'resurrected' Stone: 'The same will soe appeare if you destill / The horne of stagge or fallow deere with skill / Of *destillation laterall*: to th' side / Of the receaver shall you then see slide / The salt, and there in forme of hart's hornes clinge' (AP, 264). Ruland's *Lexicon* defined the deer's antler as both 'the Beak of the Alembic' and 'a healing herb for wounds in Paracelsian medicine' (117). The *beak of the *alembic is also called the stag's horn.

den   one of the names given to the alchemical vessel. Philalethes' *The Marrow of Alchemy* instructed the alchemist to 'Seal up the neck [of the vessel] with *Hermes* seal, and then / The Spirits are secur'd within their den' (bk 1, 26). The vessel is called the serpent's or dragon's den during the *nigredo, the first primitive stage of the opus when the *putrefaction process blackens the matter of the Stone. The *Verses belonging to an Emblematicall Scrowle* attributed to Sir George Ripley state: 'Thus ye shall go to Putrefaccion, / And bring the *Serpent* to reduction' which 'downe in his Den shall lye full lowe' (TCB, 378–9).

descension   see **distillation**.

devil   see **sulphur.**

devour   The alchemical opus was represented by a series of dramatic emblems, which included images of violent, ravenous beasts or people devouring each other, or devouring themselves, in the case of the *uroboros or serpent which consumes its own tail. In these emblems *bird eats bird, *dragon consumes dragon, *lion devours lion, eagle devours lion, lion devours sun, *Saturn consumes the mercurial *child, *wolf devours king, *king ingests his own son, and the *Hermes bird eats its own feathers. In the emblems of devouring birds and beasts, one of the pair is always winged, symbolizing the volatile nature of the substance, while the wingless creature symbolizes the fixed matter. The aim of the alchemist is to unite the opposing, quarelling pair (sulphur and argent vive/mercury) by simultaneously fixing the volatile (coagula) while spiritualizing the fixed matter (solve) (see **peace and strife** and **chemical wedding**). This devouring union is frequently represented as an *incestuous act, as in Jean de la Fontaine's 'The Pleasant Founteine of Knowledge', where the alchemist is advised to 'Make thy Sulphure penetrative, / By fire to become attractive; / And then make itt eate itts mother'. The 'mother', Fontaine informs us, is mercury: 'When thy Sulphure hath devoured / Thy mercury mortified / For forty dayes imprison these / And in transparent glasse inclose' (*AP*, 108–9). The image of devouring admirably expresses the violent nature of the opposing substances (or qualities) and the paradoxical nature of the *solve et coagula, the separation and union necessary for the creation of that pure new substance known to the alchemists as the philosopher's stone. The crystallization of a new, pure form necessarily required the 'death' or deconstruction of the earlier form. Burckhardt wrote of the death or separation necessary for the coniunctio and rebirth to take place: 'any given union presupposes an extinction of the earlier, still differentiated state' (*Alchemy*, 156). Psychologically, the act of devouring represents the death of the lower or earthly nature of man (symbolized by the image of beasts). The idea of death and rebirth occurs in all metaphysical systems, but the imagery used by the alchemists is peculiarly their own.

dew   the beneficial, healing aspect of the *mercurial water which magically transforms the *black nigredo (the death and *putrefaction of the old form of the metal) into the *white albedo. Jean de la Fontaine wrote: 'This Mercury . . . in likeness of a dew is found' (*AP*, 94). The albedo is reached through the miraculous washing of the dead, blackened forms or bodies at the bottom of the alembic (see **ablution**). At the fearful nadir of the nigredo, the mercurial waters of death are suddenly transformed into the waters of life. Through the celestial influence of the descending dew or *rain during *distillation, inert matter (the 'body' or 'earth') is cleansed and re-animated. The motto to the eighth woodcut of *The Rosary of the Philosophers* says: 'Here the dew falleth from heaven, / And washeth the black body in the sepulchre' (McLean, *Rosary*, 51). *Zoroaster's Cave* said of this process: 'With the Water of Paradise bedew the Earth now clarified, and that Water will again Ascend to heaven, and Descend againe to the earth to make it fertil and bring forth White Citrine, and Flamye Red Flowers' (74). The narrator of *The Golden Tract* witnesses the vapours rising 'from the earth through the heat of the sun' which 'when night fell ... watered the earth as fertilizing dew, and washed our bodies which became more beautiful and white the oftener this sprinkling took place' (*HM*, 1:48). Here the cycle of the day and night with the sun's evaporative heat and the descent of dew is a metaphor for the *sublimation and distillation of the matter in the alembic. A similar idea occurs in Andrew Marvell's 'Eyes and Tears': 'So the all-seeing Sun each day / Distills the World with Chymick Ray; / But finds the Essence only Showers, / Which straight in pity back he powers' (lines 21–4). The *ablution of rain or dew always precedes a new coniunctio or *chemical wedding, preparing the bodies (or body) of the Stone for the reunion with the animating soul (or with the united soul/spirit). Philalethes' *The Marrow of Alchemy* indicated that after the death of the bodies they are revived by 'dew and rain' and 'joyn'd in union' (bk. 1, 26). Likewise John Dastin wrote that after the rain of 'Dew-droppes ... there schalbe a glad *Conjunccion*' (*TCB*, 258). From this coniunctio the third principle, the *philosopher's stone, is generated: 'The Earth therefore doth not germinate without the watering humidity of May dew, that doth wash, penetrate, and whiten Bodies, like rain water, and of two Bodies make a new one' (Artephius, in *FC*, 103). In agreement with ecclesiastical symbolism, the alchemists' cleansing water is 'a dew of grace'. John Dee quoted on the title page of his alchemical work, *Monas hieroglyphica*, the biblical words, 'De rore caeli, et pingedine terrae, det tibi Deus' ('God give thee of the dew of heaven, and of the fatness of the earth' (Genesis 27:28)).

diadem   see **king**.

Diana   the matter of the Stone when it has reached the pure white lunar stage of the opus at the *albedo; the white stone; the female principle of the opus, *argent vive. The alchemists appropriated the virgin moon goddess of classical mythology, the daughter of Jupiter and Latona born on the isle of Delos, to symbolize their matter when it has been cleansed of its blackness and corruption and has become the pure, virgin matter of the *white stone or elixir. The pure and perfect elixir of Diana was thought to be able to transmute all imperfect metals into silver (Luna). The physician and poet John Collop was referring to this phenomenon when he wrote, 'But oh from th' silver forge Diana comes' (*Poesis Rediviva*, 13). Isaac Newton said concerning the preparation of philosophical mercury: 'Another secret is that you need the mediation of the Virgin Diana (a quintessence, most pure silver): otherwise the mercury and the regulus are not united' (Keynes MS 18, in Dobbs, *Foundations*, 182). Martin Ruland wrote of Diana in his *Lexicon of Alchemy*: 'The dominion of the Moon in the operation begins when the Matter, after putrefaction, changes its colour ... into that of white. When the Sages speak of their Moon in this state they call it *Diana Unveiled*, and they say that happy is the man who has beheld Diana naked, that is to say, the Matter at the Perfect White Stone' (400). Like many other tales of metamorphosis, the myth of Diana and Actaeon was drawn into the pantheon of alchemical symbolism. Diana and Actaeon are the subject of an emblem in Johannes Mylius's *Basilica philosophica* (pl. 6, row 4, no. 2). Pernety explains that this myth indicates that the alchemist must be very discreet and circumspect if he wishes to behold the purity at the white stage of the opus (*Fables*, 117). The white albedo is sometimes symbolized by Diana's white *doves: 'le couleur blanche' is 'les Colombes de Diane' (Pernety, *Dictionnaire*, 111). In Michael Sendivogius's 'A Dialogue of the Allchymist and Sulphur', Diana represents the female principle, argent vive, who must be married to the male principle, sulphur, represented by the 'Prince' (*AP*, 526).

digestion the refinement or maturation of an uncooked substance by a gentle heat; the separation of the pure from the impure matter; sometimes, the dissolution of crude matter by heat. Digestion is performed in the *athanor by filling up the turrets with coals at the top, kindling the fire in the furnace and increasing the heat by using the register or poker (Ruland, *Lexicon*, 126). A recipe for making the elixir in Colson's *Philosophia maturata* states: 'Then set the circulatory in a Furnace, and with gentle heat digest the red *Mercury* into a red and fixed calx, then adde thereto as much more of that *Mercury*, circulate and dry as before' (56). Ripley also used the term 'digestion' when describing the process of bringing the matter to the stage of the *albedo, and then to the *rubedo: 'And so our *Stone* by Drynes and by Hete, / Dygested ys to Whyte and Red complete' (*TCB*, 163). Face in Ben Jonson's *The Alchemist* assures Subtle that the matter in the *bolt's-head has been 'nipp'd to *digestion* / According as you bad me' (2.3.73–4). (See **boil**.) In Milton's *Paradise Lost*, Raphael compares angel digestion to the work of 'the empiric alchemist' who 'can turn, or holds it possible to turn / Metals of drossiest ore to perfect gold' (5.439–43).

discord see **peace**.

disease see **medicine, leprosy, Naaman the leper**.

dismemberment see **beheading**.

dissolution see **nigredo, solve et coagula**.

distillation and **sublimation** the process of purification and clarification whereby the volatile spirit is extracted from the impure matter or body. This process of refinement is achieved by rapid vaporization through applied heat, followed by cooling and condensation. Synesius wrote: 'Thus when our stone is in the vessel, and that it mounts up on high in fume, this is called *Sublimation*, and when it falls down from on high, *Distillation*, and Descension' (*The True Book*, 171). In 'Lithochymicus' Bassett Jones defined sublimation as 'that wherby the flower or subtile partes of a body are Elevated unto the topp of the Vessell and there, by vertue of the Ayer, congeal'd' (AP, 354). Lancelot Colson's *Philosophia maturata* likewise says of the Stone: 'after the third day he shall ascend and descend, first to the Moon, and then to the Sun' (35). This process of vaporization and condensation is sometimes referred to as the driving of the soul of the metal up and down from its body. During this phase the body is made spiritual and the spirit made corporeal.

The beads of liquid which accumulate on the sides of the vessel during distillation are referred to as *sweat or *tears. John Cleveland used the distillation metaphor in 'On the Arch-bishop of Canterbury': 'Verse chymically weeps, that pious raine / Distill'd with Art, is but the sweat o' the brain' (38). Joseph Hall's satire on the Paracelsian doctor in *Virgidemiarum* includes images of distilling and subliming: 'And with glas-stils, and sticks of *Iuniper*, / Raise the *Black-spright* that burns not with the fire: / And bring *Quintessence* of *Elixir* pale, / Out of sublimed spirits minerall' (37–8). In Milton's *Paradise Lost* Raphael speaks of sublimation in an alchemical context. He discourses on the convertibility and refinement of matter, giving as examples his own ability to 'convert' earthly fruits into heavenly substance, and the way that plants may be 'by gradual scale sublimed' into the animal and thence the intellectual state: 'flowers and their fruit / Man's nourishment, by gradual scale sublimed / To vital spirits aspire, to animal, / To intellectual' (5.482–7). Chaucer's Canon's Yeoman tells his listeners 'of the care and wo / That we hadde in our matires sublyming' (*Canon's Yeoman's Tale*, lines 769–70). Metaphysically, the descent of the soul into dense matter is seen as a part of the necessary experience which leads to the ascent into full 'philosophical' consciousness. The paradox that the way down is the way up (illustrated by the journey down to hell, to purgatory and thence up to paradise in Dante's *Divine Comedy*) is stated by Sendivogius in 'A Dialogue of the Allchymist and Sulphur': 'For what has not descended never can / Ascend to heaven's bright Meridian' (AP, 531).

division see **divorce**, **separation**.

divorce the same as dissolution, division, separation. The purification of the matter of the Stone is accomplished by a reiterated cycle of *solve et coagula (dissolve and coagulate), also known as separation and union, division and conjunction. Calid wrote: 'Division is a separation of the parts of the compound, and so separation hath bin his conjunction' (*Booke of the Secrets*, 33), and John Dastin said: 'If the first work proceed not, how is the second attained to? Because if no division be made, there is no conjunction' (in FC, 15). This cycle was also known as the chemical divorce and wedding. The male and female opposites, body and spirit (sometimes body and soul), *philosophical sulphur and argent vive, cannot be united at a refined level until they have first been separated or divorced. This division of the essence or spirit from the body was accomplished by dissolution. The separation or divorce must then be followed by the *chemical wedding of *king and *queen, the perfect mixing of body and soul (or the united soul/spirit) so that a new incarnation can come into existence. This is the birth of the *philosopher's stone.

Musgrove has argued that the chemical divorce is lamented in Robert Herrick's 'To the King and Queene, upon their unhappy distances': 'Like Streams, you are divorc'd but 'twill come, when / These eyes of mine shall see you mix agen' (lines 5–6) (Musgrove, 'Herrick's alchemical vocabulary', 240–65). (See **streams**.) Psychologically, an expansion of consciousness and growth of discrimination cannot take place until the soul is released from its total identification with the body or dense matter. The divorce of the soul enables it to understand, from an impartial distance, the nature of matter and spirit. The separated soul in John Donne's 'The Exstasy' proclaims: 'This ecstasy doth unperplex . . . [we] know, / Of what we are composed, and made' (lines 29–46).

doctrine of signatures   the theory that nature has put a mark or 'signature' on every natural object, providing a clue to the 'virtue' or property contained within that object. These signs were perceived to be woven into the tapestry of nature by the hand of God, giving nature intelligibility and meaning. It was thought, for example, that the wine-coloured amethyst prevented drunkenness, and that the herb *scorpius* was a remedy against a scorpion sting. Every star, creature, tree, plant, metal and stone was seen as a 'hieroglyph', a 'letter' or 'character' in the alphabet which constituted the book of nature, which was there for man to decode. According to Paracelsian theory the hieroglyph or signature was an outward sign which, rightly interpreted, revealed the inner essence of the particular object. The outward signature had only to be examined for the occult 'virtue' to become evident. Paracelsus wrote: 'Hereto also do refer the vertues and Operations of all creatures, and their use, they being stamped or markt with their arcanums, signs, characters and figures, so that there's scarce left in them the least occult point which becomes not evident by examination' (*Aurora*, 11). In the Paracelsian view the perception of a 'signature' did not consist merely of a literal identification of the outward appearance of an object with its significance. For instance, if a plant were 'heart' or 'kidney' shaped it did not necessarily mean that the plant contained a cure for the heart or kidneys. The Paracelsians insisted on a far more subtle and intuitive interpretation of nature – one that would reveal a truly objective reality.

In the sixteenth and seventeenth centuries it was thought that the way to regain man's original, paradisal state could be found by studying the two books of the Creator – the book of divine revelation (the Scriptures) and the book of divine creation (nature). This idea was brought into full focus through the work of the Christian Hermeticists, the neo-Platonists and alchemical philosophers. According to this tradition Adam was seen as the original, illumined philosopher of nature. Before the Fall, Adam was able to speak and understand the 'original' language of nature. He could directly read the secrets in nature's mystic book without need of interpretation. Andrew Marvell referred to this tradition in 'Upon Appleton House' when he wrote of his 'easie Philosopher': 'Thrice happy he who, not mistook, / Hath read in *Natures mystick Book*' (lines 583–4). Sir Thomas Browne, who was familiar with the work of Paracelsus, wrote in *Religio Medici* that every plant, vegetable and face displays 'some outward figures which hang as signes or bushes of their inward formes. The finger of God hath left an inscription upon all his workes, not graphicall or composed of Letters, but of their several formes, constitution, parts, and operations, which aptly joyned together, doe make one word that doth expresse their natures. By these Letters God calls the Starres by their names, and by this Alphabet *Adam* assigned to every creature a name perculiar to its nature' (30, 35, 57). After the Fall, it was thought, man's capacity to understand the language of nature and directly read her secrets was lost. But this knowledge was not irretrievable, and could be rediscovered by a diligent, intuitive study of nature's book.

dog and bitch   *philosophical sulphur (male, hot, dry) and *argent vive (female, cold, moist), which must be united at the first, primitive chemical wedding or *coniunctio in order to create the mercurial waters or aqua permanens. The copulation of dog and bitch is equivalent to the cannibalistic copulation of the wingless and winged *dragons or lions. The wingless dragon (dog) which symbolizes sulphur has the power to coagulate or fix the volatile spirit, while the winged dragon or argent vive (bitch) has the power to dissolve fixed matter. The union of the copulating dog and bitch produces the miraculous *mercurial water. Philalethes wrote: 'Therefore saith the Philosopher, Take the *Corascene Dog* and *Bitch* of *Armenia,* joyn them together, and they shall beget thee a Son of the colour of heaven' (*Secrets Reveal'd,* 81). Flamel described the violent copulation of dog and bitch which ends in bloodshed and death: 'These two then, (which *Avicen* calleth the *Corassene bitch* and the *Armenian dogge*), these two I say, being put together in the vessel of the *Sepulcher,* doe bite one another cruelly, and by their great poyson, and furious rage, they never leave one another, from the moment that they have seized on one another . . . till both of them by their slavering venome and mortall hurts, be all of a goare bloud . . . and finally killing one another be stewed in their proper *venome,* which after their death, changeth them into living and *permanent water*' (HE, 68–9). Michael Maier used the image of wolf and dog, rather than dog and bitch, to represent this first primitive union of sulphur and argent vive (AF, 285). See **devour**.

dough   see **paste**.

dove   a symbol, like the swan, of the pure white stage of the opus, the *albedo. The stage of the dove succeeds the corruption, putrefaction and sublimation of the black matter (the *caput corvi) at the *nigredo. Saturnius said: 'After the first fifty dayes, the *Caput Corvi* shows it self; from thence in an hundred and fifty, the Dove is made' (in ZC, 82). Philalethes wrote that 'after thy Matters begin to be boiled in a continual decoction, Putrefaction will be compleat, and then Sublimation or Circulation will begin again, which in 46 or 50 days will end a white Dove' (RR, 174). In Salomon Trismosin's *Splendor Solis* the eleventh plate shows the dove poised on the head of the *king in a tub. The king in his *bath represents the putrefying matter of the Stone and the dove indicates that the white

12 The alchemical dragon

stage or albedo is at hand. The dove is also a symbol for the transforming arcanum, Mercurius, because it reconciles and unites the opposite substances, male *Sol and female *Luna; it brings peace to the quarrelling elements. This is illustrated in the second emblem of *The Rosary of the Philosophers* (see **peace and strife**, **bird**). See fig. 9.

dragon the dual-natured *Mercurius in his first dark chthonic phase (fig. 12). Chaucer's Canon's Yeoman says: '[Hermes] seith, how that the dragoun, / douteless, / Ne deyeth nay, but-if that he be slayn, / With his brother; / and that is for to sayn, / By the dragoun, Mercurie and noon other / He understood' (*Canon's Yoeman's Tale*, lines 1435–9). At the beginning of the opus alchymicum the alchemist dissolves the metal or the matter for the Stone into the original stuff of creation, the *prima materia, in order to obtain the double seed of metals from which the *philosopher's stone is created and gold is grown. These two seeds, philosophical *sulphur (male, hot, dry) and philosophical *argent vive or quicksilver (female, cold, moist), are compared to two dragons, one winged, the other wingless. Nicolas Flamel wrote: 'Looke well upon these *two Dragons*, for they are the true principles or beginnings of this *Phylosophy* ... The first is called *Sulphur*, or heat and driness, and the latter *Argent-vive*, or cold, and moisture. These are the *Sunne* and *Moone* of the Mercurial source' (*HE*, 70). Elsewhere Flamel explains that 'The wingless dragon is sulphur because it never flies away from the fire. The winged serpent is quicksilver, which is borne away through the air (the female seed which is composed of water and earth) – because in a certain degree it flies away or evaporates' (*HM*, 1: 142). These two separated seeds must be united spermatically by means of *Mercurius, the mother of metals, in order to produce the magical mercurial or permanent water which 'may overcome every thing *Metallick*, how solid and strong soever it bee' (*HE*, 65–6). This water is called 'dragon's blood'.

The union of the male and female seeds is presented in alchemical texts as a most violent and bloody copulation in which two dragons kill each other in order to engender their offspring. After their quarrel the dragons are transformed into the harmonious serpents entwined around the caduceus of Mercury (see **caduceus**). Equivalent symbols of the initial violent copulation are the dragon or bird eating its own wings, the dragons keeping watch over the golden apples in the garden of the Hesperides, the two serpents which Hercules strangled in his cradle, the two serpents around Mercurius's caduceus, the amorous birds of prey, the Corascene bitch and Armenian dog, and the uroboros or serpent devouring its own tail. Metaphysically, the dragon is the lower, earthly self which the soul must learn to subdue and train, so that the higher self (the golden apples) may at last reign (Hodgson, *Astrology*, 46–8). In *A Fig for Momus* Thomas Lodge complained of the vain enigmas employed by the alchemist, including the uroboric dragon: 'First aske they where the flying eagle dwels ... Then of the Lyon greene, and flying hart. / Next of the Dragon, swallowing his tayle' (*Works*, 3: 69). The 'great dragon of the four elements' is philosophical mercury (Mercurius) which is composed of the four elements. 'Dragon's teeth' is the name for mercury sublimate, as Ben Jonson's Sir Epicure Mammon points out in *The Alchemist*: 'The Dragons teeth, *mercury* sublimate, / That keepes the whiteness, hardnesse, and the biting' (2.1.95). See **blood, dog and bitch, devour; serpent**.

dragon's blood, dragon's teeth   see **dragon, blood**.

dragon's tail   see **cloud**.

dregs   see **dross, faeces**.

dropsy   the swollen, glutted state of the Stone's body when too much *mercurial water has been added to it too quickly and without first drying or desiccating the body. During the *cibation or *imbibation the distilled liquid ('milk') is returned to the body of the Stone (also known as *earth and *ashes) to moisten it. But if this process is carried out without also drying the body (symbolized by feeding it with 'meat') or done too quickly and in too large quantities, the Stone becomes hydropic or dropsical and is said to be drowned. Sir George Ripley wrote of the feeding of the Stone with milk and meat: 'But geve yt not so much that thou hyt glut, / Beware of the Dropsy, and also of *Noyes* Flood; / By lyttyll and lyttyll therfore thou to hyt put / Of Mete and Drynke as semyth to do hyt good'. (*TCB*, 45–6). John Dastin likewise warned the adept: 'As often as ye moisten the Ashes, desiccate them by turns, but if it be moistened before it be desiccated and made Dust, it is drowned; inebriated, and reduced to nothing; for he makes it without weight (as *Trismegistus* saith) kills and strangles it, because who drinks and thirsts not, cherishes ingestion, and doth invite and induce Dropsie' (in *FC*, 103). In John Donne's 'A Nocturnal upon S. Lucy's Day' the poet describes a nihilistic 'new alchemy' in which he has become 'A quintessence even from nothingness'. In this opus the earth has become 'hydroptic' (dropsical) and the alchemical lovers have 'by love's limbeck' wept so much water that they have 'drowned the whole world' (lines 6–24). See **Naaman the leper**.

dross   the earthy impurities separated from the metal or matter of the Stone during the process of dissolution and *sublimation. Arthur Dee cites Aristotle: 'that which ascends higher is efficacious purity but that which fals to the bottome, is drosse and corruption' (*FC*, 70). The alchemical dross is also known as the dregs, *faeces or terra damnata. The 'Clangor Buccinae' states that when the pure earth or snow ascends to the top of the vessel 'the Ashes remaining in the bottome are dregs, and the vilified drosse of Bodies, and to be cast away' (in *FC*, 78). Artephius likewise explained the process of purification: 'For in such a dissolution and natural sublimation or lifting up, there is a loosening or untying of the elements, and a cleansing and separation of the pure, from the impure. So that the pure and white substance ascends upwards, and the impure and earthy remains fixed in the bottom of the water and the vessel. This must be taken away and removed, because it is of no value, taking only the middle white substance flowing and melted or dissolved, rejecting the foeculent earth, which remains below in the bottom. These faeces were separated partly by the water, and are the dross and *terra damnata*, which is of no value, nor can do any such service as the clear, white, pure and clean matter' (*SB*, 20–1). Elizabeth Melville, Lady Culross, uses the term metaphysically in a poem sent to John Welsch, a political prisoner in Blackness Castle: 'My dear Brother, wt courage bear the crosse / Joy shall be joyned with all thy sorrow here / High is thy hope disdain this earthly drosse' ('A Sonnet sent to Blackness to Mr. John Welsch, by the Lady Culross' (lines 1–3, in Greer, *Kissing the Rod*, 33)). Following a long tradition of presenting the act of writing as an alchemical act of creation, Michael Wilding describes a character illicitly reading a friend's stories in manuscript: 'But the old flatness was still there. He could find traces of it, of the old over explicitness, the clumsiness: gold amongst the dross, the silt, the rubble … He registered the redundancies, the spelled out endings, the unrealised and untransmuted autobiography, and said nothing' (*Aspects of the Dying Process*, 52) (see **faeces**).

duenech   see **king**, **laton**.

dung, dunghill   Used to make a gentle heat for the alembic. The decoction or *digestion of the matter of the Stone was accomplished by placing the vessel in a very gentle heat provided by either a *balneum mariae or horse dung. Paracelsus advised the alchemist to shut the matter 'in the best glasse' and 'set it in horse-dung for a moneth then distil it wholly off with a gentle fire, that the matter may be coagulated in the bottom' (*Archidoxis*, 22). In the 'Toothless Satyrs' section of *Virgidemiarum*, Joseph Hall writes that the Paracelsian doctor 'would coniure the *Chymick Mercurie*, / Rise from his hors-dung bed and upward flie' (37). Sir George Ripley noted that the putrefaction was accomplished 'Wyth hete of Balne, or ells our Dounghyll' (*TCB*, 149). John Dee recorded in his Diary that during an alchemical experiment in Trebon, Bohemia, on 24 March 1588, 'Mr K.

put the glas in dung' (*Private Diary*, 26) ('Mr K.' is Edward Kelly). In 'To the Countess of Bedford', John Donne compared the springing forth of 'sublime ... refined' honour from humble places to the winning of the pure parts of herbs: 'From gross, by stilling ... is better done / By despised dung, than by the fire or sun' (lines 1–12). The alchemical treatises stress that the dung-hill or balneum is really philosophical mercury, the secret fire which burns within the alchemical vessel, not outside it. Synonyms for the dunghill are balneum, bath, horse-belly, aqua vitae, fire, blood of the *green lion and *Mercurius. Colson's *Philosophia maturata* says of philosophic mercury: 'This is our Fire always equally burning in one measure within the Glass, and not without: This is our Dunghill, our Aqua vitae, our Balmy, our Horse-belly' (32).

The alchemists frequently stated that the precious *first matter or raw stuff of the Stone was to be found anywhere and everywhere, even in the despised dunghill. Dung thus became a name for the matter from which the miraculous, rejuvenating elixir or Stone was made. Material alchemists, *puffers and charlatans mistakenly interpreted this term literally and frequently worked with dung as their first matter. In *Pantagruel* François Rabelais parodies this belief that alchemy can produce the elixir from dung: 'But Panurge fairly threw up his food when he saw an archasdarpenim fermenting a great tub of human urine in horse-dung, with plenty of Christian shit. Pooh, the filthy wretch! He told us, however, that he watered kings and great princes with this holy distillation, and thereby lengthened their life by a good six or nine feet' (651). A miniature from a fifteenth-century manuscript of the *Aurora consurgens* shows a man defecating into a crucible, which, according to Jacques van Lennep, symbolizes the purification of mercury by *sublimation (*Alchimie*, 64). In Jonson's *The Alchemist* Subtle uses the alchemical metaphor of the purification of matter out of dung when berating Face for ingratitude after Subtle has rescued him from obscurity: 'Thou vermine, have I tane thee, out of dung ... Rais'd thee from broomes, and dust, and watring pots? / *Sublim'd* thee, and *exalted* thee, and *fix'd* thee / I' the *third region,* call'd our *state of grace*?' (1.1.64–9). See **bath**.

dungeon   see **prison**.

dust   the whitened, purified body of the Stone attained through *sublimation, also known as *ash, *snow, *white foliated earth and *Bird of Hermes. *The Rosary of the Philosophers* says of the dust: 'when it shall ascend most white as Snow, it will be compleat, therefore gather it carefully, lest it fly away into smoke, because that is the very sought for good, the white foliated Earth' (in FC, 72). The *Clangor Buccinae* advised the alchemist to sublime the body of the Stone and boil it with mercury 'until it ascends in likenesse of most white Dust, adhering to the sides of the Vessell in manner of Snow, But the Ashes remaining in the bottome are dregs.' These dregs are also called 'dust': 'in the bottome are dregs, and the vilified drosse of Bodies, and to be cast away, in which there is no life because it is a most light Dust, which with a little blast vanisheth' (in FC, 78). Arthur Wilson referred to the alchemical dust, meaning 'dregs', in a dedicatory poem to Edward Benlowes: 'By sacred Chymistrie, the *Spirit* must / Ascend and leave the Sediment to Dust' (Benlowes, *Theophila*, C3r). Aristotle equated the purified body or white dust with the Hermes Bird: 'Whiten the Earth, and Sublime it quickly with Fire, untill the Spirit which thou shalt finde in it goe forth of it, and it is called *Hermes Bird*; for that which ascends higher is efficacious purity but that which fals to the bottome, is drosse and corruption. This therefore is Dust drawn from Dust, and the begotten of the Philosophers, the white foliated Earth, in which Gold is to be sown' (in *FC*, 70). See **white foliated earth**.

dye   the transformation of the white stone (attained at the *albedo) into the blood red or purple of the red stone (at the *rubedo); the transmutation of metals. These processes are often compared by the alchemists to the dyeing of cloth. There was a close relationship between the chemical laboratory, the dyer and the alchemist. The Stockholm Papyrus (an Egyptian papyrus from the late third or early fourth century AD) applies the succession of operations – washing, mordanting and colouring – to the transmutation of metals as well as to the dyeing of fabrics. Artephius stated that the reddening of the Stone is 'like as the tinctures or colours in dyeing cloth are by water put upon, and diffused in through the cloth' (*SB*, 24). Ripley told the alchemist desiring to learn about tincturing metals: 'Att the Dyers craft ye may learn this *Science* / ... So dieth Mettals with Colours evermore permanent, / After the quality of the Medycine Red or White' (*TCB*, 155). Certain colours which dyers used were rare because the source of the dye was difficult to obtain. The 'Tyrian purple', which was very rare, was often used by the philosophers to symbolize the colour of the precious red tincture or stone. The Tyrian purple robe symbolizes the attainment of the goal of the opus, the purple elixir. In a recipe for making the tincture the *Turba philosophorum* said: 'Then leave it for several days in its own vessel, until the most precious Tyrian colour shall come out from it to the surface' (48). The fact that Tyrian purple was a permanent dye made it an apt symbol for the stone-tincture which transmutes all that is transient into a permanent, eternal state.

During the alchemical dyeing, the volatile spirit is fixed or congealed by union with the body. The dyeing or staining of the pure white matter red means that it has been given new life and form. It signifies that the previously separated spirit has revivified the body and is now united with it, and that a new creation or incarnation has come into existence (i.e. the philosopher's stone). The new incarnation is sometimes symbolized by the dyeing of the matter with red blood, as in Bernard Trevisan's 'Practise of the Philosophick Stone' where the final red stage is compared to 'Hercules on Oeta ... Fird with the shirt dy'd in the Centaur's Blood' (lines 194–5, *AP*, 454). The meadow cleared of mown hay in Andrew Marvell's 'Upon Appleton House' is compared to the newly created world and to the arena in Madrid where the blood of bulls is shed, staining it red. In this creation scene, and in an alchemical context, Marvell alludes to the alchemical dyeing or staining which symbolizes the conferring of form on pure matter (white into red): 'This *Scene* again withdrawing brings / A new and empty space of things; / A levell'd space as smooth and plain, / As Clothes for *Lilly* stretcht to stain. / The World when first created sure / Was such a Table rase and pure. / Or rather such is the *Toril* / Ere the Bulls enter at Madril' (lines 441–8). (Marvell's eighteenth-century editor, Thomas Cooke, annotated Lilly as an 'eminent Cloth Dyer'. See Cooke (ed.), *Marvell*, I,22.)

E

eagle philosophic mercury which has been *sublimated, the white tincture or water also known as the *virgin's milk; sometimes philosophical sal ammoniac. Thomas Lodge wrote of the alchemists' enigmatic riddles: 'Let us marke their misteries and spels ... First aske where the flying Eagle dwels' (*Works*, 3:69). Lancelot Colson's *Philosophia maturata* refers to the 'white water, which we call our white tincture, our Eagle, our white *Mercury*, and Virgin's milk' (38). The alchemical eagle is sometimes referred to in the plural, and their number is anything from three to ten, according to the number of sublimations. Philalethes wrote: 'and therefore every sublimation of the Philosophers, let be one *Eagle*' (*Secrets Reveal'd*, 15). During the process of the opus alchymicum, the earliest stage of *Mercurius's manifestation is known as the *dragon or serpent. After the death of the dragon Mercurius is transformed into the *lion. In the succeeding stage Mercurius becomes the flying white eagle – the wings signifying that mercury is in a volatile state. Paracelsus wrote of the *red lion: 'This by the aid of Nature and the skill of the Artist himself, can be transmuted into a White Eagle' (*PW*, 22). He explains that the 'Tincture of the Philosophers' is created from the coagulation of 'the rose-coloured blood from the lion and the gluten from the Eagle' (*PW*, 25–6). The lion and the eagle are often paired together, demonstrating the process of transformation from one stage to the next: 'their *Eagles* are brought to devour the *Lion*' (Philalethes, *Secrets Reveal'd*, 14–15). The devouring of the lion by the winged eagles signifies the 'solve' aspect of the *solve et coagula cycle where the volatile spirit dissolves the fixed matter or body, spiritualizing it. At the same time, the volatile spirit must be captured and fixed by the inertia of the body, corporealizing it. Thomas Vaughan wrote: 'The *greene Lion* is the *Body* or *Magicall earth* with which you must clip the *wings* of the *Eagle*, that is to say, you must fix her, that shee may fly no more' (*VW* (R), 463) (see **beheading**). Gabriel Harvey's *Pierces Supererogation* mentions the pairing of the eagle and green lion in a discussion of Thomas Nashe's wit and Edward Kelly's alchemy: Nashe's 'witt must not enter the listes of comparison with Kelleyes Alchimy: howsoever he would seeme to haue the Greene Lion, and the Flying Eagle in a boxe' (Harvey, *Works*, 2:68–9). The toad and the flying eagle are also often paired in alchemical symbolism, signifying

the *sublimation of the fixed matter by the volatile. An emblem from
Michael Maier's *Symbola aureae mensae* shows Avicenna pointing to the
pair, saying: 'Join together an earthly toad and a flying eagle' (Stolcius,
Viridarium, 132). The high-flying eagle is also a symbol for the initiate
who has spiritualized the earthly serpent or scorpion, the power of
the instinctive urge in man.

earth one of the four *elements, the mastery of which brings the ability to give
divine service. The term 'earth' is used in alchemy to denote the dense,
heavy 'body' of the metal as distinct from the soul and spirit. Michael
Sendivogius wrote of this cold, dry element: 'The Earth is of great worth
in its quality and dignity: in this Element, the other three, especially the
fire, rest ... it is grosse, and porous, heavy in respect of its smallness, but
light in respect of its Nature' (*New Light of Alchymie*, 83). See **elements,
black earth, dross, white foliated earth, green lion**.

east and west a name for two of the subtances involved in the process of *solve et
coagula (dissolve and coagulate), which is reiterated many times to
achieve the purification and refinement of the matter of the Stone in the
alembic. The east signifies the red, dry, coagulating aspect (*philosophical sulphur) while the west signifies the cold, moist, dissolving aspect
(philosophical *argent vive). Abu'L-Qasim wrote that the alchemists
'often indicate by their phrase "Eastern" a substance which is hot and
dry as is the nature of the region of the East, and is also the nature of the
sun which appears from the East. Similarly by the "West" ... they mean
the moistness extracted from their stone as the West is related to moisture' (*Book of Knowledge*, 56). The alchemist's task was to unite these
opposing qualities and substances, sulphur and argent vive, in order
to create a perfectly integrated and balanced state embodied as the
*philosopher's stone. This is illustrated in emblem 47 of Maier's
Atalanta fugiens where 'The wolf, coming from the east, and the Dog,
coming from the West, have bitten each other.' These animals (symbols
of sulphur and argent vive) are described as biting each other in rage
and bloodshed, until they are united as one (*AF*, 285). See **dog and bitch**.

eat see **devour, cibation**.

eclipse a striking image used to portray the dark *nigredo, a time when the
body of the impure metal or matter for the Stone is dissolved and
putrefied in order that its seed or virtue may be released and a new form
(or state) created. It is an alchemical law that all nature must first die
away before it can be renewed. Philalethes wrote: 'But before the renovation of these Natures, they must in the first place pass through the
Eclipse, both of Sun and Moon ... which is the Gate of Blackness, and
after that they shall be renovated with the Light of Paradise' (*RR*, 15). The
Scala philosophorum likewise says of the Stone's matter: 'When it has
stood under an Eclipse for five months, and the Darknesse recedes,
the Light supervening, Encrease your fire' (in *ZC*, 82). In making the
*philosopher's stone the alchemist unites the seeds of *Sol (sulphur,

gold) and *Luna (argent vive, silver) in the *chemical wedding. Sol and Luna are united (coagulated), then killed (dissolved), and their bodies placed in a coffin or grave to blacken and putrefy while their souls rise to the top of the vessel. *The Sophic Hydrolith* says: 'At first the earthly Body of the Sun is totally solved and decomposed, and robbed of all strength … and is thus despoiled of its soul' (HM, 1:82) (see fig. 38). See **sol niger**, **green lion**.

The time of the eclipse is a time of suffering, mourning and *melancholy. A profound darkness reigns, as if the light will never return. *Bloomfield's Blossoms* says: 'The *Sun* and *Moone* shall lose their light, / And in mourning Sables they shall them dight' (TCB, 323). The eclipse of the sun described in *The Hunting of the Greene Lyon* is represented by the image of the lion devouring the sun. The lion 'soone can overtake the sunne, / And suddenly wyll hym devoure … And hym eclyps that was so bright' (TCB, 279). The green lion is the mercurial solvent which 'devours' the sun or sulphur/gold at the nigredo. The nox profunda of the soul which occurs when the old state of affairs dies, making way for new spiritual understanding, is powerfully conveyed through the image of the sun's eclipse in Shakespeare's thirty-third Sonnet. The sonnet describes the lover's suffering over his friend's sexual relation with someone else. The friend is compared to the sun, whose splendour gilds all it sees with 'heavenly alcumy' (line 4), but with the friend's betrayal the splendour is eclipsed in 'basest clouds' (line 5) and the lover is plunged into darkness. The experience, however, leads to new understanding and forgiveness: 'Yet him for this, my love no whit disdaineth, / Suns of the world may staine, when heavens sun staineth' (lines 13–14) (see **sun and shadow**).

education the nourishment and growth of the infant Stone, born of the union of opposite substances, male and female, sulphur and argent vive (see **chemical wedding**). The feeding of the infant Stone with the mercurial arcanum is compared to the education of a child because it must be carried out in a gradual and unhurried manner. *The Mastery of the Philosophers* said that 'first the earth must be nourished with a little water and afterwards with more, as is seen in the education of an infant' (85–6). Andreae's *The Chymical Wedding* stated that the alchemical 'child should be tenderly nursed' and committed to the care of 'an ancient Tutor' (112).

egg the alchemist's vessel of transmutation in which the birth of the *philosopher's stone takes place (fig. 13); also known as the griffin's or gripe's egg. The creation of the philosopher's stone is frequently compared to the hatching of a chick from its egg. In order to keep the hermetically sealed vessel from breaking, the alchemist, when making his fire, attempts to emulate the gentle warmth of nature, like that of the hen or bird brooding on her eggs. The fire is the incubator which generates the kind of warmth necessary for hatching the chick (Stone) from the egg (vessel). Bassett Jones calls the required heat 'this fiery hen' (AP, 247) (see **philosophical bird**). Charles Nicholl has observed that 'the

13 Philosophical egg

variety of chemical ware – retorts, alembics, cucurbites' in which the
opus takes place – is compressed 'into a single prototype vessel known
as … the Philosophers' Egg' (*Chemical Theatre*, 30). Ripley's *A Compound
of Alchymie* says of the vessel: 'And in one Glasse must be done all thys
thyng / Lyke to an Egg in shape, and closyd well' (*TCB*, 138). *Zoroaster's
Cave* says: 'Our vessel is a Glasse, firmely shut, round bellied, of a neck
strict and long, halfe a foot or thereabout. This vessel is called an Egge,
a Sublimatory, a Sphear, a Sepulchre, a Cucurbit' (79). In Andreae's *The
Chymical Wedding* Christian Rosencreutz and his companions open their
alchemical globe to find 'a lovely great snow-white egg' from which the
philosophical bird eventually issues (65). In Ben Jonson's *The Alchemist*
Surly says to Subtle: 'you should hatch gold in a fornace, sir, / As they doe
egges in Egypt' (2.3.127–8). In certain instances, as in *The Sophic Hydrolith*,
the contents of the vessel are identified with the vessel itself, and the
'Egg of the Sages' is synonymous with the philosopher's stone (*HM*,
1:83).

egg shells an ingredient of the *philosopher's stone. A recipe in Colson's
Philosophia maturata instructs the alchemist to 'put into a Circulatory
an ounce of the calx of the Egg-shells very well reverberated, and pour
thereon of white or red *Mercury* to cover it; then nip the glass, or stop it
close with lute' (54). Other alchemists, however, state that the use of
such material to make the Stone is mistaken. Sir George Ripley tells of
his early, deluded experiments: 'Eggs shells I calcenyd twise or thryse, /
Oylys fro Calcys I made up ryse; / And every Element fro other I did
twyne, / But profyt found I ryght none therein' (*TCB*, 190). Gerhard Dorn
stated that the material alchemists were deluded in interpreting such

materials as urine, egg shells and blood literally, when they were symbolic names (in *AS*, 290). In Ben Jonson's *The Alchemist* Surly scornfully lists the materials of the deluded alchemist: 'With all your broths, your *menstrues,* and *materialls,* / Of pisse, and egg-shells, womens termes, mans bloud' (2.3.193–4).

elements   earth, air, fire and water. The idea of the four elements was derived from Empedocles (492–432 BC) and Plato's *Timaeus* (*c.* 360 BC), but came to alchemy through Aristotle's theories of matter. According to Aristotle everything was created from one original substance, the *prima materia, and the first 'forms' which arose from this original chaos were the four elements, from which all bodies were created in differing proportions and combinations. These four elements, which the alchemists used in their theory of the generation of metals, were not the material earth, air, fire and water which we know, but subtle abstract principles or qualities emanating from the source of all creation (and are obviously present in the familiar material elements). These principles are said to display four fundamental properties – hot, dry, cold and moist – and each of the elemental principles possesses two of the primary properties: earth is cold and dry, water is cold and moist, air is hot and moist, and fire, hot and dry. Aristotle maintained that each element is transformable into the others and that each is potentially latent in the others. The transformation is able to take place by virtue of the fact that each element shares a property in common: earth and water share coldness, water and air share moistness, air and fire share heat, and fire and earth share dryness. This transformation process in alchemy is known as the circle, the wheel, or the rotation of the elements (see **opus circulatorium**).

The idea of transmutation is based on the theory that all bodies, including metals, are constituted of the elements in differing proportions, that these proportions are alterable, and that the elements may be transformed into each other. Robert Fludd wrote in 'Truth's Golden Harrow': 'ffor when ther is a mutation of elements by a compleat rotation of them, wherin earth will be turned into water and water into invisible aer, and it into fire, then doth fire conclud all with a spirituall celestiall, and a bright golden earth which is the tabernacle wherin is the light of wisdome, so much mentioned of the wise Kinge aboundeth, the which is full of lif and multiplication. Thus the elements agreed among themselves in this change' (123). The elemental proportions of bodies are changed through the processes of *calcination, burning, *dissolution, *distillation, *sublimation and *coagulation. The matter, metal or body is first putrefied – broken down into its original matter, the prima materia – and the elements are then differentiated from this unified matter and combined in such a way as to create a new, purer form. Sir George Ripley wrote in *The Compound of Alchymie*: 'And lykwyse wythout thy Matter do Putrefy, / It may in no wyse trewly be alterate, / Nor thyne Elements may be devyded kyndly' (*TCB*, 148). The theory of the elements supported Geber's sulphur/mercury theory of the generation of metals which was adopted by most alchemists (see **prima**

materia). Sulphur, the principle of combustibility, possessed the hotness and dryness of fire and so was analogous with fire, while mercury was cold and moist and analogous with water. All metals were thought to be composed of varying proportions of sulphur and mercury. If the sulphur and mercury were pure and combined in perfect equilibrium of hot, dry, cold and moist, the result would be the perfect metal gold.

Another theory was that the greater the proportion of mercury in the combination of sulphur and mercury, the purer the metal. Such metals as copper, lead, tin and iron were thought to be deficient in the purity of the mercury and sulphur in their make-up, and unbalanced in the proportions of these constituents. Since these metals were made of the same substance as gold it was thought that these deformities could be remedied by altering the proportions, and applying the healing power of the *philosopher's stone or *medicine. The making of the Stone itself involved bringing about the union or 'agreement' of the four contrary elements into one perfect harmonious element known as the fifth element or quintessence (*TGH*, 123). See **fifth element, opus circulatorium, peace, dragon.**

elixir see **red elixir, white elixir.**

Elysian Fields, Elizium the *white foliated earth attained at the pure white stage of the opus, the *albedo. Ruland calls the 'white stage' the 'Elysian fields' (*Lexicon*, 347). Ripley likewise wrote that souls 'enter the Elysium' at the albedo (in *AF*, 86). Andrew Marvell's fawn in 'The Nymph Complaining' passes, after its death (*nigredo), to the pure white stage: 'fair *Elizium* to endure, / With milk-white Lambs, and Ermins pure' (lines 105–8). One of twelve alchemical engravings in *Chymica vannus* (1666) illustrates the expanses and plains of Elysium (van Lennep, *Alchimie*, 229). In 'The Philosophicall Aenigma' Michael Sendivogius call the *garden of the philosophers 'Our blest Elysium' (*AP*, 500), the garden being the sacred place or vessel where the *solar and lunar trees grow and the *lily and rose of the *white and red stages of the opus bloom. To sow the seed of gold in the pure white Elysian fields means to unite the soul/spirit of the Stone with the purified body at the *chemical wedding. Robert Boyle described his laboratory as an Elysium: 'Vulcan has so transported and bewitched me as to make me fancy my laboratory a kind of Elysium' (in Gunther, *Early Science in Oxford*, 1:11). See also **Hesperides.**

embryo see **philosophical child.**

Emerald Table one of the most important sources of medieval alchemy, attributed to Hermes Trismegistus or the Egyptian Thoth, and said to be inscribed on an emerald tablet in Phoenician characters. Legend has it that Noah carried the tablet with him in the ark during the flood, and that Sarah, Abraham's wife, found it in the hands of Hermes Trismegistus as he lay in his tomb in a cave. Hortulanus wrote: 'The wordes of the secrets of *Hermes* . . . were written in a Smaragdine Table, and found betweene his hands in an obscure vaute [*sic*], wherin his body lay buried' (*A Briefe Commentarie*, 16). Others said that Apollonius of Tyana or Alexander the Great was the discoverer of the tablet. It was considered to be the alchemist's book of laws and was still being used as a basic text in the seventeenth century. The earliest known version by Jabir ibn Hayyan was discovered by E. J. Holmyard in an eighth-century Arabic text, translated into Latin around the thirteenth century. The first English translation appeared in Roger Bacon's *The Mirror of Alchimy* (London, 1597), with a commentary by Hortulanus. Sometime between 1680 and 1684 Isaac Newton wrote a commentary (of about 1,000 words) on the *Emerald Table*. A decade or so later he translated 'La Table d'Emeraude' from the first volume of *Bibliothèque des philosophes* [*chymiques*] (Paris, 1672–8) (Dobbs, *Janus*, 15, 274).

The *Emerald Table* is much quoted and referred to in alchemical texts. Lines 1003–36 of Jean de la Fontaine's 'The Pleasant Founteine of Knowledge', for example, are a translation of the *Table* (*AP*, 109–10). An emblem of Hermes Trismegistus pointing to the sun and moon, in Michael Maier's *Symbola aureae mensae,* is accompanied by a motto based on the third law of the *Table*: 'Sol est eius coniugii Pater et alba Luna Mater, terius succedit, ut gubernator, Ignis' (5). The first two emblems of Maier's *Atalanta fugiens* are based on the fourth law: 'Portavit eum ventus in ventre suo' (emblem 1) and 'Nutrix ejus terra est' (emblem 2) (*AF*, 377–8). Bassett Jones's 'Lithochymicus' alludes to the first law of the *Table*: 'The only *All* above and soe below' (*AP*, 263). The text of the *Table* follows:

True it is, without falsehood, certain and most true. That which is above is like to that which is below, and that which is below is like to that which is above, to accomplish the miracles of one thing.

And as all things were by the contemplation of one, so all things arose from this one thing by a single act of adaption.

The father thereof is the Sun, the mother the Moon.

The Wind carried it in its womb, the Earth is the nurse thereof.

It is the father of all works of wonder throughout the whole world.

The power thereof is perfect.

If it be cast onto the Earth, it will separate the element of Earth from that of Fire, the subtle from the gross.

With great sagacitie it doth ascend gently from Earth to Heaven.

Again it doth descend to Earth, and uniteth in itself the force from things superior and things inferior.

Thus wilt thou possess the glory of the brightness of the whole world, and all obscurity will fly far from thee.

The thing is the strong fortitude of all strength, for it overcometh every subtle thing and doth penetrate every solid substance.

Thus was this world created.

Hence there will be marvellous adaptions achieved, of which the manner is this.

For this reason I am called Hermes Trismegistus, because I hold three parts of the wisdom of the whole world.

That which I had to say about the operation of Sol is complete.

(Holmyard, *Alchemy*, 98).

14 The Ethiopian

enemies see **peace**.

engender see **generation**.

Ethiopian symbol of the black stage or *nigredo (fig. 14). Deriving their symbolism from the Bible (Acts 8), the alchemists used the Ethiopian or black man to represent the blackened matter of the Stone while it is still corrupt and unclean, before it is washed at the *ablution and restored to a state of whiteness and purity at the *albedo. Jung wrote that this powerful symbol of the Moor or Ethiopian represents the activated darkness of matter, the *shadow of the sun or *prima materia, something that must be experienced consciously before renovation and integration can take place. According to Melchior, the union of the lovers (the seeds of metals, *sulphur and *argent vive) is followed by the appearance in the bottom of the vessel of 'the mighty Ethiopian, burned, calcined, discoloured, altogether dead and lifeless. He askes to be buried, to be sprinkled with his own moisture and slowly calcined till he shall arise in glowing form from the fierce fire ... Behold a wondrous restoration and renewal of the Ethiopian! Because of the bath of rebirth he takes a new name, which the philosophers call the natural sulphur and their son, this being the stone of the philosophers' (in PA, 402). In Thomas Charnock's 'The Breviary of Naturall Philosophy', the alchemical quest is presented as a sea-journey in a ship of glass. During the nigredo of this journey the men are burnt black: 'The Moone shall us burne so in process of tyme, / That we shalbe as black as men of Inde / But shortly we shall passe into another Clymate, / Where we shall receive a more purer estate' (TCB, 292). Trismosin's *Splendor Solis* recounts how at the nigredo the philosopher 'saw a man black like a negro sticking fast in a black, dirty and foul smelling slime or clay; to his assistance came a young woman, beautiful in countenance ... most handsomely adorned with many-coloured dresses, and she had wings on her back, the feathers of which were equal to those of the very finest white Peacock' (31). The 'many-coloured dresses' and wings like peacock's feathers refer to the *peacock's tail or rainbow stage of the opus which follows the nigredo and leads to the white albedo. At the peacock's tail stage the black, unclean matter has been washed to whiteness. The beautiful winged woman symbolizes the 'soul' of the Stone stepping forward to reunite with the now purified, whitened 'body' (the Ethiopian). In *Pantagruel,* François Rabelais parodies the process of whitening the blackened matter, using the image of the Ethiopian. The narrator, having reached 'The Kingdom of the Quintessence', is shown the 'Officers of the Quintessence' carrying out various alchemical operations: 'After this I saw a great number of these officers, engaged in the rapid whitening of Ethiopians by merely rubbing their bellies with the bottom of a basket' (651).

Eve counterpart of Adam, the feminine aspect of the *prima materia, *philosophical mercury, the *radical humidity, the female principle in the opus, the *white foliated earth, equivalent of *Diana, the alchemical *queen, and *Luna. The frontispiece of Arthur Dee's 'Arca arcanorum' depicts the extraction of the prima materia, with Eve on the left side of the *philosophical tree and Adam on the right. The silver moon pours down its moist, cold, white receptive influence on Eve while the crow of the *putrefaction aims its beak at her head, and two lions, one red, the other gold, sit at her feet (see fig. 31). See **Adam**.

exaltation the vaporization of the Stone, a process very similar to *sublimation. Ripley wrote of the exaltation: 'Full lyttyll yt ys dyfferent from *Sublymacion*' (TCB, 178). During the exaltation the substance of the Stone is raised to a higher degree of purity and potency through a reiterated cycle of dissolution and coagulation of the Stone in its own mercurial *blood. It is generally agreed that this stage occurs after the *fermentation and before the *multiplication (or augmentation) of the Stone, but sometimes it is identical with the multiplication. Johannes Mylius represented this stage of the opus with the image of the crowned *king and *queen, Sol and Luna, elevated upon a stage with multiple lions forming a guard of honour on the five steps leading up to the stage (*Philosophia reformata*, 126). In 'Windsor Forest' Alexander Pope wrote of the happy man who gathers herbs in the shades of the forest and 'With chymic art exalts the mineral powers, / And draws the aromatic souls of flowers' (lines 243–4).

eyes see **Argus eyes, fishes' eyes**.

F

faeces the impure parts, the dross or terra damnata which the alchemist separated from the pure matter of the Stone. Ramon Lull stated that the alchemist must separate the 'feces and dregges from the most pure substance' (in *FC*, 65). Philalethes likewise advised the adept 'be sure / By *Vulcan's* aid to purifie, till (free / From Faeces) the metalline part be pure' (*Marrow*, bk. 1, 17). As the matter in the vessel is dissolved and sublimed, that which is pure and white ascends to the top of the vessel, casting off the impure faeces to the water in the bottom. These faeces have to be discarded while the 'middle white substance' (the purified body also known as the caelum, quintessence, a corpus glorificatum) is retained. Artephius wrote: 'These faeces ... are the dross and *terra damnata*, which is of no value, nor can do any such service as the clear, white, pure and clean matter' (*SB*, 21). In Ben Jonson's *The Alchemist* Subtle assures Face that '*Terra damnata* / Must not haue entrance, in the *worke*' (2.5.5–6). Faeces or dung was also the name which the sceptics called the despised matter from which the alchemist supposedly made his elixirs and medicines. Colson's *Philosophia maturata* explained that because the Stone 'is cast out into the Dunghill, and trodden under men's feet, it is counted a most vile and contemptible thing' (15). It also warns of the danger of literally working with dung or faeces as the materia of the opus: many men 'make choice of several stinking things, which with great labour they distil, calcine and joyn together. But let such hear what the Philosophers say, *whosoever seeks the Philosophers Secrets in Turds looseth his Labour*, and in the end finds nothing but deceit' (14) (see **dung**).

fawn see **cervus fugitivus, hart.**

feathers When the *philosophical child or stone is born from the union of the male and female lovers at the *chemical wedding, it is placed in a heated *bath of mercurial water which it drinks up and plays in until dissolved. This process, known as the cibation or feeding, involves the impregnation or saturation of the Stone's matter with the mercurial tincture (see cibation). In the instances when the birth of the Stone is compared to the birth of the chick from the *egg of the alembic, the dissolution of the Stone in the heated bath is depicted as the consuming of the bird's feathers. Christian Rosencreutz in Andreae's *The Chymical Wedding* participates in the bathing of the bird: 'We therefore clapt a cover on the kettle, and suffered him to thrust his head out through a hole, till he had in this sort lost all his feathers in his bath, and was as smooth as a new-born child, yet the heat did him no further harm, at which I much marvelled, for in the bath the feathers were quite consumed' (157). A variant of this is found in the 'Emblematicall Scrowle' attributed to Ripley, where the bird eats his own feathers under the sweating heat of the sun (see fig. 7). The title of the verse accompanying this emblem is 'The Bird of Hermes is my name, Eating my wings to make me tame' (see **Bird of Hermes**). Peacock's feathers or 'cauda pavonis' is a name given to the multi-coloured rainbow stage which follows the black *nigredo and heralds the white *albedo stage. Paracelsus wrote: 'It is necessary that you persevere in the work until the peacock's tail is quite consumed … and the vessel attains its degree of perfection' (PW, 86). See **bird**.

feeding   see **cibation**.

ferment, fermentation   the stage following the *sublimation, during which the soul of the Stone is driven up and down from the body in a process of vaporization and *distillation. During the sublimation, the body is made spiritual and the spirit is made corporeal. In the fermentation which quickly follows, the soul and the purified body are chemically and permanently joined together in the *coniunctio to create the perfect *tincture or elixir. This is the chemical marriage of *Sol and *Luna. Sir George Ripley wrote: 'But Fermentacion trew as I the tell / Ys of the Soule wyth the Bodys incorporacyon' (TCB, 176). The process of sowing the ferment or soul into the earth or body is often compared by the alchemists to the process of adding leaven to dough (or *paste) to make bread, or to the *sowing of the seed of gold in a field. *The Sounding of the Trumpet* calls the ferment which activates the Stone's body, philosophical gold. The body is called white earth: 'Sow gold, i.e. the soul and quickening virtue, into the white earth, which by preparation has been made white and pure and freed from all its grossness. The natural gold is not the fermenting matter, but the philosopher's gold is the quickening ferment itself' (cited in HM, 1:35). Maier likewise says: 'Sow your gold in the white foliated earth' (AF, 81). The fermentation of the *white foliated earth by the soul results in the re-animation of the purified body of the Stone lying at the bottom of the alembic. The ferment or soul is the equivalent of the form, while the earth or body is the formless matter upon which the new form is conferred.

According to most philosophers, a third principle is involved in the union or chemical wedding of soul and body, and that is the spirit which is thought to tie or glue the otherwise irreconcilable soul and body together (though in some instances the third uniting principle is called the soul which unites body and spirit). Both *The Golden Tract* and Edward Kelly's *The Philosophers Stone* affirm that the Stone is composed of body (the imperfect matter), spirit (the aqua permanens) and soul (the ferment which gives life to the imperfect body and makes it into a more beautiful form) (HM, 1:15; Kelly, *Two excellent Treatises*, 43). Whatever the terms employed, the fermentation involves the infusing of the life force and form into lifeless, formless matter. Chaucer's Canon's Yeoman mentions the fermentation in a list of related alchemical processes: 'our citrinacioun / Our cementing and fermentacioun' (*Canon's Yeoman's Tale*, lines 814–15). The ferment is the food with which the *philosophical stone or infant is fed after its birth during the stage known as the *cibation. Ramon Lull said: 'Ferment is made after the *Ortus*, or Birth of the Infant. And *Ferment* is nothing but meat Disposed to a Convertibility into the Essence of the Infant' (in ZC, 83). Arthur Dee likewise wrote:

'And when it is prepared, then it shall be the first proper Dish, of which our Infant is nourisht, and by Philosophers, shall have the name of Ferment' (*FC*, 125). Isaac Newton referred to this same process in his 'Index chemicus': 'Cibation ... is the nutrition of the stone with milk and food i.e., with *terra alba foliata* and the soul of gold ... cibation, fermentation and multiplication are the same' (Keynes MS 30, f. 23, in Westfall, 'Index', 179).

fifth element   (also known as the quintessence and *azoth) ,the product of reconciling the four warring, quarrelling elements into one harmonious and perfect unity, the very essence of the body of the metal or Stone, the incorruptible, pure and original substance of the world magically able to preserve all sublunar things from destruction and corruption. When the body of the stone has been separated from its soul and lies 'dead' at the bottom of the alembic, it is the alchemist's task to purify that body. Gerhard Dorn (cited in *MC*, 487) stated that the quintessence was needed for the purification and preparation of the body. The purified body or caelum became the corpus glorificatum, a substance capable of being united with the already united soul and spirit, in the final coniunctio or *chemical wedding of the opus. The dross left over from this operation was known as the dregs, *faeces or terra damnata. The purified body, which is attained through sublimation, is also known as the *white foliated earth (or *ash, *snow, *dust, *Bird of Hermes, the first matter of metals). It is also known as the quintessence or white stone which can transmute base metal to silver. The *Clangor Buccinae* says of the sublimation of the Stone's body: 'Then the dregs being cast away, iterate the Sublimation of the most white Dust by itself without dregs, till it be fixt, and till it send out no dregs, but ascend most purely, like Snow, the which is our pure Quintessence; And then thou shalt have the Soul Tincting, Coagulating, and Cleansing ... which the Alchimists may use, that with it they might make silver' (in *FC*, 78–9).

The fifth element is frequently identified with the final goal of the opus, the *philosopher's stone. The philosopher's stone cannot be created until the alchemist has first united the four contrary elements – earth, air, fire and water – into an integrated, harmonious whole (see **opus circulatorium**). Mylius described the fifth element as 'a mixture of all the elements, and a reduction of them to one pure substance' (*AE*, 8). Isaac Newton wrote in his 'Index chemicus' that 'Quintessence is a thing that is spiritual, penetrating, tinging, and incorruptible, which emerges anew from the four elements when they are bound to each other' (Keynes MS 30, f. 70, in Westfall, 'Index', 179). This perfect substance or *balsam, thought to be beyond the realm of change and decay, was believed to be a panacea with miraculous healing properties and the power to transform the impure into the pure, the perishable into the imperishable. Jung has written that the process by which the four elements become united into the fifth element is frequently represented by the image of a great tree (*AS*, 332). The four elements, the constituents of the philosopher's stone, are often compared to the radices or roots from which the great tree of the fifth element grows. Andrew Marvell used the image in 'Upon Appleton House': 'When first the Eye this Forrest sees / It seems indeed as *Wood* not *Trees*: / As if their Neighbourhood so old / To one great Trunk them all did mold. / There the huge Bulk takes place as ment / To thrust up a *Fifth Element*' (lines 497–502). This quintessence is also symbolized by the image of the crowned maiden. Ripley wrote in verse 30 of his alchemical 'Cantilena': 'Four Elements, Brave Arms, and Polish'd well / God gave him, in the midst whereof did dwell / The Crowned Maid, ordained for to be / In the Fifth Circle of the Mysterie.' The maiden as elemental quintessence is illustrated in emblem 17 (first series) of Mylius's *Philosophia reformata*. In François Rabelais's *Pantagruel* (1532) Pantagruel meets the 'Lady Queen Quintessence' on arrival at the 'Kingdom of the Quintessence' (647). Henry Cotiril, who advises Pantagruel's company about sailing safely to this kingdom, answers Pantagruel's questions 'where have you come from? Where are you going? What are you carrying? Have you smelt the sea?' with 'From the quintessence . . . To Touraine. Alchemy. To the very bottom' (644–5).

filing   see **limation**.

fire   one of the four elements, the mastery of which brings the ability to express divine love; the chief agent of transmutation in the opus alchymicum. According to Michael Sendivogius, 'Fire is the purest, and most worthy Element of all, full of unctuous corrosivenesse adhering to it, penetrating, digesting, corroding, and wonderfully adhering, without, visible, but within invisible, and most fixed, it is hot and dry and tempered with Aire' (*New Light of Alchymie*, 99). Alchemy is known as the art of fire. Paracelsus referred to the fire as the 'Great Arcanum of Art' and compared it to the sun in the natural world: 'It heats the furnace and the vessels, just as the sun heats the vast universe' (PW, 74). Nicolas Flamel also compared the fire 'to that of the *Sun* itself – a gentle and even warmth', explaining that the fire is called natural 'not because it is made by the Sages, but because it is made by Nature' (HM, 1:145). The secret fire (the fiery water and the watery fire) lies hidden in the alchemist's raw matter ('gold') and is stirred into action by the application of the outer material fire. The alchemist in John Lyly's *Gallathea* says of the outer fire: 'Ay, Rafe, the fortune of this art consisteth in the measure of the fire, for if there be a coal too much or a spark too little, if it be a little too hot or a thought too soft, all our labour is in vain' (3.3.13–16). According to Pontanus, the inner fire is 'found by deepe and profound Meditation onely, and then it may be gathered out of Bookes and not before' (in HE, 244). It is generally agreed that there is only one fire employed in the work, though there are three different aspects to this fire, sometimes called three fires. The first operation of the opus requires a mild, warm, moderate fire which continues until the matter of the Stone in the vessel turns black (*nigredo) and then white (*albedo). With the appearance of the white colour, the heat is increased until the Stone is dried up and calcined. When the matter is completely dried, the fire is made even stronger and more fierce until the Stone is transformed into its perfect ruby red colour (*rubedo). Arthur Dee, following Artephius, referred to the three fires as 'Natural, not Natural, and against Nature, which Fires are of the Philosophers' (FC, 64). According to Artephius, the third fire is 'called the fire against nature, because it is water … [it] is the fountain of living water where the king and queen bathe themselves' (SB, 35) (see **bath, fountain**). This is the mercurial water, the water which burns, the water which does not wet the hands, the magical transformative substance which can dissolve gold without violence, and coagulate it. Philalethes wrote: 'O *Mercury*, thou wonder of the world … This is our water, our secret fire' (*Marrow*, bk. 3, 42). And Dardarius said: 'Argent vive is a Fire, burning, mortifying, and breaking Bodies more then Fire' (in FC, 52). Such *weaponry as sword, scissors, knife and arrow signify the dissolving action of the philosophical fire. John Dryden referred to the transformative power of the 'chymical' fire in *Annus Mirabilis*: 'Me-thinks already, from this Chymick flame, / I see a City of more precious mold: / Rich as the Town which gives the *Indies* name, / With silver pav'd, and all divine with Gold' (lines 1169–72). Guillaume du Bartas wrote of the purifying power of the alchemical fire in man himself: 'Fire, that in Lymbec of pure thoughts divine, / Doost purge our thoughts, and our dull earth refine' (*Divine Weeks*, 1:328, lines 427–8).

firmament   see **heaven**.

first matter   see **prima materia**.

fishes' eyes   the appearance of the matter of the Stone when it has reached the stage of the *ablution, and also the *albedo. Some alchemists say that, during or after the washing or whitening of the blackened earth or body of the Stone at the ablution, there appear pearls or fishes' eyes in the vessel. This is the appearance in the dark solution of the spark or light of pure consciousness. Trithemius wrote that 'before the True whitenesse comes, thou shalt see all about the margin of the Glass as it were Oriental pearls, in the matter of the Stone, glittering like the Eyes of fishes' (in ZC, 80). According to the *Sophic Hydrolith* the 'granular bodies like fishes' eyes' appear after the black *nigredo but before the many colours of the *peacock's tail, the stage which heralds the coming of the white albedo (HM, 1:83). Other alchemists say that the matter looks like fishes' eyes after the appearance of the peacock's tail when the matter has already become white and dry at the albedo. Roger Bacon's *Mirror of Alchimy* touches on the whitening of the matter: 'When it hath bin decocted pure and clean … it shineth like the eyes of fishes' (13). Benjamin Lock advised the alchemist that after the washing of the putrefied body he should 'somwhat strengthen the fyer, and in that manner continew yt untill the water be dryed up and there appeare upon the earthe like perles or the eyes of fishes, then with the continuance of the fyer the water will be dryed up into a whyte powder cleare and shyninge' and 'when you shall see the whytenes appear like to the eyes of fishes, then the work is complete in the first parte' ('Picklock', ff.

20v, 28v). The alchemists also used the fishes eyes (which never shut) as a symbol of the perpetual attention necessary for the accomplishment of the opus.

fixation   the *coagulation or *congelation of the volatile spirit of the Stone, the converting of spirit into body so that it can endure the fire and not fly away. John Hall's encomiastic poem to Bassett Jones's 'Lithochymicus' indicates that fixation is one of the alchemist's crucial achievements: 'Haile mighty priest of Nature, who hast done / That miracle which learned Ignorance / Sleights 'cause it cannot reach, and dost advance / To fix the spirit and multiply the Sunne' (*AP*, 230). Most of the alchemical texts indicate that the fixation of the volatile spirit occurs simultaneously with the volatilization of the fixed body of the Stone, or very closely afterwards. Calid wrote: 'We have taught how a Body is to be changed into a Spirit; and again how the Spirit is to be turned into a Body, *viz.* how the fixed is made volatile, and the volatile fixed again' (*Booke of the Secrets*, 121). The fixation is frequently symbolized by the capturing and taming of the volatile *Mercurius so that it can be used in the production of the *philosopher's stone. Andrew Marvell used this chemical process as a simile in 'The Loyall Scot': 'And would like Chymists fixing Mercury, / Transmute indifference with necessity' (lines 211–12). John Collop uses the image jokily in 'To Eugenia, a defence of juvenile wildnesse': 'Chymists say, who fix *Mercury* can make gold, / Fix me *Eugenia* thou art rich if 't hold' (lines 39–40). Nailing, binding, tying and freezing are synonyms for the fixation. See **congelation, solve et coagula, bind, Bird of Hermes, volatile**.

flood   a symbol of the dissolution and putrefaction of the matter of the Stone during the black *nigredo stage when water is the dominant element. Mylius wrote: 'And this blackening is the beginning of the operation and indication of putrefaction … a sign that the body is dissolving … And as its says in the story of Noah, "The waters prevailed over the earth and had dominion over it" so for one hundred and fifty six days it is concealed in the blackness before the time of whitening' (*AE*, 53). Sir George Ripley likewise said the matter must 'passe the Waters of *Noyes* flod / On Erth, whych were a hundred dayes contynuate / And fifty' (*TCB*, 151). During this stage the alchemical vessel is sometimes symbolized by the *ark which rides on the flood and becomes a vessel of generation, of new life. The ark as alchemical vessel on the flood is illustrated in Goosen van Vreeswijk, *De Goude Leeuw* (1675), embl. 2. In a variation on the flood theme, *The Golden Tract* tells of the bride hermetically sealed with her husband in the 'prison' of the vessel, dissolving into endless tears when she sees her husband melted with excessive ardour: 'she wept for him, and, as it were, covered him with overflowing tears, until he was quite flooded and concealed from view' (*HM*, 1:47). At this stage in the opus the cold, moist, feminine aspect is said to dominate the proceedings. The black waters of dissolution (mercury) threaten to drown every living creature, and yet, at the nadir, these deathly waters are miraculously transformed into the waters of life, which wash the blackened body of

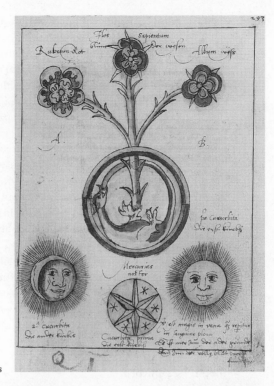

15　The alchemical flowers

the Stone at the bottom of the alembic and resurrect it into life (see **ablution**). The *rainbow, the sign of promise sent at the end of the flood, is, in alchemy, a symbol of the stage of many colours, the *peacock's tail, which follows the *nigredo and precedes the *albedo. The drying up of the flood waters represents the stage where the earth or body has passed through the nigredo and the peacock's tail and is transformed into the *white foliated earth of the albedo, ready to receive the 'seed' of gold, the previously separated soul and spirit, back into itself at the *chemical wedding.

flowers　the powdery form of substances obtained by sublimation. Bassett Jones refers to the 'flowers or subtile partes of a body' which rise to the top of the vessel during *sublimation (*AP*, 354). Artephius warned the adept that 'by reason of too much heat, you will burn the *flores auri*, the golden flowers' (*SB*, 34). In one of his experiments St Dunstan says: 'take in the Name of the Lord, of *Hungarish* Gold, which hath been cast thrice thorow *Antimony*, and be laminated most thinly, as much of it as you will, and make with quick *Mercury* an a Malgame, then calcine it most subtilly, with flowers of Sulphur' (*Recipes*, 89–90). Michael Drayton wrote of a mountain in the Derbyshire Peak District playing the subli-mating alchemist in *Poly-Olbion*: 'For shee a *Chimist* was, and Natures secrets knew / And from amongst the *Lead*, she *Antimony* drew, / And *Christall* there congeal'd (by her enstyled Flowers)' (*Works*, 4: 531, lines 386–8). The flower is also a symbol for the *philosopher's stone. The matter of the Stone is often compared to a tree or plant, because it is a growing, organic thing (see **philosophical tree**). The beautiful colours which appear in the vessel at the fullest perfection of the work are represented as flowers blossoming from the plant of the Stone. Sir George Ripley wrote of these flowers: 'If also thy Water be equall in proportion with the Earth and measured Heat, there will at once come forth a new Budde both White and Red' (in FC, 44) (see also **green**, **red**, **white**). The 'flower' is that which is an essential part of the matter, that which has attained the fullest perfection (fig. 15). Paracelsus wrote: 'so the matter of the stone doth discover most fair colours in the production of its Flower' (*Aurora*, 18). *Zoroaster's Cave* says that the opus brings forth 'White, Citrine, and Flamye Red Flowers' (74) (see **colours**). The flower of wisdom is the perfect elixir at the white or red stage. The *white stone or elixir attained at the *albedo is symbolized by the *white rose or lily, while the *red stone or elixir of the *rubedo is symbolized by the *red rose. The golden flower signifies the citrinitas, the yellow stage of the opus which occurs between the albedo and rubedo. It can also symbolize the philosopher's stone itself and the wisdom obtained at the culmination of the opus. William Bloomfield called his alchemical treatise *Bloomefield's Blossoms: or, The Campe of Philosophy* (TCB, 305–23).

foes   see **peace**.

forest   see **unicorn**.

form and **matter**   see **argent vive, chemical wedding, harvest, prima materia**.

fort, fortified city   one of the names of the alchemical vessel. The seventh key of Basil Valentine uses the siege and fort metaphor: 'If you would perform our task rightly, take the spiritual water . . . and preserve it in a closely shut chamber. For the heavenly city is about to be besieged by earthly foes. You must, therefore, strongly fortify it with three impassable and well-guarded walls, and let the one entrance be well protected' (HM, 1:339). The vessel acts as a defence to keep the contents well protected and hermetically sealed so that there is no invasion by the outside influences of the world and no danger of the contents themselves escaping. Spiritually, the siege represents a turning away from the desires and demands of the lower earthly self, a withdrawal from the outside world and its distractions into a state of contemplation in the cave or castle of the innermost self (see also **castle**).

forty days   the philosophical month, the symbolic time of *putrefaction, blackening and gestation of the matter of the Stone in the vessel. This stage is often compared to Noah's flood and thus to the time the ark rode the flood waters (see **ark**, **flood**). Arthur Dee quoted the *Turba*, which said of the body of the Stone: 'then let it be put in a kindled Fire forty days, untill it putrefie, and the colours thereof appear with the Ashes' (FC, 104). *Zoroaster's Cave* likewise said: 'When the matter has stood for the space of forty dayes in a moderate heat, there will begin to appear above a blacknesse like to pitch, which is the *Caput Corvi* of the Philosophers'

(80). The number forty is biblically significant (Jesus was in the wilderness for forty days, the Israelites for forty years). In alchemy the period of forty days is less a precise than an approximate term. In another metaphor expressing the same process the *king (Sol) puts on his black shirt (symbol of the putrefaction) and enters the *bath of dissolution and cleansing (sometimes the sweat bath) for forty-two days (RR, 20).

foster-parent see **orphan**.

fountain a name for the magical transforming substance, the *mercurial water or aqua permanens. From the mercurial fountain all other metals are said to be generated. In 'The Pleasant Founteine of Knowledge', Jean de la Fontaine wrote that 'This mercury is of mettall / The matter and the principall' and that 'bredd they [the metals] are of the founteine / When earth them deeper doth retrieve' (AP, 94, 89). The mercurial water is said to be both a *poison which kills or dissolves the metal or matter of the Stone into the *prima materia, and the life-giving *dew or rain which washes the blackened matter at the bottom of the alembic and resurrects it. *The Sophic Hydrolith* referred to the 'water of mercury (also called … the never-failing fountain, or the water of life, which nevertheless contains the most malignant poison)' (HM, 1:84). Arthephius called this water 'the royal fountain in which the king and queen bathe themselves' (SB, 15). The bathing of the king and queen (male *sulphur and female *argent vive) may occur before their first union as well as after their death, which leads to their resurrection at the *chemical wedding. The fountain is synonymous with the bath or spring into which the *king, as the raw matter of the Stone, steps to be purified of his blackness. In Bernard Trevisan's 'The Practise of the Philosophick Stone' the mercurial water is called 'a Fountain … with limpid Water', 'the Spring', and 'the Bath' (lines 39–40, 46, 61, 84, 62, 91; AP, 450–1).

four elements see **elements**.

fragrance the signal that the pure *quintessence of the *albedo has been attained. The advent of the sweet fragrance is the sign of resurgent life, indicating that the matter of the Stone is cleansed and wholly purified by the mercurial waters (or 'sea') and brought from the stinking *putrefaction of the *coffin to the resurrection of the white stage. Norton's *Ordinall* said of the albedo: 'All sweete smelling things have more puritie, / And are more spirituall than stinking maie be' (TCB, 69) (see **smell**). Colson's *Philosophia maturata* stated that when the Stone is whitened the 'dignified matter of Philosophers abounds with unspeakable sweetness, having power to cure the leprosie, and other grievous Diseases' (12). In Shakespeare's *Pericles,* Cerymon says of the sea-washed coffin in which the apparently dead Queen Thaisa lies prior to her resurrection: 'it smels most sweetly in my sense', and the Second Gentleman replies, 'A delicate Odour' (3.2.60–1). See **smell**.

frog see **toad**.

fruit   the precious raw gold or material before it is dissolved and coagulated into the *philosopher's stone; the *seed of gold from which gold was thought to have been grown; the arcane transforming substance when it has matured from *prima materia into the philosopher's stone. Isaac Newton made the following abstract from *La Lumière sortant par soy même des tenebres*: 'So vulgar gold has its own seed very perfect and digested but resembles a fruit perfectly ripe and separated from the tree' (Dobbs, *Janus*, 283).

     The growth of the arcane transforming substance, *Mercurius, is frequently compared to the growth of a tree with infinite branches. The maturation of the philosopher's stone is represented by the appearance on the *philosophical tree of the fruits of sun (gold) and moon (silver), the *red and white tinctures of the Stone. Nicolas Flamel wrote of the tree in the garden of the Sages: 'There our tree is watered with the rarest dew and fruit which hangs upon the tree which swells and ripens and expands from day to day ... Or, to drop metaphor, let the mercury be taken and warmed day and night, in an alembic over a gentle fire' (HM, 1:145). Saturn, in Michael Sendivogius's 'The Philosophicall Aenigma', throws 'the blessed Solar Fruit' into the vessel with ten parts of water, and dissolves it. He explains to the narrator that the fruit, while marvellous in itself, is not fully empowered until it has been putrefied in the mercurial water and transformed into the philosopher's stone: 'in this Water, and this onely, wee / Can putrefy the Product of the Tree / The Fruit it self is wonderfull, but yet / If here it putrefys, it does beget / The Salamander living in the Fire' (lines 218–45). He states that the fruit is 'sweet and living, yet whereas but one / Can with this Fruit (as now it is) be fed, / When in this Water reincrudated, / Reincrudation will encrease the Store / Enough to feed and feast a thousand more' (lines 252–7, AP, 502–3). An emblem commemorating Michael Sendivogius in Michael Maier's *Symbola aureae mensae* shows Saturn watering the philosophical trees on which hang the fruit of sun and moon (Maier in Stolcius, *Viridarium chimicum*, 164). The golden fruit is sometimes referred to as the apples from the garden of the Hesperides, which is guarded by a *dragon. Artephius wrote: 'every good and wise man may happily gather those desirable apples of the Hesperides from our philosopher's tree' (SB, 31). Sendivogius referred to the golden fruit as 'Apples of the Sun' (AP, 502). Psychologically, the growth of the tree and the appearance of the fruit symbolize the soul's increasing awareness and consciousness, and the bringing of this knowledge into operation in everyday life.

fugitive   see **cervus fugitivus**.

fume   see **green lion**.

furnace   the oven or *athanor in which the alembic is set to be heated. It is frequently identified with the purifying effect of the secret *fire which it contains. By undergoing the fire of the furnace the metal (or soul of man) experiences suffering and mortification yet at the same time is cleansed of its impurities and corruption. One of the earliest important treatises on furnaces, mentioned by Zosimos and entitled *On Furnaces and Apparatus,* was thought to have been written by Maria Prophetissa (third century AD). A later influential treatise on furnaces, the *Liber fornacum,* is attributed to Geber (pseudo-Jabir ibn Haiyan). Roger Bacon advised that in the building of the furnace the alchemist should be guided by nature, who engenders metals by means of a continual heat within the mountainside: 'If therefore wee intend to immitate nature, we must needes have such a furnace like unto the Mountaines, not in greatnesse, but in continual heate, so that the fire put in, when it ascendeth, may find no vent: but that the heate may beat upon the vessell being close shutte, containing in it the matter of the Stone' (*Mirror,* 11–12). *The Sophic Hydrolith* tells of the metaphysical furnace through which base, earthly man must pass to become the true illumined philosopher: the humble, regenerate man 'is placed by God in the furnace of affliction, and (like the hermetic compound) is purged with the fire of suffering until the old Adam is dead, and there arises a new man created after God in righteousness and true holiness' (*HM,* 1:110). Philip Sidney referred to the alchemical furnace of affliction in the last sonnet of *Astrophil and Stella*: 'When sorrow, using mine own fire's might, / Melts down his lead into my boiling breasts, / Through that dark furnace to my heart oppressed / There shines a joy from thee, my only light' (*Selected Poems,* 188). See **athanor, castle.**

G

games   see **ludus puerorum.**

gander   a name for the *Bird of Hermes (*Mercurius) at the *white stage of the opus alchymicum. Artephius wrote of the *ashes at the stage of *putrefaction: 'These ashes then are those of which the philosophers have spoken so much, which remained in the lower part of the vessel, which we ought not to undervalue or despise. In them is the royal diadem, and the black and unclean argent vive, which ought to be cleansed from its blackness, by a continual digestion in our water, till it be elevated above in a white colour, which is called the gander, and the bird of Hermes' (*SB,* 52). See also **goose.**

garden   the alchemists' secret vessel. 'The Garden of the Philosophers is the vessel which contains the Matter of the *Magnum Opus*', wrote Ruland in his *Lexicon of Alchemy* (364). The garden is the matrix in which the alchemical plant or *tree grows, blossoms and comes to fruition (see **flowers, fruit**). The tree is a symbol of the process of the opus and its fruit symbolize the goal of the opus, the *philosopher's stone. In his *Philosophical Summary* Nicolas Flamel wrote of 'the garden of the Sages' where 'our tree is watered with the rarest dew' (*HM,* 1:145). The *dew is the mercurial water with which the infant Stone is fed. *The Golden Tract* described this process as 'a little rain' falling on a 'small square garden … surrounded by a rose hedge covered with beautiful roses' (HM, 1:45). The rose garden is one of alchemy's best known emblems and is the title of a famous alchemical treatise, *Rosarium philosophorum,* attributed to Arnold of Villanova and first printed in 1550. The rose garden is generally depicted as an enclosed garden in which the red and white flowers of the elixir or Stone blossom. Psychologically, the blooming of the roses in the garden symbolizes the attainment of wisdom or inner knowledge. The 'Rose Garden of Wisdom' is illustrated in emblem 27 of Maier's *Atalanta fugiens* and on the fifth leaf of the hieroglyphs in Flamel's *Exposition* (12).

Geber's cooks alchemists who worked in a laboratory using ordinary chemicals to make gold and were considered inferior by the philosophical, metaphysical alchemists. Also a name for false or ignorant alchemists. Geber, an author of alchemical treatises which began circulating at the end of the thirteenth century, and who is associated with Jabir ibn Haiyan (eighth century Arabic), was one of the most important sources for the medieval alchemists. In the Renaissance there was a reaction against Geber's works, and thus the laboratory experimenters became known as Geber's cooks. Thomas Vaughan referred to them as 'the broyling frying Company, who call themselves Chimists but are indeed no Philosophers' (VW(R), 313). In the last section of *A Compound of Alchymie* George Ripley declared that when he first began the opus he carried out erroneous experiments with such substances as urine, eggs, hair and blood: 'Thus I rostyd and boylyd as one of *Geber's* Cooks' (TCB, 191). He described them thus: 'Their Clothes be bawdy and woryn threde bare, / Men may them smell for Multyplyers where they go; / To fyle theyr fyngers with Corrosyves they do not spare / Theyr Eyes be bleryd, and theyr Chekys both lene and bloe: / And thus for (*had I wyst*) they suffer losse and wo; / Such when they have lost that was in theyr purse, / Then do they chyd and *Phylosophers* sore accurse' (TCB, 153).

generation, generation of metals the generation or engendering of metals within the earth's crust, the incubation and birth of the *philosopher's stone in the laboratory. Metals were thought to grow within the earth like a great tree, warmed by the gentle heat of the sun's rays penetrating the earth. All metals were thought to be created from two subtle principles known as philosophical *argent vive and *sulphur. Gold was seen as the perfect metal, created from pure argent vive and sulphur in perfect proportion. Roger Bacon wrote: 'I will perfectly declare the naturall principles and procreations of Minerals: where first it is to be noted, that the naturall principles in the mynes, are *Argent-vive* and *Sulphur*. All mettals and minerals, whereof there be sundrie and divers kinds, are begotten of these two: but I must tel you, that nature alwaies intendeth and striveth to the perfection of Gold: but many accidents comming between, change the mettalls, as it is evidently to be seene in divers of the Philosophers bookes. For according to the puritie and impuritie of the two aforesaid principles, *Argent-vive*, and *Sulphur*, pure, and impure mettals are ingendred: to wit, Gold, Silver, Steele, leade, Copper, and Iron' (*Mirror*, 4) (see **prima materia**).

The process of creating the philosopher's stone in the laboratory is known as the generation of gold, and is sometimes compared to the birth of a *child, or the hatching of a chick from its *egg. After the union of the male and female seeds of metals (philosophical sulphur and argent vive) at the *chemical wedding, the united pair are killed and their bodies lie putrefying in the bottom of the alembic while their vital seed or virtue (sometimes called soul, other times spirit) is released. Alchemical theory stated that generation could not take place unless there had first been a death and corruption of the body to release the vital seed. An abstract made by Isaac Newton from *La lumière sortant par soy même des tenebres* stated: 'But this seed is unprofitable unless it rot and become black for corruption always precedes generation and we must make black before we can whiten' (Dobbs, *Janus*, 281). At the death of the body or bodies, the seed or soul flies to the top of the vessel while the blackened body below is washed and cleansed of its impurities. At the *albedo the matter has become completely white and pure and ready for reunion with the soul (or united soul/spirit) (see **chemical wedding**). At this reunion of the body and soul, usually portrayed by the wedding of *Sol and *Luna, the third principle or philosopher's stone is born. This whole process is referred to as the generation. The colour associated with the generation is *green, the colour of fertility, new life and growth. During this stage the vessel is sometimes referred to as the 'Vas Naturae' or 'Matrix of Nature' (Vaughan, *VW* (*R*), 474). For the generation of metals, see **prima materia**.

glass the alchemical vessel. Ripley wrote: 'And in one Glass must be done all thys thyng' (*TCB*, 138). The alchemical couple, *philosophical sulphur (male, hot, active) and argent vive (female, cold, receptive) must be united at the *chemical wedding to produce the *philosopher's stone. When they are first joined they are shut up in the glass to *putrefy. Philalethes wrote of the alchemist's task: 'therefore they married these two together, and shut them in a glass, and placed them at the fire' (*Secrets Reveal'd*, 30). Sir William Davenant referred to the alchemist's vessel as the 'glass' in 'The Christians Reply to the Phylosopher': 'Cannot Almighty Heaven (since Flowers which pass / Thaw'd through a Still, and there melt mingled too, / Are rais'd distinct in a poore Chymists Glass) / Doe more in Graves then Men in Lymbecks doe?' (lines 4–8). The glass was also referred to as the glass prison or the glass house. Artephius spoke of closing the matter 'in a house of glass, well shut and stopped with Cement' (*SB*, 39). The explosion of the alchemical glasses during laboratory experiments is a frequent topic in accounts of the alchemists' practice. In 'Upon the Death of the Lord Hastings', Andrew Marvell compared the Paracelsian physician, Sir Theodore Turquet de Mayerne, to an alchemist whose experiment has failed and whose glasses have broken: 'and *Mayern*; / Like some sad *Chymist*, who, prepar'd to reap / The *Golden Harvest,* sees his Glasses leap' (lines 48–50). The familiar explosion scene is parodied in Ben Jonson's *The Alchemist*. Face reports to Mammon, who expects the philosopher's stone to be produced at any moment: 'all the *workes* / Are Flowne *in fumo*: euery glasse is burst. / Fornace, and all rent downe! as if a bolt / Of thunder had been driuen through the house. / *Retorts, Receiuers, Pellicanes, Bolt-heads,* / All strooke in shiuers!' (4.5.57–62). For the transformation of the refined matter of the Stone into 'glass', see **vitrification**.

glass house see **glass, house**.

glue the medium of conjunction. The union of opposite qualities and states, portrayed by the *chemical wedding of male *Sol and female *Luna, is said to take place by means of a third uniting substance. This medium is named *Mercurius, who is variously described as the bond, *cement, ligament, gum, glue, spirit and soul of the world. Mercurius acts as the intermediary or messenger between heaven and earth. He plays the role of the mediating soul which unites the separated body and spirit of the Stone's matter. Happelius's *Aphorismi basiliani* described Mercurius as the 'life-giving power like a glue, holding the world together and standing in the middle between body and spirit' (in *AS*, 213–14). In some alchemical texts Mercurius is called the mediating 'spirit', rather than 'soul' (see, for example, *FC*, 111). The mercurial glue which is necessary for the uniting of male and female is also known as the seminal matter or seed because it holds the seeds of metals – sulphur and argent vive. Thomas Vaughan called it 'the true sperm of the great world' and 'this blessed cement and balsam' (*VW (W)*, 250, 230). In Andrew Marvell's 'To his Coy Mistress' the 'morning glew' sits on the mistress's skin ready for the union of the male and female lovers: 'Now therefore, while the youthful hew, / Sits on thy skin like morning glew, / And while thy willing Soul transpires / At every pore with instant Fires, / Now let us sport us while we may' (following the text of *Misc. Poems*, lines 33–7).

gluten see **eagle**.

gold and silver the two most precious metals. Roger Bacon wrote of gold: 'Gold is a perfect body, engendred of *Argent-vive* pure, fixed, cleare, red, and of *Sulphur* cleane, fixed, red, not burning, and it wanteth nothing', and of silver: 'Silver is a body, cleane, pure, and almost perfect, begotten of *Argent-vive*, pure, almost fixed, cleare, and white, and of such a like *Sulphur*. It wanteth nothing, save a little fixation, colour, and weight' (*Mirror*, 4, 5). Geber likewise says that gold is made from a combination of the most subtle, fixed and bright mercury with some clear, fixed, red sulphur, and silver made from a combination of mercury and white sulphur (Geber, *Summa*, 471) (see prima materia). The alchemists are famous for claiming that they were able to transmute base metal into the precious metals gold and silver by means of the magical *philosopher's stone. The idea of transformation is based on the theory that all metals are made from the same basic matter and grow within the crust of the earth like a giant tree or plant. Such metals as lead, iron and copper were thought to be imperfect but with the potential to develop into gold. It was thought that, given the right conditions and enough time, these metals could grow or ripen into gold: 'Now the perfection of metals and the final intention of Nature in regard to them, is gold. For all metals show that Nature has done something for them towards ultimate perfection; no metal is so base as not to contain a single grain of gold or silver' (HM, 1:17). Ben Jonson's Subtle expresses the same view when he answers Surly's assertion that an egg is a chicken *in potentia*: 'The same we say of lead, and other metals, / Which would be gold, if they had time ... Nature doth, first, beget th' imperfect; then / Proceedes shee to the perfect' (*The Alchemist* 2.3.135–6, 158–9).

Gold is seen as the perfect immutable metal which is able to withstand the test of the fire. But when the alchemists speak of gold they mean more than material gold. In the microcosmic–macrocosmic law of correspondences, gold is the metallic equivalent of the sun, the image of the sun buried in the earth. The sun in turn is the physical equivalent of the eternal spirit which lodges in the heart (the 'sun' of the human microcosm). Nicaise Le Fevre wrote that 'the chymists' give gold 'the name of the *Sun*, because that they believe it hath some correspondency and harmonical relation not onely with the celestial Sun of the Great World, but also by reason that it has a sympathetical affinity with the Sun of the Little World, which is the Heart of Man' (*Discourse*, 58). Michael Maier's *Lusus Serius* referred to gold as the 'shadow' of the eternal spirit: 'Gold, which is in it self incorruptible, is on earth accounted the symbol, the marke and the shadow of that eternity, which we shall enjoy above' (122). When the alchemists speak of the substance which can eternally endure the trials of the fire, they are referring to the ultimate fixation of the spirit, the embodiment of divine spirit in man made perfect. In *Religio Medici*, Sir Thomas Browne compared the imperishable, immortal body to 'that mysticall mettle of gold, whose solary and celestiall nature I admire' and which, when 'exposed unto the violence of the fire, grows onely hot and liquefies, but consumeth not' (48). The real transmutation is that of the earthly man into the enlightened man, whose purified lunar soul and body perfectly reflect the gold of divine spirit.

Gold is also the name of the alchemists' raw stuff or *prima materia, the original matter from which all things were thought to have been created. The philosopher's stone is created from this living gold, known as philosophical or 'green' gold, not from dead material gold, which is incapable of generation. The Stone is conceived by uniting the hot, dry, male principle (sulphur or 'our gold') with the cold, moist, female principle (argent vive or mercury, 'our silver'), the male and female seeds of metals contained in the prima materia. From these seeds the philosopher's stone, and thus gold and silver, can be grown. Paracelsus's *A Short Catechism of Alchemy* answers the question 'What do the Philosophers understand by their gold and silver?' with the reply, 'The Philosophers apply to their Sulphur the name of Gold, and to their Mercury the name of Silver' (PW, 302). These are the philosophical gold and silver which grow into the coveted red and white tinctures of sun and moon, the double components of the philosopher's stone. Sol is the name given to the *ferment that is sown into the *white foliated earth, known as Luna, at the third major coniunctio or *chemical wedding necessary for the birth of the Stone. This is the wedding of sun and moon, gold and silver, *king and *queen. The red stone is often personified by the king (Sol) and the white stone by the queen (Luna).

The philosopher's stone itself is sometimes referred to as 'gold', while the elixir is sometimes symbolized by *aurum potabile, drinkable gold. John Milton wrote of the kingdom of the 'arch-chemic' sun in *Paradise Lost*: 'What wonder then if fields and regions here / Breathe forth elixir pure, and rivers run / Potable gold' (3.606–9). Robert Herrick plays on 'aurum' and 'laurels' (*laureate*) in 'To the right honourable, *Philip*, Earle of Pembroke, and Montgomerie' when he employs the transmutation metaphor to express the idea of perfect poetry: 'You ... who hug our Poems (honoured Sir) and then / The paper gild, and laureate the pen. / Nor suffer you the Poets to sit cold, / But warm their wits, and turn their lines to gold' (141). See also **silver**.

golden age see **return**.

golden apples see **fruit, Hesperides**.

golden fleece the goal of the opus alchymicum. The opus was sometimes perceived as a perilous journey or labour, a quest for treasure. The Greek myth of Jason and the Argonauts undertaking the perilous quest for the golden fleece was used as a type of the alchemists' pursuit of the golden goal of alchemy. Nicolas Flamel called the Stone 'this inestimable good ... this *rich golden Fleece*' (HE, 36) and Baptista Lambye (Giovanni Agnelli) wrote of the trials of the opus: 'The golden fleece is not given unto Iason, unlesse first he undergoe the sure and dangerous labours' (*Revelation of the Secret Spirit*, 46). The 'golden fleece' is also the name given to the parchment on which the secrets of the opus are written. Salomon Trismosin's treatise on alchemical transmutation, *Aureum vellus* (*The Golden Fleece*), was published in 1598–9 and became almost as popular as Nicolas Flamel's treatise on the hieroglyphic figures. A few years later, in 1613, it was translated into French as *La Toyson d'Or* and published in Paris. Sir Walter Raleigh wrote in his chapter 'Of the expedition of the Argonauts' in *The History of the World*: 'Some there are, that by this journey of Jason understand the mystery of the philosopher's stone, called the golden fleece; to which also other superfine chymists draw the twelve labours of Hercules. Suidas thinks, that by the golden fleece was meant a book of parchment, which is of sheep's skin, and therefore called golden, because it was taught therein how other metals might be transmuted' (bk. 24, 413). Ben Jonson jokes about this tradition in *The Alchemist* when he has Mammon boast: 'I have a peece of IASONS fleece, too / Which was no other, then a booke of *alchemie*, / Writ in large sheepe-skin, a good fat ram-vellam' (2.1.89–91). (For Jason's helm, see **helm**.)

golden flower see **flower**.

golden fruit see **fruit.**

golden harvest see **harvest.**

golden tree see **philosophical tree.**

goose a retort like a *pelican with a long neck bent forward. See **alembic, bird, gander.**

grain the seed of metals; a measure of weight used in experiments. *Zoroaster's Cave* said: 'The Incombustible Grain of metalls, is their radicall humidity, and is a certain Seed of Sol, and Luna, which nature has inserted to them, that upon opportunity they may be Excocted to Sol and Luna by Nature in a long, by Art in a very short, Time' (65) (see seed). The matter for the Stone is often compared to a grain of corn which must first die before it can produce more corn. Hortulanus wrote that the Stone 'is also called a graine of corne, which if it die not, remaineth without fruit: but if it doo die (as is above said) when it is joyned in conjunction, it bringeth forth much fruit' (*A Briefe Commentarie*, 26–7). 'Gold grain' is one of the names of alchemical gold (Ruland, *Lexicon*, 184), and 'purple grain' a name for the *red tincture or *blood of the *red stone which is said to *dye or tinge base metals to perfect gold. Nicolas Flamel called the tincture the 'all-perfect *purple* colour' which is 'like the pure and cleere *skarlet* in graine' (HE, 137, 139). Philalethes likewise spoke of the tincture's 'grains' of 'transcendent redness' (*Secrets Reveal'd*, 109).

'Grain' was also a measure of weight used in 'chymical' experiments. It was said that just one grain of the elixir could transmute immeasurable quantities of base metal into gold. Referring to Edward Kelly's elixir, Elias Ashmole wrote: '*Sir Edward Kelley* made *Projection* with one small *Graine* thereof (in proportion no bigger then the least graine of Sand) upon one *Ounce* and a Quarter of *Common Mercury*, and it produced almost one *Ounce* of most pure *Gold*' (TCB, 481). In Joseph Hall's *Virgidemiarum*, the Paracelsian doctor is said to 'bring *Quintessence* of *Elixir* pale, / Out of sublimed spirits minerall. / Each poudred graine ransometh captive kings, / Purchaseth Realmes, and life prolonged brings' (37–8).

grapes the raw matter for the Stone, the fruit of the *philosophical tree; the prima materia, the matter from which the alchemist extracts mercury. The juice of the grapes, then, is the philosophical or *mercurial water which dissolves the old metal or matter for the Stone into the *prima materia, the original stuff of creation. Martin Ruland's *A Lexicon of Alchemy* defines grapes ('Uvae Hermetis') as 'Philosophical Water, Distillation, Solution' (325). Arthur Dee cites Aristotle on the dissolution of the united male/female body of the Stone: 'Pour on them sweet Wine till they be inebriated, and divided into smallest parts' (FC, 44). Sir George Ripley's *Vision* begins: 'A *Toade* full rudde I saw did drinke the juce of grapes so fast, / Till over charged with the broth, his bowells all to brast' (TCB, 374). Philalethes commented on this passage: 'Thus the

Body drinks in the water, or Juice of Grapes, not so much then when they are first mingled: but most especially, when by decoction it pierceth radically to the very profundity of it; and makes it to alter its Form; This is the Water which teareth the Bodies, and makes them no Bodies' (RR, 4). The *toad symbolizes the body of the Stone at the *putrefaction, when it is dissolved and blackened. The juice of grapes or wine is the aqua permanens or mercurial water, also known as the alchemist's secret *fire. Hoghelande's *De alchemiae difficultatibus* stated: 'Man's blood and the red juice of the grape is our fire' (cited AS, 279). The first emblem of Ripley's 'Emblematicall Scrowle' shows the toad in the alembic spouting the rich red grape juice. The second emblem illustrates the philosophical tree with the abundant grape vine growing around it out of the mercurial water. In the Middle Ages the philosophical tree was symbolized by the vine, and the opus was known as the purple vintage (see also **golden harvest, purple tincture**). Ripley's *A Compound of Alchemy* compares the cultivation of the red grapes on the vine to the production of the red stone of the alchemists: 'Sone after that *Noe* plantyd hys Vyneyard, / Whych really floryshed and brought forth Graps anon ... For in lykewyse shall follow the floryshyng of our *Stone*: / And sone uppon that thyrty dayes overgone, / Thou shalt have Graps ryght as the Ruby red' (TCB, 151). The first of a group of four images in 'De Alchimia' (*c.* 1526) illustrates the grape-picker culling the fruit of the vine (van Lennep, *Alchimie*, 100).

grave the alchemists' vessel during the *nigredo, when the matter of the Stone, the united *sulphur (male) and *argent vive (female) undergoes death, dissolution and putrefaction. Other names for the vessel at this stage are the tomb, coffin, sepulchre, tumulus, prison and ark. Ruland's *Lexicon* calls the vessel the 'Sepulchre and Tomb' and 'Grave, Churchyard, because the Stone lies hidden there' (413, 323). Ripley wrote of burying male sulphur and female argent vive in a grave: 'Therefore at the begynnyng [of Putrefaction] our Stonys thou take, / And bery ech on wyth other wythin ther Grave' (TCB, 150). Emblem 6 of Mylius's *Philosophia reformata* shows the dead bodies of the united lovers in the coffin as vessel (see fig. 10). The emblem of the lovers and the tomb occurs as a three-dimensional tableau in Shakespeare's *Romeo and Juliet*. Juliet, already secretly married to Romeo, begs her mother to 'Delay this marriage for a month, a week, / Or if you do not, make the bridal bed / In that dim monument where Tybalt lies' (3.5.199–201). Indeed, Romeo and Juliet finally do unite in Tybalt's tomb after Romeo obtains poison from an apothecary whose shop is adorned with alchemical insignia (5.1.40–4; 5.3.101–20). In alchemy the souls of the dead bodies, sometimes depicted as one *hermaphrodite body, are released and fly to the top of the alembic, leaving the blackened, putrefied bodies to be washed and purified so that they become the *white foliated earth of the *albedo. This earth (or cleansed body) is then pure enough to reunite with the soul (or united soul/spirit), and from this union the *philosopher's stone is born. Thus the vessel which is the tomb of death is also the womb of new life, of generation (see **generation**). John Donne equates the grave and the alembic in the 'Elegy on the Lady Marckham': 'So at this grave, her limbeck, which refines / The diamonds, rubies, sapphires, pearls and mines' (lines 23–4), and in 'A Nocturnal upon S. Lucy's Day' he wrote: 'I, by love's limbeck, am the grave / Of all, that's nothing' (lines 21–2).

green The appearance of the colour green in the alembic indicates that the infant Stone is animated and is growing to maturity. Roger Bacon wrote of 'our Stone': 'It is also greene: whereon another sayth, Concoct it, till it appeare greene unto thee, and that is the soule' (*Mirror*, 13). Although green is not one of the three main colours of the opus (black, white and red), it is nevertheless an important colour in the symbolism of alchemy. Green is the colour of fertility, of spring-time growth, of new life, and is associated with the alchemical *generation which occurs after the *chemical wedding of the two seeds of metals, male *sulphur (Sol) with female *argent vive (Luna). Colson's *Philosophia maturata* states: 'I say, such green *Sol* and *Lune*, in which the vegetable virtue is not extinguished, but is living, hot and moist, and hath power to reduce all Bodies to their vegetability; for by this, with God's permission, bodies extinct, and not multipliable, may more easily get the habit and vertue to germinate, which of the Phylosophers is called the beginning and tearm from whence the Stone is generated' (20). Philalethes wrote of the opus: 'When you see the *green* colour, know that the substance now contains the germ of its highest life' (HM, 2:194). *The Rosary of the Philosophers* also associated green with the generation of the *philosopher's stone: 'O Blessed greenness which engendered all things. You know that no vegetable and fruit appeareth in growing but it is of a green colour. Know therefore, that the generation of this thing is green wherefore the Philosophers have called it their growing and springing' (McLean, *Rosary*, 19). The alchemists sometimes called the greenness of the matter at this stage the bud. Calid wrote: 'this blessed might, power or virtue, which generates all things, will not yet cause a vegetation, springing, budding forth, or fruitfulness, unless there be a green color. Wherefore the Philosophers call it their Bud' (*Booke of the Secrets*, 111).

The alchemists' raw material or unclean matter is described as being 'green gold', the fertile matter from which gold may be grown. Thomas Vaughan wrote in *Aula Lucis*: 'by *Gold* I meane our *Spermatick green gold*, not the ador'd Lump, which is dead, and ineffectual' (VW (R), 464). Calid warned the alchemist that the greenness of the unclean body (also known as Laton) is not leprosy but should be recognized as the very colour needed for generation: 'But you strive to expel the Greenness, thinking that our Latten or Brass, is a Leprous Body, because of that Greenness, but I tell you, that that Greenness is all that is perfect therein, and all that is perfect is in that Greenness only, which is in our Latten or Brass. For that Greenness, by our Magistery, is in a very little time transmuted into the most fine Gold' (*Booke of the Secrets*, 110–11). Green in alchemy indicates that the matter in the vessel is in a state of unripeness, immaturity or youth, just as in nature green fruit is unripe fruit. Until the metal has been dissolved into its first matter or *prima materia, then purifed and transmuted, it has not yet 'ripened' into gold and is thus still green. Green is also the colour of verdigris on copper, a substance frequently linked with the disease or *leprosy of metals which must be washed away so that regeneration may occur. See **green lion, venus**.

green lion raw antimony ore, the unclean matter of the Stone, philosophical mercury, the *prima materia in the earliest stage of the opus alchymicum (see **Mercurius**). In Anthony Powell's *Temporary Kings*, Dr Brighton refers to the green lion. Observing that the spirit of the alchemist, Thomas Vaughan still haunts Venice, he says: 'His spirit was moving there. The Lion of St Mark could symbolize that green lion he calls the body, the magical entity that must clip the wings of the eagle' (243). According to most alchemical texts, the green lion is the ore from which philosophical mercury is extracted and is also known as terra (earth), the unclean body, or *Latona (Ripley, in TCB, 125). St Dunstan wrote: 'Of this very Body the matter of the Stone, three things are chiefly spoken, viz. *The green Lion, Assa foetida, and white Fume*' (in FC, 9). Michael Maier likewise referred to this lion as 'the ore of Hermes', 'the stinking water' and 'the white smoke, that is, water' (AF, 248). *The Crowning of Nature,* too, associates the lion with 'a smoke and a cloud' (20). St Dunstan clarifies the relationship of three aspects of the lion: 'By the green Lyon, all Philosophers whatsoever understood, green Gold, multiplicable, spermatick, and not yet perfected by Nature; having the power to reduce Bodies into their first matter, and to fix volatile and spiritual things, and therefore not unfitly called a Lyon. By Assa foetida, we understand a certain unsavory Odor, exhaled from the unclean body in the first operation, which may be likened to stinking Assa foetida. The reason why it is called white fume is this: In the first distillation, before the Red Tincture ascends, there arises a smoak truly white, whereby the receiver is darkened or filled with a certain milky shadow, whence it receives the name of virgin's milk. Therefore where ever thou findest a substance endowed with these three properties, know that it is the matter of the Philosophers Stone' (in FC, 9). Some alchemists identified the green lion as vitriol, but Ripley disagreed: 'Vitriall' is that which 'folys [fools] doe call the *Grene Lyon*' (TCB, 190)

There are several reasons why the lion was said to be green. Firstly, it is thought that the mercurial spirit (the vital essence) extracted from the lion is that force or virtue which makes all things fertile, green and growing, as they are in nature. 'Green' also refers to the fact that the matter of the Stone in the alembic at this early stage of the opus is still in a state of immaturity and unripeness, just as unripe fruit is green. *The Hunting of the Greene Lyon* says: 'But our *Lyon*, wanting maturity, / Is called *greene*, for unripenes trust me' (TCB, 279). From this unripe but fertile seed (the prima materia of metals), living gold may be 'grown'. Thus St Dunstan calls the green lion 'green gold, multiplicable, spermatick, and not yet perfected by Nature' (in FC, 9) (see **prima materia**). F. Sherwood Taylor identifies the green lion with the dissolving mercurial water extracted from it and observes that it is green 'no doubt because of the colour imparted to it by copper compounds always present as impurity in the mixture of gold and silver' (*The Alchemists*, 119).

Two crucial spirits or mercuries are extracted from the lion ore. One of these is red with a stinking smell, known as the *blood of the green lion. When the alchemists speak of their green lion devouring metals as the lion devours other animals, they are referring to the way in which the mercurial blood is able to dissolve and reduce all metals into their prima materia or first matter. Colson's *Philosophia maturata* says: 'And thus thou hast the Bloud of the Green Lyon, called *The Secret Water*, and most sharp Vinegar, by which all Bodies may be reduced to their first Matter' (31–2). In his 'Praxis', Isaac Newton wrote of 'the Green Lyon which easily destroys iron and devours also the companions of Cadmus' (Dobbs, *Janus*, 297). The devouring aspect of the lion is represented in an emblem which was first attached to a sixteenth-century manuscript of the *Rosarium philosophorum* and was then printed with it in 1550 (fig. 16). It shows the lion devouring the sun, with the blood of the lion issuing from its mouth. Here the sun symbolizes the alchemists' raw stuff, 'gold', which is devoured and dissolved in order to obtain the 'sperm' of gold, the living seed from which pure gold may be grown. In *A Compound of Alchymie*, Sir George Ripley stated that when the water is extracted from the lion 'the Son hydyth hys lyght' (*TCB*, 166). *The Hunting of the Greene Lyon* indicates that, in its act of consuming the sun, the lion is involved not only in a dissolution (solve) but also in a coniunctio or wedding (coagula): the lion 'soone can overtake the *Sun*, / And suddainely can hym devoure ... And hym Eclipse that was so bryght ... And yet wythin, he hath such heate / That whan he hath the *Sun* up eate, / He

16 The green lion swallowing the sun

Ich bin der war grün vnnd guldisch Löwe ohn sor-
(gen/
Inn mir steckt alle heimlichkeyt der philosophen
verborgen.

Y iij

bringeth hym to more perfection, / Than ever he had by Natures direc-
cion / This Lyon maketh the *Sun* sith soone, / To be ioyned to his Sister
the *Moone* / By way of wedding' (*TCB*, 279) (in MS Wellcome 436 'direc-
cion' reads 'coction'). The dissolution is symbolized by the lion's
engulfing the sun and eclipsing it in the darkness of the *nigredo (the
death). The body of the sun, the gold, must be dissolved so that its
fertile, male, active seed be released ready for the union with the seed
of its female, receptive aspect, the moon. *The Hunting of the Greene Lyon*
also refers to the lion as being the priest who facilitates the *chemical
wedding of the sun and moon: 'The *Lyon* ys the Preist, the *Sun* and *Moone*
the wed, / Yet they were both borne in the *Lyons* Bedd' (279–80) ('the wed'
reads 'to wed' in MS Wellcome 436). As priest he is the necessary mercurial medium of conjunction (see **glue**).

The mercurial blood is used not only as a solvent but also as a drink
for nourishing the *philosophical child or stone which is generated
from the union of sun and moon. This water with which the child is fed
is that arcanum which is the principle of life and growth, that virtue
which makes all things in nature green and flourishing. Benjamin Lock
wrote: 'you must understand this drinke to be no other thinge but onely
the bloode of the Lyon' (Picklock', f. 22) (see **red lion**). (For a detailed
study of the alchemical green lion, see Dobbs, *The Foundations of Newton's
Alchemy or The Hunting of the Greene Lyon*.)

griffin (griffon, gryphon)   a symbol of the cold, moist lunar or female principle known in alchemy
as *argent vive or mercury. In Abraham Eleazar's *Uraltes Chymisches
Werck*, griffins and poisonous dragons are said to guard the 'well of the
ancients' which is the first essence of metals or mercury (*JA*, 256). This
mythical creature, with the head and wings of an eagle and the body
of a lion, is usually paired with the hot, dry, male principle known as
*sulphur and personified by the *red lion. In Johann Andreae's *The
Chymical Wedding*, Christian Rosencreutz witnesses the pairing of griffin
and lion at an alchemical 'comedy' performed at the 'House of the *Sun*':
'In the interlude a *Lyon* and griffon were set at one another to fight, and
the *Lyon* got the victory, which was also a pretty sight' (112). The fighting
lion and griffin represent the simultaneous dissolution (separation) and
coagulation (coniunctio) of the matter of the Stone at an early stage in
the opus (see **devour, hen** and **cock**). The griffin also symbolizes *antimony. See **gripe's egg**.

gripe's egg   a name for an oval-shaped alchemical vessel. 'Gripe' is a name for the
griffin or vulture. In Ben Jonson's *The Alchemist* Subtle orders Face to 'let
the water in *Glasse E.* be *feltred*, / And put into the *Gripes egge*' (2.3.39–40).

gum   the *prima materia which contains the seeds or sperm of metals, the
mercurial medium of conjunction synonymous with the glue or mercurial sperm of the philosophers, which unites *Sol (male) and *Luna
(female) at the *chemical wedding (see **glue**). A treatise attributed to
Maria Prophetissa says of the chemical wedding, where the white
woman (argent vive) is joined with the red man (sulphur): 'Take white

gum and red gum, which is the Kybric of the philosophers, and their gold, and join the gum with the gum in a true marriage' (Patai, 'Maria', 192). An epigram from 'The Practice of Mary the Prophetess in the Alchemical Art' conveys the binding quality of this matter: 'She with two Gumms makes in the Bottome stay / What else would fly away' (AP, 423). *The Sophic Hydrolith* says of the first matter of the Stone: 'they call it a stone and not a stone; they liken it to gum and white water' (HM, 1:78). In other contexts the cleansing, transforming mercurial *tears were referred to as the weeping gum or *balsam of the *philosophical tree. The weeping gum of the tree signifies the precious life essence needed for the creation of the Stone. Red gum is the name of the magical elixir or tincture attained at the final red stage of the opus, the *rubedo. A verse in *Theatrum chemicum Britannicum* says that the mercurial water is first 'Lyke a Gumm that Floweth lyte' and then becomes that 'red Gumm: / Whych ys our Tincture' (TCB, 429). See also **amber**.

H

halcyon   philosophical mercury, the quintessence of celestial azure hue. Paracelsus stated that there were four great arcana in the opus alchymicum: the *prima materia, the *philosopher's stone, Mercurius vitae and the *tincture. The third arcanum is the great transformer and rejuvenator which 'cast off from a man the Nails of his Hands and Feet, also his Hairs, Skin and everything that is thereto subject and causeth them to grow up again and renovates the whole body'. Paracelsus compared this arcanum to 'the *Halcion* or *King Fisher* ... the which Bird is in its *Annual* season renewed, and clad with new Feathers' (*Archidoxis*, 64).

hart   see **cervus fugitivus**.

hart's horn   see **deer**.

harvest   the attainment of the *philosopher's stone. Ripley wrote of the culmination of the opus in *A Compound of Alchymie*: 'there ys Harvest, that ys to say an end / Of all thys Warke after thyne owne desyre: / Ther shineth the Son up in his owne sphyre, / And after the Eclyps ys in rednes wyth glory / As Kyng to raygne upon all Mettals and Mercury' (TCB, 138). Alchemy is an 'art' which follows the blueprint of 'nature' in order to bring her to perfection, and so the opus is sometimes compared to the 'art' of agriculture, especially the cultivation, harvesting and *winnowing of grain (see art and nature). Calid likened the process of the opus to the sowing of corn: 'Now when they [husband-men] sow their Corn, then they sow not the Matter, which is the Straw and the Chaff, but the *Corn* or *Grain*, which is the *Form* or *Soul*: So if we reap *Sol* or *Luna*, we must use their *Form* or *Soul*, and not the *Matter*' (*Booke of the Secrets*, 126). The alchemists frequently speak of sowing their *gold into the *white foliated earth. By this they mean the union of the separated soul of the Stone (the volatile matter) with the body or earth (the fixed matter) which has now been purified in the vessel. From this *chemical wedding of sun and moon, the philosopher's stone is generated. Colson's *Philosophia maturata* said of this process: 'Put thy *Amalgam* carefully into a Glass vessel of such capacity, that thy earth that is sown and harrowed, may take up only the Third part of it ... Close up the orifice with the wise lute' (78). The production of the Stone, or illumination of man by divine knowledge, is termed the gathering of the golden harvest (see also **fruit, flower, philosophical tree**). In 'Upon the Death of the Lord Hastings', Andrew Marvell compares the Paracelsian physician, Sir Theodore Turquet de Mayerne, to an alchemist who has failed to attain the goal of the opus: 'and *Mayern*; / Like some sad *Chymist*, who, prepar'd to reap / The *Golden Harvest*, sees his Glasses leap' (lines 48–50). See **autumn**.

head the vessel in which the process of separation and putrefaction occurs, identical with the *alembic. Calid instructed the alchemist to take a 'Cucurbit, on which you must place an Alembick or Head, through which the Vapours may ascend' (*Booke of the Secrets*, 115). *The Tomb of Semiramis* speaks of placing the matter of the Stone which must be *digested into 'a Head or Alembick' (CC, 17). In the *Consilium coniugii* the vapour during *sublimation is described as ascending 'through the neck to the head of the vessel, that is like a living man' (in AS, 88). The alchemical vessel is analogous to man's body since the true vessel in which the transformation takes place is man himself. From the late sixteenth to mid seventeenth century the verb 'to alembic' meant 'to rack (the brain)' (OED). Shakespeare compared the brain to the alembic as 'head' in *Macbeth*. Lady Macbeth plans to intoxicate Duncan's guards so that 'memory, the warder of the brain, / Shall be a fume, and the receipt of reason / A Limbec only' (1.7.66–8). The 'Moor's head' is the name given to a still with independent firing and a water-cooled helm, because of its resemblance to a Moorish turban (ALA, 76).

The severed head is also a symbol in alchemy. The death and dissolution of the metal (or matter for the Stone) is sometimes signified by the beheading of the *philosophical bird or the *king (see **beheading, nigredo**). In Johann Andreae's *The Chymical Wedding* Christian Rosencreutz witnesses the head of the slaughtered king being placed 'in a little chest' with an axe (123). Later, Christian is present at the beheading of the bird: 'the poor Bird of himself submissively laid down his Neck upon the Book, and willingly suffered his Head (by one of us thereto chosen by lot) to be smitten off' (159). The *crow's or raven's head is also a symbol of the *putrefaction and nigredo. The severing of the head symbolizes the necessary separation (*separatio) of the soul from the influence of the earthly pull of the body so that it can gain wisdom and illumination from the spirit. The separation before illumination is experienced by the adept as a deep loss, a 'death' to the world.

The 'red head' is a symbol of the consummation of the opus, since red is the colour of the *rubedo, when the ultimate *red stone is attained. An old alchemical dictum says that the *magistery of the whole work is that which has black feet, a white body and a red head. (Black, white and red are the three main colours of the stages of the opus; see **colours**.) The eighth plate of Salomon Trismosin's *Splendor Solis* shows an Ethiopian with a black body, white arm and red head emerging from the mud of a stream and being offered the *Tyrian robe by his queen.

heaven the top of the alembic; the *quintessence, the *philosopher's stone. During the *sublimation or vaporization of the Stone, the volatile spirits rise to the top of the alembic, which is called the 'coelum spagyricum' (spagyric heaven). The bottom of the alembic is referred to as the earth. The terms 'heaven' and 'earth' also refer to the state of the matter's refinement. When the matter is 'earth' it is gross; when it is 'heaven' it is subtle. Calid wrote of the sublimation and *distillation of the Stone's matter: 'Ascend from the Earth into Heaven and descend from the Heaven to the Earth; to the intent to make the body which is Earth, into a Spirit which is subtil, and then to reduce that Spirit into a Body again which is gross, changing one Element into another' (*Booke of the Secrets*, 121). Ripley described the sublimation process as the *exaltation of the Stone into 'Hevyn . . . Ther to be in Body and Soule gloryfycate' (TCB, 179). Isaac Newton wrote of the Stone's matter in his commentary on the *Emerald Table* of Hermes: 'Thus it ought first to be cleansed by separating the elements sweetly and gradually, without violence, and by making the whole material ascend into heaven through sublimation and then through a reiteration of the sublimation making it descend into earth' (Dobbs, *Janus*, 276–7). *The Chymicall Dictionary* defined the 'Coelum philosophorum' as 'any quintessence, or universal medicine, especially the Philosophers Stone'. The *fifth element or quintessence is termed 'our Heaven' because of its brilliant azure hue, its incorruptibility and its high level of refinement (Ruland, *Lexicon*, 225) (see **azure, fifth element**). Tauladanus gives the name heaven to the quintessence, equating it with the spirit Mercurius who, as mediator, rebinds the Stone's soul (form) and body (matter) together after the purification of the body: 'This Spirit is nothing else then that liquor attenuating the Form and Matter of the Stone, and reducing it to a spirituall Nature, which Spirit is sometimes called of the Philosophers, Heaven, sometimes solutive Mercury, sometimes menstruous Matter, sometimes Quintessence and infinite other names' (in FC, 112). The heaven or 'caelum' for Gerhard Dorn was the secret 'truth' and 'sum of virtue' hidden within man himself (MC, 487).

hell a name for the *prima materia, the *black colour which appears during the *putrefaction of the matter of the Stone at the *nigredo, the torture through which the 'body' of the Stone passes while being dissolved by the secret fire. *Zoroaster's Cave* said: 'The Fire against Nature must torment the bodyes, That is the Dragon burning violently, like the Fire of hell' (76). The 'Author' in Bassett Jones's 'Lithochymicus' cites Cephalus on the matter during the black stage: 'First make the match, then give the wound, / Then burne the ashes well; / And fourthly, 'n

Nero's napkin bound, / Convay it strayght to hell. / And wash it in the Stygian trough / Unto an unctuous redd, / Or 'till it be as white as snow:/ And then be sure th' ast spedd' (*AP*, 274). The nigredo stage is also known as 'Tartarus'. During the process of the nigredo the colour of the putre-faction is said to be as black as pitch, and the shades of hell appear. A pro-found blackness reigns both over the matter in the alembic and over the alchemist who may experience the torments of hell while witnessing the shadow or underworld of the psyche (see **nigredo**).

helm, helmet a name for the alembic, the upper part of the still. In Ben Jonson's *The Alchemist,* Face recommends Dol's amorous charms to Mammon, com-paring her to quicksilver rising up over the alembic: 'O, the most affa-blest creature, sir! so merry! / So pleasant! shee'll mount you vp, like *quicksilver, / Ouer the helme*' (2.3.253–5). And Mammon informs Surly that argent vive and mercury sublimate 'are gather'd, into IASON'S helme, / (The *alembicke*) and then sow'd in MARS his field' (2.1.98–9). See **alembic**.

hen see **cock and hen, egg.**

Henry see **lazy Henry.**

hermaphrodite *Mercurius and the *philosopher's stone, which are composed of both male *sulphur and female *argent vive. Bassett Jones wrote: 'But this *Nocopa* [Lightfoot, i.e. mercury] when you know aright, / You'l finde to be a true *Hermaphrodite*' (*AP*, 243). In the production of the Stone the alchemist must join sulphur, the hot, dry, active male aspect of the *prima materia, to the cold, moist, receptive female aspect, *argent vive or mercury. The union of these two metallic seeds is presented as the copulation of two lovers, and later, at a higher level of union, the *chemical wedding of *Sol and *Luna, sun and moon, king and queen. This complete, undivided unity, known as the rebis or hermaphrodite, is the perfect integration of male and female energies (fig. 17). Nicolas Flamel described the product of the union as 'the Androgyne, or Hermaphrodite of the Ancients' (*HE*, 86). In alchemy, the colour repre-senting the male principle is red, and the female, white. Sir George Ripley spoke of the joining of 'the *Red Man* and the *Whyte Woman*' at the coniunctio (*TCB*, 186). The resultant hermaphroditic being is thus rep-resented in alchemical emblems as red and white. The philosopher's stone contains both the red and white tinctures capable of transmuting base metal into gold and silver. The red and white hermaphrodite is sometimes said to be composed of roses and lilies. See, for example, the mercurial fawn in Andrew Marvell's 'The Nymph complaining', which is 'Lillies without, Roses within' (line 92). Mercurius is named the her-maphrodite since he is the prima materia which contains both the male and female seeds of metals (philosophical sulphur and argent vive). The *Liber de arte chymica* stated that 'Mercurius is all metals, male and female, and an hermaphroditic monster' (in Fabricius, *Alchemy*, 92). Of all the planets and metals, only the symbol for mercury is androgy-

17 The alchemical hermaphrodite with the tree of sun and moon

nous, containing the symbols for both sun (male) and moon (female), the circle and crescent. Flamel wrote of mercury that it contains 'a two-fold metallic substance, namely, the inner substance of the Moon and that of the Sun' (*HM*, 1:143). In Jonson's *The Alchemist*, Subtle says of the prima materia, 'some doe beleeve [it] hermaphrodeitie' (2.3.159–64).

Hermes   the Greek equivalent of Mercury. See **Mercurius, Hermes Trismegistus.**

Hermes Bird   see **Bird of Hermes.**

Hermes' seal   the hermetic seal which closes the alchemical vessel and keeps it airtight by either fusion or welding. The sealing not only keeps the mixture in the glass vessel secure from the intrusion of outside influences, but also makes sure the mercurial contents do not escape. Philalethes wrote in his *Secrets Reveal'd*: 'Let the glass be sealed at the top, and so great caution, that there be not the least hole or chinck, else the work would be destroyed' (14). St Dunstan wrote in a recipe for the elixir: 'Take of the best Oar of Gold, pulverize it very well, seal it with *Hermes* his Seal, set it so long into the vaporous fire, till you see it spring up and grow a white and red rose' (*DSP*, 89). Arthur Dee stated that in 'every Digestion, the Glasse must be sealed with the Seal of Hermes' (*FC*, 147). Mercury, in Ben Jonson's *Mercurie Vindicated,* comically accuses the alchemist of torturing and capturing him and using his own Hermes' seal to do it: 'I know what your aymes are, Sir, to teare the wings from my head, and heeles, and lute me up in a glasse, with my own seales' (lines 121–4). In her 'Epitaph. On her Son H. P. at St. Syth's Church', Katherine Philips compares the flight of her dead son's spirit from his body to the escape of alchemical spirits from the hermetically sealed alembic: 'Yet, in less than six weeks, dead. / Too promising, too great a Mind / In so small room to be confin'd: / Therefore, fit in Heav'n to dwell, / He quickly broke the Prison shell. / So the Subtle Alchymist, / Can't with Hermes-seal resist / The Powerfull Spirit's subtler flight' (lines 10–17, in Greer, *Kissing the Rod*, 196). The 'seal' is also known as the 'signet'. Edward Cradock's 'A Treatise Touching the Philosopher's Stone' says: 'Seale fast thy glasse with *Hermes*' Signet sure' (*AP*, 25). The metaphysical significance of the sealed vessel which keeps out all intruders is explained by Joan Hodgson: at first the adept's 'desire nature, with its headstrong wilfulness, passion and egotism crowds out the little light – the child of the Sun. The heart centre of the soul living only for itself is crowded – there is "no room in the inn". Then through some bitter sorrow or denial of desire, the soul begins to yearn for God and seeks spiritual help ... gradually the soul discovers the small cave or sanctuary in the heart from which all intruders are shut out. This is the purpose of true meditation' (Hodgson, *Astrology*, 56).

Hermes tree the mixture of substances acted on by acids in the third stage of calcination (*OED*). In many alchemical texts the Hermes tree is synonymous with the *philosophical tree, a symbol for the matter of the *Stone growing to maturity in the alchemical vessel. The alchemist must feed and nourish the matter or 'tree' with the *mercurial waters during the stage known as *cibation. In *A Compound of Alchymie* Sir George Ripley wrote: 'Therwith dyd *Hermes* moysture hys Tre: / Wythyn hys Glas he made to grow upryght, / Wyth Flowers dyscoloryd bewtyosely to syght' (*TCB*, 141). Concerning the *multiplication of the Stone by both *fermentation and *dissolution, Ripley also wrote: 'And in such wyse thou may that so augment. / That in thy Glas yt wyll grow lyke a Tre, / The *Tre of Hermes* namyd, seemly to se' (*TCB*, 182). Elias Ashmole uses the term metaphorically in an ode to his alchemy teacher, 'To my worthily honour'd William Backhouse Esquire Upon adopting of me to be his Son' (1651): 'My Fathers hand with 's Blessing to my Head / And leave it there. His leaves of Hermes Tree / To deck the naked Ash bequeath to me' (Bod. Ashm. MS 36–7, ff. 241v–242). See **philosophical tree**.

Hermes Trismegistus the father of alchemy, the thrice-great god. He was called thrice-great because he was king, philosopher and priest and held 'three parts of the wisdom of the whole world' (see **Emerald Table**). Hortulanus called Hermes 'the Father of Philosophers' (*A Briefe Commentarie*, 18). He was identified with Thoth, the Egyptian god of revelation and wisdom. Thoth also invented the alphabet and taught the Egyptians the occult arts and sciences. Hermes Trismegistus is the purported author of the alchemical book of laws known as the *Emerald Table*, and of various technical tracts on alchemy, astrology, natural history, medicine and magic. He is also said to be the author of the *Hermetica* or *Corpus Hermeticum*, Hermes' philosophical revelations concerning the creation, written at Alexandria in the second and third centuries AD. The *Hermetica* was translated from Greek into Latin by Marsilio Ficino and published in 1471, and into English by the puritan John Everard (1650).

The *Hermetica* was a highly influential force in Renaissance thought. John Milton wrote in 'Il Penseroso': 'Oft, on a plat of rising ground, / I hear the far-off curfew sound ... Or let my lamp, at midnight hour, / Be seen in some high lonely tower, / Where I may oft outwatch the Bear, / With thrice great Hermes, or unsphere / The spirit of Plato' (lines 74–89). A tradition imbibed from the early church fathers considered that the source of all teachings of wisdom was one and the same and that Hermetic and Christian teachings greatly resembled one another. Hermes Trismegistus, along with the sibyls, was thought to be a contemporary of Moses and was regarded as a Gentile prophet of Christianity. The mosaic pavement laid down at the Cathedral of Siena during the 1480s shows Hermes flanked by two sibyls holding their prophecies of the coming of Christianity, with the inscription 'Hermes Mercurius Contemporaneus Moyse' (Yates, *Bruno*, 42–3). In 1614 Isaac Casaubon demonstrated that the language of the *Hermetica* dated from the post-Christian era, not from the time of Moses. This does not necessarily mean, however, that the teachings did not originate from a long oral tradition. The preface to John Everard's translation of *The Divine Pymander* (published in 1650) claims that the texts were written 'some hundreds of yeeres before *Moses* his time'. Numerous books and treatises in the alchemical corpus are attributed to Hermes or Hermes Trismegistus. The narrator of 'Hermetick Raptures' finds himself, in Part 3, at an assembly of alchemical sages headed by Hermes and including Zadith Senior, Artephius, Geber, Raymund Lull, Arnold of Villanova, Nicolas Flamel, Bernard Trevisan and Michael Sendivogius: 'I alone / With reverence approached tow'rd the throne / Of auncient Hermes, who in Royall state – / Chief president of this great Counsell – sate: / Hermes, the father of Philosophers ... Hermes, in nature's threefold wisdom known, / Whom matchless Aegypt for her chief did own, / And grac't his learning with a royall crown' (*AP*, 600).

Hesperides the place or *garden in which the *philosopher's stone is found. The mythological Hesperian gardens were a favourite symbol in alchemy, because they contained a tree that grew golden apples. The image of the golden apples was used by the alchemists to symbolize gold and the philosopher's stone, which was thought to be able to transmute all base metal into gold. This image relates to the popular alchemical symbol which compares the growth of the philosopher's stone to the growth of the *philosophical tree and the production of golden fruit. Philalethes wrote: 'With a due fire, I may be bold to say, / That they may go to the Hesperian tree, / And pluck its apples, these are such as may / Advance gold corporal to such degree, / That it all metals which imperfect are, / May enter, tinge, and fix to gold most rare' (*Marrow*, bk. 4, 68) (see **fruit**). The sixth plate of Salomon Trismosin's *Splendor Solis* shows the alchemist collecting the golden apples from the tree in the garden of the Hesperides. Robert Herrick, son of a prosperous goldsmith and, in his youth, apprenticed as a goldsmith, named his collection of poems *Hesperides* (1648). Musgrove has explored the alchemical imagery in this collection ('Herrick's alchemical vocabulary', 240–65).

18 The alchemical homunculus

homunculus a small, diminutive person; a dwarf (OED); a symbol for the *philosophical child or infant, the *philosopher's stone. The alchemists believed that it was possible to create little creatures in the image of man by artificial means in the womb of the alembic. An emblem from the *Aurora consurgens* shows the philosophical child safely tucked in its cradle (fig. 18). In some contexts the homunculus occurs as the personification of a deeply sacred conception – the birth of the babe of light and knowledge in the illumined soul of man, while in other contexts he is little more than a mischievous sprite. The Paracelsian treatise *De vita longa* emphasized the intimate relationship of homunculus and creator: 'a homunculus is generated like in all respects in body, blood, principal and inferior members, to him from whom it issued' (PW, 334). In Goethe's *Faust*, the scene in which Faust attempts to create a homunculus is thought to be based on Paracelsus's *De natura rerum* (Gray, *Goethe the Alchemist*, 206–14). The homunculus encapsulates the purely human aspect of the opus, the birth of the Christ child from the divine spark in the heart of the adept, which parallels the growth of the Stone from the metallic seed into the perfect philosopher's stone. The image of the embryonic manikin developing *in vitro* draws attention, not only to the organic, gestatory nature of the opus, but also to the fact that the alchemist's work involves the reproduction of God's very creation in microcosm, in the little universe of the alembic.

In Andreae's *The Chymical Wedding*, Christian Rosencreutz takes part in the making of the king and queen homunculi: 'Then we cast [the thin dough] thus hot as it was into two *little* forms or moulds, and so let it cool a little ... We having opened our little forms, there appeared two beautiful bright and almost *Transparent little* images, the like to which Mans Eye never saw, a male and female, each of them only *four* inches long ... limber and fleshy, as other human Bodies, yet had they no Life' (199–200). The little forms are then fed with the blood of the *Hermes bird, whence they begin 'to grow so *big* that we lifted them from the little Cushonets, and were fain to lay them upon a long Table ... They had Gold-yellow curled hair' (200–1). Shakespeare uses the image of the homunculus in Sonnet 114, where the speaker wonders whether the beloved's love consists of flattery or truth: 'Or whether shall I say mine eye saith true, / And that your love taught it this alchemy, / To make of monsters, and things indigest / Such cherubins as your sweet self resemble' (lines 3–6). The image of the alchemical homunculus continues to persist in literature of the twentieth century. A purely fictional account of John Dee creating a homunculus occurs in Peter Ackroyd's novel, *The House of Dr Dee* (189, 240). In Lawrence Durrell's *The Alexandria Quartet*, Capodistria, who has read the Paracelsian treatise *De natura*, reports that he has seen homunculi which have been created by an alchemist: 'this Baron had ... *actually produced* ten homunculi which he called his "prophesying spirits". They were preserved in huge glass canisters which they use hereabouts for washing olives or to preserve fruit, and they lived in water ... They were exquisitely beautiful and mysterious objects, floating there like sea-horses. They consisted of a king, a queen, a knight, a monk, a nun, an architect, a miner, a seraph, and finally a blue spirit and a red one! They dangled lazily in those stout glass jars' (809). The schizophrenic son in Kingsley Amis's *Stanley and the Women* tells his father that he was not born of natural parents but as an alchemical homunculus: 'Yeah, I was put together by these alchemists using the philosopher's stone ... Kept in a vault in Barcelona till needed, then triggered off by radio beam. And here I am, ready to begin my task' (224).

honey   a name of the philosophical solvent *Mercurius, and also the all-healing *elixir. Honey is an epithet for the elixir because it is both sweet and gold. Philalethes wrote in *The Metamorphosis of Metals*: 'Mercury is our doorkeeper, our balm, our honey' (HM, 2: 192). Here honey is not only equated with mercury, but also with *balm, a name for the elixir or universal panacea. Sir George Ripley likewise wrote that when the 'quadrangle' has been converted into 'a Figure round' (i.e. the opus is completed) 'then have ye honie of our bene [*sic*] hive' (TCB, 112) (see **square and circle**). Honey is associated with the quintessence or elixir in Herrick's 'The captiv'd Bee; or little Filcher': 'But when [the bee] felt he suckt from thence / Hony, and in the quintessence; / He drank so much he scarce co'd stir' (*Works*, 71) (see **bee**). Honey is also an ingredient used in making the *lute with which the alchemist stops up the mouth of the vessel. A recipe in Colson's *Philosophia maturata* states that lute can be made 'of powder of Iron, Vitriol, and Honey, well boyled together, circulating in balneo, till it be dryed up into powder' (54).

horse-belly   a slow, moist heat of dung used for *putrefaction and *distillation. Horse-belly is a euphemistic term for horse dung. Paracelsus wrote in his *Archidoxis*: 'Make the water boil, by an horse-belly, or dunghill, and the earth itself will settle in the bottom, putrefie that which ascends' (30). Synonyms for horse-belly are balneum, *bath, *aqua vitae, moist fire, *philosophic mercury and blood of the *green lion. Colson's *Philosophia maturata* states: 'Whosoever therefore keeps not this our heat, our fire, our balnium, our invisible and most temperate flame, and of one regiment, and continually burning in one quality and measure within our Glasse; I say, whosoever understands not this Dunghill, horsebelly, and moist fire, shall labour in vain, and shall never attain this Science' (19). See **bath, dung**.

horse dung see **horse-belly, dung**.

house the alchemical vessel, the vas rotundum in which the birth of the *philosopher's stone takes place. The epigram to emblem 9 in Michael Maier's *Atalanta fugiens* advised the alchemist to take the matter of the Stone and lock it up 'in a glass house, wet with dew' (61). When the matter of the Stone is *sublimated and distilled, the vessel or 'house' is said to *sweat with the droplets which condense from the rising vapour. The alchemist is advised to construct the perfect house for the opus in accordance with the proportions of the mystic *'square and circle' principle. The square symbolizes the four elements whose opposing qualities – hot, dry, cold and moist – must be harmonized and converted during sublimation into the perfect spiritual substance, the fifth element or quintessence, symbolized by the circle or sphere. Lord Fairfax's house in Marvell's 'Upon Appleton House' is an example of such a house or vessel: 'Yet thus the laden House does sweat, / And scarce indures the *Master* great: / But where he comes the swelling Hall / Stirs, and the *Square* grows *Spherical*' (lines 51–2). See **alembic, castle, fort**.

humidity see **radical humidity**.

humours see **philosopher's stone**.

I

iatrochemistry (from the Greek *iatros* meaning physician), alchemy or chemistry applied to medicine and physiology, a field pioneered by Paracelsus (Theophrastus Bombastus von Hohenheim, 1493–1541), and adopted by others in the sixteenth and seventeenth centuries. The followers of Paracelsus were called spagyrists or iatrochemists. Paracelsus took the pre-Socratic idea of the macrocosm–microcosm and used it as a model for the scientific enquiry into nature. It is thought that he may have been the first to coin the term 'macrocosm'. Based upon this mystical idea of correspondences, his research into nature and medicine was a valid form of scientific enquiry which insisted on practical experimental techniques and rigorous observation – a revolutionary position at a time when other forms of 'science' were based on speculative theory. It is to Paracelsus that we owe the modern conception of medicine and health. He was the first physician to emphasize the importance of the external cause of disease and its seat in a particular organ. Towards the end of the sixteenth century, Paracelsian iatrochemistry began to make its way into the mainstream of medicine in Europe. The first general edition of Paracelsus was published at Frankfurt, beginning in 1603 and completed in eleven volumes by 1605. Chemical therapy was introduced into the pharmacopoeia, challenging the traditional Galenic medicine with its herbal remedies. The debate between the ancients and the Paracelsians is alluded to in a contemporary poem by the physician John Collop, 'On Dr. George Bowle of Oundle': 'Nor thy self only but thy Art mak'st friends, / While Artists discords in best musique ends. / Thou *Paracelsus* makest *Galens* friend; / While Chymicks now *Botanicks* do commend' (lines 15–18).

The first English Paracelsian work had already been written by R. Bostocke in 1585, following the renewed publication of Paracelsus's work by a group of German disciples in the 1560s and 1570s. Sir Walter Raleigh practised Paracelsian medicine. Lucy Hutchinson records that her mother, wife of Sir Allen Apsley, lieutenant-governor of the Tower, paid for the experiments Raleigh conducted in a henhouse converted into a little distillery while imprisoned in the Tower (1605–16): 'Sir Walter Raleigh and Mr Ruthven being prisoners in the Tower, and addicting themselves to chemistry, she suffered them to make their rare experiments at her cost, partly to comfort and divert the poor prisoners, and partly to gain the knowledge of their experiments, and the medicines to help such poor people as were not able to seek physicians' (*Memoirs*, 13). During his experiments, Raleigh concocted a medicinal 'cordial' which became famous. In 1661 the French Paracelsian Nicaise Le Fevre became professor of chymistry and apothecary-in-ordinary to Charles II, who ordered him to recreate the celebrated cordial of Sir Walter Raleigh. Le Fevre subsequently wrote *A Discourse upon Sir Walter Rawleigh's Great Cordial* (1664). The Paracelsian John Hester dedicated his *A Hundred and fourteene Experiments and Cures of … Paracelsus* (1596) to Raleigh. Gabriel Harvey was a patient of Hester, and Sir Francis Drake, Sir Francis Walsingham, Henry, second Earl of Pembroke, and Henry's wife Mary were patients of the Paracelsian Thomas Moffet. Sir Theodore Turquet de Mayerne, who wrote the preface for the new *Pharmacopoeia Londinensis* (1618), became the Paracelsian physician to James I, Charles I, and later to Cromwell. His work on the English pharmacopoeia helped to ensure the acceptance of iatrochemical medicine in England (see Debus, *The Chemical Philosophy*). In Andrew Marvell's 'Upon the Death of the Lord Hastings', Mayerne's failed attempt to save the life of Lord Hastings is recorded: 'And *Aesculapius*, who, asham'd and stern, / Himself at once condemneth, and *Mayern*: / Like some sad *Chymist*, who prepar'd to reap / The *Golden Harvest*, sees his Glasses leap' (lines 47–50).

Icarus   see **metamorphosis**.

imbibation   the return of distilled liquid to the residue or 'earth' at the bottom of the alembic, followed by further distillation, also known as cohobation and often identified with *cibation. Edward Kelly wrote: 'Consider that

Cibation is but imbibation' (BL Sloane MS 3631, f. 60). Chaucer's Canon's Yeoman refers to 'our materes enbibing' (*Canon's Yeoman's Tale*, line 815). According to Sir George Ripley the imbibation of the earth or body of the Stone should be carried out seven times (TCB, 163). Geber wrote: 'Imbibe Calx or Body often-times, that thence it may be sublimed, and yet more purified then before' (in FC, 34). In Johann Andreae's *The Chymical Wedding*, the process is symbolized by the image of the *philosophical bird drinking his own bath-water: 'In this Room a Bath was prepared for our Bird, which was so coloured with a fine white Powder, that it had the appearance of meer Milk … He was mighty well pleased with it, drinking of it, and pleasantly sporting in it' (157). John Dastin used the image of the *king eating 'meat' and drinking his own bath-water to represent this process: 'It is meet the King rest in a sweet Bath, till by little and little he hath drunk the Trinity of his Nourisher, and let Drink be after Meat and not Meat after Drink' (in FC, 100). The drinking symbolizes the moistening of the Stone's body, while the eating symbolizes its drying or dessication. See **cibation**.

incest   The alchemical union of opposite forces and substances in the *chemical wedding is often portrayed as an incestuous union. The alchemist first unites the hot, dry, active male seed of metals, known as philosophical *sulphur, with the cold, moist, receptive female seed, *argent vive. This united pair, represented as lovers, are then placed in a coffin, their bodies killed and their souls and spirits released to the top of the vessel. The second major union takes place when the soul unites with the spirit, and the third union when the blackened dead bodies (the 'earth' in the bottom of the alembic) are washed and purified and joined again with the united soul and spirit. In alchemy all forms were believed to be created from the same formless substance, the *prima materia or original first matter. The fact that the two participants in the wedding are personified as coming from the same family emphasizes the essential similarity of the substances being joined even though they appear to be opposites of unlike nature. Paracelsus wrote enigmatically of the processes undergone by the matter in the vessel: ''Tis dissolved by it self, coupled by it self, marries it self and conceives in it self' (*Aurora*, 53).

The incestuous coniunctio is most frequently represented as the union of brother and sister, but it is also represented as the union of mother and son, father and daughter, and king and son. *The Tomb of Semiramis* informs us that Aristotle said in *The Rosary of the Philosophers*, 'joyn your Son Gabricius (dearer to you then all your children) with his sister *Beja,* who is a tender sweet and splendid virgin' (CC, 18). Isaac Newton wrote concerning the preparation of philosophic mercury: 'Grind the mercury for a quarter of an hour with an iron pestle and thus join the mercury, the doves of Diana mediating, with its brother, philosophical gold, from which it will receive spiritual semen' (Keynes MS 18, in Dobbs, *Foundations*, 182). In *Hesperides*, a sequence of poems which Musgrove argues is alchemical, Robert Herrick wrote: 'A sister (in the stead / Of Wife) about I'le lead; / Which I will keep embrac'd, / And kisse, but yet be chaste' (*Works*, 13). In *The Golden Tract* the couple who are married and

19 Incest: the king crawling under his mother's skirt

'charged with incest' are both mother and son *and* brother and sister (HM, 46). The *king in Sir George Ripley's 'Cantilena' says that he has to 'dissolve to my First Matter', which means uniting with his mother (mater, matter) in order to be reborn as the 'Ruddy Son' of the philosophers (fig. 19) (see **philosophical child**). Likewise the prince in William Backhouse's 'The Magistery' must enter 'Into his *Virgin-Mothers* wombe' in order to be reborn as the king (TCB, 243). Artephius wrote of the process whereby the mother must be sealed up within the 'belly of her infant; and that is Sol himself, who proceeded from her, and whom she brought forth; and therefore they have loved one another as mother and son, and are conjoined together, because they come from one and the same root, and are of the same substance and nature' (SB, 16). (See **devour**.) Incest is a union which is forbidden by society, by the outer world; thus the term is used to indicate a union that must be performed secretly, within the soul.

infant see **philosophical child**.

ingestion see **devour**.

inhumation a method of distillation in which vessels were buried in earth within a circular fire, or placed in animal dung. During this process the matter for the Stone in the vessel is dissolved and putrefied. John Dastin's 'Speculum philosophiae' states: 'But thou shalt distill all things with moisture, because driness corrupts the work with combustion: And the Philosophers advise that every distillation be always made seven days with inhumation, meaning that inhumation be made seven days between every distillation' (in FC, 23).

inversion   the continuous process of *solve et coagula (dissolve and coagulate).
Maria Prophetissa stated: 'Invert nature and you will find that which
you seek' (Patai, 'Maria', 180). During the process of solve et coagula, the
states of matter are being constantly reversed – hard matter must be dissolved, while soft or flowing substance must be hardened. The solve et
coagula is accomplished by the *secret fire, of which Artephius said: 'it
overturns all things, dissolves, congeals and calcines' (SB, 33). Trismosin
compared the solve et coagula to the games of children because of its
topsy-turvy nature: 'Wherefore is this Art compared to the play of children, who when they play, turn undermost that which before was
uppermost' (*Splendor Solis*, 39). The theme of reversal can be seen in the
idea of the alchemical work as the *opus contra naturam – the work
which must go against nature in order to progress, the work which must
go backwards before going forwards. Old outmoded forms of body and
thought must return or dissolve into their original state, the *prima
materia, before they can become purer, more beautiful forms. At the
peak of the opus the glories of the coniunctio (coagula) fade and the
alchemist finds himself in the throes of yet another dissolution (solve)
or reverse movement of the work, which enables him to regain the original state of the prima materia from which a new form can be coagulated.
Thus the prima materia is often said to be found in a topsy-turvy place.
Abu'L-Qasim wrote that the prima materia was to be found in a rocky
mountain where everything is upside down: 'the top of this rock is confused with its base, and its nearest part reaches to its farthest, and its
head is in the place of its back, and vice versa' (in PA, 433). The paradoxical motif can also be seen in the dual role played by the transforming
arcanum, *Mercurius, who is both dissolver and coagulator, slayer and
resurrecter, *poison and *medicine, demonic and divine. The principle
of irony and paradox is characteristic of the opus alchymicum. See
inverted tree.

inverted tree   the *philosophical tree. The inverted tree is an ancient symbol not
confined to any one culture or tradition. It occurs in *The Bhagavadgita*, in
The Perfect Sermon or the Asclepius and in Plato's *Timaeus*, and found its way
into alchemy via the Cabbala. The inverted tree is one of a number of
inversion motifs found in representations of the alchemical opus (see
inversion). The alchemists compare the growth of the arcane substance
into the *philosopher's stone to the inverted tree because the roots
receive nourishment from a heavenly source, i.e. Mercurius. The sixteenth-century alchemist Laurentius Ventura wrote of the inverted tree:
'The roots of its ores are in the air and the summits in the earth' (in AS,
311). Calid wrote of the matter of the Stone which is to be found in
'mountains': 'And thou must know, that the rootes of their mynes are in
the ayre, and their tops in the earth, and it wil easily be heard when they
are pluckt out of their places, for there will be a great noyse' (*Booke of the
Secrets*, 41). *The Glory of the World* says: 'For when our Stone rises upward in
the alembic, it has its roots in the air, but if it would regain its virtue and
strength, it must once more return to its earth, and then it has its head
and perfect potency in the earth' (HM, 1: 218). The inverted tree image

occurs in the wood sequence in Andrew Marvell's 'Upon Appleton House' when the poet undergoes a merging with nature, an *inversion (the *solve et coagula), and becomes a 'natural tree' with its roots in the earth: 'Or turn me but, and you shall see / I was but an inverted Tree' (lines 567–8). Psychologically, the growth of the tree symbolizes the unfolding of the soul, the expansion of consciousness. See **inversion**.

iris   see **peacock's tail**.

island   see **philosophical tree**.

J

jackdaw   a symbol of the stage known as the *nigredo, the putrefaction which leads to the stage of the *peacock's tail. Equivalent terms are crow, crow's head and raven. The raven and jackdaw are both members of the crow family. The jackdaw is depicted in plate 20 of Salomon Trismosin's *Splendor Solis* illustrating the putrefaction of the Stone at the nigredo. Gradus, the killer of John Shade in Vladimir Nabokov's *Pale Fire,* plays the role of jackdaw and raven at the nigredo. He 'called himself variously Jack Degree or Jaques de Grey, or James de Gray, and also appears in police records as Ravus, Ravenstone, and d'Argus' (77). The name given to the vessel during the stage of the nigredo when the Stone is in putrefaction is the *'grave'. It is only a short associative leap through Gradus's aliases, Gray to (G)Ravenstone to gravestone, raven and stone. Thus 'Ravenstone' links him firmly to the first grade of the opus in a novel whose centre-piece, a manuscript, is described by a dethroned *king as 'so many ingots of fabulous metal' (101). Through Gradus's alias 'Jacques d'Argus' (Jackdaw), the blackness of the nigredo is transformed into the rainbow colours of the mythological Argus, whose eyes were transferred to the peacock's tail by Hera. The peacock's tail is the rainbow stage in the opus which follows the blackness of the raven at the nigredo. Richard Devine, in Marcus Clarke's *His Natural Life*, also plays the role of the jackdaw. When the alchemist Devine takes the first step in his opus, he discards his original name and takes on the name of Rufus Dawes, a name which he retains for the duration of his corruption and mortification in the hell of the convict prisons. Maurice Frere and others refer to him at this stage as 'Jack' Dawes (635). As the transformation in his outer and inner life takes place, he discards the name 'Jack Dawes' and eventually re-inherits his divine name, 'Devine'. See **Argus, crow, peacock's tail, raven**.

Jason   see **golden fleece, helm**.

juice of grapes   see **grapes**.

Jupiter   the planet, the metal tin, the fire of nature, the colour grey in the opus. In 'The Pleasant Founteine of Knowledge', Jean de la Fontaine wrote: 'By Gold our meaning is the *Sunne* . . . and by tynne / Understand *Jupiter* the thinne' (lines 381–8, *AP*, 93). Salmon's *Dictionaire Hermetique* states that Jupiter (tin) is the most perfect of the imperfect metals and that it takes only a little work to convert it into the perfect metal, gold (88). It also states that the philosophical sublimation is symbolized by the myth of Jupiter, transformed into an eagle, transporting Ganymede to heaven (87), and that the shower of gold into which Jupiter has been converted symbolizes the distillation of philosophical gold (153). The god Jupiter and the golden shower are alluded to in emblem 23 of Michael Maier's *Atalanta fugiens*. The epigram to this emblem states: 'May then, also, when Pallas breaks out of Jupiter's head, / The gold descend into the retort destined to it, / Like a rainshower' (*AF*, 181). Klossowski de Rola interprets Pallas Athena in this emblem as signifying mercury sublimated by coction to the highest degree and Jupiter as 'the innate generative heat of bodies (the Natural Fire) which brings metals to maturity' (*Golden Game*, 100). The god Jupiter also appears in emblem 46 of *Atalanta fugiens*, as the father of Apollo who symbolizes the *philosophical son.

K

kemia   see **chymia**.

king   the raw matter for the Stone; the *philosopher's stone itself; the hot, dry, active, male principle of the opus, the masculine seed of metals known as 'our sulphur', 'our gold' and *Sol. In order to produce the philosopher's stone the king has to be united with (or married to) the cold, moist, receptive female principle, known as 'our argent vive' (or mercury), 'our silver' and *Luna. Usually the male and female substances which participate in the *coniunctio are called king and queen in the later unions, when the matter is in a more refined state than at the beginning of the opus (see **chemical wedding**). In the alchemical myth of the rex marinus the name 'king' is applied to the matter of the Stone from its conception until its ultimate perfection. *Semita semitae* applies the name 'king' to the newly born *philosophical infant: 'then is born our Stone which of the Philosophers is called a King' (in *FC*, 67). The child is said to be fed on kingly food, with which nourishment 'he will become a King, stronger than a King' (*FC*, 110). This nourishment is the transforming arcanum or mercurial *blood, as William Backhouse makes clear: 'from the *Cradle* to his *Crowne*' the king 'is fed with his owne *bloode*' (*TCB*, 343).

During the process of becoming the Stone, the king has to undergo a death and resurrection. In the early stages of the opus, the king, as 'our gold' or the alchemist's raw stuff, suffers death and *putrefaction as he is

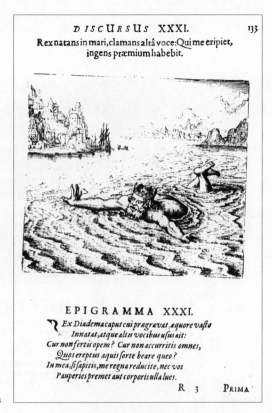

DISCURSUS XXXI. 133

Rex natans in mari, clamans altâ voce: Qui me eripiet,
ingens præmium habebit.

EPIGRAMMA XXXI.

Ex Diadema caput cui prægravat, æquore vasto
Innatat, atque altis vocibus usus ait:
Cur non fertis opem? Cur non accurritis omnes,
Quos ereptus aquis sorte beare queo?
In mea, si sapitis, me regna reducite, nec vos
Pauperies premet aut corporis ulla lues.

R 3   PRIMA

20 Rex marinus

dissolved into the original matter of creation, the prima materia. This
was the death which necessarily preceded rebirth. In the myth of the rex
marinus, the king is almost drowned in the sea but is saved, renewed
and united in the coniunctio with his queen (fig. 20). Plates 7 and 8 of
Salomon Trismosin's *Splendor Solis* depict the marinated king in both
his drowning and regenerated state, restored by the alchemical queen.
Shakespeare's Pericles enacts this very process when he is almost
drowned and is restored by Thaisa, who becomes his queen in the
*chemical wedding (*Pericles*, Act 2). The dissolution of the king in the sea
is alternatively depicted as the *eclipse of the sun (Sol), the beheading of
the king or, more frequently, the placing of the king in a *sweat bath so
that his impurities may be cleansed. At this stage the matter is at its
blackest black and is known as the black king, King Duenech or *Laton.
Maier wrote of King Duenech in his *bath (emblem 28 of *Atalanta
fugiens*): 'Herein he bathes and bathes, under the glass arch, / Till by the
wet dew he is freed from all bile' (AF, 206). In Trismosin's *Splendor Solis*
the black king is depicted as the Ethiopian who is cleansed of his filth
by a beautiful crowned lady (plate 8).

The death and resurrection of the king occur in a number of versions
in *Atalanta fugiens,* as Heleen de Jong has noted: 'In emblem 24 the king
is devoured by the wolf and thrown into the fire, from which he rises,
crowned. In emblem 31 the sea-king is in danger of sinking into deep
waters and promises great treasures to his servants, if they save him. In

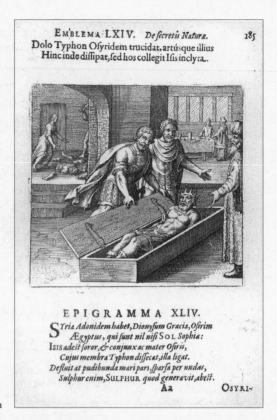

EMBLEMA LXIV. *De secretis Naturæ.* 185
Dolo Typhon Osyridem trucidat, artúsque illius
Hinc inde dissipat, sed hos collegit Isis inclyta.

EPIGRAMMA XLIV.

SYria Adonidem habet, Dionysum Græcia, Osirim
Ægyptus, qui sunt nil nisi SOL Sophia:
ISIS adest soror, & conjunx ac mater Osiris,
Cujus membra Typhon dissecat, illa ligat.
Defluit at pudibunda mari pars, sparsa per undas,
Sulphur enim, SULPHUR quod generavit, abest.

Aa   OSYRI-

21 The king rising from his coffin

emblem 48 the Merlini king dissolves in the water and rises as the
Philosopher's Stone. The *Rosarium Philosophorum* ends with a picture in
which the Philosopher's Stone is compared with the risen Son of God,
represented by Christ rising from a Sarcophagus' (*AF*, 212) (fig. 21). In Sir
George Ripley's 'Cantilena' and William Backhouse's 'The Magistery',
the king's death and renewal are accomplished by his 'incestuous' re-
entry into his virgin mother's womb (i.e. the prima materia) (see fig. 19).
In yet another version, the 'Visio Arislei', the king's kingdom is barren
because like sex mates with like. The kingdom is renewed when the
king follows the alchemical philosopher's advice to have the opposite
sexes marry instead. The king orders the wedding of his son and daughter, Thabritius and Beya (*AA*, 146–54) (see **incest**). After the black king's
putrefied body is washed and cleansed of its impurities the white stage
or *albedo is attained. The whitened body (symbolized by the queen) is
then married to the previously separated soul (or soul/spirit), symbolized by the king, leading to the birth of the *philosopher's son, himself
a king, stronger and purer than his father (i.e. his earlier unregenerate
state) (fig. 22). At this stage the alchemist increases the heat of the fire
until the matter is transformed into a 'deep ruby colour' known as the
'Mighty King' or red king, the red stone which can transmute all base
metals into pure gold (Kelly, *Two excellent Treatises*, 142) (see fig. 34). Sir
George Ripley wrote of the king in the final stages of the opus: 'His
second Vertue as Gold is Red, / In his Vessell bright shining, / A Diadem

22 The birth of the king as philosopher's stone

set on his head, / Richer then any earthy thing. / His third Vertue is Purple pure, / Like Sun-beames he shineth bright and clere, / Of Red tincture then be you sure' ('The Mistery of Alchymists', in *TCB*, 382).

L

labyrinth the dangerous journey of the alchemist through the opus alchymicum. The alchemists use the image in a symbolic way to designate a place of confusion, geographical or mental, which has to be negotiated with great care in order to avoid becoming lost without thread or clue. While in the labyrinth of the opus, illusion and confusion reign and the alchemist is in danger of losing all connection and clarity. Nicolas Flamel wrote: 'This operation is indeed a *labyrinth*, for here there present themselves a thousand wayes at the same instant' (*HE*, 1:106). Elias Ashmole described the alchemical books themselves as 'Labyrinths' to which the reader needs a 'clew' (*TCB*, Prolegomena). The *Arcanum* makes it clear that the thread or clue which leads man out of the labyrinth of illusion is divine illumination (*FC*, 157), and *The Six Keys of Eudoxus* says of the alchemical opus: 'without the inspiration of Heaven ... one remains undoubtedly in this labyrinth, without being able to find a happy deliverance from thence' (in Regardie, *Philosopher's Stone*, 107). When the alchemist learns to discriminate between the true and the false, he emerges from the labyrinth unscathed.

lac virginis see **virgin's milk**.

lapis philosophorum see **philosopher's stone**.

laton, Latona, latten   a natural alloy of gold and silver resembling brass or bronze; also philosophical gold, which is the unclean body or raw stuff of the philosopher's stone which must be cleansed of its impurities. Calid wrote: 'Know also that our Brass, or Latten, is the Philosophers Gold, is the true Gold' (*Booke of the Secrets*, 110). The alchemists personified laton as the goddess Latona who, with Jupiter, was the parent of Apollo (sun, gold) and Diana (moon, silver). Latona is the matrix or interior part of the earth in which the metals are engendered and nourished. Michael Maier described Latona as 'an imperfect body composed of *Sol* and *Luna*' and stated that 'this Latona is dark with black stains on the face which can only be washed away by making Latona white' (*AF*, 114). Arthur Dee equated Laton with the 'unclean body' known as the green lion (*FC*, 121) (see **green lion, lead**). The imperfect Latona who must have her stains or spots washed away is a symbol of the impure body (also known as earth or King Duenech) which the separated soul and spirit have abandoned at the bottom of the alembic during the initial stage of the opus, the black *nigredo. This black and putrefying body must be purified before it can reunite with the soul (or the united soul/spirit entity) at the white *albedo. The cleansing process, called the *ablution, is accomplished by washing the body with the *mercurial waters also known as the secret *fire ('our water' or *Azoth). Artephius wrote: 'our brass or latten is prepared with our water, purified, and brought to a white colour'. He advised the alchemist to 'wash away the blackness from the latten, not with your hands but with … our second mercurial water'. He explained that 'laten', the unclean body, is made to ascend by *sublimation until it is whitened and 'changed into spirit' (*SB*, 45–7). Edward Kelly wrote in *The Stone of the Philosophers*: 'Purify Laton, i.e. copper (ore), with Mercury, for Laton is of gold and silver, a compound, yellow, imperfect body' (*Two excellent Treatises*, 31). Kelly then quotes Morienus: 'Azoth and fire purify Laton, that is to say, wash it and thoroughly remove its obscurity; Laton is the impure body, Azoth is quicksilver' (*Two excellent Treatises*, 43).

As with *Naaman the Leper, another symbol of cleansing, the washing of the stains from Latona's face refers to the purification of the soul by baptism, so that it may rise above the darkness of the earth into the light of the spirit. The poet Marcellus Palingenius wrote of *Mercurius, the effective agent of the philosopher's stone: 'O *Titan*, beauty of the worlde, O fairest God in sight, / O thou *Latona* driving hence the shadowes of the night, / *O swiftly fleeting restless Impe of Iove and Maia* borne / That able art to change thyselfe, to shapes of sundry forme' (*Zodiacus vitae*, in Smith, *Business of Alchemy*, 54). White Laton of the Sages is philosophical *Luna or the purified, whitened matter attained at the *albedo. Red Laton of the philosophers is their bronze, and sometimes a symbol of the red stone attained at the perfect red stage or *rubedo. A story about Shakespeare and Ben Jonson, alluding to Shakespeare's alleged ignorance of Latin, plays on the alchemical meaning of 'translate' (transmute) and 'Latin' (latten): 'Shake-speare was Godfather to one of *Ben:Johnsons* children, and after the christning being in a deepe study, Johnson came to cheere him vp, and askt him why he was so Melancholy. no faith *Ben*: (sayes he) not I, but I haue beene considering a great while

what should be the fittest gift for me to bestow vpon my Godchild, and
I haue resolu'd at last; I pry'the what, sayes he? I faith *Ben*: I'le e'en giue
him a douzen good Lattin Spoones, and thou shalt translate them'
(Chambers, *Shakespeare*, 2:243, 17).

laundering　the philosophical *sublimation by which the perfect white stage of the
opus is accomplished, the process of cleansing the impurities of the
matter of the Stone and regenerating it through immersion in the transforming *mercurial waters. In an Egyptian papyrus from the late third
or early fourth century AD, known as the Stockholm Papyrus, the succession of operations applied to the dyeing of fabrics (washing, mordanting and colouring) is also applied to the transmutation of metals (see
dye). Emblem 3 of Maier's *Atalanta fugiens,* which depicts a woman bent
over a large washing tub, has the motto: 'Go to the woman who washes
the sheets and do as she does' (*AF*, 66). Plate 21 of Trismosin's *Splendor
Solis* shows laundresses washing linen in tubs and in a river while others
lay out the clean laundry in a meadow to dry. Ruland declared the circulation of the matter in the vessel with its ascent of vapour and descent of
rain to be 'like a shower upon new linen at the fullers'. He explained that
when the alchemists say, 'Go and look at the women who are employed
over the washing and fulling of linen: see what they do, and do what
they are doing', it simply means 'to cleanse the matter of its impurities'
(*Lexicon*, 384). A jokey version of laundering which plays with alchemical
concepts occurs in Shakespeare's *The Merry Wives of Windsor* where the
'gross' and 'unclean' matter, Falstaff, is tricked into escaping a jealous
husband by being shut in a laundry basket. Falstaff says: 'To be stopped
in, like a strong distillation, with stinking clothes ... think of that – that
am as subject to heat as butter, a man of continual dissolution and thaw'
(3.5.81–100). See **ablution**.

laundry　see **laundering**.

lavement　see **laundering**.

lazy Henry　a nickname for the distillatory furnace. Paracelsus referred to the 'piger
Henricus' in his *Aurora* as 'the accidia or slow Henry' (25). In Jonson's *The
Alchemist* Subtle warns Ananias to give him satisfaction 'or out-goes /
The fire: and downe th' *alembekes*, and the fornace, / *Piger Henricus*, or
what not' (2.5.80).

lead　the heavy metal which the alchemists believed could be transmuted
into pure silver or gold through the agency of the *philosopher's stone;
the raw material for making the Stone, the *prima materia. Roger Bacon
wrote of the heavy metal: 'Leade is an uncleane and imperfect bodie,
engendered of Argent-vive impure, not fixed, earthy, drossie, somewhat
white outwardly, and red inwardly, and of such a Sulphur in part
burning. It wanteth puritie, fixation, colour, and fiering' (*Mirror*, 5).
Michael Drayton wrote of the refining of lead by a mountain in the
Derbyshire Peak District in *Poly-Olbion*: 'and oft to th' earth bow'd

downe her aged head, / Her meager wrinkled face, being sullyed still with lead, / Which sitting in the workes, and poring o'r the Mines, / Which shee out of the Oare continually refines: / For shee a *Chimist* was, and Natures secrets knew / And from amongst the *Lead*, she *Antimony* drew' (*Works*, 4:530, lines 381–6). In John Lyly's *Gallathea* Peter boasts of his master's power to transmute lead into silver: 'Why, of the quintessence of a leaden plummet he hath framed twenty dozen of silver spoons' (2.3.84–5).

The 'lead of the philosophers', on the other hand, refers to 'gold', the raw material for the Stone from which the seed of metals is extracted. Thus philosophical lead (as distinct from common lead) is a most valuable substance without which the philosopher's stone cannot be made. Lead is associated with the deathly beginnings of the opus, the *nigredo stage where the matter for the Stone is dissolved into the original stuff of creation, the *prima materia. This 'lead' is synonymous with the unclean body, the matter of the Stone (see **Latona**), and also with the prima materia (or *Mercurius). Artephius wrote: 'Wherefore let our body remain in the water till it be dissolved into a subtle powder in the bottom of the vessel and the water, which is called the black ashes: This is the corruption of the body which is called by the philosophers or wise men, *saturnus, aes, plumbum philosophorum, and pulvis discontinuatus,* viz, Saturn, Latten or brass, the lead of the philosophers, the disguised powder' (*SB*, 51). As the unclean body and prima materia, lead is naturally thought of by the alchemists as the father of gold. Old man Saturn with his scythe is synonymous with Mercurius senex who brings forth Mercurius puer or gold. When the lead or matter is cleansed of its blackness and corruption, it is called the white lead of the wise. In his 'Praxis', Isaac Newton wrote that when Latona becomes white 'you shall have the plumbum album sapientum, the white Diana' (Dobbs, *Janus*, 304). At the attainment of white lead it is said that a new light dawns. Sir Philip Sidney used this metaphor in the last poem of *Astrophil and Stella*: 'When sorrow, using mine own fire's might, / Melts down his lead into my boiling breast, / Through that dark furnace to my heart oppressed / There shines a joy from thee, my only light' (188). Lead, Saturn and melancholia are inextricably linked in alchemy. The nigredo is a time of suffering and lamentation as the dark shadow of melancholia is cast over the alchemist witnessing the events in the alembic.
Psychologically, lead represents the fragmented, chaotic state of the soul or psyche, which has then to be separated from the body so that it can become detached from earthly conditions, gain equilibrium, and then receive illumination. White lead is a name for philosophical mercury.

leaven see **fermentation**, **paste**.

leprosy the disease of metals, the impurity which metals have contracted in the mines of the earth where they are formed. The alchemists apply the epithet 'leprous' to the 'imperfect' metals (iron, copper, tin and lead), which have not yet matured into silver or gold (see prima materia). Thomas Tymme wrote: 'Imperfect metalls are in fact Gold and Silver, but their sicknes and imperfeccions do hide their properties, whiche imperfeccions and sicknesses proceede of these causes ... All these leprousies come by the mixture of divers Sulphurs corrupting them, which was in their Mynes.' According to the alchemists, ordinary fire cannot purge and cleanse the impurity from metals. This can only be done through the secret fire of the opus. These sick metals, wrote Tymme, can only be transmuted into silver and gold if they are cured by the true medicine: 'Therefore as a sick man taking medicine is made sounde, only by alteracion ... so mettaline bodies, by the true medicine altering them, are made perfect and become pure and good Gold and Silver' (*Light in Darkness*, 24–5). The miraculous panacea or *medicine which cures the leprous metals of their corruption and transmutes them into gold is the *philosopher's stone or elixir. *The Golden Tract* said of the Stone: 'it is a subtle spirit which tinges bodies, and cleanses them of their leaprous infirmities' (HM, 25) (see **Naaman the leper**). The initial unclean body of the Stone which must be cleansed is also said to suffer from leprosy (see **green lion**, **Latona**). In William Warner's *Albion's England*, Queen Elizabeth is presented as the alchemist who can cure the world's leprosy and turn it to gold: 'Our world ... Of whose faire-cured leaprosie / From former twaine to golde, / (For in a Quintessence was all / Eare Gods world's-curse of olde) / The vndeluding alcumist / Is that Elizabeth' (Chalmers, *English Poets*, 4:509).

lily The white lily is a symbol of the pure white elixir and stone attained at the *albedo, the white stage of resurrection which follows the blackness and death of the *nigredo. Like the white rose, the lily is a symbol of purity. *Philosophical mercury is known as the juice of the white lily. The Paracelsian 'Lilium' is defined as 'Mercury and its Flowers. Also Tincture of the Philosophers, Quintessence of Sulphur, Fixed Flowers, Fixed Sulphur' (Ruland, *Lexicon*, 207). But most commonly the lily is known as a symbol of the perfect white of the albedo. Bassett Jones referred to the white stone as 'The *Lilly white*', and the silver, lunar stage as 'the lunar Lillie-whitened mine' ('Lithochymicus' in AP, 284, 296). John Collop referred to the alchemical lily in 'The praise of his Mistris': 'Admire no more these downy breasts, / Where Candors pure Elixir rests / Praise not the ... subtile lillies which out-vie / Calcining arts choice chymistry' (71). The lily is frequently coupled with the red lily or red rose, which signifies the red stone or elixir attained at the final stage of the opus, the *rubedo. These are the male and female flowers that bloom on the philosophical plant or arbor philosophica (the *prima materia). Robert Fludd noted in 'Truth's Golden Harrow' that the alchemists' use of the rose and the lily derives from the biblical 'Song of Songs'. He wrote of 'the rose of the field and lilly of the valley, after the patterne whereof the Alkimists have shaped their red and white Elixir, or Stone' (Josten, 'Truth's Golden Harrow', 122) (see **flower**). Plate 7 of Johann Mylius's *Basilica philosophica* shows the white lily and the red rose in either hand of the alchemical *hermaphrodite (the united male and female substances forming the philosopher's stone). The white lily, associated with the feminine, moon aspect of the opus, is united with the red rose (sometimes the red lily), the male, sun aspect at the *chemical wedding.

lily (red)   see **lily**.

limation   the dissolution of a body with a file; commonly called filing (Jones, in *AP*, 351–2). In *Fasciculus chemicus* Arthur Dee cites a prose version of Ripley's *Compound*: 'that thou maist not spoil the work, let the Bodies be both subtilly limated with Mercury, and subtilized with equall proportion, one of the Sun, another of the Moon, till all these things be reduced to Dust' (46). In his own copy of his translation of Dee's work, Elias Ashmole has underlined 'limated' and written 'fyled' in the margin (*FC*, 46).

limbeck   see **alembic, head**.

linen   see **laundering**.

lion   see **green lion, red lion**.

liquefaction   the reduction of a solid into a liquid. In alchemy this is synonymous with the dissolution (at the black *nigredo) of the impure metal or matter of the Stone into the original substance of creation, the *prima materia. 'The Golden Rotation' stated that the decoction of the matter must be done in a gentle, temperate fire until there is 'a certaine shew of blacknes, which is the signe of the liquefaction of the Stone, and the beginning of the Arte' (f. 24v). Artephius wrote of 'the reiterating of the liquefaction or dissolution in this our dissolving water' on 'gold, our body' (*SB*, 4). According to Musgrove, Robert Herrick used the image of liquefaction in an alchemical context in 'Upon Julia's Clothes': 'When as in silks my *Julia* goes, / Then, then (me thinks) how sweetly flowes / The liquefaction of her clothes' (Musgrove, 'Herrick's alchemical vocabulary', 261).

lovers and the tomb   see **chemical wedding, grave**.

ludus puerorum   the process of *inversion in the opus, the *solve et coagula (dissolve and coagulate). Salomon Trismosin's *Splendor Solis* illustrates the alchemical 'games of children' (pl. 20). The text accompanying this emblem says: 'Wherefore is the Art compared to the play of children, who, when they play, turn undermost that which before was uppermost' (39). The solve et coagula is a paradoxical process whereby that which is hard is made soft (body dissolved into spirit) and that which is soft is made hard (spirit is congealed into form). In this way these opposites may become mingled into one entity – spirit and body are united. *The Glory of the World* explained that this process of softening the 'earth' and hardening the 'water' is compared to 'boys in the street' when they 'pour water on dry dust, and knead the whole into one mass. For this reason the Sages call our process child's play' (*HM*, 1:239). The term 'play of children' is also used to describe the simplicity of the opus. *The Golden Tract* said: 'If you understand it, it is mere child's play' (*HM*, 1:40). Edward Kelly wrote in a letter of advice to an unknown recipient: 'To regulate the fire is mere child's play' (*Two excellent Treatises*, 53). The epithet *"women's work' is used interchangeably with 'child's play' in this context. The words 'Ars nostra est ludus puerorum cum labor mulierum' appeared in an inscription on the study wall of the house in Prague rented by John Dee in 1584, which belonged to Rudolph II's alchemical adviser, Dr Tadeus Hajek (Casaubon, *True and Faithful Relation*, 212). 'Ludus puerorum' is the title of an alchemical treatise collected in the anthology *Artis auriferae* (Basel, 1593).

Luna   the female principle of the opus, *argent vive, the female seed of metals. Luna, the moon, or *Diana, symbolizes philosophical silver (fig. 23). Chaucer's Canon's Yeoman explains to his audience: 'Sol gold is, and Luna silver we threpe [affirm]' (*Canon's Yeoman's Tale*, line 826). Philosophical silver is a different substance from vulgar silver. Marcilius Ficinus is cited in *Zoroaster's Cave*: 'All the metals when they are prepared by Art, then they are call'd Sol, Luna, Mercurius, etc. For before they were onely Gold, Silver, and Quicksilver' (65). Calid explains that this 'Luna is made of a pure fine Mercury, and a pure white Sulphur by the Influence of the Moon' (*Booke of the Secrets*, 126). Colson's *Philosophia maturata*, explains that '*Sol* and *Lune*, is nothing else, but *Red* and *White Earth*, to which Nature hath perfectly joyned *Argent vive*, pure, subtile, white and Red, and so of them hath produced *Sol* and *Lune*' (2–3). Luna is also the name of the white elixir and the white stone which transmutes base metal into pure silver. It symbolizes the attainment of the perfect white stage, the *albedo, where the matter of the Stone

23 Luna

reaches absolute purity. Philalethes wrote that, after accomplishing the
*peacock's tail or multi-coloured stage of the opus, 'expect *Luna* perfect,
the whitest white, which will grow more and more glorious for the
space of twenty days' (RR, 23).

Luna is the bride, the white *queen and consort of King Sol. She is the
moist, cold, receptive principle which must be united with *Sol, the dry,
hot, active principle, in the *chemical wedding. Edward Kelly quoted
the alchemical authority Senior on this subject: 'I, the Sun, am hot and
dry, and thou, the Moon, art cold and moist; when we are wedded
together in a closed chamber, I will gently steal away thy soul' (*Two excellent Treatises*, 38). Luna is sometimes described as the field or *white foliated earth into which the seed of Sol (gold) is sown. From the marriage
of Sol and Luna, the philosopher's stone is born. Thus Luna is the
mother of the *philosophical child or stone. The third law of the *Emerald
Table* says of the Stone: 'The father thereof is the Sun, the mother the
Moon.' Edward Cradock confirmed the long tradition of this alchemical
idea in 'A Treatise Touching the Philosopher's Stone': 'For as our *Sol* is
father of our Stone, / Soe *Luna*, mother those writers every one / That
learned bee doe commonly itt name' (AP, 16–17). In Ben Jonson's *The
Alchemist* Surly lists amongst the innumerable alchemical terms: 'Your
sunne, your *moone*, your *adrop*' (2.3.191). Luna is also identified with a
milky humidity which accumulates on the receiver when the *green
lion is heated in a sand-bath. Colson's *Philosophia maturata* states: 'from
the first appearing of the White Fume, the fire must be discreetly
increased by little and little: This same tingeth the Receiver with
a certain thick and milky humidity which is our Lune' (31).
Psychologically, Luna governs the realm of the imagination. The white
work of the albedo involves the cleansing of the subconscious and the
automatic activities of the body controlled by the subconscious. When
this is accomplished, the purified soul may become illumined.

lunar fruit, lunar plant or **tree**   see **fruit, philosophical tree**.

lunaria   see **philosophical tree, white stone**.

lute   the impervious matter used by the alchemists to seal the stopper of
a retort or alembic. *The Hydropyrographum Hermeticum* said that 'the
vessel must be well "luted" and closed so the spirit will not fly away'
(Houpreght, *Aurifontina*, 27). This substance is often called the 'lute of
wisdom', as Calid writes: 'thou shalt take the precious stone, and put it
in a Cucurbite, covering it with an Alembicke, being well closed with
the lute of wisdome, and set it in verie hote dung' (*Booke of the Secrets*, 46).
The *Hermetis Trismegisti Tractatus Aureus* gives a recipe for the lutum sapientiae: 'Take Glue dried into powder, one ounce, Barly flower, Crocus
martis, or caput mort, of Vitriol one ounce, all being in fine powder, let
them be mixed with juice of Comfrey, and Whites of Eggs, to the just
consistency of Lute' (Salmon, *Medicina Practica*, 236). In Chaucer's *Canon's
Yeoman's Tale* the Yeoman tells of 'the pot and glasses enluting, / That of
the eyre might passe out no-thing' (lines 766–7). Mercury, in Ben

Jonson's *Mercurie Vindicated*, says accusingly to his persecutor, Vulcan, the alchemist: 'I know what your aymes are, Sir, to teare the wings from my head, and heeles, and lute me up in a glasse' (lines 121–4). Musgrove has argued that Robert Herrick plays on the musical and alchemical meanings of 'melt' and 'lute' in 'Upon Julia's Voice' where the poet listens 'to thee . . . Melting melodious words, to lutes of Amber' (lines 3–4). He explains that the chemical lute used by Lavoisier was made of resin (amber) melted with wax (Musgrove, 'Herrick's alchemical vocabulary', 258). Herrick continues the melt/lute metaphor in the poem following 'Upon Julia's Voice': 'Then melted down, there let me lye, / Entranc'd, and lost confusedly: / And by thy Musique strucken mute, / Die, and be turn'd into a lute' (lines 5–8).

M

magistery, magisterium a potent medicine, a name for the opus alchymicum or magnum opus, the attainment of the *philosopher's stone. In Jonson's *The Alchemist* Subtle expresses amazement at Sir Epicure Mammon's sleeping when 'This is the day, I am to perfect for him / The *magisterium*, our *great worke*, the stone' (1.4.13–14). The magistery, literally meaning the quality of mastery, is also a name for the 'virtue' or concentrated essence of a substance. Paracelsus wrote: 'This therefore is a *Magistery*, viz that which can be Extracted out of things without any separation or Preparation of the Elements, and yet notwithstanding, the Powers and virtues of things, are by the addition of some thing, attracted into that matter and conserved there' (*Archidoxis*, 78). In *Theophila or Loves Sacrifice. A Divine Poem*, Edward Benlowes compared the potency of God's word to alchemical or 'magisterial gold': 'All *Vaticans* are drosse; This, Magisterial *Gold*' (13). See **medicine**.

magnesia a term which covers a number of mineral substances, including magnesium, magnetite and manganese dioxide and the *star of antimony ; a name for the perfect white earth or matter of the Stone attained at the *albedo, the quintessence. *Zoroaster's Cave* said: '*Terra Alba*, White Earth, White Sulphur, White Fume, Auripigment, Magnesia, and Ethel, signifie the same in this Art' (66). Synesius wrote of this substance: 'For that is the White Mercury, White Magnesia, Foliated Earth' (*The True Book*, 173). In his 'Propositions', Isaac Newton gave the code name 'magnesia' to the active, vitalistic alchemical agent Mercurius, and in his treatise 'Praxis', 'magnesia' is the quintessence of the alchemists (Dobbs, *Janus*, 24–5, 162). 'The Golden Rotation' likewise equated magnesia with the *fifth element or quintessence produced from the union of the four elements: 'made of foure equall natures . . . yt is a matter compounded and congealed which will evermore resiste the fyre. And preserveth all things from burning and fixeth all that is volatile' (f. 50). Chaucer's

Canon's Yeoman tells the tale of a disciple enquiring of his master Plato: '"What is Magnesia, good sir, I yow preye?" / "It is a water that is maad, I seye, / Of elementes foure" quod Plato' (*Canon's Yeoman's Tale*, lines 1458–60). *Zoroaster's Cave* states that philosophical mercury is composed of magnesia and the 'spume of silver': 'Our water, the Spume of Silver mingled with Magnesia, rids away the Darke Umbra of the body' (75).

marble   a symbol for the *white stone of the philosophers. *The Glory of the World* advised the alchemist to 'Subject our Stone to coction till it becomes as bright as white marble. Then it is made a great and effectual Stone' (HM, 1:205). Marble is also used as a surface on which to perform the grinding of substances. Colson's *Philosophia maturata* gives a recipe on how to *calcine *Sol and *Luna: 'Amalgame *Sol* and *Lune*, and grind it on a Marble with powder of salt, prepared without any moisture, until no *Mercury* appear' (75). See **albedo**.

marriage   see **chemical wedding**.

Mars   the planet, the god, the metal iron. Chaucer's Canon's Yeoman explains to his audience that 'Mars yron, Mercurie is quyksilver' (*Canon's Yeoman's Tale*, line 827). Jean de la Fontaine comments on Mars's qualities in 'The Pleasant Founteine of Knowledge': '*Mars* he is hard, weighty and Bad, / And above all others most sadd' (i.e. solid, dense) (AP, 107). B. J. T. Dobbs has observed that iron was especially popular as a reducing agent and when applied to antimony ore it caused it to crystallize in a star pattern, producing the regulus of antimony (Dobbs, 'Newton's "Clavis"', 199). Mars appears in the epigram accompanying the eighth emblem of Michael Maier's *Atalanta fugiens*. It says of the Stone's matter in the vessel: 'Attack it cautiously with a fiery sword (as is the custom); / Let Mars assist Vulcan; the bird arising from it / Will be a conqueror of iron and fire' (AF, 95). In this context Mars signifies iron, *Vulcan the fire and the *bird the *philosophical child or stone born from the *egg or vessel. According to Heinrich Khunrath, the regimen of Mars follows the regimen of Venus in the process of the opus. The reign of Mars is associated with the stage when the rainbow colours of the *peacock's tail (the cauda pavonis) appear in the vessel, heralding the advent of the white stage or *albedo (MC, 289).

Mary's bath   see **bain-marie**.

massa confusa   see **chaos**.

matrass   a glass vessel with a round (sometimes oval) body and a long neck, used by the alchemists for distillation (OED). In Victor Hugo's *Notre-Dame de Paris*, Claude Frollo's cell is cluttered with alchemical vessels: 'Upon the stove were heaped in confusion all sorts of vessels – earthen flasks, glass retorts, and charcoal matrasses' (361).

May dew   see **dew**.

medicine   the *philosopher's stone or elixir. The Stone is perceived as a miraculous, eternal substance which can cure such 'diseased' or imperfect
metals as lead, tin, copper and iron, and transmute them into pure
and perfect gold (see **leprosy, prima materia**). Francis Bacon records
Sir Edward Dyer saying to the Archbishop of Canterbury: 'I saw Mr
[Edward] Kelly put of the base metal into the crucible; and after it was
set a little upon the fire, and a very small quantity of medicine put in,
and stirred with a stick of wood, it came forth in great proportion,
perfect gold; to the touch, to the hammer, to the test' (*Apophthegms*,
I:122). All metals were perceived to be potential gold, and the impurities
which they contracted in the mines of the earth where they were formed
were thought of as a state of disease or leprosy which could be cured by
the perfect medicine or philosopher's stone. Calid wrote that 'our
Medicine transmutes infinitely imperfect Metals, and that he who
attains once to the perfection of it, shall never have any need to make
more' (*Booke of the Secrets*, 120). At the same time the 'medicine' is the universal panacea capable of curing man of all weaknesses and diseases,
rejuvenating him and transforming him from earthly into illumined
man. Philalethes wrote that the adept who has won the tincturing Stone
'hath a Medicine Universal, both for prolonging Life and Curing of all
Diseases' (*Secrets Reveal'd*, 119). Shakespeare uses the metaphor of the
alchemical medicine in *Antony and Cleopatra* when Cleopatra says to her
attendant, Alexas: 'How much unlike art thou Mark Antony! / Yet,
coming from him, that great medicine hath / With his tinct gilded thee'
(1.5.34–6). In *Volpone*, Jonson has Mosca and Corbaccio jokily assert that
material gold is the universal cure-all. Gold is 'your sacred medicine . . .
this great *elixir*' (1.4.69–72) (see **venom**).

melancholia   the state of mind associated with the initial deathly stage of the opus,
the *nigredo or melanosis. During the death and dissolution of the
metal or matter of the Stone (or old state of being) into its *prima
materia, the alchemist witnesses and experiences suffering and melancholy. This time of lamentation and sacrifice is often referred to as the
reign of *Saturn. Jung wrote: 'The nigredo not only brought decay,
suffering, death, and the torments of hell visibly before the eyes of the
alchemist, it also cast the shadow of its melancholy over his own solitary
soul' (*MC*, 350). The acknowledgement of the previously hidden shadow
of the psyche which leads to the death of the old state of being is experienced by the alchemist as a nox profunda, a state of deep blackness from
which it is almost impossible to imagine emerging. The narrator of *The
Golden Tract* witnesses the embrace of bride and groom (*argent vive and
*sulphur) in the heated alembic and is overcome by fear and anguish at
their death: 'the husband's heart was melted with excessive ardour of
love, and he fell down broken in many pieces. When she who loved
him . . . saw this, she wept for him, and, as it were, covered him with
overflowing tears until he was quite flooded and concealed from view.
But those complaints and tears did not last long, for being weary with
exceeding sorrow, she at length destroyed herself. Alas! what fear and
anguish fell upon me, when I saw those who had been so straitly

committed to my change, lying as it were, melted and dead before me' (*HM*, 1:47). See **beheading, flood, night**.

menstruum   the *mercurial solvent of the philosophers. It is the means by which the alchemists dissolve metals into the *prima materia, and by which they ripen their matter into gold. *The Golden Tract* quoted Lull: '"For the knowledge of the menstruum", says Raymond, "is a thing without which nothing can be done in the magistery of this Art. Nothing preserves the metals while it dissolves them, but our menstruum" which, as he further states in his "Codicil" is "the water by which the metals are solved, while all their essential properties are conserved"' (*HM*, 1:38). This solvent is named menstruum because it releases the seed or sperm from the dissolved metal. From this seed the *philosopher's stone and gold are generated in the *womb of the alembic. The menstruum is often personified by the mercurial *lion, *serpent or *dragon. It is also known as the *blood of the *green lion, the Hermetic stream and the *fountain. Colson's *Philosophia maturata* says that when the green lion is heated in a sand-bath a white fume arises 'and therewith shal also ascend a most red oyl, called Philosophers aureal Gold, a stinking menstruum, the Philosophers Sol, our Tincture, Burning Water, the Blood of Green Lyon' (31). In Jonson's *The Alchemist* Subtle asks Face: 'Are you sure, you loos'd 'hem / I' their owne *menstrue*?' (2.3.70–1). (To 'loose' means to dissolve.)

mercurial water   see **bath, dew, fire, fountain, Mercurius, rain, sea, tears**.

Mercurius   the central symbol in alchemy, also known by the equivalent Greek name Hermes, symbolizing the universal agent of transmutation (fig. 24; see also fig. 3). The alchemists most emphatically distinguish between common mercury (Hg) and philosophical mercury, Mercurius ('our Mercury'), which is made by the union of *sulphur and *argent vive (first mercury). *The Golden Tract* stressed that 'Our mercury is not the mercury of the vulgar herd' (*HM*, 1:27). Colson's *Philosophia maturata*, speaks of the deluded state of the purely material alchemists: 'in these our Times, we know no man who doth diligently and truly find out the Philosophers Tinctures, but most of them labour absurdly and vainly in vulgar *Mercury*' (6). Philosophical mercury is mercury that has been prepared by the alchemist's art, as *Zoroaster's Cave* noted: 'All the metalls when they are prepared by Art, then they are called Sol, Luna, Mercurius, etc. For before they were onely Gold, Silver, and Quicksilver' (65).

   Mercurius is a symbol for the alchemists' magical arcanum, the transformative substance without which the opus cannot be performed. Mercurius is the mother of all metals, the substance from which all other metals are created. Jean de la Fontaine stated: '*Mercury* is the vive Argent, / The which hath the whole governmente / Of mettalls Seven, and is mother / To all, as well as stepmother, / Who can the imperfect perfect' (*AP*, 93). Mercurius or Hermes is also the name of the divine spirit hidden in the depths of matter, the light of nature, the anima

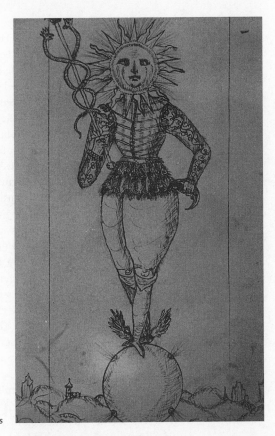

24 Mercurius

mundi, the very spirit of life which must be released in order to make the *philosopher's stone. Mercurius is most frequently described as a water (divine water, our water, water that does not wet the hands, aqua ardens, aqua vitae, aqua permanens), but is also referred to as a fire (noster ignis), and as water *and* fire ('For this a water is which yet is fire' – Philalethes, *Marrow*, 68) (see **fire**). In other instances Mercurius is seen as an aerial spirit or soul symbolized by clouds or fume, indicating that the alchemists were aware of the psychic nature of their transformative substance. Calid said: 'Our Mercury is Aereal; look for it therefore in the Ayre, and in the Earth' (ZC, 59).

Mercurius is present everywhere and at all times during the opus. From the dark chthonic beginnings of the opus to the divine, triumphant completion, Mercurius is not only the *prima materia (the 'mother' of metals) which is sought at the beginning of the work, but also the ultima materia (the philosopher's stone), the goal of his own transformation. Mercurius is not only the matter of the work but stands also for all the processes to which this materia is subjected. He is simultaneously the matter of the work, the process of the work, and the agent by which all this is effected. The epigram to emblem 14 of Maier's *Atalanta fugiens* says of this paradoxical and enigmatic force: 'it devours itself and spits itself out, kills itself and generates itself again' (66). And Rhasis, cited in *Zoroaster's Cave*, states: 'For it dissolves, and conjoyns It selfe, makes it selfe Black and Citrine, White and Red, espouses Itselfe, Conceives, brings forth, and does all to the perfect end' (67). Mercurius is the grand master of the reiterated cycle of *solve et coagula (dissolve and coagulate) which constitutes the alchemical work of purification. Through him matter is spiritualized (solve) and spirit materialized (coagula). The *Rosary of the Philosophers* said of Mercurius: 'It is the water which killeth and reviveth ... It is the water which dissolveth and congealeth' (McLean, *Rosary*, 18). At the beginning of the opus Mercurius takes the form of a dark, destructive force which 'kills' the old metal or outmoded state of being and dissolves it into the prima materia (also called Mercurius). In this role Mercurius is the ultimate solvent. He then transmutes himself and is transmuted from being the poisonous waters of death into the divine life-giving elixir. He is the water of life, (the *tears, *rain or *dew) which descends in showers upon the blackened dead body (of metal or soul) lying at the bottom of the alembic, washing it, purifying it and re-animating it, preparing it for its union with the united soul/spirit at the *chemical wedding. Metaphysically, Mercurius carries that divine love essence which kills falsehood and illusion and allows truth to arise. As the swift messenger-god, Mercurius opens up a path of light, a line of communication between the greater self and the limited personality of every day. Through this contact the body can eventually be transmuted from fleshly mortality to immortality (Hodgson, *Astrology*, 40).

Mercurius appeared to the alchemists as a dual-natured, ambivalent force, both destructive and creative. Basil Valentine indicated that the great secret of the opus is 'double Mercury' (HM, 1:352). Mercurius indeed consists of all conceivable opposites. The texts describe him as both dark and light, visible and invisible, young and old, hard and soft, fixed and volatile. He is said to run around the earth enjoying equally the company of the good and the wicked. Bassett Jones's Dr Allslagen called him 'that light-heeld God', 'this Truant' with 'Nimble winge', and 'the flyinge thief' (AP, 284, 248). He is a protean, elusive, duplicitous, inconstant, teasing spirit which, when captured and *tamed by the alchemist, is magically transformed into a willing, faithful, helpful ally or ministering servant (see fig. 3) (see also **cervus fugitivus**). 'Inconstant' mercury must be made 'constant' by the alchemist. In *Paradise Lost* Milton refers to the fixation of philosophic mercury as the binding of Hermes: 'by their powerful art they bind / Volatile Hermes, and call up unbound / In various shapes old Proteus from the sea, / Drained through a limbeck to his native form' (3.602–5). The cutting off of the feet of mercury (usually by the *scythe of Saturn) also symbolizes the fixation of elusive, volatile mercury.

The elusive, duplicitous Mercurius who consorts with the devil is at the same time a redeeming psychopomp. The fact that he can freely participate in both light and dark worlds without taint makes Mercurius the perfect mediating bridge, able to unite the division in man which was thought to have occurred at man's fall from the garden of Eden. As an ancient pagan god Mercurius possesses a natural undividedness despite his ambiguity, perhaps even because of it. The alchemists realized that this unity within flexibility was the very quality needed for healing the divided post-lapsarian state. It is for good reason that the alchemists chose the wily pagan god of revelation, commerce, communication and thieving as the symbol for their transforming arcanum. Another way in which Mercurius's duality manifests itself is in his role as the hermaphrodite. In Michael Maier's *Lusus Serius*, Mercury, contending for the title of 'King' from amongst all nature's creatures, claims that he has the advantage of being a hermaphrodite: '*Mercury* is an Hermaphrodite, he is Father and Mother to other Mettalls' (119). In Ben Jonson's masque, *Mercurie Vindicated from the Alchemists at Court*, Mercury comically complains of the endless processes and tortures to which he is subjected, and to the multitude of roles given him, including the hermaphrodite: 'I am their Crude, and their Sublimate; their Praecipitate, and their vnctuous; their male and their female; sometimes their *Hermaphrodite*; what they list to stile me. It is I, that am corroded, and exalted, and sublim'd, and reduc'd, and fetch'd ouer, and filtred, and wash'd, and wip'd; what betweene their salts and their sulphures; their oyles, and their tartars, their brines and their vinegers, you might take me out now a sous'd *Mercury*, now a salted *Mercury*, now a smoak'd and dri'd *Mercury*, now a poudred and pickl'd *Mercury*' (lines 51–60). As prima materia, the hermaphroditic Mercurius contains the male and female seeds of metals, the hot, dry, active male principle known as philosophical *sulphur, and the cold, moist, receptive female principle, philosophical *argent vive (also mercury). *Zoroaster's Cave* said: 'in the beginning of the work [Sol and Luna] are reduced into their first nature that is, Mercury, therefore from it they took their beginning'; 'Wherefore I counsell you my friends, that you work not on anything but *Sol* and *Luna*, reducing them into their first matter, that is, Our Sulphur and Argent vive' (ZC, 68). As the ultima materia or Stone, Mercurius contains both the red and white tinctures or stones, the tincture of Sol (male, gold, spirit) and Luna (female, silver, purified body).

According to most alchemical texts, the chemical wedding of *Sol and *Luna may not take place without the presence of a third mediating principle. This medium of conjunction is Mercurius, the substance which contains both male and female seeds and unites them. In this context Mercurius is often depicted as the 'soul' (anima) which unites 'body' and 'spirit', though sometimes he is represented as the 'spirit' which joins 'soul' and 'body', form and matter, as Petrus Bonus testifies: 'When the Anima Candida is perfectly risen, the Artist must joyn it, the same moment, with its body: For the Anima without its body cannot be held. But such a Union must be made by mediation of the Spirit because the Anima cannot have life in the body nor perseverance in it, but by the Spirit' (in ZC, 85–6). Whichever way this is represented, Mercurius is always the mediator. In *The Stone of the Philosophers* Edward Kelly advised the alchemist to 'unite them [Sol and Luna] through the mediation of Mercury' (*Two excellent Treatises*, 28). In this role Mercurius is known as the priest who ties the marriage knot, as *Cupid or Eros who shoots the magnetic arrow of love, and as the gum or *glue which binds body and spirit (or soul) in the chemical wedding. The mercurial water also provides the supreme nourishment for the embryonic Stone born from the union of Sol and Luna. This nutriment, known as the mercurial *blood or *milk, is the vital force of life and growth itself which must be fed to the maturing Stone. The emblem of the *philosophical tree of sun and moon (Sol and Luna), growing on an island or directly out of the sea, symbolizes the growth of the fifth element or Stone out of this mercurial water of life.

Mercurius is endowed with an infinity of names to describe the many guises he adopts during the different stages of the alchemical work: the *dragon, *poison, sharp vinegar, *serpent, Melusina, *lion, *uroboros, prima materia, sea, *shadow, *virgo, anima mundi, spirit, fire, hart, deer, *cervus fugitivus, psychopomp, tears, dew, rain, sweat, blood, *virgin's milk, water of the wise, blessed water, golden water, aqua permanens, *fifth element, wind, *eagle, twin, *hermaphrodite, *bride, groom, lover, beloved, *microcosm, gum, glue, priest, Eros, Cupid, *bee, *tree, *flower, *tincture, *elixir, *Stone. Although the forms and names of Mercurius are diverse, he is essentially one thing, one matter (i.e. Mercurius). Laurentius Ventura's words sum up the role of Mercurius in the opus: 'Nostrum Magisterium incipitur, et perficitur, una re tantum, id est Mercurio' (Our magistery is begun and perfected by only one thing; that is Mercury) (FC, frontispiece) (see AS, 193–250).

Mercury was the god of merchants and of commerce. The words 'mercury' and 'merchant' share a common etymological source, both deriving from the Latin for merchandise (merc-, merx) (OED). Characteristically, alchemists were involved in multiple wealth-generating projects. John Dee was associated with various trading and exploration companies. Sir Walter Raleigh's Guiana voyage has recently been described as a kind of alchemical field trip, a pursuit of physical gold as well as the 'golden king' of the alchemists (Nicholl, Creature, 314–35). The alchemist, physician and entrepreneur, Joachim Becher (1635–82), generated a new discourse based on the language of alchemy to communicate to his patrons at the court of the Holy Roman Emperor the new idea of material increase through production and commerce. By employing alchemical images of regeneration and multiplication, by symbolically using the figure of Hermes/Mercurius in his multiple roles, as agent of transmutation, regenerator and multiplier of gold, and patron of merchants and trade, Becher was able to make comprehensible to the emperor a world run by commercial profit (see Smith, The Business of Alchemy).

metamorphosis The alchemists were interested in the idea of metamorphosis as a way of expressing the changes of substances from one state to another. The work of alchemy was seen as the metamorphosis of base metal into silver and gold, of infantile, bestial man into the mystical homo maximus. John Frederick Helvetius wrote in his Golden Calf that the eminent physician Dr Theodore Ketjes gave him a medal whose inscription stated that alchemy is the 'divine metamorphosis' (HM, 2:281). During the

Renaissance, the fables of the master of metamorphosis, Ovid, were appropriated by the alchemists to express the process of transmutation. They not only used Ovid as a source of enigmatic allusion but also claimed that the *Metamorphoses* and other Greek and Roman myths were consciously Hermetic, alchemical works. Bassett Jones wrote of the myth of Jove and Io: 'This feate had *Ovid* learned cunninglie / From father *Hermes*' booke of Alkhemie' (AP, 294). Maier states that, according to Petrus Bonus, Homer and Ovid were amongst those who handed down Hermetic wisdom to succeeeding generations; Ovid's *Metamorphoses*, in particular, contained the secret of the philosopher's stone (AF, 8, 37). Martin Ruland's *Lexicon of Alchemy* stated that 'the ancients commonly made use of fables, and those of the Egyptians and the Greeks were devised only in view of the Great Work, if we are to believe the Philosophers who frequently refer to them in their works' (382). In 'Lithochymicus' Bassett Jones used the myth of Phaethon's chariot as a key to understanding the reconciliation of the 'two enemies' in the alchemical opus, and observed that the alchemical art never speaks more truly than when it uses the 'store' of histories or emblems 'which in *Ovid* you may construe ore' (AP, 245, 293). Arthur Dee wrote in his 'Corollary' to chapter 5 of *Fasciculus chemicus*: 'In this Chapter is openly explained the Fable of *Phaeton*, in *Ovids Metamorphosis*. As also of *Dedalus* with his son *Icarus*; who when they had made themselves wings of Feathers, and had fastned them with Wax, and when with these they had flown through the Aire beyond the Labyrinth, it is reported *Icarus* flying too high, fell into the Sea, in which he was drowned, because the Sun melted the Wax. By his Father *Dedalus* is understood the Sulphur of Nature sublimated and Philosophically coagulated. By *Icarus* the same Sulphur sublimated, but with undue governance of the Artist, and continued violence of the Fire, melted into Water, and buried in the dead Sea' (FC, 81–2).

The title and frontispiece of Michael Maier's *Atalanta fugiens* are taken from Ovid's *Metamorphoses*. He uses the fleeing Atalanta as his symbol for the volatile, elusive *Mercurius, the agent of transformation in the opus alchymicum. Maier also makes use of Ovid's 'Venus and Adonis' in the epigram to emblem 41 of the same work. The myth of Diana and Actaeon is the subject of an emblem in Mylius's *Basilica philosophica* (plate 6, row 4, no. 2) and this myth also appears as emblem 92 in Daniel Stolcius's *Viridarium chimicum* (101). The transformation of Actaeon into a stag had been used as a symbol of transmutation since the times of Hellenistic alchemy. Likewise the myth of Cadmus and the metamorphosis of the dragon's teeth into warriors is alluded to in a number of alchemical treatises, including William Backhouse's 'The Magistery' and Philalethes' *An Open Entrance* (TCB, 342; HM, 2:166).

microcosm   the philosopher's stone. Petrus Bonus called the 'Stone of the Philosophers ... a microcosm or little world' (*New Pearl*, 238), and Thomas Norton wrote in *The Ordinall of Alchimy*: 'Noble Auctors men of glorious fame, / Called our *Stone Microcosmus* by name' (TCB, 85). The creation of the Stone involves the duplication of God's own macrocosmic creation in miniature, in the microcosmic world of the alembic. The Stone, which is said to be composed of 'body', 'soul' and 'spirit', was thought of as a perfect little world in which all the elements are united and harmonized, a perfect reflection of the macrocosm. Paracelsus wrote of the Stone: ''Tis likewise composed of body, spirit and soul. On the same account they have also called it their microcosm, because it hath the likeness of all things in the world' (*Aurora*, 22).

milk   see **virgin's milk**.

miscarriage   see **abortion**.

moon   see **Luna, Diana**.

Moor, Moorish king, Moorish ground   see **Ethiopian**.

Moor's head   see **head**.

mortification   the chemical alteration of the external form of a substance; the 'death' of the metal or the matter for the Stone so that it can be dissolved into the *prima materia. After the death of the metal its 'soul' is released to the top of the vessel, while below the body putrefies and blackens (see **putrefaction, nigredo**). *Zoroaster's Cave* said: 'Nature begins all her Actions from Seperation [*sic*]. Mortification is the first step to Separation, and the only way to that End: for, as long as Bodies remain in their old Origin, separation without putrefaction and mortification, cannot reach them' (71). The eighth emblem (series 3) of Johann Mylius's *Philosophia reformata*, illustrating the mortification, shows the king about to be bludgeoned to death by ten enemies (359). The king symbolizes the matter for the Stone while the cudgels symbolize the universal solvent or secret fire known as *Mercurius.

Moses   The alchemists considered Moses a great prophet, natural philosopher and alchemist. *The All-wise Doorkeeper* called alchemy 'the Mosaico-Hermetic science of all things above and things below' (HM, 2:301). In the alchemical texts Moses often alternates with *Hermes Trismegistus as the founder of alchemy. Philalethes wrote: 'Hermes, surnamed Trismegistus, is generally regarded as the father of this Art, but there are different opinions with regard to his identity. Some say he was Moses' (HM, 2:233). The *Turba Philosophorum*, a famous tenth-century Islamic text (probably derived from Greek sources), includes Moses as one of the exalted assembly of alchemical sages. Ben Jonson must have been sure that his audience would appreciate the satiric reference to Moses as alchemist when he had Sir Epicure Mammon say: 'I'll show you a booke, where MOSES, and his sister, / And SALOMON have written of this art' (*The Alchemist*, 2.1.81–2). Moses's Book of Genesis, and Hermes' *The Divine Pymander* were the two basic texts on creation to which the alchemists referred for the creation of the *philosopher's stone. Patai has written that in Hellenistic Egypt there seems to have been an actual alchemist by the name of Moses, who apparently wrote several alchemical treatises (JA, 30).

mould a container into which molten metal is cast in a foundry. The separation of unformed matter and its casting into a mould is a process which originated in the laboratory of the alchemist. Dryden uses 'mould' in a metallurgical and alchemical sense in *Annus Mirabilis*: 'Me-thinks already from this Chymick flame, / I see a City of more precious mold: / Rich as the Town which gives the *Indies* name, / With silver paved and all divine with Gold' (lines 1169–72). Milton uses 'mould' in its metallurgical, alchemical sense when describing the act of 'founding' Pandaemonium in *Paradise Lost*. The reprobate spirits in hell 'With wondrous art founded the massy ore, / Severing each kind and scummed the bullion dross: / A third as soon had formed within the ground / A various mould' (1.703–6). The work of the alchemical opus is sometimes compared to the making of bread – the kneading of the dough or paste (the purified 'body' of the Stone's matter), the adding of the leaven (the ferment or 'soul' of the Stone) and then the pouring of the the paste into a mould to create a new being. In *The Chymical Wedding* Christian Rosencreutz takes part in the moulding of the little homunculi: 'we were to *moisten* the Ashes with our fore-prepared *Water* till they became altogether like a very thin Dough. After which we set the matter over the Fire, till it was well *heated*, then we cast it thus hot as it was into two *little* forms or moulds, and so let it cool a little . . . We having opened our little forms, there appeared two beautiful bright and almost *Transparent* little Images, the like to which Mans Eye never saw, a Male and Female' (199).

mountains the place where the *prima materia is said to be found: 'And this prime matter is found in a mountain containing an immense collection of created things' (Abu'L-Qasim, *Book of Knowledge*, 24). Nicolas Flamel wrote that 'the real first substance of the Stone' is to be obtained from 'a glorious Regal Herb' growing on the 'summit of a mountain'. The alchemist is advised to extract the pure juice of this herb, 'the true and subtle mercury of the philosophers', from which may be prepared the 'white tincture and the red' (HM, 1:146). An anonymous poem collected in Ashmole's *Theatrum chemicum Britannicum* likewise described the alchemical plant of sun and moon with its red and white *flowers (tinctures) as growing 'a pon a Mowntayn brym' (348). The male seed of metals, philosophical *sulphur (Sol), and the female seed, philosophical *argent vive (Luna), which constititute the *prima materia (*philosophical Mercurius), are sometimes referred to as two mountains. When these male and female seeds are united, the philosopher's stone is born. *The Glory of the World* says: 'You daily behold the mountains which contain husband and wife' (HM, 1:208), and 'The Treatise of Dunstan' likewise says that 'our stone is bred between two mounteynes . . . by these little mountaynes is understood *Sol* and *Lune* . . . both which are in our mercurie' (St Dunstan, 'Treatise', ff. 3–4). Sir George Ripley's 'Cantilena'

compares the united couple at the coniunctio to 'a Hille and Aire sur-
rounding it' (178).

Roger Bacon advised the alchemist to construct his furnace in imita-
tion of the mountains where metals were thought to be engendered
from the prima materia: 'we must needes have such a furnace like unto
the Mountaines, not in greatnesse, but in continuall heate, so that
the fire put in, when it ascendeth, may find no vent' (*Mirror*, 11–12).
Metaphysically, going up into the mountains means to rise in awareness
in order to come to know the prima materia, the pure, original sub-
stance/consciousness from which all things are created. When Nicolas
Flamel advised the alchemist who wished to obtain the prima materia
to go to the seventh mountain and from its height look down upon
the sixth where the 'Regal Herb' grows (*HM*, 1:46) he meant that the
alchemist had to rise high enough in awareness to be able to observe
the very matter of creation.

mountebank   see **theatre**.

mud   see **black earth**.

multiplication   the penultimate stage of the opus alchymicum, also known as the augmentation. At this point the *red stone (tincture) is repeatedly redissolved and coagulated in the *mercurial water upon which it has been
nourished at the *cibation. Some alchemists equate the cibation with
the multiplication. Isaac Newton wrote: 'cibation, fermentation and
multiplication are the same' (in Westfall, 'Index', 179). During the multiplication the weight, volume and potency of the Stone are greatly augmented and all the colours of the opus are said to appear in rapid
succession. Artephius advised the alchemist to take the red elixir and
reiterate the operation of dissolution and coagulation: 'Thus also is the
virtue thereof increased and multiplied both in quantity and quality; so
that, if after the first course of operation you obtain a hundred fold; by a
second course, you will have a thousand fold; and by a third, ten thousand fold increase. And by pursuing your work, your projection will
come to infinity, tinging truly and perfectly, and fixing the greatest
quantity how much soever' (*SB*, 42). As illustrated in this passage from
Artephius, the augmentation or multiplication is often merged with or
included as part of the final stage of the opus, the *projection, where the
tincture is thrown over base metal to transmute it into gold. In *Paradise
Lost* Milton plays with this alchemical metaphor when he speaks of
Venus and the other stars in the creation scene: 'they augment / Their
small peculiar' (their own inherent light) 'by tincture or reflection' of
the sun's 'quintessence' of light (7.367–9). A bawdy pun on 'multiplication' (and other alchemical terms) occurs in John Lyly's *Gallathea* when
Raffe and his brother Robin gossip about the alchemist's sex life: 'I sawe
a prettie wench come to his shoppe, where with puffing, blowing, and
sweating, he so plyed her, that hee multiplyed her' (5.1.18–21).

One of the most common symbols of the multiplication is that of the
*pelican who wounds her own breast to feed her many young with her

25 Pelican as symbol of the multiplication

blood (fig. 25). The Hydra or serpent, whose head when cut off produces ten more heads, is also a symbol of the multiplication, as is the spreading of colour in a substance when saffron is added. Colson's *Philosophia maturata* says of the white and red elixirs during multiplication (here identified with *projection): 'that as we see a great quantity of Water coloured with a little Saffron, so they may in the least quantity abundantly tinge every metal. And moreover, that themselves they may be infinitely multiplied, able to free the body of Man from the worst and most deadly diseases' (3–4).

multiplier   a person who transmutes base metal into silver or gold by alchemy. A multiplier is also a coiner or maker of counterfeit coins. The name is derived from the alchemical process known as *multiplication, which is often identified with the final stage in the opus, the *projection, when the *tincture is thrown over base metal to transmute it into gold. John Gower uses the verb 'multiply' to mean 'transmute': 'And also with great diligence, / Thei fonde thilke Experience: / Which cleped in *Alconomie*, / Whereof the Silver multeplie; / Thei made, and eke the Gold also' (TCB, 368). The term 'multiplier' is generally used pejoratively, referring to the charlatan trickster or to the deluded alchemist who frequently lost wealth and health in the attempt to make the *philosopher's stone. Sir George Ripley wrote of these alchemists in *The Compound of Alchymie*: 'Their Clothes be bawdy and woryn threde bare, / Men may them smell for Multiplyers where they go' (TCB, 153).

mundification   see **ablution**.

N

Naaman the leper the unclean metal or matter of the *philosopher's stone which must be washed and regenerated at the *ablution. The washing of the leprous Naaman seven times in the river Jordan refers to the purification of the body of the Stone, which is killed at the *nigredo and left to blacken and putrefy while the freed soul flies to the top of the alembic. Nicolas Flamel wrote that to cleanse the leprous body the alchemist 'must make it goe downe seven times into the River of regeneration of Iordan, as the Prophet commanded the Leprous Naaman the Syrian' (HE, 103). The motto to emblem 13 of Maier's *Atalanta fugiens* reads: 'The ore of the philosophers is dropsical and wants to be washed seven times in the river, just as Naaman, the Leper, washed in the Jordan' (AF, 124). The washing of Naaman refers to the *cooking of the black matter in the philosophical *fire (mercury) until it becomes white. The river Jordan is a symbol of the medicinal, purifying *mercurial water or aqua permanens with which the cooking and ablution are performed. See **leprosy.**

nail see **bind, cross.**

nature and art see **art and nature.**

nature's mystic book see **doctrine of signatures.**

neck see **crow's beak.**

nest the alchemical vessel. This is the place where the *philosopher's stone is incubated and generated. A popular symbol for the birth of the Stone is that of the *philosophical bird or chick hatching from the *egg in the nest of the philosophers. The treatise 'Aristeus Pater' says of the fire: 'let it be gentle, moist and sweet / Like that of Birds when on their Eggs they sit' while the Stone lies 'quiet in the Nest below' (lines 141–6, AP, 476). The 'Liber sapientiae' advised that the nest be made of strong material to withstand the rigours of the opus: 'Therefore their Nest must be made of a strong kinde, / Of the most hardest and cleerest Body ... For if it so be that Chamber or Nest begin to Breake, / Anon out thereof they will begin to Creake' (TCB, 202). See **alembic.**

night a symbol for the initial stage of the opus, the *nigredo. During the nigredo the old form or body of the metal is killed and dissolved into its original substance, the *prima materia. At this stage the body becomes blackened and putrefies. The nigredo is a time of blackness and death and is often conceived of as the night of the opus. Ripley referred to the nigredo as the 'shade of Night' (TCB, 180), and Synesius called it 'the sable Robe [and] Night' (*The True Book*, 171). At this point of blackness and death it is as if the sun has been eclipsed forever and the adept may experience the deep despair associated with the black night of the soul (see **eclipse, melancholia, sun and shadow**). The opus alchymicum consists of a reiterated cycle of dissolutions and coagulations of the Stone's matter in the alembic, and this cycle is sometimes compared to the sun's continual rotation around the earth (according to the Ptolemaic system). In this particular metaphor of the *solve et coagula, night signifies the time of dissolution (the nigredo) while day signifies the coagulation. See opus circulatorium.

nigredo the initial, black stage of the opus alchymicum in which the body of the impure metal, the matter for the Stone, or the old outmoded state of being is killed, putrefied and dissolved into the original substance of creation, the *prima materia, in order that it may be renovated and reborn in a new form. The alchemists, along with popular seventeenth-century belief, held that there could be no regeneration without corruption. Nature could only be renewed after first dying away. The biblical parable of the grain of wheat was cited to support their theory: 'Chryst do it wytnes, wythowt the grayne of Whete / Dye in the ground, encrease may thou not gete' (Ripley, in *TCB*, 158). In the process of generating the *philosopher's stone, the two seeds of metals, philosophical *sulphur (hot, dry, male) and philosophical *argent vive (cold, moist, female), must be obtained from the prima materia and then joined together. After they are united in the *chemical wedding, they are then killed and dissolved into their first matter by the universal solvent, *Mercurius. At the dissolution, the soul and spirit of the matter rise to the top of the alembic, separated from the body, which lies below, blackening and putrefying. The body is then washed by the *dew of mercurial water so that it may become pure and white, ready for reunion with the soul (or with the soul and spirit which have already united to form an entity).

The dissolution that takes place at the nigredo – sometimes called the mortification – is said to smell of the stench of graves and is frequently represented by the image of the bodies of the united lovers (sulphur and argent vive) lying in a coffin or grave while their souls float above them. Sometimes their united bodies are depicted as one hermaphroditic body (see **hermaphrodite**). Other symbols of the dissolution and putrefaction at the nigredo are the skeleton, the skull, the angel of death, *Saturn with his scythe, the *eclipse of sun and moon, the beheaded king or bird, the crow's head, the severed head, and all things black – *night, *the crow, *the raven, coal, pitch, ebony, the black man, Moor or *Ethiopian. Ripley wrote of the nigredo: 'But hyt hath Names I say to the infynyte, / For after each thyng that Blacke ys to syght' (*TCB*, 134) (see **black**). The dissolution is also symbolized by the *flood, tears, the *sweat bath, the dismemberment of the mercurial *serpent or *dragon, the truncated *tree, the *beheading of the bird or chopping off of the *lion's paws and the death of the *king (sometimes compared to Christ's crucifixion).

The beginning of the opus is a time of bloodshed and lamentation. Fabricius commented on the opening emblem of Trismosin's *Splendor Solis*: 'Its season of spring is a season of sacrifice, its river a life stream of blood' (*Alchemy*, 17). During this black time of suffering, despair and melancholia may cast their shadow over the alchemist. In Johann

Andreae's *The Chymical Wedding* the adepts become sad as they watch the beheading of the *philosophical bird: 'His Death went to the heart of us' (160). The beginning of spiritual realization is always accompanied by some kind of sacrifice or death, a dying to the old state of things, in order to make way for new insight and creation. Burckhardt observed that the turning away from the outer world to the inner to face the shadow of the psyche is frequently experienced as a nox profunda, before the dawning of the new light of illumination (*Alchemy*, 186). The nigredo is a difficult phase, but only through experiencing it can the adept gain the wisdom and humility necessary for illumination.

Nile   the arcane transforming substance or *mercurial water, known as the mercurial *serpent; the name of an Egyptian retort. In the Western world alchemy had its origins in Alexandria, so the river Nile (and the *crocodile) became readily absorbed into alchemical symbolism. Thomas Vaughan called the mercurial water 'the Originall of Nilus' (*vw (W)*, 247). In Michael Maier's *Lusus Serius: or Serious Passe-time*, Mercury, contending for the title of king amongst nature's creature's, compares himself to the Nile: '[My utility to man] is so immense and so rich, that like the Prince of Rivers, the *Nile* (which dischargeth itselfe by a seven-fold streame unto the Mediterranean Sea) spreads and divides it self into so many branches, according to the number of Metallick formes, which merely draw their rise and being from me' (91). The mud of the Nile, which was thought to possess alchemical properties, was one of the symbols of the *prima materia. In 'Upon Appleton House' Andrew Marvell wrote of the subsiding *flood waters as both serpent and Nile in an alchemical context: 'No *Serpent* new nor *Crocodile* / Remains behind our little *Nile*; / Unless it self you will mistake / Among these Meads the only Snake' (lines 629–32).

Noah   In alchemical legend Noah is said to have kept the *Emerald Table safe from the *flood waters in the *ark. He is also supposed to have preserved the *philosopher's stone from destruction by the flood. *The Sophic Hydrolith* remarks that by the aid of the Stone 'Noah is said to have built the Ark' (*HM*, 1:86). Noah's flood is also a symbol for the *dissolution of the Stone's matter into the *prima materia during the *nigredo. At this stage of the opus the cold, moist, feminine principle (*Luna, argent vive) is said to dominate the hot, dry, coagulating male aspect of the opus (*Sol, sulphur). Sir George Ripley wrote: 'the Waters of *Noyes* flud / On Erth, whych were a hundred dayes contynuate / And fyfty, away or all thys Waters yode, / Ryght so our Waters as wyse men understode / Shall passe' (*TCB*, 151). During this time of dissolution, the alchemical vessel is symbolized by Noah's ark (see **ark, flood**). In *A Compound of Alchemy* Ripley compared the growth of the Stone into the red elixir to Noah's cultivation of grapes: 'Sone after that *Noe* plantyd hys Vyneyard, /Whych really floryshed and brought forth Graps anon … For in lykewyse shall follow the floryshyng of our *Stone*: / And sone uppon that thyrty dayes overgone, / Thou shalt have Graps ryght as the Ruby red' (*TCB*, 151).

nose   the tube-like part of the alembic which is sometimes called the 'head'. In *Fasciculus chemicus* Arthur Dee quotes Arnold of Villanova's description of the mercurial water descending 'by the Nose of the Alembick' (16) (see **head**).

O

oak   a name for the *philosophical tree. The image of the hollow oak is also used to designate the alchemical vessel or the oven in which the vessel is placed (see **tree (truncated)**). In Bernard Trevisan's 'Practise of the Philosophic Stone', the king places a hollow oak over the magic fountain or spring (the mercurial water): 'Around the Top he plact an aged Oak / Which had been with an artificiall Stroak / Cleft in the middle' (*AP*, 451). The hollow oak against which Cadmus pierced the serpent with his lance is said to signify the completion of the operation of making the *philosopher's stone. In the alchemical interpretation of this myth, Cadmus symbolizes the alchemist, the serpent, philosophical mercury, the lance, the fire, and the oak, the *athanor in which the alchemical *egg or vessel sits. Philalethes advised the alchemist: 'learn then, who are the friends of Cadmus ... what the hollow oak to which Cadmus spitted the serpent' (*HM*, 2:166). Isaac Newton likewise wrote in 'Praxis': 'The Serpent must then devour the companions of Cadmus and be fixed by him to an hollow Oak' (Dobbs, *Janus*, 301). Musgrove has argued that Robert Herrick's 'To the King and Queene, upon their unhappy distances' is alchemical and that the oak is 'a common type of the life-giving alchemical tree' (Musgrove, 'Herrick's alchemical vocabulary', 253): 'Like Streams, you are divorc'd; but 'twill come, when / These eyes of mine shall see you mix agen. / Thus speaks the Oke, here; C. and M. shall meet, / Treading on *Amber*, with their silver feet' (lines 5–10). The alchemical oak is illustrated in 'De Alchimia' (*c.* 1526) (van Lennep, *Alchimie*, 98).

odour   see **fragrance, smell**.

open and shut   the same as dissolve and coagulate. In *The Marrow of Alchemy* Philalethes wrote: 'For all our Art is but to ope and shut, / To loose, and after that to recongele' (bk. 3, 56). See **solve et coagula**.

opus circulatorium   the opus alchymicum, also known as the circular work of the elements. Simple circulation consists of the continuous distillation of liquid for the purpose of refinement. During the opus the matter for the Stone must be dissolved and returned to its primal state before it can be recreated or coagulated into the new pure form of the *philosopher's stone. This cycle of *solve et coagula or *separation and union has to be reiterated many times throughout the opus. During this circulation, the

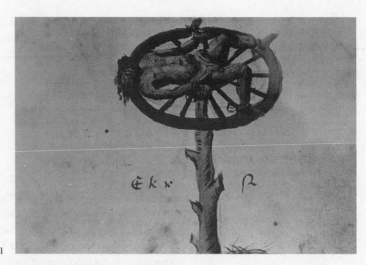

26 The philosophical wheel

elements earth, air, fire and water are separated by *distillation and converted into each other to form the perfect unity, the *fifth element. This conversion takes place by unifying the qualities that each element has in common: earth which is cold and dry may be united with water through the common quality of coldness since water is cold and moist (or fluid), water may be united with air through fluidity since air is hot and fluid, and air is united to fire through heat, since fire is hot and dry. In another alchemical metaphor, this process is described as the transformation of the square (four elements) into the circle (the united fifth element) (see **square and circle**).

This process of transformation, of successively converting the elements into each other, is often compared to the turning of a great wheel. An emblem from the 'Buch von Vunderverken' shows a man symbolizing the matter to be converted being tortured on the wheel (fig. 26). Colson's *Philosophia maturata* states that 'nothing can be made an *Elixer*, untill it hath pass'd the Philosophical Wheel; which being unknown, all labour comes to nothing' (44). Sir George Ripley described the rotation of the 'Wheele of the Elements': 'But fyrst of these Elements make thou Rotacyon, / And into Water thy Erth turne fyrst of all; / Then of thy water make Ayre by Levygation; / And Ayre make Fyre' (*TCB*, 133). In Jonson's *The Alchemist* Face likewise tells us that the process which Subtle has described as the turning of 'the philosopher's wheel' involves 'shifting, sir, your elements / Drie into cold, cold into moist, moist into hot, hot into drie' (2.5.36–9). The contrary qualities of the four elements are likened to quarrelling foes who must be reconciled and united in order for harmony to reign (see **peace**). The circulation of elements is identical with the process the alchemists describe as the conversion of body into spirit, and spirit into body, until each is able to mingle together, or unite in the *chemical wedding to form a new perfect being, the *philosopher's stone (see **conversion**). Other images used to represent the circular work are the *uroboros (the serpent which ingests its own tail, thus forming a circle) and the sun's circular course around the earth (in the Ptolemaic view of the universe). Benjamin Lock compared the turning of the 'wheele of philosophy' to the passage of the sun's 'fyery chariot' ('Picklock', f. 28). Ruland wrote that the alchemists likened the circulation of the elements (the solve et coagula) to 'the Movement or Revolution of the Heavens' (*Lexicon*, 347).

opus contra naturam   the work against nature, a name for the opus alchymicum. The process of creating the *philosopher's stone requires that the alchemist consciously turn back to the divine source, against the outward thrust of nature, in order to know the secret of creation and its laws. In order for regeneration to occur, the imperfect metal (or outmoded state of being) has first to be destroyed. It must be dissolved into the original stuff of creation, the *prima materia, before a new, purified *microcosm or Stone can be reconstructed or created. This apparently destructive and backward-turning movement of the *wheel of the philosophers which occurs at the beginning of the opus is known as the opus contra naturam. Ripley advised the alchemist that in order to go forward he must first 'go backward, turnyng thy Wheele againe' (*TCB*, 133). Metaphysically, the opus contra naturam requires that the adept first turn inward to experience pure consciousness so that he can acknowledge and integrate the dark aspect of the pysche.

orphan   one of the names of the *philosopher's stone. The Stone is born from the union and death of its parents, *sulphur and *argent vive, and so it is said to be an orphan found ready formed by the alchemist, who acts the part of its foster parent, nurturing it until it grows to maturity (see **cibation, education**). Paracelsus wrote: 'The most wise *Mercurius* the wisest of the Philosophers affirms, the same, hath called the Stone an Orphan' (*Aurora*, 51). In Johann Andreae's *The Chymical Wedding* the alchemical babe is found floating on the water in 'a little *Chest*' and is brought to the king who becomes her foster-parent (111–12). Martin Ruland wrote of the alchemical foster-parent in his *Lexicon of Alchemy* that 'The Chemical Philosophers find their infant ready formed by nature' (378). Musgrove has argued that Robert Herrick's poem 'Orphan' is alchemical: 'A Lamb / I keepe (tame) with my morsells fed, / Whose Dam / An Orphan left him (lately dead)' (lines 1–4). According to Musgrove, Herrick's poem alludes to the *taming of the mercurial beast, the feeding or *cibation of the Stone (the lamb), and the fact that the *philosophical child or stone is an orphan because the alchemical mother and father must die before the child is born (Musgrove, 'Herrick's alchemical vocabulary', 245). See **chemical wedding**.

our   The possessive adjective 'our' is regularly used in alchemical texts in front of any noun denoting a material, substance, force or vessel which performs philosophical operations, as opposed to 'vulgar' or merely physical operations. 'Our gold', for example, refers not to common gold (Au) but to the seed of gold or the *prima materia from which gold may be grown (see gold, green lion). 'Our sulphur' refers not to common *sulphur (S) but to the masculine 'seed' of metals, the hot, dry, active principle of the opus which must be united with the cold, moist, receptive female seed or principle, philosophical *argent vive, in order to produce the *philosopher's stone. Bloomfield wrote of 'Our greate *Elixir* most high of price, / Our *Azot*, our *Basaliske*, our *Adrop*, and our *Cockatrice*' (TCB, 312). In Jonson's *The Alchemist*, Surly, who takes a cynical view of Subtle's alchemy, parodies the alchemists' possessive 'our' with the repeated ironic 'your' attached to an endless list of alchemical terms: 'What else are all your termes, / Whereon no one o' your writers grees with other?/ Of your *elixir*, your *lac virginis*, / Your *stone*, your *med'cine*, and your *chrysosperme*, / Your *sal*, your *sulphur*, and your *mercurie*, / Your *oyle of height*, your *tree of life*, your *bloud*, / Your *marchesite*, your *tutie*, your *magnesia*, / Your *toade*, your *crow*, your *dragon*, and your *panthar*, / Your *sunne*, your *moone*, your *firmament*, your *adrop*' (2.3.182–190). The term 'nostrum' (Latin neuter singular of *noster*, our), meaning 'A quack remedy, a patent medicine, *esp.* one prepared by the person recommending it' (OED), derives from alchemical usage.

oval   (from the Latin *ovum*), the alchemical vessel, also known as the philosopher's *egg. Jodocus Greverius wrote that during the first decoction of the Stone's matter, 'there will rise from the earth a certain humidity of Argent vive like a Cloud, and will stick to the upper part of thy vacant Oval by its sides' (ZC, 71). Edward Kelly described the multiplication of the Stone: 'And now yt is the perfect Stone Elixir fully compleat yet must you easily Multiply it by feeding it with more mercury still as you did before … and then again mixt up in an ovall Glasse, begin with an Easey heate to procure blackness first' ('Exposition', f. 61).

P

panacea   see **medicine**.

panther   see **toad**.

paradise   see **Adam, albedo, Elysian Fields, heaven**.

paste   the purified, whitened body (or earth) of the Stone. The coniunctio or *chemical wedding of the Stone's soul with its purified body during *fermentation is often compared to the making of bread. The ferment or soul sown into the white earth of the body is likened to the addition of leaven to paste or dough. Ripley wrote: 'For lyke as flower of Whete made into Past, / Requyreth Ferment whych Leven we call / Of Bred … Ryght so thy Medcyn Ferment thou shall / That yt may tast wyth the Ferment pure, / And all assays evermore endure' (TCB, 175). The soul or ferment is the vital force which re-animates the amorphous purified matter (or body) of the the Stone and gives it a new and more beautiful form. In Johann Andreae's *The Chymical Wedding*, Christian Rosencreutz tells of the 'thin Dough' which is cast 'hot as it was into two *little* forms or moulds'. After cooling, the moulds are opened and 'there appeared two beautiful bright and almost *Transparent little* images, the like to which Mans Eye never saw, a male and female ... yet they had no Life'. The life force is then supplied by the re-entry of the souls into the bodies through a tube (199, 203). Texts such as *The Six Keys of Eudoxus* (in Regardie, *Philosopher's Stone*, 114) and Philalethes' commentary on Ripley's 'Vision' (RR, 9) compare the feeding of the dissolved body with mercurial water during the *nigredo to the addition of leaven to bread. The corroding solvent makes the blackening body of the Stone puff and swell in the same way as dough is puffed up by leaven.

peace and **strife**   Peace is the harmonious state attained when the opposing principles of the opus, *sulphur (male, hot, dry, active) and *argent vive (female, cold, moist, receptive), are united in the *chemical wedding. Benjamin Lock wrote: 'peace is made by ioyning 2 extremes together, that is to say sulph: and arg: vive' ('Picklock', f. 25). Sulphur contains the elements air and fire, while argent vive is composed of earth and water, which are 'enemies' to air and fire. During the early, primitive stages of the opus, sulphur and mercury, body and spirit, are often referred to as the quarrelling couple. Thus the chemical wedding paradoxically comes about through a process of strife. The reconciliation of the couple is also known as the conversion of the four elements (see **opus circulatorium**). The elements with their opposing qualities are said to be warring, conflicting foes until reconciled and united in peace. This union may take place by the reconciliation of that quality which each element has in common with the other: earth is cold and dry and thus shares coldness with water which is cold and moist, water shares moistness (or fluidity) with air which is hot and fluid, and air shares heat with fire that is hot and dry. Nicolas Flamel wrote that the warring elements 'by meanes of the *Mediators* and Peace-makers lay downe by little and little, the ancient enmity of the old *Chaos*' (HE, 84). Benjamin Lock wrote that 'after long strife [the elements] are made frendes, concluding in such a perfecte unity as can not be broken' ('Picklock', f. 25). In John Donne's 'An Anatomy of the World: The first Anniversary', Elizabeth Drury's perfection is described as a harmonious union of the elements: 'Both elements and passions lived at peace / In her, who caused all civil war to cease' (lines 321–2). In the alchemical process, a sign that 'peace' is beginning to reign is the advent of the *rainbow and the appearance in the vessel of 'drops of perle or the eyes of fishes, firmely standing upon the earthe' (Lock, 'Picklock', f. 26). See **pearls, fishes' eyes, peacock's tail**.

peacock's flesh   see **peacock's tail**.

peacock's tail   the stage occurring immediately after the deathly black stage or *nigredo, and just prior to the pure white stage or *albedo. After the nigredo, the blackened body of the Stone is washed and purified by the *mercurial water during the process of *ablution. When the blackness of the nigredo is washed away, it is succeeded by the appearance of all the

27 Peacock's tail

colours of the *rainbow, which look like a peacock displaying its lumi-nescent tail (fig. 27). Jung has suggested that the basis for this phenome-non may be the iridescent skin that often forms on the surface of molten metal (MC, 285). Philalethes wrote: 'after black, / The colours of the Rainbow did appear / the Peacock's-Tayl' (*Marrow*, bk. 2, 30); and Roger Bacon observed that 'there appears also before whiteness, the peacock's colour, whereon one saith this. Know thou that all the colours in the world, or may be imagined, appeare before whiteness, and afterward true whitenesse followeth' (*Mirror*, 13). The appearance of the peacock's tail is a welcome sign that the dawning of the albedo is at hand, that the matter is now purified and ready for re-animation by the illumined soul. The image of eating or consuming the peacock's flesh which occurs in Ripley's 'Cantilena' (verse 17) represents the integration of the many rainbow colours into the single, pure, white colour symbolizing a state of purity and unity. The peacock or peacock's tail is one in a succession of bird images which the alchemists employ to represent the stages of the opus: the black *crow or *raven for the nigredo, the peacock for the many-coloured stage, the swan or dove for the white *albedo, and the phoenix for the red *rubedo. In Ben Jonson's *The Alchemist*, Face assures Mammon that he has put the matter of the Stone through the three stages of black, rainbow and white: 'the *crow*, / The *peacock's taile*, / and *plumed swan*' (2.2.102).

pearls   a sign that the matter of the Stone has reached the *ablution, during which stage the matter is washed of its impurities; also a symbol of the succeeding white stage or *albedo. Some alchemists compared the rising and descending vapours and waters in the alembic during the washing process of the *ablution to *dew, *rain or pearls. Philalethes wrote that at this stage of the opus there 'shall rise a vapour, like pearl orient, / which shall the Dark earth from its filthiness / With gentle showers wash' (*Marrow*, bk. 3, 55). In Thomas Vaughan's alchemical poem 'Hyanthe', the washing of the blackened matter is compared to tears which 'In *Chaines* of *liquid Pearle* did fall' (*VW* (R), 205). Other texts apply the image of pearls to the stage after the many colours of the peacock's tail, just before the true whiteness of the albedo. Trithemius wrote: 'Before the clear Splendent colour comes, all the Colours in the world will appear and disappear: then ... before the True whitenesse comes, thou shalt see all about in the margin of the Glass as it were Oriental pearls, in the matter of the Stone, glittering like the Eyes of fishes' (in *ZC*, 80). Pearls are also used to symbolize the albedo and the *white stone or elixir (see Locke', Picklock', f. 12v). After cleansing and purification, the previously corrupted, putrefied body (the earth) of the Stone is said to appear shining white, like pearls. (See **fishes' eyes**.) Trismosin's *Splendor Solis* describes the first fruit of the *philosophical tree (a symbol for the process of the opus) as pearls: 'The First are the very finest Pearls. The second are called by the Philosophers TERRA FOLIATA. The Third is the very purest Gold' (28).

pelican   a form of circulatory still which resembles a pelican with its beak to its breast (fig. 28); a symbol for the red elixir and for the stage in the opus known as the *multiplication. Bassett Jones wrote of the circulatory still: 'Circulation is the exaltation of a liquor by a circular motion ... *per pelicanum* (by pelican)' (*AP*, 355). Edward Kelly mentioned the pelican as a vessel in a letter to Edward Dyer, 14 September 1595: 'I was wont with the spirit of wine in glasses, and especially in such vessels as they commonly call pelicans, by the means of the gentle vapour of the bath, to elevate the calces of metals' (Bod. Ashm. MS 1420, 328). A recipe for making the *elixir in Colson's *Philosophia maturata* instructs the alchemist to 'Dissolve the red Calx of *Sol* and *Mercurie* in the first most strong corrosive composed of Salt-Peter and Vitriol the common way; put the Solution in a pelican in balneo, drawing off the one half, then stop it most close, dry it up with a gentle heat' (60). In Jonson's *The Alchemist*, Face informs Subtle that 'the Retort brake, / And what was sau'd was put into the *Pelicane*' (2.3.77–8).

28   The pelican vessel

The pelican is also a symbol of the *red elixir. The red elixir, issuing like a *fountain of blood from the *white stone, was thought to resemble the pelican who pierces her own breast to nourish her young with her blood without diminution of her strength. The pelican nourishing her young naturally became a symbol of the *cibation, when the infant Stone is fed with the mercurial *blood. It also symbolizes the stage known as the multiplication, sometimes identified with the cibation (see fig. 25). During the multiplication, the penultimate stage in the opus, the potency and quantity of the red elixir or stone are augmented by more than a thousandfold through the reiterated dissolution and coagulation of the matter in the *mercurial water. An emblem illustrating the multiplication in Johann Mylius's *Philosophia reformata* shows the alchemical queen riding on a lion who feeds numerous young cubs and holding in her left hand the hermetic vessel containing the pelican wounding her breast. The image depicting the pelican's generosity to her young admirably symbolizes the quality of abundance which occurs at this stage when the opus is reaching its culmination.

persecution see **torture.**

Phaethon see **chariot of Phaethon.**

phial see **vial.**

philosopher an alchemist, as seen in the terms *philosopher's stone, *philosopher's egg, *philosopher's earth, philosophical mercury. In the sixteenth and seventeenth centuries one of the definitions of the term 'philosophy' applied to alchemy. 'The publisher's epistle to the Reader' prefaced to 'Hermetick Raptures' referred to alchemy as 'the Metallick Philosophy' (*AP*, 566). The alchemists were known as natural philosophers because they were concerned not only with researching the outer aspect of the workings of nature but with discovering nature's inner essences and subtle virtues. The alchemical philosophers were concerned not merely with material alchemy but with medical and spiritual alchemy. Allen Debus writes in *Chemistry, Alchemy and the New Philosophy* that the Paracelsians 'have too often been dismissed either as a very difficult medical sect or as chemists who failed to bring about a chemical revolution. It is surely more correct to think of them as Chemical Philosophers – a term they used with regularity themselves' (236). B. J. T. Dobbs has written that the 'seventeenth-century epithet "philosopher by fire" distinguished the serious philosophical alchemist from the empiric "puffer" or the devious charlatan or the amateur "chymist"' (*Janus*, 1). In his prolegomena to Arthur Dee's *Fasciculus chemicus*, Elias Ashmole, for example, makes a distinction between the material 'chymist' and the philosophical alchemist: 'the *Philosophers* tell us, *One Glass, one Furnace, one Fire*, (and that an *immaterial* one, not to be found in the *Furnace* of the *Chymists*), is *sufficient to perfect the work*' (*FC*, n.p.). Arthur Dee wrote in the preface to 'Arca arcanorum' of the rarity of the true philosopher: 'But truly I found not one Man for Thirty yeers together, that wrought upon the proper Matter, and consequently not any who deserved the name of a *Philosopher*' ('Arca', n.p.).

philosopher's earth   see **ashes, black earth.**

philosopher's egg   see **egg.**

philosopher's stone   the much sought-after goal of the opus alchymicum and the most famous of all alchemical ideas. The Stone is the arcanum of all arcana, possessing the power to perfect imperfection in all things, able to transmute base metals into pure gold and transform the earthly man into an illumined philosopher. It is the figure of light veiled in dark matter, that divine love essence which combines divine wisdom and creative power, often identified with Christ as creative Logos, or with the Eastern idea of the *atman* symbolized by the jewel in the lotus. Edward Benlowes wrote of the philosopher's stone as divine love and grace in his *Theophila or Loves Sacrifice. A Divine Poem*: 'Convert dull *lead* to active *Gold* by LOVE-CHYMIE' (9), and 'Turn Sense to *Spirit*, Nature's chang'd alone / By GRACE; THAT is the *Chymick-stone*' (12). During the transformation in man, the aspect of the psyche which is unconscious (the shadow) is illumined by consciousness. The two previously separated aspects of the psyche become integrated, creating harmonious unity. The Stone is known as the universal *medicine because it can dispel all corruption, heal all disease and suffering, and bestow youth, longevity and wisdom. *The Sophic Hydrolith* described it as 'the cure for all unsound and imperfect metals – the everlasting light – the panacea for all diseases – the glorious Phoenix – the most precious of treasures' (HM, 1:97). *The Book of Lambspring* said of the mercurial 'blood' used to make the Stone: 'From it the Sages derive their science, / And through it they attain the Heavenly Gift, / Which is called the Philosopher's Stone, / Possessing the power of the whole world' (HM, 1:294). The *Clangor buccinae* says of the Stone's power to bestow youth: 'Wrincles of the face, every litura or spot, gray haires, it takes away, and keeps us in perpetual youth and cheerfulnesse' (ZC, 88).

   This supreme substance of the philosophers is always referred to in a most paradoxical, enigmatic and riddling way. Such statements as 'It is a stone and not a stone' (probably originating with Democritus, d. ?357 BC, but perhaps with Zosimos of Panopolis *c*. AD 300 or 'Aristotle') and 'It costs nothing, is vile and mean but is the most valuable treasure on earth' ('noble and worthless, valuable and of small account' – *The Golden Tract*, HM, 1:10) are recurring refrains in the alchemical texts. Calid wrote: 'This Stone is vile, blacke and stinking: It costeth nothing' (*Booke of the Secrets*, 40). Colson's *Philosophia maturata* states that the Stone is 'cast out into the Dunghill, and trodden under mens feet, it is counted a most vile and contemptible thing' (15) and 'the Stone is equally common both to the Poor and Rich. These things considered, thou shalt understand, that our Stone lyeth hidden, and secretly lurketh, often in places least suspected, and nothing esteemed, whose matter and nearness, if it should be known, would produce most great danger' (66). The statement that the Stone is a stone but not a stone occurs in nearly every treatise. Calid wrote: 'Take the Stone, no Stone, or that is not a Stone, neither is of the nature of a Stone' (*Booke of the Secrets*, 41). Face, in Ben Jonson's *The Alchemist*, says of the *lapis philosophicus*: "'Tis a *stone*, and not / A *stone*' (2.5.40–1). Although often described as being in powder or tincture form, the philosopher's stone is referred to as a 'stone' because it is the supreme crystallization in form of the precious life-essence. For this reason it is sometimes compared to such precious stones as ruby, pearl, sapphire and diamond.

In many instances the Stone is described as having two forms: the white stone attained at the *albedo (the lunar stage) which can transmute base metal into silver, and the red stone of the *rubedo (the solar stage) which can transmute base metals into gold. In order to make the philosopher's stone the alchemist must understand the laws of nature so that he can reproduce God's macrocosmic creation in the microcosm of the alembic. The first step in this task is to obtain the very stuff of creation, the *prima materia, from which, in alchemical theory, all metals (and all created things) are thought to be made. This materia is the principal substance of the Stone and is known as philosophical mercury (*Mercurius), a substance distinct from vulgar or physical mercury (Hg). The philosopher's mercury is obtained through the reduction of gold and silver into their elementary substance, which contains the living male and female seeds, *sulphur and *argent vive (mercury), necessary for the generation of the Stone in the dialectic of creation. *The Golden Tract* stated that 'the substance of our Stone should be pure and perfect mercury combined with pure, subtle and incombustible sulphur' (HM, 1: 24). When male sulphur (the hot, dry, active principle of the prima materia) is combined with female argent vive (the cold, moist, receptive principle), the philosopher's stone is conceived and born. It is said to be born, like a child, from the union of the archetypal opposites, *Sol and *Luna (sulphur and argent vive), in the *chemical wedding. Sol represents the active, male force of the universe (creative will), while Luna represents the receptive female force (wisdom). The infant Stone is sometimes personified as a male, and at other times as a female when the alchemist wishes to stress the divine knowledge/wisdom aspect of the pure love essence which arises from the union of opposites. John Collop wrote in 'On Dr. George Bowle of Oundle': 'Knowledge is th' Suns Child, true Philosophers Stone' (line 6). The Stone is said to be composed of a perfect balance of elements and forces. *Zoroaster's Cave* said of the Stone's perfect balance of the elements: 'All defections from natural Symmetry are reduced by it to Temperament, because there is a perfect Aequation of Elements' (88). John Pontanus's *Epistle upon the Mineral Fire* states: 'It is then the Philosophers Stone, but is called by various names, and thou shalt find it hard to know: For it is Watry, Aery, Fiery and Earthy; Phlegmatic, Choleric, and Melancholic; it is Sulphureous, and is likewise argent vive' (93–4).

The alchemists also stated that the Stone, like a man, is composed of body, soul and spirit. The body has the power to fix or coagulate the spirit. The spirit has the power to dissolve and penetrate the body. The soul has the power to re-animate the body and unite the body and spirit in perfect harmony: 'The Sages have affirmed that our Stone is composed of body, soul, and spirit, and they have spoken truly. For the imperfect part they have compared to a body, because it is weak. The water they have called spirit ... The ferment they have termed soul, because it gives life to the imperfect body (which before was dead) and makes its form more beautiful' (HM, 1:150). In Jonson's *The Alchemist* Face reiterates this theory when he answers Subtle's query, 'Your *lapis philosophicus?*' with ''Tis a *stone*, and not / A *stone*; a *spirit*, a *soule*, and a *body*' (2.5.40–1).

Jung has written that by the fourteenth century it had begun to dawn on the alchemists that the Stone was something more than an alchemical compound (MC, 475). But the spiritual component of Alexandrine and Islamic alchemy entered Europe as an integral part of that science. Zosimos of Panopolis (third–fourth century AD) had written that the alchemist must seek his origin in order to 'obtain the proper, authentic, and natural tinctures' and that this was accomplished by 'plunging into meditation' (JA, 55). Calid had stated that 'This Stone is to be found at all times, in everie place, and about every man' (*Booke of the Secrets*, 40). This tradition was inherited by the medieval alchemists and the alchemists of Renaissance Europe. Many were aware of the fact that the Stone or the matter for making the Stone was to be found in man himself. Ripley wrote: 'Every-ech Man yt hath, and ys in every place, / In thee, in me, in every tyme and space' (TCB, 123), and Philalethes wrote that Morienus informed his pupil, the king, that he must 'descend / Into himself the matter for to finde / Of this our stone' (*Marrow*, bk. 4, 62). Gerhard Dorn likewise indicated that panacea was the truth to be found in man (MC, 478). Colson's *Philosophia maturata*, states that the Stone 'is generated between Male and Female and lieth hide [*sic*] in Thee, in Me, and in such like things' (15). In the production of the Stone, the alchemist was advised to employ his imagination as the major tool. Arnoldus is cited in *Zoroaster's Cave*: 'Follow it with the Instance of Labour, but first exercise thyself in a diuturnity of Intense Imagination: for so thou mayst find the compleat Elixir; but without that never at all' (89).

It is generally thought that the elixir and philosopher's stone are of the same essence, the elixir being in liquid form, the Stone being in solid or powder form. Chaucer's Canon's Yeoman identifies the two: 'the philosopher's stoon, / Elixir clept, we sechen faste echoon' (*Canon's Yeoman's Tale*, lines 862–3). Colson's *Philosophia maturata* indicates that there is a difference between them: 'betwixt the Elixer and the Stone there is this difference; for the Stone rejoyceth in unity and simplicity, but the Elixer in plurality' (22). The Stone is endowed with many names, some of which are: elixir, tincture, medicine, panacea, balsam, arcanum, quintessence, tree, rose, lily, hyacinth, east, morning, living fountain, white stone, red stone, ruby, crystal, diamond, sapphire, Adam, paradise, Sophia, hermaphrodite, man, red king, red lion, microcosm, salvator, servator, filius macrocosmi, homunculus, sun, son, daughter, orphan, bird, Hermes bird and phoenix. John Read has suggested that the alchemical authors seem to have regarded it as 'a mark of their originality to advance a new name for the Stone' (*Prelude*, 127). Despite the many names of the Stone, the alchemists stressed that it personified unity and consisted in one thing and one thing only. Morienus wrote: 'For it is one Stone, one med'cin, in which consists the whole magistery', and the *Scala philosophorum* stated: 'The Stone is one: Yet this one is not one in Number, but in kind' (zc, 66, 68). The idea of the philosopher's stone was so well known in the Renaissance that Shakespeare could depend on the audience of *Timon of Athens* to respond to the bawdy joke made by the Fool in answer to Varro's servant's question, 'What is a whore master, fool?' The Fool replies that he is 'sometimes like a philosopher, with two stones more than's artificial one' (2.2.111–15). In *The Jew of Malta* Christopher Marlowe has Barabas sarcastically challenge the high price asked for a young Turk in the market-place with 'What, hast the philosopher's stone? An thou hast, break my head with it; I'll forgive thee' (2.3.114–17). When Satan in Milton's *Paradise Lost* first lands on the sun and experiences its dazzling brilliance, he finds it difficult to describe but reports that it might be something like the philosopher's stone, which is 'Imagined rather oft then elsewhere seen, / That stone, or like to that which here below / Philosophers in vain so long have sought' (3.599–601). The idea of the alchemist in search of the philosopher's stone still persisted in literature in the nineteenth century. Balzac wrote of his hero Balthazar Claes: 'Balthazar was put under the ban of society; he was a bad father, who had run through half-a-dozen fortunes, who had spent millions of francs on the search for the Philosopher's Stone in this enlightened nineteenth century, the century of incredulity' (*The Quest of the Absolute*, 219–20). P. G. Wodehouse must also have expected his twentieth-century audience to understand his comic reference to the Stone when he wrote of the obsessive golfer: 'Confidence! That was what Wallace Chesney lacked, and that, as he saw it, was the prime grand secret of golf. Like an alchemist on the track of the Philosopher's Stone, he was for ever seeking for something that would really give him confidence' (*The Heart of a Goof*, 105).

philosophical bird   see **Bird of Hermes**.

philosophical child   the *philosopher's stone when it is first born from the union of *Sol and *Luna at the *chemical wedding. The *Emerald Table* states of this child that 'the father thereof is the Sun, the mother the Moon'. Isaac Newton wrote in his commentary on the *Emerald Table*: 'And this generation is similar to the human, truly from a father and a mother, which are the Sun and the Moon. And when the Infant is conceived through the coition of these, he is borne continuously in the belly of the wind until the hour of birth, and after birth he is nourished at the breasts of foliated Earth until he grows up' (Dobbs, *Janus*, 276). The generation of the philosopher's stone is frequently likened to the birth of an infant or *homunculus (fig. 29; and see fig. 18). An anonymous treatise says that after the wedding of Sol, the 'red man', and Luna, the 'white woman', 'she will come to him again and lye with him on bed and then she shall conceive and bear a Son, that shall worship all his Kin ... For this Man

29 The birth of the philosophical child

and this Woman getteth our Stone' (GU Ferguson MS 238, f. 2v). *The Glory of the World* observed: 'Hence it is well, though somewhat enigmatically said by the Sages, that there takes place a conjugal union of husband and wife, and that of the two a child is born after their likeness, just as men generate men' (*HM*, 1:232–3). Morienus wrote: 'For the conduct of this operation you must have pairing, production of offspring, birth and rearing. For union is followed by conception, which initiates pregnancy, whereupon birth follows. Now the performance of this [alchemical] composition is likened to the generation of man, whom the great Creator most high made not after the manner in which a house is constructed, nor as anything else which is built by the hand of man' (*Testament*, 29).

The infant Stone is also sometimes personified as a female child representing sophia or wisdom (see Andreae, *The Chymical Wedding* (48), and Mylius, *Philosophia reformata*, embl. 17, second series). During the conception and birth of the Stone the alembic is known as the *womb or the *bed of birth. The Stone is known as the *orphan and the alchemist plays the role of its foster-parent. As Ruland noted, 'The Chemical Philosophers find their infant ready formed by nature' (*Lexicon*, 379). During the *cibation, the alchemist must gradually nourish the infant Stone with 'milk' and 'meat' (the white and red mercurial waters) so that it may become sweet and strong. When it has grown to maturity this infant has the power to conquer all disease and transform all things to perfection. Arthur Dee wrote of the infant Stone's maturation into the spiritual warrior: 'he will become a king, stronger than a king, and so stout in Battell, that he alone being a most powerful Conqueror, will obtain the Victory against ten thousand Enemies' (FC, 110).

philosophical mercury see **Mercurius**.

philosophical tree an ancient symbol used to represent the course of the opus alchymicum, the growth of gold and maturation of the *philosopher's stone, the alchemical process itself, and the unfolding of the psyche during the the opus. Paracelsus wrote: 'Gold, through industry and skill of an expert Alchymist may bee so far exalted that it may grow in a glass like a tree, with many wonderful boughs and leaves ... which the Alchymists call their Golden hearb, and the Philosophers Tree' (*Nine Books*, 16–17). The tree symbolizes growth and fruition, in both a physical and spiritual sense. It represents the development of the arcane substance from the *prima materia (the original stuff of creation) to the ultima materia, the all-transforming philosopher's stone. Michael Maier wrote that the 'philosophers call their stone vegetable, because it grows and multiplies like a plant' (AF, 226).

The alchemical tree takes many forms, from a tiny plant to a great old oak or world tree. The *arbor inversa, with its roots in the air to receive the heavenly nourishment or *virgin's milk from above, is one version of this tree. Michael Maier's *Atalanta fugiens* compared the maturing philosopher's stone to *coral growing in water: 'For just as coral grows in water and gets its food out of the earth, in the same way the Philosopher's Stone grows out of the mercury water' (227). One of the most popular forms of the alchemical tree is that of the tree of sun and moon. At the culmination of the opus this tree bears the fruits of sun and moon, gold and silver on each branch (see fig. 17). In Michael Sendivogius's 'The Philosophicall Aenigma', the philosopher is shown these trees growing in a garden on an island: 'One / Had fruit as glittering as the radiant Sun. / The Stemm was golden and the Root below, / And golden leavs adorned every Bough. / The next had silver leavs and Fruit as white / As lillys in the Lawn of pure untinctur'd Light. / I stood amaz'd. Said Neptune then to me / "This is the Lunar, that the Solar Tree"' (lines 184–91, AP, 501). The trunk of the tree is the symbol of the union of sun and moon (*Sol and *Luna) from which the great unity, the philosopher's stone, is born. Sometimes the tree takes the form of a small bush or herb on which bloom *roses or *lilies (see fig. 15), representing the attainment of the solar and lunar tinctures, the red and white stones. Maria Prophetissa wrote of the lunar plant: 'Take the white clear, honoured, finest hearb which exists on the small mountain tops, and pound it when fresh just as it is in the hour of its birth, and it is the true fixed body which does not flee from the fire' (Patai, 'Maria', 192). An anonymous treatise collected by Elias Ashmole describes the alchemical plant as a herb called 'Lunarye' growing on the mountain brim, having a black root, red stalk, round leaves that 'wexsyth and waynyth as the Mon [moon]', and flowers that shine (TCB, 348–9)

In some instances, the tree represents the prima materia, and takes
the form of a great tree growing inside the earth's crust. Trismosin's
Splendor Solis described the alchemical tree growing in the earth:
'Therefore the Earth flowers and bears manifold coloured blooms
and fruits, and in her interior has grown a large Tree with a silver stem,
stretching itself out to the earth's surface. On its branches have been
sitting many kinds of birds, all departing at Daybreak, when the
Ravenhead became white' (28). The tree as prima materia is also
depicted as a golden tree with seven branches, signifying the seven
metals and planetary influences: mercury (Mercury), copper (Venus),
iron (Mars), lead (Saturn), tin (Jupiter), gold (Sun) and silver (Moon).
Paracelsus wrote of this tree: 'But whereas the Philosophers do compare
their matter to a certain Golden Tree of seven boughs, they mean that it
(viz. the matter) doth conclude the seven mettals in its sperm, and that
there they lye hidden' (*Aurora*, 17–18).

The philosophical tree is said to grow in various habitats, including
the sea (either in the sea, on the sea, or on an island in the sea). Saturn in
Michael Sendivogius's 'The Philosophicall Aenigma' says of the tree
growing on the blessed isle: 'And know / The Solar Tree did from this
Water grow' (lines 278–9, *AP*, 503). The *sea symbolizes the arcane mercurial water with which the tree is nourished in its growth from prima
materia to ultima materia (fig. 30). Some alchemical texts say that the
tree grows on a *mountain. Nicolas Flamel's *Philosophical Summary*
states: 'On the summit of that mountain they will find the glorious
Regal Herb' (*HM*, 1:146). The same text testifies that the tree grows in the
philosopher's *garden: 'But in the garden of the Sages ... our *tree* is
watered with the rarest dew' (*HM*, 1:145). The watering of the tree with
dew symbolizes the nourishing of the *philosophical child or stone
with the mercurial water ('milk') during the *cibation. Both mountain
and sea are symbols of the prima materia. See **tree (truncated)**.

30 The alchemical tree growing on an
island in the mercurial sea

phoenix   a symbol of renewal and resurrection signifying the *philosopher's stone, especially the *red stone attained at the *rubedo, capable of transmuting base metal into pure gold. *The Sophic Hydrolith* says: 'The Philosopher's Stone . . . is described as . . . the glorious Phoenix' (*HM*, 1:97). The *Chymicall Dictionary* defines phoenix as 'the quintessence of Fire; also the Philosopher's Stone'. Toutguerres in Bassett Jones's 'Lithochymicus' says: 'I know full well Sir! now what you would have; / You would reduce your Kinge out of his grave / To a young *Phoenix* that nere more shall die' (*AP*, 261). The phoenix is the final bird in the set of bird images representing the four main stages of the opus: the crow symbolizing the *nigredo, the peacock symbolizing the cauda pavonis (*peacock's tail), the swan (sometimes dove) symbolizing the *albedo, and the phoenix symbolizing the resurrection of the Stone at the rubedo. Lambsprinke wrote of the final stage, where the whiteness of the albedo develops into the redness of the rubedo: 'And of the Dove is born a Phoenix' (*HM*, 1:290). The phoenix is also a symbol of the alchemical *multiplication, where the quality and quantity of the elixir are infinitely multiplied by dissolution and coagulation.

piss   see **children's piss**.

pitch   see **nigredo, putrefaction**.

plant   see **flower, fruit, lily, philosophical tree, rose**.

poison   see **venom**.

pontic   see **sea**.

poppy   a name for the deep red colour of the elixir or Stone attained at the final stage of the opus, the *rubedo. Philalethes wrote of this stage: 'And then in a moment comes the Tyrian colour, the sparkling Red, the fiery Vermilion and Red Poppy of the Rock' (*RR*, 23).

pot   a generic name for the alchemical vessel; a specific utensil used in making the *elixir. Colson's *Philosophia maturata* states: 'This work ought to be done in a Circulatory placed in an Earthen Pot, wherein it must stand covered with dung to the middle; This Pot must be full of holes in the bottome, and must be placed upon the mouth of a Copper Vessell half fill'd with hot water' (61). In 'Love's Alchemy', John Donne referred to the vessel in which the coition of 'male' *sulphur and 'female' *argent vive takes place as the 'pregnant pot' (line 8). Chaucer's Canon's Yeoman tells of the misfortune of the shattered alchemical vessel: 'ful ofte it happeth so, / The pot to-breketh, and farewel! al is go! / This metals been of so greet violence' (*Canon's Yeoman's Tale*, lines 906–8).

potable gold   see **aurum potabile**.

powder   see **red powder**.

pregnancy   see **bed, philosophical child, square and circle, womb.**

priest   see **green lion.**

prima materia   first matter, the original, pure substance from which it was believed the universe was created and into which it might again be resolved. The alchemical prima materia is the receptive matter upon which the forms of all things were thought to be imprinted in the process of creation. In Aristotelian and scholastic philosophy this matter is 'the component of a thing which has bare existence but requires an essential determinant (*form*) to make it a thing of a determinate kind' (OED). The alchemical concept of the prima materia derives from the Hellenistic alchemists, who based their theory of nature on Aristotle's idea of the prima materia and on his idea of the four elements from which the fifth element or quintessence was synthesized. In François Rabelais's *Pantagruel*, an inhabitant of the 'Kingdom of the Quintessence' where Lady Quintessence dwells informs Pantagruel that 'Aristotle, that first of men and pattern of all philosophers, was our Lady Queen's godfather' (646).

According to the alchemists, the *philosopher's stone could not be made, nor base metals transmuted into silver and gold, without their first being dissolved into the original substance or first matter. *Zoroaster's Cave* said: 'Solution turns the Stone into its Materia prima, that is, into Water' (73). And Isaac Newton wrote in his 'Index chemicus' (Keynes MS 30) that '*Materia prima* is that which has been stripped of every form by putrefaction so that a new form can be introduced, that is, the black matter in the regimen of Saturn' (in Westfall, 'Index', 180). Once dissolved into this pure, basic stuff of creation, a new 'metallic' form could be imprinted upon the materia – the form, for instance, of the perfect metal – gold. Alchemy and popular Renaissance thought maintained that the world was a living organism with metals growing like plants and trees inside the earth's crust. The growth of gold is mentioned in 'On the Victory obtained by Blake' (sometimes attributed to Andrew Marvell): 'With fatal Gold, for still where that does grow, / Neither the Soyl, nor People, quiet know' (lines 57–8). It was thought that metals developed gradually through the action of the generating warmth of the sun's rays penetrating the substances inside the earth. 'Imperfect' or 'unripe' metals such as lead, iron, tin and copper were thought to ripen gradually within the womb of the earth into the perfect metal, gold. This idea occurs in a literary context in Dryden's *Annus Mirabilis* (1666): 'As those who unripe veins in Mines explore, / On the rich bed again the warm turf lay, / Till time digests the yet imperfect Ore, / And know it will be Gold another day' (lines 553–6). John Donne wrote of the sun's power to ripen metal into gold in the 'Eclogue' of 1613: 'The Earth doth in her inward bowels hold / Stuff well-disposed which would fain be gold / But never shall, except it chance to lie / So upward, that heaven gild it with his eye' (lines 61–7). In 1676 Joachim Becher wrote in his Kunsthaus Referat to the Emperor Leopold: 'Thus in this laboratory the truth and use of alchemy will also be demonstrated by means of various processes, such as the ripening of lead into silver . . .

Thus this laboratory is securer and richer than mines or exchange banks, and it alone will return the costs of the project' (cited in Smith, *Business of Alchemy*, 192–3).

Instead of waiting thousands of years for nature to complete the work of digesting imperfect ore to gold, the alchemist employed artificial means in the laboratory to accomplish this process in a considerably shorter time. Colson's *Philosophia maturata* states: 'Philosophers have made *Sol* in the space of one day, which Nature cannot do underground in a thousand years' (63–4). In order to generate gold the alchemist must first obtain the prima materia, also known as 'our Mercury' or *Mercurius. Mercurius contained within it the two seeds of metals, male sulphur (hot, dry, active) and female argent vive (cold, moist receptive). Ramon Lull is cited in *Zoroaster's Cave*: 'Wherefore I counsell you my friends, that you work not on anything but *Sol* and *Luna*, reducing them into their first matter, that is, Our Sulphur and Argent vive' (68). It was thought that the 'heat' of various different varieties of sulphur inherent in the prima materia acted upon the cold, moist aspect, argent vive, to form the different types of metal in the earth. The greater the proportion of argent vive or mercury in a metal, the greater its perfection, the closer to being gold or silver. Sulphur constituted the 'form' of the metal, argent vive its 'matter'. This theory, which was based on Aristotle's account of the generation of metals, first occurred in the writings of Geber (i.e. pseudo-Jabir ibn Haiyan) and remained as the basis of alchemical practice well into the seventeenth century. Philosophical 'sulphur' and 'mercury' do not refer to the substances we now call by those names, but are internal, constitutive principles or abstract, essential qualities. Edward Kelly wrote in *The Stone of the Philosophers*: 'The Sages have it that gold is nothing but quicksilver perfectly digested in the bowels of the earth, and they have signified that this is brought about by sulphur which coagulates the Mercury and digests it by its own heat. Hence the sages have said that Gold is nothing but mature quicksilver' (*Two excellent Treatises*, 18). Guillaume du Bartas wrote of the seeds of metals: 'Pray sing thy Heat, which subtilly doth pierce / The solide thicknes of our Universe: / Which in th' Earth's kidneys *Mercurie* doth burne, / And pallid *Sulphur* to bright Mettall turne' (*Divine Weeks*, 1: 222, lines 573–6). The alchemist's task is to unite these opposing substances in the *chemical wedding. From the union of the two a third, new, perfect entity known as the philosopher's stone comes into being. Isaac Newton wrote in his commentary on the *Emerald Table* of Hermes Trismegistus: 'Sulfur is mature quicksilver, and quicksilver is immature sulfur; and on account of this affinity they unite like male and female, and they act on each other, and through that action they are mutually transmuted into each other and procreate a more noble offspring to accomplish the miracles of this one thing' (Dobbs, *Janus*, 276).

Alchemy operates at a metaphysical as well as a physical level. The alchemist is concerned not only with the transmutation of base metal into gold, but most importantly with the transformation of the natural or earthly man into the illumined philosopher. The process of purifying the imperfect metal was analogous to the purification of man's soul and

31 Prima materia

body – the subject of much Renaissance metaphysical poetry. In alchemy the prima materia or first matter from which the universe was created is identical with the substance which constitutes the soul in its original pure state. In the metaphysical work of the opus, corrupt, rigid thought forms, and old habits of being, have to be resolved so that the soul can regain its original pure state, undisturbed by impressions and desires. When this process of refinement is accomplished, the divine spirit may illuminate the soul, creating the possibility of a new, freer, and more spiritual form or state of being. In Milton's *Paradise Lost*, Raphael informs Adam that God created everything from 'one first matter all, / Indued with various forms, various degrees / Of substance, and in things that live, of life; / But more refined, more spirituous, and pure, / As nearer to him placed or nearer tending' (5.472–6).

The prima materia, like the philosopher's stone, is sometimes spoken of as a substance deemed worthless, unnoticed and despised by the ignorant. Colson's *Philosophia maturata* said of the tincture or elixir which cannot be made without the prima materia: 'Behold thou understandeth this Tincture, which we draw out from a vile thing of no price' (67). The prima materia is referred to as a common thing because it can be found everywhere and costs nothing. *The Sophic Hydrolith* enigmatically observed that: 'by the ignorant and the beginner it is thought to be the vilest and meanest of things ... seen by all, but known by few' (*HM*, 1:78). This matter was said to be found in the *philosophical tree which grows on the surface of the ocean in the lands of the west, or in a topsy-turvy mountain (see Abu'L Qasim, *Book of Knowledge*, 23–4). The topsy-turvy nature of the mountain symbolizes the 'inverted' action of the *solve et coagula, the apparently backward-turning revolution of the *opus contra naturam which leads the alchemist back to the source of creation and the prima materia (see **inversion**). The prima materia is known by many names, some of which are: Adam (the original, uncorrupted man), the sea (which carries within it all forms), the moon, mother, earth (which as mother nourishes nature), the virgin (pure, receptive), lion, seed, sperm, menstrue (containing the seeds of all things), the shadow, cloud, hidden Stone, buried treasure, the tree whose fruits are sun and moon (i.e. silver and gold), 'our mercury' (see **Mercurius**), ore, lead, Saturn, poison, chaos, spirit, fountain, water and dew. The frontispiece of Arthur Dee's 'Arca arcanorum' is a coloured circular emblem depicting the extraction of the prima materia (fig. 31).

prison the stage of the the opus known as the *putrefaction and *nigredo; the name of the vessel during this stage. During the putrefaction the matter in the alembic is said to be captured in a dungeon or in prison. In order to make the *philosopher's stone, the old metal or matter for the Stone must first be dissolved so that the alchemist can obtain the mercurial spirit imprisoned in matter. This spirit is known as the mercurial serpent or dragon. Thomas Charnock wrote: 'and all for my prevayle / [ma]ny years I keapt this dragon in pryson strounge' (Aubrey, *Brief Lives*, 2:167). Philalethes equated the vessel with the 'prison' and stated that, at the opening of the opus, 'the *Artist* must in the first place expect to be in Prison a long time' (Klossowski de Rola, *Alchemy*, 27). When the matter for the Stone is dissolved, the male and female seeds of metals known as the bride and bridegroom are released from the mercurial prima materia. In order for the philosopher's stone to be conceived, the seeds or bride and bridegroom, Sol and Luna, must be united in the *chemical wedding. Their united, hermaphroditic body must be killed, blackened and putrefied, while the soul is released to float at the top of the alembic. An anonymous manuscript refers to this stage as 'the black prison'. It continues: 'For if this soul be freed from the body then blackness appeareth as a sign of a good and right operation' (BL Sloane 3631, f. 14). In 'Compositor huius libri ad lectorem', Simon Forman wrote of the united Sol and Luna: 'But I will leave them Imprisoned nowe / Untill one unto another they yeald and bowe ' (lines 45–7, *AP*, 67). Martin Ruland wrote that the vessel at this stage is referred to as 'a Prison, because the Bride and Bridegroom are shut in there by force' (*Lexicon*, 323). The convict prison in Marcus Clarke's *His Natural Life* acts as the prison house of the alchemical nigredo. The protagonist, Richard Devine, who has worked as an alchemist's laboratory assistant in Amsterdam, plays the role of the alchemical matter which must be corrupted at the nigredo before it can be redeemed. Under the alias of Rufus Dawes, he undergoes a long series of imprisonments, first in 'the prison cage' of the ship transporting him to Australia (199), ending up in the prison of Norfolk Island in which 'hot foul air rushed out like a blast from a furnace' (579). Having passed through the trial of the prison-furnace, 'steeled in the slow fire of convict labour' (329), he escapes and is transformed into the wealthy gold prospector living at the Victorian goldfields, under the name of Tom Crosbie. He is finally restored to his alchemical laboratory and to his original name, Richard Devine, symbolizing the regaining of the consciousness of the divine self.

projection the final operation of the opus alchymicum, when the *philosopher's stone or tincture is thrown over the base metal to transmute it into silver or gold; the instant exaltation or *augmentation of a substance by the *medicine or philosopher's stone. Colson's *Philosophia maturata* says of the white elixir which can transmute base metal into silver: 'before thou make projection, congeal it (our Mercury) into an oily powder, one part thereof converts a thousand, nay ten thousand parts of *Argent vive*, and the other Mettals into pure *Lune*, enduring all trialls' (40–1). Likewise, at the final red stage when the *rubedo is attained, the powder of projection may be cast onto the heated mercury, copper or other matter to be transmuted. John Dee recorded that at Trebon, on 19 December 1586, Edward Kelly made alchemical projection in the presence of himself and Edward Garland: 'E. K. made projection with his powder ... and produced nearly an ounce of best gold; which gold we afterwards distributed from the crucible' (*Diary*, 22; trans. in Smith, *John Dee*, 22). In a document sent to Elias Ashmole (received 29 March 1674), Sir Thomas Browne wrote that, while in Bohemia with Edward Kelly and his father John Dee, Arthur Dee 'had seen projection made and transmutation of pewter dishes and flaggons into sylver which the goldsmiths at Prague bought of them. and that Count Rosenberg playd at Quaits with sylver quaits made by projection as before' (Bod. Ashm. MS 1788, f. 151r–v).

It was said that just one ounce of the Stone could transmute a hundred, two hundred, or even a thousand times its own weight of base metal into gold. The treatise *Pearce the Black Monke upon the Elixir* stated that 'One ounce of thys Medycine worthy / Cast upon two hundred owncees of Mercury: / Schall make Gold most royall' (TCB, 276). In Jonson's *The Alchemist* Mammon exclaims that 'one part [of the Stone] proiected on a hundred / Of *Mercurie*, or *Venus*, or the *Moone*, / Shall turne it to as many of the *Sunne*; / Nay to a thousand, so *ad infinitum*' (2.1.38–41) (Venus signifies copper, the moon, silver, and the sun, gold). Artephius claimed that 'by pursuing your work, your projection will come to infinity, tinging truly and perfectly and fixing the greatest quantity by how much soever' (SB, 42). The emblem illustrating the projection in 'Coronatio naturae' (GU Ferguson MS 208) shows the red tincture projected from the heart of the *red king (the red stone) onto his subjects, who personify the base metals (fig. 32). In 'Paradox. That Fruition destroys Love', Henry King compared the post-coital disillusionment of sexual love to the alchemical opus which miscarries and fails to achieve projection: 'After Fruition once, what is Desire / But ashes kept warm by a dying fire ? / This is (if any) the Philosopher's Stone / Which still miscarries at Projection' (lines 73–6). Edward Benlowes stressed the

PROIECTIO.

galli cantus

32 The projection of the red tincture from
the heart of the king onto the base metals

spiritual aspect of the alchemical projection in *Theophila*: 'Nature's
chang'd alone / By GRACE; THAT is the *chymick-stone*: / And thy all-
pow'rful WORD is pure Projection' (12).

In tracing the development of the word 'projection', Pamela Smith
writes that for Leibniz and his contemporaries the original meaning of
'to project' was to effect alchemical transmutation by casting the philosophical powder or stone over base metal. The word 'project' also began
to be used at this time to mean a plan, sketch or concept that could be
transferred onto the material world. By the end of the century in
Germany, 'projector' had taken on the negative meaning of 'deceptive
artificer'. This meaning was already in use in the early seventeenth
century in England (*Business of Alchemy*, 269).

projector   see **projection**.

prostitute   see **Venus**.

Proteus   one of the names of *Mercurius, the prima materia. The volatile, elusive
spirit Mercurius who takes on many guises during the process of the
opus is sometimes compared to the Greek sea god who could assume a
variety of forms. In order to make the *philosopher's stone the alchemist
must capture the elusive Mercurius (Hermes) and tame him. In other
words, the alchemist must obtain the first matter of the work, the prima
materia, sometimes symbolized by the *sea. In *Paradise Lost* Milton wrote
of the alchemists: 'by their powerful art they bind / Volatile Hermes, and
call up unbound / In various shapes old Proteus from the sea, / Drained
through a limbeck to his native form' (3.602–5).

33 The purple robe and crown

puffers   alchemists who make excessive use of the bellows to keep the fire going in the alchemical furnace or *athanor. In Ben Jonson's *The Alchemist*, Mammon calls Face, the puffer, 'Lungs' and 'Puffe': '*Lungs*, I will manumit thee, from the fornice; / I will restore thee thy complexion, *Puffe*, / Lost in the embers' (2.2.18–20). Sir Epicure Mammon likewise says of Subtle's puffer: 'That's his fire-drake, / His lungs, His *Zephyrus*, he that puffes his coales' (2.1.26–7). See bellows.

pumpkin   a gourd-shaped alchemical distilling vessel, also known as the *cucurbite (Latin *cucurbita*, gourd). *The Gloria Mundi* stated that the alchemist should place the matter of the Stone 'in a glass (pumpkin shaped) distilling vessel and calcine until it becomes dry and white yet liquid withal'. Then the alchemist will have obtained 'the treasure of this world, which has virtue to purify and perfect all earthly things' (HM, 1:179).

purification   see **ablution, albedo, refine, solve et coagula.**

purple tincture   the same as the red elixir or stone. The Latin *purpureus -a -um* means purple-coloured; dark red, dark brown. The *red stone or elixir, which can tinge all base metals to gold and restore man to perfect health and consciousness of God, is frequently described as the precious purple tincture. Basil Valentine wrote that 'this Tincture is of a colour intermediate between red and purple' (HM, 1:348). Nicolas Flamel called it 'the true red purple' (HE, 1:126). John Cleveland jokily plays with the image of the purple or violet tincture in 'Fuscara; or The Bee Errant', where the bee 'whose suckets are moyst *Alchymie*' lands on Fuscara's sleeve: 'The ayrie Free-booter distreins / First on the Violets of her Veins, / Whose tinckture, could it be more pure, / His ravenous Kiss had made it bluer' (lines 11–14). The colour of the tincture is frequently compared to the

Tyrian purple of costly fabrics worn by persons of royal or imperial rank, and made from molluscs called (in Greek) *porphura* (see **dye**). In *A Relation of a Iourney*, George Sandys wrote about the 'invention' of the purple dye of Tyre and its distillation in a 'Limbeck' or alembic (215). One of the most frequently occurring images symbolizing the attainment of the purple tincture is that of the king putting on the purple robe. The purple robe and crown of the king as *red stone are illustrated in GU Ferguson MS 271 (fig. 33). Joan Hodgson explained the metaphysical symbolism of the purple robe of the adept who has mastered himself and the elements: 'The fully-evolved child of the seventh ray does indeed wear the kingly purple, not the dark heavy shade symbolising material power, but a robe of rich amethyst light, indicating his dominion over the kingdom of the self. He has reached the state of mastery where the lower self has become completely absorbed into the higher. In the words of the old alchemists, the base metal has been transmuted into fine gold' (*Astrology*, 174).

putrefaction the conversion of a metal into an apparently inert mass or powder (Holmyard, *Alchemy*, 278), the decomposition of a substance. Calid wrote: '*Putrefaction* is to rost, grinde, and water, so long till all be mingled together and become one' (*Booke of the Secrets*, 42). Putrefaction, the corruption that changes one thing into another, occurs during the initial stage in the opus known as the *nigredo. During the nigredo the impure body of the metal or Stone is dissolved by the application of a gentle heat which stimulates the internal heat of the matter, causing it to be reduced into blackness and into its first matter or *prima materia (the substance from which it was originally created). *Zoroaster's Cave* states that 'Putrefaction is made by a most Gentle fire hot and moyst, and no other, so that nothing ascend' (73). The appearance of the black colour in the alembic is a sign that the putrefaction process is under way. Roger Bacon wrote: 'in the first operation of our Stone, it is called putrifaction, and our Stone is made blacke' (*Mirror*, 12). A recipe in Colson's *Philosophia maturata* describes the details of this operation: 'take an ounce of this calx hidden before in the Philosopher's eg, and thereon put of the red tincture to cover it two fingers; then seal it, and set it to putrefie eight daies in a most cold place; which being ended, it will drink up the humidity; again pour on as much of the tincture, and let it stand as before for other eight daies, continuing again the said imbibations and times: let it stand till it cease to drink any more tincture; remove it not from its place untill it be blacker then any pitch; which being seen, set it into a natural balmy, that the moisture with the black Earth may be digested, and fixed into a white mineral; then divide it into two equal parts, and work the one for the white, and the other for the red stone' (37).

The alchemical principle of putrefaction is based on the idea that nature is renewed only after first dying away. The conception of new life is seen as a 'death' which is then followed by rebirth or resurrection. *Zoroaster's Cave* stated: 'Desponsation and Conception is made by a kind of putridnesse in the Bottom of the Vessell' (73). Edward Kelly wrote: 'all things that are to grow and receive life, must first putrefy' (*Two excellent Treatises*, 140). According to Robert Fludd the putrefaction 'is effected by corruption and dyeing after the naturall patterne observed in the grayne of corne which after it is dead (for by dying his elements are parted by subtiliation, and that by vertue of the centrall and incorruptible agent) doth rise againe in a manifold multiplication' (*TGH*, 141). The putrefaction of the 'body' of the metal releases the spark of divine light and life which is hidden in it. Robert Fludd wrote that the art of alchemy 'doth nothinge else but by adaption putrify the dark matter to free the hidden formal spark or grayne of light hidden in obscurity and darknes' (*TGH*, 113). The alchemists believed that only on the freeing of this life spark could life be increased and multiplied.

The putrefaction is said to be accompanied by a fetid odour 'rather intellectually than sensuously perceptible' (Kelly, *Two excellent Treatises*, 138), and is represented both verbally and visually in the alchemical texts by various images of death: *Saturn with his *scythe, the angel of death, a skeleton standing on a *coffin or on a *black sun (see fig. 38), the *raven or *crow, the bodies of the dead lovers (*sulphur and *argent vive) lying in their grave (see fig. 10), the ashes of Hermes' tree, the toad and Hades. Sir George Ripley wrote: 'And *Putrefaccyon* ... ys of Bodyes the sleying ... The kyllyng Bodyes into corrupcyon forth ledying, / And after unto Regeneratyon them ablying' (*TCB*, 148). In Jonson's *The Alchemist* Subtle asks Face to 'name the vexations, and martyrizations / Of mettalls, in the worke' and Face begins his list with 'Putrefaction' (2.5.20–1). The narrator in Rabelais's *Pantagruel* witnesses the various parodic 'forms of alchemy' practised in the 'Kingdom of the Quintessence' amongst which is putrefaction: 'I saw one calcinator artificially extracting farts from a dead donkey, and selling them at five pence a yard. Another was putrefying sechabots or abstractions' (651).

Q

quarrel see **peace**.

queen (white) a name for the white elixir or stone attained at the *albedo; a symbol of the receptive, cold, moist, female principle of the opus. The white elixir has the power to transmute base metal into silver. Edward Kelly wrote in *The Theatre of Terrestrial Astronomy* that 'this tincture, or elixir is also called the Virgin's milk, the everlasting water, and water of life, because it is as brilliant as white marble; it is also called the White Queen' (*Two excellent Treatises*, 142). The white queen as the receptive, female principle (*Luna), must be united with the *red king or *Sol, the active male principle, in the *chemical wedding. This wedding represents the union of the universal male and female forces, which the alchemists speak of as either the union of spirit and soul, or the union of the already united soul and spirit with the purified body of the Stone. From this union a new, perfect entity arises, which the alchemists call the *philosopher's stone. The wedding of king and queen is illustrated in emblem 2 (second series) of Johann Mylius's *Philosophia reformata* and in *The Rosary of the Philosophers* (see fig. 9).

quicksilver *argent vive or mercury. A name mainly applied to philosophical argent vive, the moist, cold, female seed of metals, which the alchemist must unite with philosophical *sulphur, the dry, hot, male seed, in order to produce the *philosopher's stone. Chaucer's Canon's Yeoman tells of the 'amalgaming and calcening / Of quik-silver, y-clept Mercurie crude' (*Canon's Yeoman's Tales*, lines 771–2). Quicksilver is a name applied to *Mercurius in his role as the slippery, elusive spirit which the alchemist must *tame or fix in order to make the *philosopher's stone. In John Lyly's *Gallathea*, Peter teaches Rafe that the 'first spirit [in alchemy] is quicksilver' and Rafe replies: 'That is my spirit, for my silver is so quick that I have much ado to catch it, and when I have it, it is so nimble that I cannot hold it. I thought there was a devil in it' (2.3.52–5). The *prima materia, the pure, first matter which contains the male and female *seeds of metals, is sometimes called 'quicksilver'. 'The Golden Rotation' states that the matter of the Stone must be 'reduced into his first beginning, which is quicksilver the first matter of metals' (f. 33) (see also **chemical wedding, Mercurius**). The alchemist Marco Antonio Bragadini, known as Mamugnano, was renowned for his transmutations of quicksilver into gold. The newsletters of the banking house of the Fuggers reported his arrival in Venice in November 1589. He 'holds banquet daily for five hundred people and lives in princely style in the Palazzo Dandolo on the Giudecca. He literally throws gold about in shovelfuls. This is his recipe: he takes ten ounces of quicksilver, puts it into the fire and mixes it with a drop of liquid, which he carries in an ampulla. Thus it promptly turns into good gold' (*Fugger News-Letters*, November 1589).

quintessence see **fifth element**.

R

radical humidity the soul of metals, *argent vive, philosophical mercury, the moist matter or 'divine water' which is the origin of the *philosopher's stone. Arthur Dee quotes the treatise *Ludus puerorum*: 'By Argent vive is understood the humidity of that unction, which is the radicall humidity of our Stone' (*FC*, 31). Since the soul in alchemy is associated with water and moisture and is symbolized by dew, the radical moisture is sometimes referred to as the may-dew which the alchemists are shown collecting on *sheets laid out in a meadow in Altus's *Mutus Liber* (pl. 4). The radical humidity or philosophical mercury is the anima mundi, the spirit imprisoned in matter. This divine water is sometimes identified with the prima materia from which it must be extracted and freed. *The Rosary of the Philosophers* says of the radical humidity: 'The matter of Metalls is a certain smoaky substance, and it is the first matter of Metalls, containing in itself an unctuous or oyly moisture, from which substance the Artist separates the Philosophicall humidity, which is fit for the work, which will be as clear as a water drop, in which is coucht the metallick Quintessence' (FC, 10). It is extracted not only by means of the fire's torment (the dissolution of the matter into the four elements or 'roots' (Latin *radices*)), but also by the alchemical process known as *cooking or *digestion. François Rabelais treats this concept satirically in *Pantagruel* where the Lady Queen of the Quintessence addresses her gentlemen alchemists: 'The orifice of the stomach, the common ambassador for the alimentation of all the members, both inferior and superior, importunes us to restore to them, by the application of suitable nourishment, what they have lost through the continuous action of the natural heat on the radical humidity' (653).

rain   see **cloud, dew.**

rainbow   the attainment of the *peacock's tail stage which occurs after the black *nigredo and heralds the coming of the the white *albedo. During the process known as the *ablution, when the cleansing showers of mercurial water descend from the top of the alembic to purify the blackened body below, a rainbow appears to show that the testing time of the nigredo is past and the perfect white stage, the albedo, is in sight. When the albedo or white stone is reached the multi-colours of the rainbow are integrated into the single white colour, a sign that a state of pure stillness and receptivity of soul has been attained. Sir George Ripley wrote that at the peacock's tail, 'Shyning Colors therein thou shalt espye: / Lyke to the Raynbow mervelose unto syght' (TCB, 150), and 'Pekok's fethers in color gay, the Raynbow whych shall overgoe . . . / These shall appere before the parfyt Whyte' (TCB, 188). In some treatises, the dissolution of the body or bodies at the nigredo is compared to the advent of *Noah's flood where the waters threaten to overwhelm the matter completely and drown it. The sighting of the rainbow and the landing of the *ark on dry land symbolizes the alchemist's successful arrival at the albedo when the matter in the alembic becomes dried and whitened (see **flood**).

rarefaction   purification, refinement of the matter of the Stone. An anonymous treatise advised the alchemist to take the 'Earth, lying in the bottom [of the vessel] and purifye it subject to the continual operation of the Water upon it, which when it once ascendeth on high and again descendeth to the bottom, by drops, and by gentle Rarefaction is at last coagulated' (BL Sloane MS 3631, f. 7). See **distillation.**

raven, raven's head   a symbol of the *nigredo, the initial step of the opus, where the impure body of the metal, or matter for the Stone, is killed, dissolved and putrefied (see fig. 38). The alchemists believed that metals could be regenerated or transmuted by first being dissolved into their original substance or *prima materia. Their dictum was 'only through corruption can generation be made'. The nigredo is referred to as the raven or raven's head because it is a time of death and putrefaction, when the body of the Stone at the bottom of the alembic becomes blackened and fetid. Edward Kelly wrote: 'The beginning of our work is the Black Raven, which, like all things that are to grow and receive life, must first putrefy' (*Two excellent Treatises*, 140). *The Sophic Hydrolith* described the 'earth' or dead body of the metal 'changing to a coal-black colour, called by the Sages the Raven's Head, within the space of forty days' (HM, 1:82). See also crow. In Vladimir Nabokov's *Pale Fire*, which alludes to the alchemical opus, Gradus, the killer of John Shade, plays the role of the raven of the nigredo when the stone is killed and blackened. Gradus calls himself 'Gray' and 'appears in police records as Ravus, Ravenstone, and d'Argus' (77). It is only a short verbal leap from Gray to (G)Ravenstone to gravestone, raven and stone. The name given to the alchemical vessel during the nigredo is the *grave. 'Raven-stone' is also a poetical term for the place of execution, the gallows. See **jackdaw, crow**.

rebis   see **hermaphrodite**.

receiver   a vessel, usually glass, for receiving and condensing the product of distillation. A recipe for fixing sublimed mercury in Colson's *Philosophia maturata* tells the alchemist to 'put two or three pound [of mercury, saltpetre and vitriol tempered with distilled *acetum*] in a long receiver, stop the mouth, place it in ashes, so as the Globe may be wholly covered' (51). In Ben Jonson's *The Alchemist,* receivers are mentioned amongst the alchemical equipment Face claims to have lost in an explosion: 'O sir, we are defeated! all the *workes* / Are flowne *in fumo*: every glasse is burst ... *Retorts, Receivers, Pellicanes, Bolt-heads,* / All strooke in shiuers!' (4.5.57–62). John Donne plays on 'receiver', referring both to the alchemical apparatus and to the impotency of mankind to receive the transmuting influence of Elizabeth Drury, in his poem 'An Anatomy of the World: The First Anniversary': 'She, from whose influence all impressions came, / But by receivers' impotencies, lame, / Who, though she could not transubstantiate / All states to gold, yet gilded every state' (lines 415–18).

reconciliation   see **peace and strife**.

rectification   purification or refinement by repeated distillation or by chemical process. In an appendix to 'Lithochymicus', Bassett Jones wrote that '*Rectification* is the repetition [*sic*] of a destillation; and usd either when a destillation by longe keepinge or otherwise is become dull, or else where the flegme, Spirits and Oyle are confusedly destill'd. Then it is rectifyed, to the end they may be easyer severed' (AP, 353–4). Arthur Dee wrote in *Fasciculus chemicus* that 'The Philosophicall Work may be begun with an equall Proportion of earth prepared, and pure Water seven times rectified; which are joined up in an Ovall Glasse Hermetically Sealed' (101).

red   see **rubedo**.

red earth   philosophical *gold; a name for the base matter which is dissolved into the *prima materia; the prima materia also known as *Adam (thought to be derived from the Hebrew *adom* meaning 'red earth'). *The Golden Tract* says: 'For what are gold and silver (says Avicenna) but pure red and white earth' (HM, 1:39). The red earth is the reddened matter from which the *red elixir and stone are made, the substance which can transmute base metal into gold. In 'The Litany' John Donne uses 'red earth' in its sense as the Adamic base matter which must be purified before it can become resurrected as the true tincture or spiritual quintessence (line 7): 'Father ... re-create me, now grown ruinous: / My heart is by dejection, clay, / And by self-murder, red. / From this red earth, O father, purge away / All vicious tinctures, that new fashioned / I may rise up from death' (lines 1–9) (see also **Adam**).

red elixir   from the Arabic *al-iksir*, the universal panacea or miraculous *medicine, synonymous with the *philosopher's stone, which can transmute all base metal into pure gold, cure all disease, confer longevity, and resurrect the dead to eternal life. Roger Bacon wrote: 'The red Elixir doth turne into a citrine colour infinitely, and changeth all mettals into pure gold' (*Mirror*, 14). 'The Golden Rotation' says of this elixir: 'For yt is the Riches of all Riches, and onely miracle of Nature. Not onely that yt changeth all metalls into gold, or silver, but that yt encreaseth naturall strength in all living creatures, curing all sicknes and infirmatye, restoring virtue and comfort to the aged and worne bodyes. In shorte yt is the medicine that hath more virtues then all the medicines of the earth' (f. 62). John Donne wrote of this elixir in his 'Elegy on the Lady Markham': her soul shall inspire 'Flesh of such stuff, as God, when his last fire / Annuls this world, to recompense it, shall, / Make and name then, th' elixir of this all' (lines 26–8).

The red elixir is attained at the final stage of the opus, the *rubedo, when the white matter of the *albedo has been decocted in a dry fire until it transforms into a deep red or purple colour. The reddening of the white matter in the alembic symbolizes the conferring of form onto the pure but hitherto formless matter of the Stone (the white earth or body). The alchemists speak of two elixirs, one white and the other red, but insist that there is essentially one elixir, not two. Benjamin Lock wrote on this subject: 'The firste parte of the Elixir: is made of whyte earth and therefore is whyte. The second parte is red for yt is made of red earthe, yet nevertheless yt is one Elixir and no more' ('Picklock', f. 34v). The red elixir, which is equivalent to the consolamentum (or comforter), is symbolized by the red *rose, the red lily, hyacinth, *ruby, red *blood, *red king, *Sol, the *sun, the *phoenix, the *Tyrian purple, and the purple robe (see **purple tincture**). The attainment of the red elixir is illustrated in the last emblem of the 'Pretiosum Donum Dei' which

34 The red elixir, red rose and red king

shows the red king standing knee-deep in the elixir with the red rose
blossoming above the alembic (fig. 34). Robert Herrick stressed the
metaphysical aspect of the elixir when he wrote of the healing power of
penitence: 'There is no evill that we do commit. / But hath th' extraction
of some good from it: / As when we sin; God, the great *Chymist*, thence /
Drawes out th' *Elixar* of true penitence' (*Works*, 386). In Mary Astell's
poem 'Awake my Lute', virtue is the transmuting, converting elixir:
'Who has the true Elixir, may impart / Pleasure to all he touches, and
convert / The most unlikely grief to Happiness. / Vertue this true Elixir
is' (lines 100–3, in Greer, *Kissing the Rod*, 340).

red gum   see **gum**.

red head   see **head**.

red king   see **king**, **red elixir**.

red lily   see **lily** (white).

red lion   red *sulphur, the hot, dry, male seed of metals, *Sol (the masculine principle of the opus) in its early primitive stage. Paracelsus wrote that 'the
matter of the Tincture [i.e. Stone] . . . is called by many the Red Lion' (PW,
22). The alchemist begins the preparation of the *philosopher's stone by

35 The red lion

obtaining the living seed of metals, which is differentiated into 'Male and Female, Mercury and *Sulphure vive*' (Ripley, in *TCB*, 145). Masculine sulphur (fire and air) and feminine mercury or argent vive (earth and water) then have to be reconciled and chemically combined for the philosopher's stone to be conceived and born (see **chemical wedding**). Sulphur, associated with Mars, is the masculine substance *par excellence*, a substance which scourges and burns all that come into contact with it. Synesius referred to it as 'devouring sulphur' (*The True Book*, 171). The violence of sulphur is aptly personified by the red lion (fig. 35). Mercury (argent vive), sulphur's marriage partner, is personified as the lioness. The two together symbolize the quarrelling couple who must be united in the early, primitive stage of the opus. When depicted with crowns on their heads, the lions prefigure the royal pair who unite at a refined level at the completion of the opus. The red lion may also symbolize the goal of the opus, the elixir or Stone which has attained perfect redness and which can transmute base metal into gold (see **red elixir**).

red man and **white woman**   names given to the hot, dry, active male principle or seed of metals (*sulphur) and the cold, moist, receptive female principle (mercury or *argent vive) which the alchemist must join together in the *chemical wedding in order to create the *philosopher's stone (see fig. 8). Sir George Ripley wrote that the 'Red Man and the Whyte Woman' should be 'made one' (*TCB*, 186). On a wall in the house of Rudolf II's alchemical adviser, Dr Tadeus Hajek, where John Dee stayed in Prague, the following words were written in Latin: 'If a white woman is married to a red husband, they embrace and conceive. They dissolve of themselves, they sooner or later are perfected of themselves' (Casaubon, *True and Faithful Relation*, 212). An anonymous treatise (GU Ferguson MS 238) instructs the alchemist: 'therefore take a Red Man and a White Woman and Wed them together, and let them go to Chamber both, and look that the door and Windows be fast barred for else the Woman will be gone away from her Husband ... For this Man and this Woman getteth our Stone' (f. 2v). Surly, in Jonson's *The Alchemist*, sarcastically refers to 'your red man, and your white woman' as one of the alchemists' countless enigmas (2.3.192). In the early primitive stage of the opus the couple to be united are symbolized by the aggressive lion and lioness, dog and bitch, or hen and cock. Later, at a more refined level of operation, the couple are symbolized by the lovers, the red man and the white woman, who are sometimes referred to as the brother and sister (see **incest**). Though more refined than the relationship of the bestial participants in the initial union, the relationship between the red man and the white woman is not an easy one and they are sometimes referred to as the quarrelling couple. An anonymous treatise warns the alchemist that if the man 'be boisterous to her in the beginning she will flee away from him and if he be easie with her in the beginning she will be his Master a good while. This is a hard Marriage nevertheless one Comfort is after she hath born a Child, and known somewhat of Disease she will be the more sober and never leave him after' (GU Ferguson MS 238, ff. 2v–3r).

red powder the red stone attained at the *rubedo, at the culmination of the opus. This Stone, which at the *projection is cast over base metal to convert it into gold, is sometimes referred to as the red powder or tincture. Synesius advised the alchemist to proceed with imbibing the *medicine 'until the force of the digestion of the fire convert it into a very red powder, which is ... the bloody Stone, the purple red Coral, the pretious Ruby, red Mercury, and the red Tincture' (*The True Book*, 175). Robert Fludd identified both a white and a red powder: 'Dorneus and Hoglandus say that the chimicall powder, wheather one calle it the Philosophers stone or fusible salt, or pure Sulphur, or the Elixir, or a medicin or Aurum potabile, hath an admirable vertue and force in the thre kingdomes of compound things, namely animall, vegetable and minerall. And Hoglandus in his proeme sayeth: The intent of the Philosophers Art is to produce artificially a certayne minerall vertue out of the pure seed of gold and silver by the benefit and assistance of nature in the forme of a subtill powder white and red which is able to propagat and multiply infinitely' (TGH, 129). Sir Thomas Browne wrote that he had often heard Arthur Dee say that Count Rosenberg, patron of John Dee and Edward Kelly, 'playd at Quaits with sylver quaits made by projection ... that this transmutation was made by a small powder they had which was found in some old place' (Bod. Ashm. MS 1788, f. 151r–v).

red sand see **sand**.

Red Sea the *prima materia, the aqua permanens or *mercurial water. The red sea is the paradoxical water of life and death. It is the great solvent and at the same time the water of baptism and rebirth. In alchemy, the dangerous crossing of the Red Sea by the Israelites signifies the death and rebirth of the matter of the Stone in the alembic. The sea is death to that which is impure and unenlightened, and life to that which is pure and regenerate. The division of the Red Sea by the Israelites symbolizes the *division of the *prima materia (the alchemist's first matter) into the four differentiated elements (earth, air, fire and water). The *Turba philosophorum* spoke of extracting the healing elixir from 'our red and most pure sea' (185). An emblem in Ripley's 'Emblematicall Scrowle' illustrates the alchemical *bath balanced on a column, standing in a red pool on the side of which is inscribed 'The red sea: The red Lune: The red Sol: the Dragon' (BL Additional MS 5025, detail).

red servant *Mercurius as *servus fugitivus; the ore from which this philosophical mercury is extracted. *The Crowning of Nature* equates the 'fugitive servant' with the *green lion, which symbolizes either philosophical mercury or the ore from which philosophical mercury is extracted (McLean, *Crowning*, 20). *The Golden Tract* says that the true philosopher would not 'extract the quicksilver [mercury] from any but the red slave' (HM, 1:33) and makes it clear that the red servant is the 'father' of the red male (the hot, dry, masculine principle of the opus) which the alchemist must unite with the white female in the *chemical wedding (see **red man and white woman**). Some treatises identify the red male with the 'servus rubeus', conflating it with the father ore. The red servant is called a 'servant' because, once captured and tamed, it serves in the generation of metals and the production of the *philosopher's stone. This substance is referred to as 'red' 'because in this last preparation he goes into red dust' (McLean, *Crowning*, 10). See **cervus fugitivus**.

red stage see **rubedo**.

red stone see **red elixir, philosopher's stone**.

red tincture a preliminary stage of the philosopher's stone as the prized red elixir, *medicine or stone which, when cast upon base metal at the *projection, tinges it to gold. Paracelsus wrote that this 'Tincture ... makes Gold out of Lune, and the other metals' (*Archidoxis,* 64). Synesius identified 'the bloody Stone' as 'the purple red Coral, the pretious Ruby, red Mercury, and the red Tincture' (*The True Book*, 175). It was thought that just one ounce of the tincture could transmute over a hundred or a thousand times its own weight of base metals into pure gold. Shakespeare used 'tinct' in its alchemical sense in *Antony and Cleopatra* when Cleopatra says to her 'base' attendant Alexas: 'How much unlike art thou Mark Anthony! / Yet coming from him, that great Med'cine hath / With his tinct gilded thee' (1.5.34–6). Milton likewise used this metaphor when, in the creation scene in *Paradise Lost*, the stars multiply their light and Venus 'gilds her horns' from the sun's quintessential source, 'By tincture or reflection' (7.364–9). See **red elixir, philosopher's stone, grain, purple tincture**.

red within the white see **rubedo**.

refine to purify a metal (or soul) by removing the defects and impurities and raising it to a more subtle or spiritual state. The alchemists purified metals through the action of their secret refining *fire. During this process the matter in the alembic is put through a reiterated cycle of *solve et coagula (dissolution and coagulation), with each cycle bringing the matter to a more subtle and pure state. The alchemists held that gold was the only metal that could endure the heat of the fire while retaining its true nature and purity. In the macrocosmic–microcosmic law of correspondences, gold was the metallic equivalent of the sun, which in turn was the physical equivalent of the eternal spirit. So when the alchemists spoke of the substance which could eternally endure the trial of the refining fire, they were referring to the ultimate fixation of the great spirit, the embodiment of the divine spirit in man made perfect. John Collop plays on the alchemical sense of 'refine' in 'To a refin'd Lady': 'But come choice piece of Nature more refin'd, / Perfection to a quintessence calcin'd. / I'le no more study the Philosophers stone, / *Eugenia* mine, th' Elixir's sure mine own' (lines 1–4). The concept of refinement in the natural order of things, as well as through trial, is a major theme in Milton's *Paradise Lost*. In a passage rich with alchemical imagery Raphael explains to Adam that everything is created from 'one first matter' (the *prima materia) but those things which are more refined are closer to God (5. 472–9): 'O Adam, one almighty is, from whom / All things proceed, and up to him return, / If not depraved from good, created all / Such to perfection, one first matter all, / Indued with various forms, various degrees / Of substance, and in things that live, of life; / But more refined, more spirituous, and pure, / As nearer to him placed, or nearer tending ... Till body up to spirit work' (5. 469–79). He reveals to Adam that man may transmute or refine his earthly state into a heavenly one by following the golden rule of love and obedience (5.491–503).

regeneration   see **blood, generation, prima materia.**

remedy   see **medicine.**

retort   a globe-shaped vessel of glass or earthenware with a long, gradually bent neck, used in distillation. A recipe by St Dunstan for making the elixir states: 'Take of the best red transparent oar [ore] of gold, as much as you can have, drive its Spirit from it through a Retort; this is the *Azoth* and the *Acetum* of Philosophers, from its proper minera, which openeth radically *Sol* that is prepared' (DSP, 82–3). In Jonson's *The Alchemist*, Face exclaims: 'O sir, we are defeated! all the *workes* / Are flowne in *fumo*: euery glasse is burst ... *Retorts, Receivers, Pellicanes, Bolt-heads*, / All stroke in shiuers' (4.5.57–62).

return   the solution or dissolution of metals or the matter for the Stone, and its coagulation into a new form. The opus alchymicum is also known as the circular work of the elements, the *opus circulatorium. Simple circulation consists of the continuous distillation of liquid for the purpose of refinement. The refinement involved a continually reiterated cycle of *solve et coagula, the dissolution and coagulation of the matter, known as the process of 'return'. Calid wrote in *The Booke of the Secrets*: 'Againe we returne to dissolve those bodies and congeale them after their solution' (36). During the opus the matter for the Stone had to be dissolved and returned to its primal state or 'first nature' before it could be moulded into a new pure form. Calid wrote of this process: 'Afterward returne back to the first natures, which ascended from it, and purifie them likewise from uncleannes, blacknesse, and contrarietie' (*Booke of the Secrets*, 40). The contrary qualities of the four elements were likened to warring foes which were reconciled and united in a new harmony. During this circulation, the elements (earth, air, fire and water) are separated by distillation and converted into each other to form the perfect unity, the *fifth element, also known as 'heaven', the 'new kingdom' or the 'golden age'. The transformation of the iron age into the golden age through the circulation or return of the elements was the main task of the alchemist. Stanton Linden has pointed out that 'even one of so tough-minded a bent as John French, for example, in the epistle dedicatory to *The Art of Distillation* (1651), sees the revival of interest in alchemy [in the 1650s] as a harbinger of a new Golden Age of moral perfection' (*Darke Hieroglyphicks*, 218). Abraham Cowley had written in his ode 'In Commendation of the time we live under the Reign of our Gracious King Charles': 'Our *Charles*, blest *Alchymist* ... did change / The Iron age of old, / Into an age of Gold' (54). Similarly, Andrew Marvell's 'An Horatian Ode upon Cromwell's return from Ireland' celebrated the return which enables Cromwell to ruin 'the great work' of time and alchemically 'cast the kingdom old / Into another mould' (lines 34–6). Cromwell is later described by Marvell in 'A Poem upon the Death of his Late Highness the Lord Protector' as the one who has presided over 'the golden years' (line 4). Shakespeare had earlier used 'ruin' and 'return' in an alchemical context in Sonnet 119. The poet, after being deceived by a faithless lover, having drunk 'potions ... of siren tears / Distilled from limbecks foul as hell within', finally realizes that 'ruined love when it is built anew / Grows fairer than at first, more strong, far greater. / So I return rebuked to my content, / And gain by ills thrice more than I have spent' (lines 1–2, 11–14). See solve et coagula, opus circulatorium, opus contra naturam.

reverberatory a furnace in which the flame or heat is forced back upon the substance which is already being heated by it. Colson's *Philosophia maturata* states that calcining the blackened matter of the Stone is not enough for its perfect cleansing to whiteness, but that the matter must be put 'into a Reverberatory, with a moderate heat, for eight dayes, and so many Nights, increasing the heat and flame, till it be white as Snow' (33). In Ben Jonson's *The Alchemist* Subtle informs Mammon that he has won the salt of mercury by '*reverberating* in *Athanor*' (2.3.66).

rex marinus see **king**.

ripen to mature (used of metals). The alchemists perceived the metals inside the crust of the earth as living organisms growing like plants and trees.

Such imperfect metals as lead, copper and iron were thought to grow slowly in the earth's womb until they eventually ripened into the perfect metal, gold. This growth was thought to be stimulated by the gentle penetration of the sun's rays into the earth. Alexander Pope wrote in *Windsor Forest*: 'And Phoebus warm the rip'ning ore to gold' (line 396). The alchemists ripened gold in the laboratory by using their secret fire (the 'sun') to reduce the metal into its *prima materia (mercury or *Mercurius) from which they obtained the metallic seeds to 'grow' gold. Thus philosophical mercury was thought of as 'unripe' or potential gold. Philalethes wrote: 'And if our *Mercury* which wee doe call / Our living water, be but unripe Gold, / Then unto Gold by Art what ever shall / Converted be' (*Marrow*, bk. 1, 11). The image of the alchemical plant blooming with *roses, and that of the *philosophical tree with its ripened fruits of sun and moon, symbolize the completion of the opus alchymicum. See **harvest**.

river   see **Nile, stream**.

river Jordan   see **Naaman the leper**.

robe   see **dye, red elixir, gold and silver, sable robe, Saturn, Sol**.

rock   the place where the *prima materia is found, the alchemical vessel, a name for the *philosopher's stone. *The Glory of the World* records the saying of an ancient philosopher: 'Our Stone is called the sacred rock' (HM, 1:172). An anonymous alchemical treatise said of the mercurial water from which the Stone is made: 'This Water I have in my first part called The Spirit of the Rock, and it is truely Rocky and Stony, for it is Coagulated Into the Stone of the Wise Men' (BL Sloane 3631, f. 9). Robert Fludd called the *quintessence (often identified with the Stone) a 'spirituall rock of pure transparent saphir' (TGH, 109). According to Abu'L-Qasim, the mercurial *prima materia is found in a topsy-turvy rock on a *mountain in India: there is 'a rock in which a devouring lion takes shelter and often he defends it. And the top of this rock is confused with its base, and its nearest part reaches to its farthest, and its head is in the place of its back, and *vice versa*' (*Book of Knowledge*, 23). In other alchemical texts the 'tumulus of rock' is a name for the alchemical vessel as *grave or sepulchre, the place where the alchemical lovers are united in the *chemical wedding and then buried and putrefied in order to bring forth the *philosophical child or stone. *The Rosary of the Philosophers* called the vessel (while the matter is in *putrefaction) 'the red tomb' or 'tumulus of rock' (McLean, *Rosary*, 110). See **cornerstone**.

roots   a metaphor to describe the four elements, earth, air, fire and water, which are the significant constituents of the philosopher's stone. They are the roots from which the philosophical tree grows, blossoms and comes to fruition (see **fifth element, inverted tree, philosophical tree**).

rose garden   see **garden**.

rose (red)   a symbol of the goal of the opus alchymicum, the perfect red stone or elixir attained at the culmination of the *rubedo (see fig. 34). The red stone has the power to transmute all base metal into pure gold and earthly man into the illumined philosopher. Both red and white roses are said to bloom in the philosopher's garden when the white and red stones appear in the alembic. Ripley wrote in his *Bosome Book* of 'the pleasant and dainty Garden of the Philosophers, which beareth the sweet smelling Roses white and red, abbreviated out of all the Work of the Philosophers, containing in it nothing superfluous or diminished, teaching to make infinitely Gold and Silver' (CC, 121). The blossoming of the roses signifies the advent of wisdom and inner knowledge as well as the attainment of the elixir or consolamentum (comforter). The image of the alchemical rose and lily (synonymous with the white rose) occurs in John Collop's 'The praise of his Mistris': 'Admire no more those downy breasts, / Where Candors pure Elixir rests. / Praise not the blushings of the Rose, / Which th' Mornings mantle doth disclose: / Nor subtile Lillies which out-vie / Calcining arts choice Chymistry' (lines 1–6). See **flower, garden, lily** (white), **philosophical tree.**

rose (white)   a symbol of the white elixir and the *albedo or pure white stage which occurs just prior to the final red stage or *rubedo. It also symbolizes the white stone which has the power to transmute base metal into silver. Calid wrote that the matter for the Stone after sublimation will become 'like unto the Matter of the White Rose, transparent and most clear as any Orient Pearl' (*Booke of the Secrets*, 126). The white rose also symbolizes the feminine silver/moon aspect of the opus which must be united with the gold/male aspect in the *chemical wedding of *Sol and *Luna. In the alchemical texts the image of the white rose is invariably coupled with that of the red *rose signifying the red stone or elixir. In a recipe for the elixir St Dunstan wrote: 'Take of the best Oar [i.e. ore] of Gold, pulverize it very well, seal it with *Hermes* his Seal, set it so long into the vaporous fire, till you see it spring up and grow a white and red rose' (*DSP*, 89). In the description of his encounter with the alchemical elixirs, the narrator of *The Golden Tract* says: 'Then lighting upon a certain place, I found white and red roses' (*HM*, 1:44). These roses are said to be found blooming in the philosopher's rose garden, the garden of wisdom. The white rose, like the white *lily, is a symbol of purity. See **flower, garden.**

rotation of the elements   see **elements, opus circulatorium.**

royal   Alchemy is known as 'the royal art'. Gold was thought of as the noble, royal metal in contrast with the 'lesser' base metals, lead, iron, copper and tin. The treatise *Pearce the Black Monke upon the Elixir* stated that one ounce of the *philosopher's stone cast on two hundred ounces of mercury 'Schall make Gold most royall' (*TCB*, 276). The final coniunctio, which involves the marriage of the the red *king (the male principle) to the white *queen (the female principle), is called the royal wedding. At this stage the matter in the alembic is in its most highly refined state.

From this royal union the philosopher's *child, the Stone, is born. Arthur Dee called the Stone 'Our Infant . . . of Royall Stock' (*FC*, 108). The royal crown is a symbol of the completed Stone at the perfect red stage (see fig. 33). Metaphysically, the royal crown symbolizes the halo of light radiating from the head of the saint or illumined philosopher.

rubedo (also known as the rubification), the reddening of the white matter of the Stone at the final stage in the opus alchymicum. Humphrey Lock's treatise says of the Stone that 'when he is fully fedd [he is] brought from whiteness into white / and after into red' (f. 4). The 'rubification' of the Stone is listed as one of the key stages of the alchemical opus by the alchemist's servant in John Lyly's play *Gallathea*: ' it is a very secrete Science, for none almost can vnderstand the language of it. Sublimation . . . Calcination, Rubification' (2.3.12–13). And Michael Sendivogius wrote in 'A Dialogue of the Alchymist and Sulphur': 'Wash and dealbate, and then rubify' (line 602, *AP*, 530). At the rubedo the silvery moonlight and dawn light of the *albedo phase develop into the golden illumination of the midday sun, symbolizing the attainment of the *philosopher's stone, the attainment of the consciousness of God, the goal of the opus. At this point the limited lunar consciousness, the brain, receives the full illumination of the spiritual sun (Hodgson, *Astrology*, 30).

When the matter of the Stone has been purified and made spotless at the *albedo it is then ready to be reunited with the spirit (or the already united spirit and soul). With the fixation, crystallization or embodiment of the eternal spirit, form is bestowed upon the pure, but as yet formless, matter of the Stone. At this union, the supreme *chemical wedding, the body is resurrected into eternal life. As the heat of the fire is increased, the divine red tincture flushes the white stone with its rich red colour, a process sometimes likened to blushing, as in Michael Drayton's *Endimion and Phoebe*. Phoebe increases her fire to the stronger heat of the sun, causing the white matter, Endimion, to be tinctured red: 'she putteth on her brave attire, / As being burnisht in her Brothers fire . . . Which quickly had his pale cheekes over-spred, / And tincted with a lovely blushing red' (*Works*, 4:146, lines 647–52). The reddening of the white matter is also frequently likened to staining with blood (see **dye**). Theophrastus compared the reddening of the slain, white Mercurius in its own blood to the dyeing of a white garment in *Tyrian purple (in Lindsay, *Origins*, 277).

The rich red (sometimes purple) of the rubedo is given many names by the alchemists. Philalethes wrote: 'And so the Red they name their Vermilion, their red lead, their Poppy of the Rock, their Tyre [i.e. Tyrian purple], their Basilisk, their red Lion, and in sum it borrows the names of all red things' (*RR*, 178). The rubedo is also symbolized by the red *rose, the red lily, *ruby, *coral, the sun (*Sol) and the red *king (see fig. 34). The red stage issues from the white stage (albedo) of the matter, and because of this it is often said that within the whiteness the red is hidden. Artephius wrote: 'And when you see the true whiteness appear, which shineth . . . know that in the whiteness there is redness hidden'

(*SB*, 52), and Roger Bacon wrote: 'When thou shalt find a whitenesse a top in the glasse, be assured that in that whitenesse, rednesse is hidden: and this thou must extract: but concoct it while it become all red' (*Mirror*, 13). Benjamin Lock explained that the elixir 'is outwardly whyte bycause of his coldness and moysture and inwardly red bycause of his drynes and heate, which rednes is hid in his center as the soul ... in his body' ('Picklock', f. 5v). In Andrew Marvell's poem, 'The Nymph Complaining for the Death of her faun', the white fawn folds itself 'In whitest sheets of lilies cold' and feeds on roses 'Until its lips e'en seemed to bleed'. The mercurial fawn, described as 'Lilies without, roses within', is slain by troopers and its purple blood is shed over its whiteness, yielding the 'Gumme' or *balsam of the sages (lines 84–97) (see **cervus fugitivus**).

rubification   see **rubedo**.

ruby   a symbol for the *red stone or elixir attained as the final stage of the opus, the *rubedo. This celestial ruby has the power to transmute base metal into gold, and earthly man into an illumined philosopher. Synesius referred to 'the bloody stone, the purple red Coral, the pretious Ruby ... the red Tincture' (*The True Book*, 175). And Bassett Jones wrote of 'th' Inceration of our Ruby Stone' (*AP*, 284). In Jonson's *The Alchemist*, Mammon addresses Surly: 'I assure you, / He that has once the *flower of the sunne* / The perfect *ruby*, which we call *elixir* ... Can confer honour, loue, respect, long life, / Giue safety, valure: yea, and victorie, / To whom he will' (2.1.46–51).

rust   the 'infection' or imperfection of the base metal before purification, before the transforming *medicine or *philosopher's stone' has been applied to it. Dastin's *Dreame* calls this disease of metals 'cancred rust' (*TCB*, 262). John Gower wrote in 'Concerning the Philosophers Stone' that the Stone 'pureth' metals from the 'vice ... Of rust' (*TCB*, 371). *Leprosy and rust are equivalent terms in alchemy. Rust is used in its alchemical, metaphysical sense by Lucy Hastings in a poem on the premature death of her son, Henry Lord Hastings: 'His Soul is he, which when his Dear / Redeemer had refin'd to a height / Of Purity, and Solid weight; / No longer would he Let it Stay, / With in this Crucible of Clay, / But meaning him a richer Case, / To raise his Luster, not imbase, / And knowing the infectious Dust / Might Canker the bright piece with Rust, / Hasted him hence' (lines 7–16, in Greer, *Kissing the Rod*, 9–10). Rust is also synonymous with the process of *putrefaction or corruption through which the metal, or body of the Stone, must pass in order to be purified or redeemed. Calid wrote: 'Know, that except thou subtiliate the bodie till all become water, it will not rust and putrefie, and then it cannot congeale the flitting soules' (*Booke of the Secrets*, 36).

S

sable robe a symbol of the black nigredo, the initial stage of the opus alchymicum; synonymous with the black shirt and black vest. Synesius spoke of the matter in the bottom of the alembic during the initial stage as 'putrefyed and black, which is called the sable Robe, Night, or the Croweshead' (*The True Book*, 171). William Bloomfield likewise wrote of the black night of the soul at the nigredo with its symbolic eclipse of light: 'The *Sun* and *Moone* shall lose their light / And in mourning Sables they them shall dight' (*TCB*, 323). See **nigredo**.

sal ammoniac (or **sal armoniac**) usually ammonium chloride used in washing and purifying processes; in alchemy it is Arabian salt or the dissolved matter of the Stone and is symbolized by the *eagle. In John Lyly's *Gallathea* Peter, trying to teach Rafe the four spirits of alchemy, names 'The third, sal armoniack' (2.3.58). The theory of the four spirits is set down in Chaucer's *Canon's Yeoman's Tale* (which may be Lyly's source): 'The firste spirit quik-silver called is, / The second orpiment, the thridde, y-wis, / Sal armoniack, and the ferthe brimstoon' (lines 822–4).

salamander a symbol of the fiery masculine seed of metals, *sulphur, the hot, dry, active male principle of the opus; the red stone or elixir, the magical *philosopher's stone which has the power to convert base metal to gold and cure all disease and imperfection. Jodocus Greverius is cited in *Zoroaster's Cave*: 'I tell thee that our Semen is the true Salamander, conceived by fire, nursed by fire and perfected by fire' (62). The red stone is compared to the fire spirit or salamander because, like this spirit, the Stone is able to live in the fire and is nourished by it. The fifth emblem of *The Book of Lambspring* shows the salamander shining in the fire symbolizing the augmentation or *multiplication of the Stone. The text informs us that the 'blood' of the salamander is 'the most precious Medicine upon earth' (*HM*, 1:294–5).

salt, sulphur and mercury the tria prima or three first principles of Theophrastus Bombastus von Hohenheim (1493–1541), the Swiss iatrochemist and physician known as Paracelsus. Paracelsus added a third principle to the two traditional alchemical principles 'sulphur' and 'mercury', which he termed 'salt' (for sulphur and mercury, see **prima materia**). According to Paracelsus all metals were made from a three-fold matter: mercury (the spirit), sulphur (the soul) and salt (the body) (fig. 36). In this theory, sulphur or the soul is the mediating principle which unites the two contraries, body and spirit, and transforms them into one essence. This differs from traditional alchemical theory, where mercury (or Mercurius) is the great uniter and binder of opposite substances and qualities (see **glue**). In the tria prima theory, sulphur is the cause of structure, substance and combustibility, and is the principle of growth. Mercury provides the vaporous and liquid quality, penetrating and enlivening things, while salt keeps matter together by giving

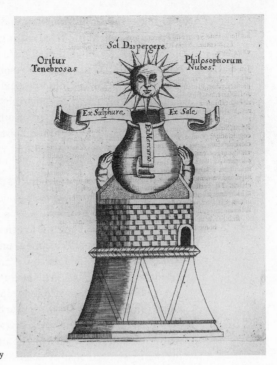

Sol Dispergere.
Oritur
Tenebrosas
Philosophorum
Nubes.
Ex Sulphure.
Ex Sale.
Ex Mercurio.

36 Salt, sulphur and mercury

it fixity and firmness, and is found in the ashes. *The Golden Tract* stated that the three constituents of the Stone were: 'The true spirit of mercury, and the soul of sulphur united to spiritual salt and dwelling in one body' (HM, 1.14). In *A Suddain Flash*, George Wither compared perfect government to the harmonious combination of the tria prima in one body: 'But this [perfection] can never be (as I have said / Elsewhere) until . . . by good and perfect *Chymestry*, / *Natures* three *principles*, *Salt, Mercury* / And *Sulphur*, be to that just *temprature*, / And such *proportion* brought, as will procure / To govern us, a *Civil-Trinity* / Made up into a *blessed Unity*' (32). John Collop plays on the idea of the three Paracelsian principles in a satirical poem on a quack chemist, 'The fugitive Chymick': 'The Knave turns quack too, blow'd the chymist coal; / As if each blast, inspir'd their *Theophrasts* soul. / He talks of salt without a grain of wit. / But *Mercury's* sure ith' lightnesse of his wit; / Nor doth he want his Sulphur, he hath got / Against the state no less then Powderplot' (lines 1–6). In traditional alchemical theory salt, like ash, is a synonym for the pure white stage or *albedo and is associated with the white stone, the *white foliated earth, the full moon, the silver lunar stage, the *white woman, the soul, the white *dove and wisdom (sal sapientiae).

sand, sand-bath   a *bath or balneum containing warmed sand for the gentle, even heating of the matter of the *Stone in the alchemical vessel. A recipe in Colson's *Philosophia maturata* instructs the alchemist to place three pounds of the *green lion into a 'glass' containing four sextaries of Wine, and then 'put it into a Furnace with sand, so as the Sand may be two fingers thick under the Glass, and about and above the Matter; then the Matter being a little dryed with a gentle heat, put a Receiver not yet luted thereto' (29). In Jonson's *The Alchemist,* Subtle informs Mammon: 'I meane to tinct C. in *sand-heat*, to morrow / And giue him [the Stone] *imbibation*' (2.3.58–9). In other contexts red sand, like red earth, is a name for the matter out of which the *philosopher's stone is made. *The Golden Tract* states of this matter: 'Nothing is more precious then the red sand of the sea; it is the distilled moisture of the Moon joined to the light of the Sun, and congealed' (HM, 12).

sapientia wisdom, divine knowledge, which is the guide and goal of the opus alchymicum. The *philosopher's stone or pure love essence is born of the union of power and wisdom, personified in alchemy by *Sol (the male principle) and *Luna (the female principle). Wisdom is the female aspect of the philosopher's stone or universal *medicine. Robert Fludd wrote in 'Truth's Golden Harrow': 'It is wisdom which is the infallible medicine' (TGH, 125), and, in his poem 'On Dr. George Bowle of Oundle', John Collop wrote: 'Knowledge is th' Suns Child, true Philosophers Stone' (line 6). In alchemy, wisdom or divine knowledge is frequently personified as a beautiful female figure. The *Aurora consurgens* opens with a description of wisdom in the form of a mystical lady (AC, 33), and the twenty-sixth emblem of Maier's *Atalanta fugiens* shows a crowned Lady Sapientia standing in a landscape (AF, 195). Thomas Vaughan personified wisdom as a beautiful lady who makes all things new, who is the perfect reflection of God: 'For Wisdom is more moving then any motion, she passeth and goeth thorow all Things by reason of her pureness. For she is the Breath of the power of God, and a pure Influence flowing from the Glory of the Almighty, therefore can no defiled thing fall into her. For she is the brightnesse of the everlasting light, the unspotted mirror of the power of God, and the image of his goodnesse. And being but One, she can do all things and remayning in her self she maketh all things new' (VW (R), 123).

Saturn the base metal lead; a secret name for the *prima materia and for *philosophical mercury; the name of the Stone's matter during its *putrefaction at the bottom of the vessel. Arnoldus is cited in *Zoroaster's Cave*: 'Our Stone . . . in the putrefaction is called Saturnus' (65). Saturn's discipline and melancholia govern the grim beginnings of the opus alchymicum. As the reaper who cuts down all in his path, Saturn is strongly associated with the initial deathly stage of the *nigredo, during which the diseased metal or matter for the Stone is killed, dissolved and putrefied into the prima materia or philosophical mercury. Maier's *Atalanta fugiens* observed that Saturn 'carries a scythe because, like time, he mows everything he produces' (120) (see **weaponry**). Old man Saturn (Mercurius senex) is that force which mercilessly destroys the old and yet miraculously makes way for the new (Mercurius puer) (see fig. 10 and fig. 26). The first emblem of Basil Valentine's *Practica with Twelve Keys* shows Saturn mowing with his scythe. The accompanying text says: 'As the physician purges and cleanses the inward parts of the body, and removes all the unhealthy matter by means of his medicine, so our metallic substances must be purified and refined of all foreign matter, in order to ensure the success of our task' (HM, 1:24–5). Philalethes described how before entering the *bath of dissolution during the black nigredo and putrefaction, the sick *king (the metal, matter for the Stone) 'pulls off his robe and gives it to Saturn from whom he receives a black shirt' (RR, 20). After the nigredo or stage of Saturn, the blackened matter of the Stone in the alembic (the 'king' in the 'bath') must be purified and whitened. In *Atalanta fugiens*, Michael Maier used the dramatic image of throwing snow in Saturn's black face to represent this whitening process: 'Whosoever wants to achieve much with little trouble, / Should throw snow in Saturn's black face: / And the whitest material of lead will fall to you' (AF, 176–7). Saturn sometimes appears in the role of guide or psychopomp to the alchemist, instructing him on the details of the opus alchymicum, as in Michael Sendivogius's 'The Philosophicall Aenigma' or in his 'A Dialogue of the Allchymist and Sulphur'. In Bernard Trevisan's 'The Practise of the Philosophick Stone', Saturn takes the role of the first chamberlain to the *king (raw matter) as the king steps into the spring (or bath) at the *black beginning of the opus (AP, 452).

scissors see **weaponry**.

scythe see **weaponry**.

sea or **sea water** a synonym for the *mercurial waters or *prima materia. The prima materia is the original stuff of creation from which it was thought all things in the universe were made. The sea is used as an image for the prima materia because it is the 'mother' (mater, matter) from which all things come. The sea's expansive, amorphous state makes it an obvious choice of image for something that is formless but contains forms within it. Saturn, in Michael Sendivogius's 'The Philosophicall Aenigma', says of this substance: 'Many and different are its names, but we / Call it the Water of our Sophick Sea: / A Water which no vulgus understands, / Water of Life, which never wets the Hands' (lines 321–4, AP, 505). As the mercurial water, the 'sea' represents the solvent of the metal or matter for the Stone. *The Sophic Hydrolith* says that the dissolution of this matter in the cycle of *solve et coagula occurs 'by means of the sweet universal ... marine water' (HM, 1:98). Plate 7 in Salomon Trismosin's *Splendor Solis* and emblem 31 in Michael Maier's *Atalanta fugens* both depict the alchemical king (the raw matter of the Stone) being marinated in sea water before he is rescued and taken to dry land (signifying the *coagula). The mercurial water is also used to feed the growing infant Stone. Numerous alchemical texts depict the *philosophical tree growing with its roots in the sea (or on an island in the sea) and this symbolizes the nourishment of the young, growing Stone (see fig. 30). See **cibation**, **red sea**.

seal see **Hermes' seal**.

seed the germinal seed or life spark, thought to be inside the hard shell of
metals, from which gold could be generated. This seed of metals was
thought to consist of an interior heat, named philosophical *sulphur,
and a moist spirit, philosophical *argent vive (the *radical humidity).
A Short Catechism of Alchemy asks: 'Q. What do you understand by the seed
in the work of the Philosophers? A. I understand the interior heat, or the
specific spirit, which is enclosed in the humid radical' (PW, 303). The
alchemists believed that gold could be produced from the seed of gold
in the same way as an acorn produced an oak tree. The seed of gold was
obtained by dissolving gold into the original stuff from which it was
created, known as the *prima materia, which contained sulphur and
argent vive, the male and female seeds of metals. Sir George Ripley is
cited in *Zoroaster's Cave*: 'The matter which we need to our work is ... the
Materia prima propinqua, The first matter in a propinquity, that is, the
second; which in Animals is Sperm, in vegetals Seed, in minerals
Sulphur and Argent vive' (62). The two opposing seeds of metals,
sulphur (hot, dry, active male; fire and air) and argent vive (cold, moist,
receptive, female; water and earth) had to be reconciled and united by
the alchemist during the process of the opus in order to create the
*philosopher's stone (the agent of transmutation). See also **grain**.

separation the same as *division; the separation of the original *chaos of the Stone
into the four differentiated elements (earth, air, fire and water); the
division of the pure from the impure. In *The New World of English Words*,
Edward Phillips defined alchemy as 'the art of dissolving metals, to
separate the pure from the impure' (no pagination). The separation is
accomplished by a reiterated cycle of *solve et coagula (dissolution and
coagulation). During this repeated process the matter of the Stone
becomes more subtle and pure. Sir George Ripley wrote that '*Separacyon*,
doth ech parte from other devyde, / The subtill fro the groce, fro the
thyck the thyn ... Makyng dyvysyon of qualytes Elementall' (TCB, 139).
Separation is the same as dissolution, division and *divorce and occurs
at the initial stage of the opus alchymicum known as the *nigredo. The
coagulation, *coniunctio, *fixation or union of the opposing elements
cannot take place unless they have first been separated. Although the
separation appears to be a time of death, sorrow and suffering, it is
nevertheless the necessary prelude to perfect conjunction and fixation.
Arthur Dee quoted Dastin: 'If the first work proceed not, how is the
second attained to? Because if no division be made, there is no conjunction' (FC, 15). During the process of separation the alchemist gains a
wider understanding of himself and the cosmos, and learns to discriminate between the true and the false, illusion and reality, thus
emerging from the initial chaos unscathed. The alchemical processes of
separation and fixation are referred to in Thomas St Nicholas's poem
'Commendable Chemistry': in spiritual alchemy (as opposed to expen-
sive material alchemy), 'when the limbeck hath by sev'ral drops / A separation made ... 'twill be no cost / To fix't in writing, that it be not lost'
(lines 63–70). Samuel Johnson used the alchemical term 'separation'
in an article in *The Rambler*: 'To expunge faults where there are no

excellencies is a task equally useless with that of the chymist who employs the art of separation and refinement upon ore in which no precious metal is combined to reward his operations' (16 July 1751).

sepulchre   see **grave, dog and bitch**.

serpent   the ancient matter with which the alchemist begins his task, *Mercurius or the divine mercurial water of transformation, and the *prima materia. The poisonous *dragon or serpent, which symbolizes Mercurius at the primitive opening of the opus, is a dark, destructive, chthonic force with the power to kill the corrupt metal or matter for the Stone and dissolve it into its first matter or *prima materia. In Sir George Ripley's *The Compound of Alchymie,* the serpent is also the name for the ancient corrupt matter or metal which the mercurial serpent destroys and reduces into the prima materia: 'Thus ye shall go to Putrefaction, / And bring the *Serpent* to reduction' (TCB, 134). The process of bringing the serpent to reduction is illustrated in Nicolas Flamel's hieroglyph of the snake nailed to the cross (GU Ferguson MS 17, f. 27). As well as representing the ancient matter and the deathly waters of destruction which reduce the matter or metal into its prima materia, the serpent is also an image for that prima materia. When reduced into the prima materia, Mercurius manifests itself as two serpents, one winged, the other wingless, which symbolize the two seeds of metals, male *sulphur and female *argent vive, which must be united to create the *philosopher's stone. These are the two serpents which, when transformed, circulate and intersect each other on the magical *caduceus of Mercurius, representing the harmonious union of the universal male and female energies. The adept must bring these complementary forces together in union for the production of the philosopher's stone. In the initial stages of the opus these two serpents simultaneously unite with and destroy each other, and their bodies are left to putrefy in the bottom of the alembic. The paradoxical Mercurius then transmutes itself, and is transmuted from being the waters of death into the divine life-giving waters which descend upon the dead, blackened matter lying in the bottom of the alembic, purifying it, cleansing and whitening it. At this stage the serpent is often identified with the river *Nile, which was thought to have magical properties and thus became a name for the waters of transformation. In 'Upon Appleton House' Andrew Marvell wrote of the river which cleanses and transforms the meadow after the nigredo of the *flood: 'No *Serpent* new nor *Crocodile* / Remains behind our little *Nile*; / Unless it self you will mistake, / Among these Meads the only Snake' (lines 629–32). At the culmination of the opus the river serpent is transmuted into the celebrated goal of the work, the elixir or Stone. The *uroboros or paradoxical serpent, which devours its own tail and begets itself, is a symbol of the circular process of the opus alchymicum. Edward Kelly wrote of Mercurius: 'It is the wanton serpent that conceives of its own seed, and brings forth on the same day' (*Two excellent Treatises*, 24). The crucified serpent of Abraham the Jew is a symbol of mercury *cooked to the perfect red stage at the *rubedo, and named the perfect elixir (GU Ferguson MS 17, f. 27). See **Mercurius**.

servant   see **cervus fugitivus, red servant.**

servus fugitivus   see **cervus fugitivus, red servant.**

severed head   see **head.**

shadow   see **sun and shadow, eclipse, gold, green lion, prima materia, venom, virgin's milk.**

sheets   the unclean matter of the Stone which must be washed and dried at the *ablution, and the matter when it has attained the pure white state at the *albedo. The process of the ablution is frequently symbolized by laundresses washing sheets or clothes which represent the unclean matter. Trismosin's *Splendor Solis* (pl. 21) shows women washing linen in tubs and in the river and laying it out to dry in the adjacent meadow (fig. 37). Fabricius observes that the laundress emblem in Mylius's *Philosophia reformata* (no. 22, first series) represents the washing of 'the foul clothes of rebirth in the sevenfold circulation or distillation' (110). In the allegory of King Duenech, represented in the twenty-eighth emblem of Maier's *Atalanta fugiens*, the white sheets in which he is wrapped become stained with the black bile of melancholy during the *nigredo. The washing and whitening of these sheets leads to the lunar stage or the *albedo. At this stage, the pure white matter of the albedo (the body of the Stone) is ready to receive the imprint of form upon it (the spirit of the Stone). The alchemists sometimes referred to this process as the staining of the white sheets with the red blood of the precious red elixir or tincture (see **dye**).

37   Washing and drying the alchemical sheets in the meadow

Sheets are also used in the process of gathering the mystical 'may dew', the mercurial water of grace needed for the accomplishment of the opus. The fourth emblem of Altus's *Mutus Liber* shows the alchemical couple wringing out sheets in a meadow. The sheets are laid out in the meadow to gather the fresh dew or *radical humidity, and then the alchemist and his 'soror mystica' wring out the dew from the sheets to collect it in the alchemical vessel ready for use.

ship a name for the alchemical vessel during the dark process of the *nigredo and dissolution. During dissolution, the water element dominates the other elements in the work, and so the nigredo is sometimes symbolized by the image of the flood, with the vessel as ark or ship floating on the waters (see **flood**). Thomas Charnock calls his alembic the 'Ship … of Glasse' (*TCB*, 292). In Andreae's *The Chymical Wedding*, Christian Rosencreutz boards one of seven ships which have the signs of the seven metals on them. Six of these ships carry the coffins of the buried 'Royal Persons' and are sailing to the tower of Olympus to obtain *medicines necessary to revive the dead (123–5). The alchemical vessel at this stage of the opus is also known as the coffin (see **grave**). Andreae here uses the images of both ship and coffin for the vessel. See ark. Referring to the distillation and sublimation of the Stone's matter, the *Philosophia maturata* records that: 'after the third Day he shall ascend and descend, first to the Moon, then to the Sun, through the round Ocean Sea, and without end, sitting in a very little Ship' (35). In Shakespeare's *Pericles,* the '*Tyrian Shippe*' with its 'banners Sable' is the vessel in which the unredeemed Pericles suffers the blackness of the nigredo before he is transformed by Marina at 'Metaline' (the place of metalline transmutation) into the king of the *Tyrian purple (5. Ch.18; 5. 1.12–14) (see **Tyrian purple**).

shirt see **colours**.

signatures see **doctrine of signatures**.

signet see **Hermes' seal**.

silver the physical metal silver; a symbol of the *albedo, the pure white stage at which the white stone and elixir are attained. Roger Bacon wrote of the metal: 'Silver is a body, cleane, pure, and almost perfect, begotten of *Argent-vive*, pure, almost fixed, cleare, and white, and of such a like *Sulphur*. It wanteth nothing, save a little fixation, colour and weight' (*Mirror*, 5). At the lunar stage of the albedo, the white stone has the power to transmute base metal into pure silver. Sir Thomas Browne wrote that Arthur Dee, while he was in Bohemia with Edward Kelly and his father John Dee, 'had seen projection made and transmutation of pewter dishes and flaggons into sylver which the goldsmiths at Prague bought of them' (Bod. Ashm. MS 1788, f. 151r). Silver is also the symbol of the female principle of the alchemical opus, *Luna, which must be united with the male principle, *Sol (or gold), in the *chemical wedding, in order to create the magical *philosopher's stone. See **gold and silver, Luna**.

sister   see **incest**.

skeleton   see **nigredo**, and figures 8, 9 and 20.

skull   see **nigredo, beheading, head**.

smell   the advent of the stinking smell of *graves is a sign that the process of *putrefaction, which occurs at the initial stage known as the *nigredo, is under way. Artephius wrote: 'in this putrefaction and resolution of the body, three signs appear, viz. a black color, a discontinuity of parts, and a stinking smell, not much unlike the smell of the vault where dead bodies are buried' (SB, 51–2). This unsavoury odour in the first operation of the opus is often linked with stinking asafoetida, the name which the alchemists apply 'to the Mercury of Ripley, because it has the smell of this substance, when newly extracted from the mineral ore' (Ruland, *Lexicon*, 337). See **green lion**. Colson's *Philosophia maturata* explained that 'By the *stinking gumme*, we mean a certain stinking smell, proceeding from the unclean Body in the first distillation, which is altogether like unto stinking *Assafoetida*, that with a certain sweetness, whereof it is said before its preparation, its smell is grievous; which is most certain: but after that in a due manner it shall be prepared and circulated into any quintessence' (11–12). See also **fragrance**.

smoke (or **fume**)   see **green lion, cloud**.

snake   see **serpent, dragon, Mercurius**.

snow   the whitened 'body' of the Stone also known as terra alba foliata (the *white foliated earth) whose 'whiteness surpasses any snow in the world' (Stolcius, *Viridarium chimicum*, 146). This is the pure matter from which the new Stone or *philosophical child is formed. In Book 3 of Edmund Spenser's *The Faerie Queene*, the witch who creates the false Florimel as an alchemical homunculus fashions the body from a substance which is 'purest snow in massie mould congeald ... tempred with fine Mercury' (3.8.6). In *Atalanta fugiens* Michael Maier used the dramatic image of throwing 'snow in Saturn's black face' in order to represent the process of whitening the blackened 'body' of the Stone, which has putrefied in the bottom of the vessel at the *nigredo (176). *The Rosary of the Philosophers* says of the white *dust or earth which adheres to the sides of the vessel during *sublimation: 'when it shall ascend most white as Snow, it will be compleat, therefore gather it carefully, lest it fly away into smoke, because that is the very sought for good, the white foliated Earth, congealing what is to be congealed' (in FC, 72). When the white earth or snow has been separated from the dregs or *faeces and has adhered to the sides of the vessel, the alchemist must collect it and continue to sublimate it, as Geber advises: 'And when thou shalt see that thing excelling in its whitenesse the whitest snow, and as it were dead, adhere to the sides of the subliming vessell, then reiterate its sublimation without dregs' (in FC, 68). At the final sublimation the snow is transformed into the philosopher's *quintessence and the white stone which can transform base metal into silver or *Luna (see **Bird of Hermes**). The *Clangor Buccinae* directs the alchemist to 'sublime the Body [of the Stone] as much as thou canst' until it is whitened. It will then 'ascend most purely, like Snow, the which is our pure Quintessence … which the Alchemists may use, that with it they might make Silver' (in *FC*, 78–9). Artephius also spoke of the *quintessence which ascends to the top of the alembic as 'more white than the driven snow' (*SB*, 44). Snow is a symbol of the pure white stage of the opus known as the *albedo. The landscape which the alchemists use to represent the albedo is cold, white, still and silver under the illumination of the moon.

Sol the sun, gold, philosophical gold (the virtue hidden in gold). Chaucer's Canon's Yeoman instructs his listeners: 'Sol is gold, and Luna silver we threpe [affirm]' (*Canon's Yeoman's Tale*, line 826). Philosophical gold or Sol is gold prepared by the art of the alchemist. Ficinus is cited in *Zoroaster's Cave*: 'All the metals when they are prepared by Art, then they are call'd Sol, Luna, Mercurius etc. For before they were onely Gold, Silver, and Quicksilver' (65). Calid explains that this 'Sol is engendred of a most pure fine Mercury, and a pure red Sulphur, by the Influence of the Sun' (*Booke of the Secrets*, 126). Colson's *Philosophia maturata* stated that '*Sol* and *Lune*, is nothing else, but *Red* and *White Earth*, to which Nature hath perfectly joyned *Argent vive*, pure, subtile, white, and Red, and so of them hath produced *Sol* and *Lune*' (2–3). Sol also symbolizes the bridegroom, the *red king, the hot, dry, active seed of metals, the male principle of the opus, which must be united with his sister *Luna (the cold, moist, receptive female principle) in the *chemical wedding (see fig. 9 and fig. 22). From the marriage of Sol and Luna (spirit and purified body) the magical *philosopher's stone is born. Thus Sol is the father of the Stone, as Bassett Jones's joking paraphrase of the *Emerald Table* in 'Lithochymicus' illustrates: '*Sol* shall be father to this Bratt' (*AP*, 245). Sol is sometimes described as the *seed of gold which is sown in the field of Luna (the *white foliated earth or 'body' of the Stone attained at the *albedo).

Sol is also identified with the blood of the *green lion, which is the great solvent known as red mercury (*Luna is the white mercury, the *virgin's milk). Colson's *Philosophia maturata* states that after putting the green lion to be heated in a sand-bath a white fume rises and 'tingeth the Receiver with a certain thick and milky humidity which is our Lune, and therewith shal also ascend a most red oyl, called Philosophers aureal Gold, a stinking menstruum, the Philosophers Sol, our Tincture, Burning water, the *Blood of the Green Lyon*, our unctuous humidity, which is the last comfort of Man's Body in this life' (31). Finally, Sol symbolizes the *red elixir, the red stone, the culmination of the opus alchymicum known as the *rubedo. Subtle, in Jonson's *The Alchemist*, says: 'The work is done: Bright SOL is in his robe. / We haue a med'cine of the *triple Soule*, / The *glorified spirit*' (2.3.29–31). According to Capodistria, the seeker of alchemy in Durrell's *The Alexandria Quartet*, Sol is associated with wisdom, while Luna is associated with fantasy (808). Metaphysically, Sol is

Putre *factio !*

38 Black sun, skeleton, angel of death and crow

the source of the perfect incarnation which follows the illumination of the soul (Luna) by the divine spirit or solar ray. See **sol niger**, **sun**, **king**.

sol niger   (the black sun), symbol of the death and putrefaction of the metal, or of united *sulphur and *argent vive at the *nigredo, the initial stage of the opus alchymicum (see **chemical wedding**) (see fig. 38). At the nigredo the metal or matter for the Stone is 'killed' and dissolved into its *prima materia so that it may be resurrected in a new form. At the death of the matter, darkness reigns. The light of the sun (gold) is said to be put out, totally eclipsed (see **eclipse**). Artephius wrote: 'But first this Sol by putrefaction and resolution in this water, loseth all its light or brightness and will grow dark and black' (*SB*, 4).

solar fruit, solar tree   see **fruit**, **philosophical tree**.

Solomon   According to the alchemists, Solomon was a Hermetic philosopher and built his temple with the aid of the *philosopher's stone (*HM*, 1:86–7). In Jonson's *The Alchemist* Sir Epicure Mammon says to Face: 'For I doe meane / To haue a list of wiues and concubines, / Equall with SALOMON; who had the *stone* / Alike, with me' (2.2.34–7). Mammon also claims to have an alchemical book written by Solomon, Moses and Maria Prophetissa: 'I'll show you a booke, where MOSES, and his sister, / And SALOMON haue written of the art' (2.1.81–2).

solution   see **solve et coagula**.

solve et coagula   dissolve and coagulate, one of the oldest axioms in alchemy, first found in Greek manuscript quotations of Maria Prophetissa (Patai, 'Maria', 183). The alchemical process of solution (or dissolution) involves the converting of a solid (a body) into a fluid substance (a spirit), while the coagulation is the turning of a fluid into a dry solid. *Zoroaster's Cave* states: 'Our Great business is to make the Body a Spirit, and the Spirit a body' (74). The opus alchymicum consists of a repeated series of dissolutions and coagulations – the dissolution of the old metal or matter of the Stone into the *prima materia (original stuff from which it was created) and the coagulation of that pure materia into a new and more beautiful form. With each cycle of solve et coagula the matter in the alembic becomes purer and more potent. A well-known alchemical dictum is 'Dissolve and congeal again and again, dissolve and congeal, till the tincture grows in the stone' (AE, 15). The alchemist must never cease in the process of dissolving the stone which has just been coagulated. Subtle in Jonson's *The Alchemist* informs Mammon that the 'medicine' (i.e. Stone) is exalted by 'giuing him solution; then congeal him; / And then dissolve him; then again congeal him; / For look how oft I iterate the work, / So many times I add unto his virtue' (2.3.104–7). The solve or dissolution is associated with the moon (moisture and coldness), while the coagula is associated with the sun (dryness and heat). Dastin wrote in his 'Speculum philosophiae': 'for in the beginning of thy operation, help the work in dissolution, by the Moon, and in coagulation by the Sun' (in FC, 41). The moon and the sun here refer to the two contrary actions of the mercurial waters (see **stream**).

Frequently the processes of *separation (division) and *coniunctio (union) are identified with the solve et coagula. When the metal or matter for the Stone is killed and dissolved (solve), its soul and spirit is separated from its body (separatio). The body is cleansed of its impurity and the soul (or soul/spirit union) may then be reunited with it. The re-entry of the soul/spirit into the purified matter at the coniunctio gives it form, coagulates it. At the simplest level, the solve is the softening of hard things, and the coagula the hardening of soft things (or the giving of form to amorphous matter). In order for a complete merging or union to take place between body and spirit at the *chemical wedding, the body (a hard substance) has to be spiritualized or made soft, while at the same time the spirit (a soft substance) is materialized or made hard. This is sometimes termed the volatilization and the fixation of the matter. Many alchemical texts claim that these two processes happen simultaneously. *The Golden Tract* stated: 'with this solution there takes place simultaneously a consolidation of the spirit' (HM, 1:40). Artephius wrote of the 'Sunne' and 'Moone', the alchemical lovers (the male and female seeds of metals) which are killed after they have been united in the *chemical wedding: 'their solution is also their congelation for they have one and the same operation, for the one is not dissolved, but that the other is congealed' (161). See **inversion**.

son of the philosophers   see **philosophical child**.

soul   the volatile vapour released when a substance, metal or matter for the Stone is dissolved. John Dryden wrote of the volatile vapour during distillation of wine as the 'soul': 'And as those lees that trouble it refine /

The agitated soul of generous wine; / So tears of joy, for your returning spilt / Work out and expiate our former guilt' ('Astraea Redux', lines 272–5). The soul plays a vital role in the creation of the philosopher's stone. The raw material for the Stone must first be dissolved into its first matter or *prima materia, and this process is referred to as the death of the 'body'. At this death the 'soul' or 'anima' is released and rises to the top of the vessel, awaiting the purification of the blackened, putrefying body which lies below (see fig. 12). In the meantime the soul unites with the spirit and is illumined by it (see **chemical wedding**). When the body is purified it can then be reunited at the coniunctio with the soul by means of the mediating spirit. From this union the philosopher's stone is conceived and born. Petrus Bonus said: 'When the Anima Candida is perfectly risen, the Artist must joyn it, the same moment, with its body: For the Anima without its body cannot be held. But such an Union must be made by mediation of the Spirit because the Anima cannot have life in the body nor perserverance in it, but by the Spirit: And such an Union and Conjunction is the end of the Work. The Soul must be joyned with the First body whence it was, and with no other' (zc, 85–6). See also **ablution**, **albedo**, **cervus fugitivus**, **fermentation**, **glue**, **Mercurius**, **nigredo**, **philosopher's stone**.

sow   see **harvest**.

spagyrist   an iatrochemical, medical chemist and follower of Paracelsus. See **iatrochemistry**.

sperm   *Mercurius, the seed of metals found in the *prima materia, from which gold and silver are grown. Benjamin Lock wrote: 'Without the sperme of Sol and Lune is made no perfect generation, nor quick fusion of medicine' ('Picklock', f. 36) (see **seed**). Mercurius, in his role as the mediator or priest joining Sol and Luna in the *chemical wedding, is known as the sperm or *glue. Thomas Vaughan calls Mercurius 'the true sperm of the great world' (vw (w), 250). The *mercurial water (or *milk) with which the body of the Stone is nourished during *imbibation is also known as sperm. The *Semita semitae* stated: 'It is nourished with its own Milk, that is, with Sperm, of which it hath been from the beginning' (in fc, 99–100).

spirit   the pure essence of a metal or person; a volatile substance which sublimes on heating (see fig. 12). In a universe of macrocosmic–microcosmic correspondences, the 'death' of a metal and the rising of volatile spirits were seen as analogous to the death of the human body and the release of the vital spirit of life. The rejoining of the united soul/spirit with the purified body of the Stone's matter constitutes the culmination of the opus. The spirits which rise up when fire is applied to the matter of the Stone during *sublimation and distillation are symbolized by *birds in alchemy. The *Aurora consurgens* says of the circulatory distillation: 'the waters are sublimed and rise like birds over the earth, which remains below as if dead, then drop down again like living rain or dew' (349). In

Paracelsus's *salt, sulphur, mercury (body, soul, spirit) theory of metals, mercury is equated with the spirit. See **albedo, chemical wedding, Mercurius, nigredo, tria prima.**

spots (or **stains**)   the unclean matter or earthiness of the Stone which has to be washed and purified in the philosophical *fire. Synesius wrote: 'Thus art thou to separate the earth from the fire, the *gross* from the *subtil* ... that is to say, the more pure substance of the stone, until thou hast got it clean and free from all spots or filth' (*The True Book*, 175). In Michael Sendivogius's 'A Dialogue of the Allchymist and Sulphur', the souls of drowned Diana and her Prince assure the narrator that the death of their bodies in the water is a necessary step in the opus: ''Tis well, 'tis very well with us ... else we / Could never have been purifyd and free / From sordid Spots of Terrestreity' (lines 472–6, AP, 527). An anonymous alchemical tract comments on the Stone's matter when purified: 'For the Earth must be Crystalline, and flowing, the soul tingeing and splendent and the spirit serene and freed from all spots, but to arrive this farr is a difficult point' (BL Sloane MS 3631, f. 11). Other alchemical images symbolizing the cleansing of the unclean matter are: the washing of the spots on *Latona's face, the cleansing of *Naaman the Leper in the river Jordan, the washing of the *Ethiopian or black man and the laundering of the dirty linen or *sheets. See **laundering, ablution.** Psychologically, the spot or stain signifies original sin, the breaking of divine law, the turning away by humankind from goodwill into self-will. A recognition and putting into action of goodwill initiates the release of pure love essence in the heart, which solves or dissolves the spots of self-will.

spring   see **bath, fountain, stream, Mercurius.**

spume of the moon   the matter of the Stone, philosophical mercury (see **halcyon**).

spume of silver   see **magnesia.**

square and circle   The transformation of the square into a circle symbolizes the transformation of the four elements into the alchemical quintessence or fifth element. The image of the square and circle also symbolizes the opus alchymicum itself, and the crystallization of the *philosopher's stone. The figure of the square and circle is a Vitruvian symbol which represents the harmonious proportions of the human body and of the universe itself. The little world or microcosm was thought to be constructed on the same principles and in the same proportions as the great world or macrocosm. Vitruvius stated that if man was to design his buildings in harmony with cosmic structures, his architecture ought to be based on the geometry of the 'square and circle' (*Ten Books*, 73). This figure became a key hieroglyph in alchemy. Around the innermost circle of Sir George Ripley's 'alchemical wheel' are inscribed the words: 'When thou hast made the quadrangle round, then is all the secrett found' (TCB, 117). As in other metaphysical systems, the square with its four sides represents the four elements, the four seasons, the four compass directions, the four arms of the earthly cross and the mutable material world perceivable through the five senses. The circle (or sphere) represents the unending perfection of divine love, the unified spiritual realm of God. In the alchemical opus the square symbolizes the four elements (earth, air, fire and water) which are to be converted into the perfection of the circular quintessence, or the *philosopher's stone which has the power to perfect all imperfections. The alchemists also say that their secret vessel of transformation is constructed according to the square and circle principle. Paracelsus wrote: 'Verily our Vessell ... ought to be framed according to a truly Geometrical proportion and measure and by a Certain (and assured) Quadrature of a Circle'. If the proportions were wrong 'the Vessel would leap into a thousand pieces' (*Aurora*, 57). See **house** for a literary example.

stag	see **cervus fugitivus**.
stag's horn	see **hart**.
stain	see **dye, blood, Latona, spots**.
star of antimony	see **antimony, star**.
star (six-pointed)	the magical transforming arcanum *Mercurius, the divine light hidden in the prison of matter; also the star of *antimony. An anonymous alchemical treatise states that during rarefaction the matter of the Stone 'breaketh and sublimeth into a Water like Gold, which is our so glorious Mercurius. This [is] the Starr of the Wise' (BL Sloane MS 3631, f. 7). Mercurius, as transforming medium, has the power to resolve and unite opposite qualities and substances, the power to create perfect balance and harmony (see **chemical wedding, glue**). An emblem in Johann Mylius's *Basilica philosophica* shows the mercurial child (with a six-pointed star above his head) uniting the opposites Sol (the hot, dry, active, male seed) and Luna (the cold, moist, receptive, female seed) (pl. 4, row 3, no. 1). Emblem 2 of *The Rosary of the Philosophers* illustrates the solar *king and lunar *queen united by the mercurial dove and six-pointed star (see fig. 9 and fig. 15). The wedding of sun and moon by the mercurial power of the six-pointed star is illustrated in a hieroglyph on the title page of Arthur Dee's 'Arca arcanorum' (fig. 39). The form of the star specifically represents the mercurial power which unites heaven above (the downward-pointing triangle) with earth below (the upward-pointing triangle). In the merging of these two triangles, heaven and earth, spirit and body, are wedded. The star is the symbol of man made perfect, the true goal of the opus alchymicum. Thomas Vaughan referred to the mercurial water (or blood) which nourishes the growth of the *philosophical child or stone as 'that starry milk' (*vw(w)*, 427). The commentary to the *Tractatus aureus* described the mercurial nourishment for the 'child' as coming from 'the philosophical heaven adorned with an infinite multitude of stars' (in *AS*, 222) (see **cibation**, see **heaven**). Regarding the 'star of antimony', B. J. T. Dobbs has written that

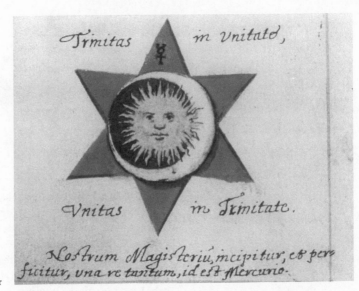

Trinitas in Vnitate,

Vnitas in Trinitate.

Nostrum Magisteriū incipitur, et perficitur, vna re tantum, id est Mercurio.

39 The six-pointed star

the crystallization of this star was produced by reducing antimony ore with iron: 'The star was antimony's natural signature or sign, demonstrating its affinity with celestial bodies and suggesting its ability to draw into itself the celestial virtues that streamed constantly toward earth from heaven' ('Newton's "Clavis"', 199).

still distillation apparatus consisting of: a vessel in which the matter to be distilled is heated; a condenser in which the vapour is liquefied; and a receiver in which the product is collected. Goodwife Faldo, whose mother looked after the Elizabethan magus John Dee during his sickness, told John Aubrey that Dee 'kept a great many stilles goeing' at Mortlake (Aubrey, *Brief Lives*, I:213). John Cleveland wrote of the alchemical still in 'Fuscara; or the Bee Errant': 'Nature's Confectioner, the *Bee*, / Whose suckets are moyst *Alchymie*, / The Still of his refining mould / Minting the Garden into Gold ... At my *Fuscara*'s sleeve ariv'd, / Where all delicious sweets are hiv'd' (lines 1–10). 'Still' is also used as a verb meaning 'to distill'. John Donne wrote of the power of spiritual crosses and metaphysical 'distillation' in 'The Cross': 'These for extracted chemic medicine serve, / And cure much better, and as well preserve / Then are you your own physic, or need none, / When stilled, or purged by tribulation' (lines 25–30).

stone see **philosopher's stone, rock.**

stork a vessel for circular distillation, like the *pelican. A diagram of the stork is found in Porta's *De distillatione* (1608) (fig. 40).

strawberries and cream see **cream.**

stream a name for the transforming arcanum, the *mercurial waters. The transforming waters, also known as streams or rivers, are dual-natured, both

40 The stork vessel

male and female. These two aspects have an opposite chemical action: one water congeals, while the other dissolves. The 'Hermetis Trismegisti tractatus aureus' stated that 'there are two Stones of the Wise, found in the Shores of the Rivers' which are 'Male and Female' (*MP*, bk. 2, 280). The *chemical wedding of the male and female lovers (the *king and *queen) is sometimes described as the union of separated streams. In Herrick's 'To the King and Queene, upon their unhappy distances', a poem which Musgrove has argued is alchemical ('Herrick's alchemical vocabulary', 240–65), the parted 'Man and Wife' are compared to separated streams which will unite again and become chemically mixed: 'Like Streams, you are divorc'd: but 'twill come when / These eyes of mine shall see you mix agen' (lines 5–6). Likewise the separated lovers in Andrew Marvell's poem 'To his Coy Mistress' are associated with two distant rivers, the Ganges in the East, and the Humber in the West, signifying the male and female aspects of the mercurial waters, the red, coagulating aspect (the East) and the cold, dissolving aspect (the West): 'Had we but World enough, and Time, / This coyness Lady were no crime . . . Thou by the *Indian Ganges* side / Should'st Rubies find: I by the Tide / Of *Humber* would complain' (lines 1–7). The drying up of the streams refers to the coagulation of the Stone's matter, after it has been dissolved in the mercurial water. Arthur Dee wrote that water and earth should be put in a *glass and 'placed in the Philosophicall Furnace, or Athanore, and cherished with a most soft Fire, whilst the Earth drinks up her Water, and (according to Ripley) the Streams are dried up' (*FC*, 152). In Michael Sendivogius's 'A Dilaogue of the Allchymist and Sulphur', the souls of the drowned Diana and her Prince (argent vive and sulphur) inform the narrator that they will not repossess their bodies 'while they are polluted so, but when / They shall be purgd to be forever clean; / And that this River shall no longer run / Dryd with the Heat of the prevaling Sun' (lines 479–82, *AP*, 527).

strife see **peace and strife**.

sublimation see **distillation**.

suffering see **beheading, melancholia**.

sulphur one of the two principles of metals, according to Geber's 'sulphur/mercury' theory of the generation of metals. Sulphur is the

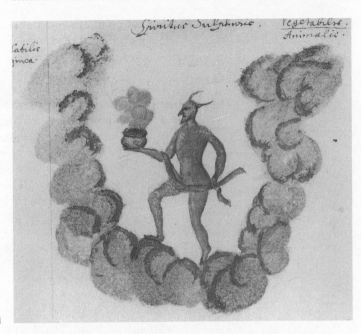

41 Sulphur and the devil

hot, dry, active seed of metals, the male principle, *Sol, in the opus alchymicum (see **prima materia**). John Dastin advised the alchemist beginning the opus: 'Minerals made of living Mercury, and living Sulphur, are to be chosen' (in ZC, 59). Philosophical sulphur is not the substance which we now call sulphur, but rather an abstract principle, an inherent constitutive element within matter. The sulphur principle constitutes the 'form' of the metal. Calid wrote: 'all Metals are compounded of Mercury and Sulphur, Matter and Form; Mercury is the Matter, and Sulphur is the Form' (*Booke of the Secrets*, 125–6). In its most primitive state sulphur is said to burn, consume and corrupt, and even have affinities with the devil (fig. 41). Sulphur's violence is aptly expressed in its image as the red lion (see fig. 35). Because it is the precursor of gold, the seed of gold, sulphur is also known as 'our gold'. Ramon Lull's *Testamentum* states: 'The Phlegm where in our Sulphur, which is called Gold, is decocted is that in which Air is included' (in FC, 17). At a more refined stage of the opus, sulphur is symbolized by the sun (see **gold and silver, Sol**). The seed from which metals were thought to grow was divided into two opposing aspects, which Paracelsus described as 'Sulphur, or living male, and . . . Mercury or living female' (PW, 293). Sulphur has the power to fix and coagulate the volatile spirit, while argent vive or mercury has the power to dissolve fixed matter. Nicolas Flamel explained: 'all metals have been formed out of sulphur and quicksilver, which are the seeds of all metals, the one representing the male, and the other the female principle. These two varieties of seed are, of course, composed of elementary substances; the sulphur, or male seed, being nothing but fire and air . . . while the quicksilver, or female seed is nothing but earth and water' (HM, 1:142). Thus sulphur is said to be the father of gold. Subtle in Jonson's *The Alchemist* says of the materia liquida: 'It turns to *sulphur*, or the *quick-*

silver: / Who are the parents of all metals' (2. 3.153). In order for the
*philosopher's stone to be conceived, sulphur and argent vive (quicksilver) must be united in the *chemical wedding. The alchemical couple
are known as the red man and white woman (see fig. 8). In the early
stages of the opus the red masculine sulphur is a violent, corrosive substance which is said to *quarrel with his white wife, argent vive or
mercury. The quarrelling couple, the hot, red man and his cold, white
wife, occur in a literary context in Marcus Clarke's novel *His Natural Life*.
The sulphuric red lion, Maurice Frere, is 'red-headed', 'ruddy' faced
with 'red whiskers' (80, 568), and the 'lion of the party' (247), while
'Mercurial Dora' (334, 365) is cold and made of 'ice . . . the artificial ice
that chemists make in the midst of a furnace' (606). Dora and Frere are
known as a quarrelling couple (596, 658).

sun   symbol of *gold, philosophical gold (the virtue or mysterious power
hidden in gold), the secret *fire, the masculine power or principle in
the opus (sulphur), the red stage or *rubedo, when the *red stone or
elixir is attained at the culmination of the opus. The sun is one of the
major symbols in alchemy. Jean de la Fontaine wrote: 'By Gold our
meaning is the *Sunne*; / Equall to him, metall there's none' (lines
381–2, *AP*, 93). Claude Frollo, the archdeacon–alchemist in Victor
Hugo's *Notre-Dame de Paris*, exclaims: 'Gold is the sun; to make gold, is
to become God!' (235). The alchemical sun is often personified by *Sol
or the *red king, who not only signifies the rubedo, but also the hot,
dry, active masculine seed of metals which has to unite with the cold,
moist, receptive seed, *Luna, in the *chemical wedding so that the
*philosopher's stone may be conceived. In this role the sun is said to be
the father of the Stone (see **Emerald Table, third law**). Dissolution
and moisture are said to be associated with the moon, while coagulation and heat are qualities of the sun. Ripley wrote: 'Helpe *Dyssolucion*
wyth moysture of the Mone, / And *Congellacyon* wyth the Son, then
hast thou done' (*TCB*, 132). The sun is also an image for the secret *fire
in the *athanor or furnace. Paracelsus wrote: 'The fire in the furnace
may be compared to the sun. It heats the furnace and the vessels, just
as the sun heats the vast universe' (*PW*, 74) (see fig. 36). The sun was
thought to have magically transformative rays which, when they penetrated the earth's crust, provided the generative warmth to ripen
such imperfect metals as iron, copper and lead into the perfect metal,
gold. In Milton's *Paradise Lost*, Satan admires the sun's generative
powers: 'What wonder then if fields and regions here / Breathe forth
elixir pure, and rivers run / Potable gold, when with one virtuous
touch / The arch-chemic sun so far from us remote / Produces with terrestrial humour mixt / Here in the dark so many precious things / Of
colour glorious and effect so rare' (3.606–12). The sun is also a name
for the *red tincture or stone which has the power to transmute all
base metal into gold. In *King John*, Shakespeare used the metaphor of
the sun as alchemist, transforming the base earth to gold with his
magical red tincture: 'the glorious sun . . . plays the alchemist, /
Turning with splendour of his precious eye, / The meagre cloddy

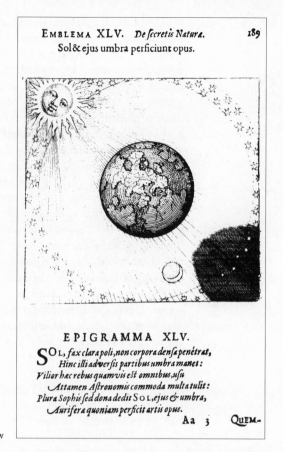

EMBLEMA XLV. *De secretis Naturæ.* 189
Sol & ejus umbra perficiunt opus.

EPIGRAMMA XLV.

SOL, *fax clara poli, non corpora densa penetrat,*
Hinc illi adversis partibus umbra manet:
Vilior hæc rebus quamvis est omnibus, usu
Attamen Astronomis commoda multa tulit:
Plura Sophis sed dona dedit SOL, *ejus & umbra,*
Aurifera quoniam perficit artis opus.

Aa 3   QUEM-

42 The sun and its shadow

earth to glittering gold' (3.1.1–6). See **fire**, **gold and silver**, **Luna**, **Sol**, **sun and shadow**.

sun and shadow   one of the most enigmatic symbols of the opus. In Michael Maier's *Atalanta fugiens* the device of the sun and shadow is presented as a cosmic image of the ultimate stage in the opus, the *projection (fig. 42). The motto to emblem 45 says: 'The sun and its shadow complete the work' (AF, 421), recalling the final law of the *Emerald Table* – 'That which I had to say about the operation of the Sun is completed'. The alchemists compare the 'shadow' to night, which alternates with day and without which day would have no definition. Maier makes it clear that the shadow is not something separate from light, but integral to it: 'What is the meaning of the Sun without Shadow? The same as a clapper without a bell ... the Sun is the tongue, the Shadow is the language' (AF, 280). Some alchemists identify the shadow as the *philosopher's stone, because it is thought to be a perfect microcosm, a perfect reflection (or shadow) of the macrocosm. Others identify the shadow with *Luna, the moon, who is in shadow until she has borrowed her light from the sun. Luna symbolizes the soul, sometimes the earth or body of the Stone. Democritus wrote of the *ablution: 'Our divine Water... rids away the Darke Umbra of the body' (ZC, 75). The identification of the shadow with Luna readily evokes the final cosmic wedding of Sun (male, active, hot, dry) and Moon (female, receptive, cold, moist) (see **chemical wedding**). The union of sun and moon gives birth to the *philosopher's stone, the tingeing arcanum which has the power to *dye all base metal to golden perfection and bring wisdom to the heart of man. Lacinius wrote: 'without the Sun and its shadow, the moon, we can have no tingeing quicksilver' (Bonus of Ferrara, *New Pearl*, 313).

The tingeing arcanum appeared at first to be a vile, undesirable thing and so was sometimes referred to as a *poison. Edward Kelly quoted Pandolphus: 'no tingeing poison is generated without gold and its shadow. Whoever tinges the poison of the Sun and its Shadow, has attained the highest wisdom' (*Two excellent Treatises*, 45). The shadow is inextricably linked with the eclipse of the sun at the *nigredo, when the gold is 'killed' and dissolved into its *prima materia or first matter. At this time a shadow is cast over the alchemist as he experiences the *melancholia of the black night of the soul, a stage which cannot be bypassed on the way to enlightenment. Psychologically, the device of the sun and shadow symbolizes the integration of the feminine, unconscious, *Luna aspect of the psyche with the male, conscious, *Sol aspect in order to produce the whole, illumined man of wisdom. The image of the sun and its shadow symbolizes the balancing or union of the two great universal energies, male and female. In Sonnet 33, Shakespeare used the alchemical imagery of the sun, the shadow and the staining, tingeing poison to express the gaining of wisdom by the lover who comes to terms with his friend's sexual relations with someone else. The sun, which gilds 'pale streames with heauenly alcumy' and is eclipsed in the shadow of base clouds, is compared to the shining friend whose betrayal eclipses the lover in shadow. The lover resolves the pain through love and forgiveness and thus attains wisdom: 'Yet him for this, my loue no whit disdaineth, / Suns of the world may staine, when heauens sun staineth'.

sun (black)   see **sol niger**.

swan   a symbol of the white stage known as the *albedo, and of the white elixir or stone which can transmute base metal to silver. Ruland wrote: 'When the Stone . . . has arrived at the perfect White Stage . . . or Swan, then all the philosophers say that this is a time of joy' (*Lexicon*, 379). The swan is one of a series of hermetic birds which represent the different phases and colours of the matter in the alembic during the opus (fig. 43). The *crow or *raven of the black *nigredo is followed by the many colours of the peacock or *peacock's tail, which is then transformed into the swan or *dove of the albedo and finally into the *phoenix of the red *rubedo. In Jonson's *The Alchemist*, Face informs Mammon that he has put the matter through the 'several colours', 'the *crow*, / The *peacock's taile*, the *plumed swan*' (2.2.26–7). The swan is sometimes depicted as swimming in a silver sea and spouting the silver arcanum or elixir. It can also signify the magical mercurial arcanum with which the *king (the male principle) is fed when he unites with the *queen (the female principle)

43 The swan

to become one body in the *chemical wedding (sixth key, Valentine, in
HM, 1:336).

sweat the beads of liquid that accumulate on the sides of the alembic during
the distillation and purification of the matter of the Stone. The matter
itself is also said to sweat in the gentle heat of the fire during this process.
An anonymous tract in Ashmole's *Theatrum* says: 'This Vessel must be set
in a kinde heat / That the Matter may kindly sweate' and by 'swetting and
bathing be made suttell' (*TCB*, 408, 414). Edward Cradock wrote in 'A
Treatise Touching the Philosopher's Stone': 'And then concoct itt with
an easy heate: / Let itt not seeth, but only lett itt sweate' (lines 479–80,
AP, 25). Thomas Vaughan likewise wrote that the secret fire 'makes the
Matter to vapour – no, not so much as to sweat' (*VW*(*W*), 220). The image
of the sweating vessel is found in Abraham Cowley's 'Weeping': 'Ah,
mighty Love, that it were *inward Heat* / Which made this precious *limbeck*
sweat' (66). The emblem of the *king being washed in his sweat bath is a
symbol of the *ablution, the cleansing of the blackened, dead body of the
Stone or metal at the bottom of the alembic. The epigram to emblem 28
of Maier's *Atalanta fugiens* says that the king in his sweatbath 'bathes and
bathes again under the glass arch, / Till by the wet-dew he is freed from
all bile' (80) (see **bath**). The sweat is both the black bile that issues from
the king (the impurity of the matter) and the sweet dew which washes
the king's body clean and purifies it (see the dual aspect of Mercurius).

sweat bath see **bath**, **sweat**.

sweet smell see **fragrance**.

sword see **weaponry**.

T

tabula smaragdina   see **Emerald Table.**

tame   see **Bird of Hermes, unicorn.**

Tartarus   the hardened dregs of wine. Martin Ruland's *Lexicon of Alchemy* defines 'Tartarus' as 'Calculus of Wine, called Wine-stone by similitude, the stone or deposit which cleaves to the sides of the vessels' (310). The *Chymicall Dictionary* also says: '*Tartarum* is a hard saltish dregs that sticks to the sides of Wine vessels'. John Milton used the image in his creation scene in *Paradise Lost*, where the spirit of God 'vital virtue infused, and vital warmth / Throughout the fluid mass, but downward purged / The black tartareous cold infernal dregs' (7:235–8). Tartarus is the underworld, the sediment or precipitate of a once living world (MC, 493). Tartarus is also a name for the hellish torment through which the matter for the Stone passes at the *nigredo (see **hell**).

tears   the *mercurial waters which cleanse the blackened, dead matter of the Stone lying at the bottom of the alembic. Tears are the the same as *sweat, *rain, *dew and *gum. The tears are an expression of sorrow at the death of the *Hermetic Bird, the *beheaded king or the *hermaphroditic body of the lovers (*sulphur and *argent vive), after they are united in the *chemical wedding. The dead, united body of the lovers is said to exude sweat or tears as it is distilled in the alembic and cleansed of its impurities. Abu'L-Qasim said of the body 'thou wilt see as it were tears flowing down the cheeks' (*Book of Knowledge*, 48). During the distillation the alembic, too, is said to weep as the droplets of moisture condense at the top of the still and fall down upon the blackened body below. The tears symbolize the mercurial waters of grace which seemingly drown the body but which in reality wash away the impurities and make it ready to receive the enlivening soul (sometimes soul/spirit) at the *albedo (see **flood**). Houpreght's *Aurifontina chymica* described the mercurial water as 'clear as the tears of eyes' (26). In Sir George Ripley's 'Cantilena', the *queen who is 'great with child' (the gestating Stone), 'Bath'd herself with the Teares which she had shed' (stanza 188). In 'On the Arch-Bishop of Canterbury', John Cleveland compared the writing process to the alchemical weeping at the distillation: 'Verse chymically weeps; that pious raine / Distilled with Art, is but the sweat o' the brain' (38).

teeth   see **dragon's teeth, weaponry.**

temple   see **ark.**

terra   see **earth, green lion.**

terra alba foliata   see **white foliated earth.**

terra damnata   see **faeces**.

theatre   Alchemy and theatre were closely associated. In sixteenth-century Italy the *ciarlatani* or mountebanks, so vividly portrayed in Ben Jonson's *Volpone*, used to set up their scaffolds in the piazzas in order to sell alchemical nostrums, salves and recipes, and present theatrical entertainments. It was from these entertainments that the *commedia dell'arte* is thought to have developed. The alchemical recipe books of secrets were often published under the *ciarlantani's* commedia names: Polcinella, Biscottino, il Zanni bolognese (Eamon, *Science and the Secrets of Nature*, 237). The alchemical mountebank was known in sixteenth and seventeenth-century England. Michael Drayton writes of the 'false' alchemist in 'The Moone-Calfe': 'Sometimes he for a Mountebanke would passe, / And shew you in a Crusible, or Glasse: / Some rare extraction, presently and runne, / Through all the Cures that he therewith had done' (*Works*, 3:190). Many alchemical treatises, like other Renaissance works, were entitled 'theatres' – meaning 'a book giving a "view" or "conspectus" of some subject' (OED). Examples include Lazarus Zetzner's *Theatrum chemicum* (1602–61), Edward Kelly's *The Theatre of Terrestrial Astronomy* (published posthumously in 1676) and Elias Ashmole's anthology of English alchemical verse, *Theatrum chemicum Britannicum* (1652).

The contents of the treatises demonstrate an awareness of the theatrical nature of the work. Salomon Trismosin's *Spendor Solis* shows the alchemical vessels representing the steps of the great work elevated on a stage. Other plates in his treatise show the alchemical events as stage scenery (plates 6, 12–18). The audience is presented in boxes, observing the performance. Trithemius wrote of the three main stages in the opus: 'the Black, White and Red, are Eminent and lasting Scenes' which do not vanish away (ZC, 80). In his *Exposition of the Hieroglyphicall Figures*, translated into English in 1624, Nicolas Flamel similarly speaks of setting the 'Philosophical Egge' in warm ashes 'in the middest of a Stage' (58). In Andreae's *The Chymical Wedding*, Christian Rosencreutz witnesses the events of the alchemical opus as a seven-act comedy (109–112). During this comedy, played upon a 'scaffold', a series of well-known alchemical emblems are brought to life. The alchemists viewed their alembic as a theatre in which the miniature creation of the Stone imitated the creation of the greater world in microcosm. The alembic was the theatre in which the cycle of solve et coagula, beheading and renovation, melting and recasting, was faithfully re-enacted. Andrew Marvell's 'An Horatian Ode' uses the theatrical metaphor in an alchemical context. In order for the new kingdom to be created, the old kingdom (the 'great work of time') must first be ruined and the chemical king beheaded: 'That thence the royal actor borne / The tragic scaffold might adorn' (lines 53–4) (see **beheading, king**).

thick and thin   the gross and subtle elements of the Stone. Hortulanus comments on the seventh law of the **Emerald Table*: '*Thou shalt separate*, that is, dissolve: for dissolution is the separation of partes. *The earth from the fire, the thinne from the thicke*: that is, the lees and dregges, from the fire, the ayre, the water, and the whole substaunce of the Stone, so that the Stone may remaine most pure without all filth' (*A Briefe Commentarie*, 22). Calid wrote of the *conversion of these elements: 'Whereupon we joyne fire and water, earth and ayre togither: when the thick hath bin mingled with the thin, and the thinner with the thick, the one abydeth with the other' (*Booke of the Secrets*, 36).

thief see **Mercurius**.

three principles see **salt**, **sulphur** and mercury.

tie the coagulation or fixation of the volatile spirit into form, also referred to as 'binding' and 'nailing'. One of the alchemist's tasks is that of capturing and taming the elusive spirit *Mercurius so that he becomes a useful ally and servant in the process of the opus alchymicum. The *Hydropyrographum Hermeticum* warned the alchemist that he must 'Tye him [Mercurius] hands and heels ... with a most puissant cord and yoke' (Houpreght, *Aurifontina*, 33). Paradoxically, it is Mercurius himself, in his role as mediating soul or priest, who ties the knot between the lovers, body and soul (or spirit), at the *chemical wedding (see **fix**, **glue**).

tincture a colouring liquid, and hence the *philosopher's stone and elixir which tinges base metals to gold. Paracelsus wrote that the 'Tincture...makes Gold out of Lune, and the other metals' (*Archidoxis*, 64). *The Sophic Hydrolith* states that the 'tincture has virtue to change, tinge, and cure every imperfect body' (HM, 1:83). Shakespeare uses this alchemical term as a metaphor in *Antony and Cleopatra* when he has Cleopatra say to her attendant Alexas: 'How much unlike art thou Mark Antony! / Yet coming from him, that great med'cine hath / With his tinct gilded thee' (1.5.34–6). It was thought that just one ounce of the tincture or Stone could transmute over a hundred or a thousand times its own weight of base metal into pure gold. Sir Epicure Mammon in Ben Jonson's *The Alchemist* remarks on the augmenting power of the tincture: 'one part proiected on a hundred / Of *Mercurie*, or *Venus*, or the *Moone*, / Shall turne it to as many of the *Sunne*' (2.1.38–40). John Donne wrote of the great transforming power of Christ in 'Resurrection, imperfect': 'He was all gold when he lay down, but rose / All tincture, and doth not alone dispose /Leaden and iron wills to good, but is / Of power to make even sinful flesh like his' (lines 13–16). See **red tincture**, **purple tincture**, **red elixir**, **rose**.

toad (or **frog**) the swelling, puffing matter of the Stone in the alembic during the *putrefaction at the *nigredo (fig. 44); philosophical earth, the alchemists' *chaos in terrestrial form; the *philosophical child or son. Like the serpent and dragon, the toad generally represents the base matter which, though poisonous, contains the precious philosopher's stone within (AP, 380). Philalethes wrote that this toad is 'most venomous ... yet highly prized' (*Marrow*, bk. 4, 69). In his poem, *A Vision*, Sir George Ripley described the initial dissolution of the matter by the

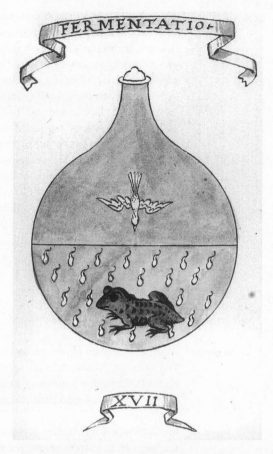

44 The toad

corrosive *mercurial water (*venom) as 'A Toade full rudde' which 'did drinke the juice of grapes so fast / (Till overcharged with the broth, his bowells all to brast)' (TCB, 374). Philalethes commented on the putrefying matter: 'They call it their Toad which crawleth on the ground, and feedeth upon the slime of the Earth, because before it is quite black, it may resemble the colours of a Toad, and its likeness, puffing and swelling, and rugged with bunches and blisters and knobs' (RR, 177). Gabriel Harvey referred to the puffing toad when writing of the alchemist Edward Kelly and of Thomas Nashe: 'But Kelley will bid him [Nashe] looke to the swolne Toade, and the daunsing Foole' (Harvey, Works, 2:69). Thomas Nashe himself referred to the alchemical frog in a witty denunciation of his literary detractors: 'I would wish them to … not grinde their colours so hard; having founde that which is black, let them not, with our forenamed Gold-falsifiers, seeke for a substance that is blacker than black, or angle for frogs in a clear fountain' (Works, 1:261). During the *ablution which follows the black stage, the toad or putrefying matter of the Stone is cleansed in the clear water of the mercurial *fountain.

Toad, frog, *serpent, *dragon, *green lion, *panther, and *crow are equivalent terms (see Ripley, in TCB, 188). In The Marrow of Alchemy Philalethes calls the dead 'body' at the putrefaction 'our Toad and Crow' (bk. 3, 55). The verses in the 'Emblematicall Scrowle' attributed to Ripley likewise equate serpent, crow and toad (*TCB*, 378–9). In Ben Jonson's *The Alchemist,* Surly taunts Subtle with an endless list of alchemical symbols which includes the synonymous terms: 'Your *toade*, your *crow*, your *dragon*, and your *panthar*' (2.3.189). See **venom**. The toad is often paired with the eagle, symbolizing the sublimation of the fixed earth by the volatile spirit. The toad and eagle pairing is illustrated in an emblem celebrating Avicenna in Michael Maier's *Symbola aureae mensae* (Stolcius, *Viridarium,* 132) (see also **eagle**). In the fifth emblem of Michael Maier's *Atalanta fugiens*, the toad is the philosophical matter or child which must be fed with the mercurial 'milk' at the *cibation. The motto to this emblem reads: 'Put a toad to the breasts of a woman, that she may feed it, / And the Woman may die, and the toad grows big from the milk' (*AF*, 75) (see **cibation**).

tomb   see **grave**.

topsy-turvy   see **inversion**.

torment   see **torture**.

tortoise   an alchemical basin sometimes identified with the secret vessel itself. The tortoise is listed in Ruland's *Lexicon of Alchemy* (195) and illustrated in Porta's *De distillatione* (40) (fig. 45). It is also a hieroglyph of the matter of the Stone which, once prepared, becomes an instrument of great power.

torture   the *calcination or reduction of the old body of the metal to a powder at the *nigredo. In order to be renewed and transformed, the matter for the Stone (the body) must first be killed and reduced into the pure matter of

45   The tortoise

creation, the *prima materia. Part of this process involves the calcination of the body, which is often referred to as the torture or persecution of the matter. Arthur Dee wrote that the *fire of the philosophers 'tortures, calcines, exanimates, and inanimates the Physicall Body, and at length renders it more then perfect' (FC, 64). *Zoroaster's Cave* likewise said: 'The Fire against Nature must torment the bodyes, That is the Dragon burning violently, like the Fire of hell' (76) (see hell). Thomas Nashe referred to the alchemists as persecutors of their matter in a witty rebuke to his literary detractors: 'Whatever they [the detractors] be that thus persecute Art (as the Alcumists are said to persecute Nature) I would wish them to rebate the edge of their wit, and not grinde their colours so harde' (*Works*, 1:261). Ben Jonson's Face likewise calls the alchemist 'you smoky persecuter of Nature!' (*The Alchemist* 1.3.100). Mercury, in Jonson's *Mercurie Vindicated*, comically complains of his treatment by Vulcan the alchemist: 'neuer Herring, Oyster or Coucumer past so many vexations: my whole life with 'hem hath bene an exercise of torture' (lines 61–2). The process of torturing the matter is symbolized by such images as the beheading of the king, the cutting off of Mercury's feet, the lion's paws or the bird's wings, the chopping down of the tree, and the torturing of the man on a wheel (see fig. 26).

tower a synonym for the *athanor or philosophical furnace. Illustrations of the furnace frequently resemble the turret or tower of a *castle (fig. 46). According to *The Golden Tract* the glass vessel in which the brother and

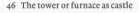

46 The tower or furnace as castle

sister lovers (*Sol and *Luna) are captured is 'situated in a strong tower, and surrounded with battlements and lofty walls, and, moreover, could be easily heated with a gentle continuous fire' (*HM*, 1:47). Edward Kelly comments on one of his emblems in *The Theatre of Terrestrial Astronomy*: 'An old man stands near the furnace, both towers are open' (*Two excellent Treatises*, 141). In Jonson's *The Alchemist* Subtle says to Ananias: 'O Are you come? 'Twas time. Your threescore minutes / Were at the last thred, you see; and downe had gone / *Furnus acediae, Turris circulatorius* ... Had all beene cinders' (3.2.1–5). See **castle, fort**.

transmutation   the conversion of one element or substance into another through the agency of the *philosopher's stone. In alchemy, true transmutation is considered to be the instantaneous change of base metal into silver or gold by the projection of the philosopher's stone or tincture (usually in powder form) over the base metal. Calid wrote of the *medicine or philosopher's stone: 'our Medicine transmutes imperfect Metals into *Sol* and *Luna*' (*Booke of the Secrets*, 120). The idea of transmutation is based on the Aristotelian concept of the *prima materia and the four elements which can be converted one into the other. It was thought that all things were created from one original substance, known as the prima materia or first matter onto which form was imprinted or moulded. If all metals were made from the same original matter, then they could be melted down into that matter and then imprinted with a new, purer form to make gold or silver. The alchemists explained transmutation as an acceleration, in the laboratory, of the natural process of metals ripening in the womb of the earth to become ultimately the perfect metal, gold. This ripening force or universal philosophical substance was known as *Mercurius. The philosopher's stone could not be made without this vital ingredient. The alchemist's first task was to capture or fix Mercurius. In 'The Loyal Scot', Andrew Marvell used the fixation and transmutation metaphor in describing the clamorous crowd: 'And would like Chymists fixing Mercury, / Transmute indifference with necessity' (lines 211–12). Elias Ashmole wrote in an ode 'To my worthily honour'd William Backhouse Esquire Upon his adopting of me to be his Son' (i.e. his alchemical disciple): 'That I'm true bred, question it he that dare, / If these my Aeglete Eyes on th' Sun can stare. / Or cause a ☿ in Crest I hold / Since my crude Mercury's transmute to Gold' (Bod. Ashm. MS 36–7, ff. 241v–242). Metaphysically, transmutation is the conversion of earthly man into the illumined philosopher through the tincture of divine love, grace and wisdom. See **prima materia, metamorphosis, Diana**.

transubstantiate   transmute. The primary meaning of transubstantiate is 'Change the substance of; transform, transmute' (OED). In Sir John Ferne's *The Blazon of Gentrie*, Paradin says of an alchemical author: 'I see his rules and precepts, practized euery day, euen by those of my owne companye, and I see that they by the skill of his book can transubstantiate Inck, parchment, yea and euen wordes also into perfect gold, goodly fayre houses and large reuenues' (4). Milton uses 'transubstantiate' in an alchemical context in *Paradise Lost*. Raphael accepts Adam's invitation to sit down and dine: 'And to their viands fell, not seemingly / The angel, nor in mist, the common gloss / Of theologians, but with keen despatch / Of real hunger, and concoctive heat / To transubstantiate; what redounds, transpires / Through spirits with ease; nor wonder; if by fire / Of sooty coal the empiric alchemist / Can turn, or holds it possible to turn / Metals of drossiest ore to perfect gold' (5.433–42). See **transmutation**.

tree see **philosophical tree**.

tree (truncated) a motif symbolizing the *dismemberment phase of the dissolution (solve) at the initial deathly stage of the opus known as the *nigredo. An emblem in Mylius's *Basilica philosophica* shows a great tree being felled by an axe (fig. 47). Two emblems of the truncated tree accompany the fifth treatise concerning the dissolution in Trismosin's *Splendor Solis* (plates 19 and 22). Ripley likewise compared the dissolution of the metal or matter of the Stone to the putrefying *oak tree (*TCB*, 151–2). The truncated tree is one of a number of images expressing the torture motif that occur in alchemical texts. Other images include the cutting off of the lion's paws, the decapitation of the bird (or cutting off of his wings) and the torture and tormenting of *Mercurius. See **beheading**, **torture**, **philosophical tree**.

tria prima see **salt**, **sulphur** and mercury.

turds see **dung, dunghill, faeces**.

turris circulatorius see **tower**.

47 The truncated tree

MORIENVS ROMAN, *Philosophus*.

twins the alchemical brother and sister who are united in the *chemical wedding in order to produce the *philosopher's stone. Male sulphur (the sun, creative power) is wedded to female argent vive (the moon, wisdom) to create the perfect Platonic union of opposites, upon which the successful outcome of the opus depends. Sometimes the alchemical couple, the *red man and *white lady, the king and queen, are depicted as an incestuous couple (see **incest**), and in some instances they are symbolized by the alchemical twins, who when united form one perfect whole. A pseudo-Lullian manuscript 'Opera chemica' (*c*. 1470–5) shows Asiatic male twins burning in a well, symbolizing the matter of the Stone in the alembic during the *putrefaction (van Lennep, *Alchimie*, 83). In 'Singing Birds', Michael Wilding writes of poets in the Bohemian milieu of the 1970s: 'They rolled on the pavements like alchemical twins, breaking each other's heads into the awaiting concrete … Their blood congealed' (*This is for you*, 45). For an exploration of alchemical twins in literature see James Bulman-May, 'Patrick White and Alchemy', on Waldo and Arthur Brown in Patrick White's *The Solid Mandala* .

Tyrian purple see **dye, rubedo**.

U

unicorn the masculine, penetrating aspect of *Mercurius, the mercurial spirit. The third emblem in *The Book of Lambspring* shows the unicorn and deer in a forest. The accompanying text identifies the unicorn as the spirit, the deer (*cervus fugitivus) as the soul, and the forest (i.e. dark place) as the body of the Stone. It advises the alchemist to 'snare and capture … tame and master' the unicorn and the deer 'by Art, / To couple them together / And to lead them in and out of the forest' (*HM*, 1:280). Here the author is referring to the *distillation and *sublimation of the matter in the alembic, a process which leads to the second union of soul and spirit in the *chemical wedding. The unicorn also appears in an emblem in Johann Mylius's *Philosophia reformata* (316, 365), and in Andreae's *The Chymical Wedding,* where Christian, in the company of 'our Virgin', witnesses the 'snow-white *Unicorn* with a golden coller' bowing down before a *lion standing on a fountain (73). In this set of images the fountain contains the mercurial waters and the Virgin represents the receptive feminine aspect of Mercurius. Jung argues that the unicorn and the lion on either side of the lady in the sixteenth-century tapestry *La Dame à la Licorne* (Musée de Cluny, Paris) represent the opposing qualities of Mercurius in the chemical wedding (*PA*, 463–4).

unicorn's horn horn of rhinoceros reputed to be an antidote against venom.

universal medicine   see **medicine, philosopher's stone.**

urinal   a glass phial (or vial) for solutions. A recipe for making the elixir in Colson's *Philosophia maturata* instructs the alchemist to 'take Vitriol, calcine it into ashes, then beat them into most subtle powder; put them in an Urinal, and pour thereto Virgins Milk to cover them, stop the Urinal with a Linnen cloth, and let it stand eight dayes' (45) (see **vial**).

urine   an ingredient in making a powerful solvent. A recipe from St Dunstan for a solvent states: 'Take the Urine of a wholesome Man, that drank meerly Wine, make of it, according to Art, the Salt of Microcosme, purifie it very well, which doth so much accuate the Spirit of Wine, that it dissolveth *Sol* in a moment' (*Recipes*, 88). Saturn, in Michael Sendivogius's 'A Dialogue of the Allchymist and Sulphur', uses 'urine' as an agent to wash and join argent vive and sulphur. He takes two argent vives which he says come from the same root and 'washt them in his Urine, and he said / "Sulphur of Sulphurs they shall be," and made / A Composition where he duly mixt / The volatile togeather with the fixt … and inclos'd it then / In an exact proportionable Den' (lines 545–54, *AP*, 529). Sir George Ripley declared that he was deluded in using such material in his first experiments: 'I provyd Uryns, Eggs, Here, and Blod, / The Scalys of Yern whych Smethys do of smyte … whych dyd me never good' (*TCB*, 190). Surly, in Ben Jonson's *The Alchemist,* ridicules the alchemists' use of such ingredients as 'your broths, your *menstrues*, and *materialls*, / Of pisse, and egge-shells, womens termes, man's blood' (2.3.193–4) (see **children's piss**). It was often said that the *philosopher's stone was made from a vile and despised substance. The *Philosophia maturata*, for example, stated that 'our Stone is … cast out into the Dunghill, and trodden under mens feet, it is counted a most vile and contemptible thing' (15). As a result of this, many alchemists mistakenly took as their material dung, piss, blood and egg shells. Gerhard Dorn stated that the frivolous alchemists or 'sophists' interpret the symbolic names of substances literally and therefore use milk, eggs, urine and hair, which are unsuitable ingredients for making the Stone (in *AS*, 290).

uroboros   the serpent which devours its own tail and gives birth to itself, a symbol for *Mercurius found in the earliest surviving Greek alchemical manuscripts. This paradoxical hieroglyph symbolizes the magical transforming arcanum which both slays and is slain, resurrects and is resurrected during the process of the opus. The uroboros is at the same time its own vessel (or womb) and its own contents (or product). In biting its own tail the uroboros makes a complete circle, aptly symbolizing the circular nature of the transformative process, the *rotation of the elements, the opus circulatorium (see fig. 15). Nicolas Flamel wrote in his *Exposition*: 'These are the *serpents* and *Dragons* which the ancient Aegyptians have painted in a *Circle*, the *head* biting the *tayle*, to signify that they proceeded from one and the same things, and that it alone was sufficient, and that in the turning and *circulation* thereof, it made it selfe perfect' (66).

V

venom   a name for the *mercurial transforming arcanum in the early, deathly stage of the opus, when the metal or matter for the Stone is dissolved into the *prima materia. During this phase, known as the *nigredo and symbolized by the *crow, *raven or *toad, the mercurial water acts as a deadly poison or venom 'killing' the matter in the alembic, dissolving and putrefying it. Edward Kelly wrote of this process in *The Theatre of Terrestrial Astronomy*: 'For solution and putrefaction begin with a fetid smell . . . the Raven's Head is called a deadly poison' (*Two excellent Treatises*, 138). As the opus proceeds, the venomous mercurial waters are enigmatically transmuted into the miraculous waters of life, which descend like the dew of grace upon the dead matter in the bottom of the alembic, resurrecting it into new life. *The Sophic Hydrolith* refers to this dual-natured water as 'the water of mercury (also called the never-failing fountain, or the water of life, which neverthless contains the most malignant poison)' (*HM*, 1: 84). A striking alchemical image occurs in Ripley's poem 'The Vision' where the *toad first drowns in his own venom before it is transmuted into the 'medicine' or elixir at the white and red stages of the opus known as the *albedo and *rubedo. Sir George Ripley wrote: 'Then of the Venom handled thus a Medicine I did Make / Which Venom kills, and saveth such as a venom chance to take' (*TCB*, 374). Philalethes referred to Ripley's venom /medicine as 'this blessed Tincture, which expelleth all Poyson, though it self were a deadly Poyson before the Preparation, yet after it is the Balsam of Nature, expelling all Diseases' (*RR*, 24) (see **dragon**). The alchemical 'shadow' and also the tincture, microcosm or Stone are also sometimes identified with the poison or venom. *The Rosary of the Philosophers* stated that 'no tincturing poison is generated without Sol and his Shadow, that is his wife' (McLean, *Rosary*, 57) (see **sun and shadow**). Metaphysically, the realization of the nature of the lower self, which comes about through the grace of divine knowledge, at first acts like a deadly poison upon the adept. But as the lower nature is overcome and slain, this knowledge acts as a panacea and bringer of new life.

Venus   In alchemy Venus variously symbolizes a planet, a goddess, a whore, an enlightened substance and copper. Jean de la Fontaine wrote: 'By Gold our meaneing is the *Sunne* . . . *Venus* and Copper is the same' (*AP*, 93). According to Geber copper is the most perfectable of all the base metals because of the large proportion of mercury in its make-up (Geber, *Summa Perfectionis*, 507). Roger Bacon wrote that 'Copper is an uncleane and imperfect bodie, engendered of Argent-vive, impure, not fixed, earthy, burning, red not cleare, and of the like Sulphur. It wanteth purity, fixation and weight' (*Mirror*, 5). In his poem 'To John Hoddeson on his *Divine Epigrams*' Dryden plays on the idea of copper being an unclean body compared with gold: 'Reader, I've done, nor longer will withhold / Thy greedy eyes; looking on this pure gold, / Thou'lt know adulterate copper; which, like this, / Will only serve to be a foil to his' (lines 23–6). The role of Venus in alchemy is characteristically paradoxical. At the beginning of the opus Venus is the whore who symbolizes the impure matter of the Stone in its initial chaotic, corrupt state. Ruland's *Lexicon of Alchemy* defines Venus as 'The Impure Stone, the Matter' (322). From this unclean matter philosophical mercury is extracted. Salmon's *Dictionaire Hermetique* describes it as 'the Prostitute of the philosophers' from which 'the alchemist draws their mercury' (159). In other contexts Venus is the 'chaste bride', the cold, moist, receptive substance (*argent vive), which must be united with Mars, the hot, dry, active substance (*sulphur), in the *chemical wedding. Mercurius is often identified with the moon and Venus because of its half-feminine nature. Jung wrote: 'As his own divine consort [Mercurius] easily turns into the goddess of love' (*AS*, 226) (see **hermaphrodite**). Furthermore, as the goddess of love and mother of *Cupid, Venus presides over the sexual union of the male and female seeds of metals at the *chemical wedding. She is associated with the colour *green and is invariably robed in green. The 'Hermetick Raptures' says: 'Bright Venus next I see: Fair beauty's queen / Whose inward tincture is the purest green' (lines 166–7, *AP*, 579). Although green is not one of the three major *colours of the opus (black, white and red), it is nevertheless a significant colour, representing new life, growth and fertility without which the *philosopher's stone cannot grow. The green colour appears in the alembic after the black of the deathly *nigredo and before the multi-coloured stage known as the *peacock's tail. Green is also the colour of verdigris, which is often found on copper.

vessel see **alembic**.

vial (phial, viol) a small glass bottle, spherical, with a straight, slender neck, used in solution and *coagulation. Nicolas Flamel notes that 'The Philosophicall Egge ... is a viall of glasse' (*HE*, 58). In *A Demonstration of Nature*, Nature rebukes the ignorant alchemist for not following her method of making metals in the inmost bowels of the earth: 'For, behold, you break vials, and consume coals, only to soften your brain still more with the vapours' (*HM*, 1:123). Thomas Vaughan wrote of distillation in his alchemical poem *Hyanthe*: 'So dy'd *Hyanthe*. Here (said shee) / *Let not this Vial part from Thee*. / It holds my *Heart, though now 'tis* Spill'd, / And into *Waters* all distill'd' (*VW* (*R*), 205–6). In *Areopagitica*, Milton compared books to vials and their contents to the alchemical *quintessence, the immortal fifth element: books 'preserve as in a vial the purest efficacy and extraction of that living intellect that bred them' and the crime of censorship 'ends not in the slaying of an elemental life, but strikes at the ethereal and fifth essence, the breath of reason itself, slays an immortality rather than a life' (578–9). 'Vial' is sometimes spelt 'viol', as in Paracelsus's *Aurora*, where he refers to: 'the Cucurbit, the Pelican, Retort, Viol, fixatory etc'. (25). Musgrove observes that Robert Herrick's musical/alchemical pun on 'viol' in 'The Voice and Viol' depends on the knowledge that small vessels called viols were attached to the alembic by strings or cords (Musgrove, 'Herrick's alchemical vocabulary', 259).

vine see **grapes**.

vinegar a name for the dissolving, penetrating *mercurial water which has the power to reduce metals and bodies into their *prima materia or first matter. Synesius wrote that the mercurial arcanum is 'the most sharp vinegar' (*The True Book*, 169). Artephius likewise wrote: 'a certaine ancient Philosopher said, *I besought the Lord, and hee shewed me a certain clear water, which I knew to be the pure vinegre, altering piercing, and digesting. The vinegar I say is penetrative, and the instrument moving the gold or the silver, to putrefy, resolve, and to be reduced into his first matter, and is the onely Agent in the whole world for this Art, that can resolve and reincrudate, or make raw againe the Mettallicke Bodies, with the conservation of their species*' (*sb*, 9). A recipe in *Philosophia maturata* for calcining *Venus (copper) and Mars (iron) states: 'Sprinkle *Venus* and *Mars* with the best Viniger well distilled, that they may gather Rust: burn this with most strong Fire in an Iron Dish' (75). Vinegar is synonymous with the blood of the *green lion. The same treatise says: 'And thus thou hast the Bloud of the Green Lyon called *The Secret Water*, and most sharp Vinegar, by which all Bodies may be reduced to their first Matter' (*Philosophia maturata*, 31–2). In Ben Jonson's *Mercurie Vindicated*, Mercury comically lists vinegar as one of the many substances with which the alchemists torture him: 'what betweene their salts and their sulphures; their oyles, and their tartars, their brines and their vinegers, you might take me out now a sous'd *Mercury*, now a salted *Mercury*, now a smoak'd and dri'd *Mercury*, now a pouldred and pickl'd *Mercury*'. (lines 56–60).

viper a name for the primitive matter of the Stone at the beginning of the opus. Equivalent terms are *serpent and *dragon. During the initial stage of the opus known as the *nigredo, the 'body' of the Stone is killed and dissolved and the poisonous mercurial spirit or serpent released. Martin Ruland's *Lexicon of Alchemy* defines the 'Viper' as 'the matter of the Philosophers in Putrefaction, because it is then one of the most violent and active poisons in the world' (437) (see **dragon, serpent, Mercurius, venom**).

virgin a symbol of the *prima materia, the pure, original stuff of creation, and of the receptive, feminine aspect of the dual-natured *Mercurius. It was thought that at the creation God imprinted the receptive prima materia with the forms of all things; thus the prima materia was looked upon as the virgin mother of all things. Arthur Dee quotes *Incertus de Chemia*: 'The Virgin is Mercury, because it never propagated a body in the Womb of this Earth, and yet it generates the Stone for us, by resolving the Heaven, that is, it opens Gold, and bringeth forth a Soul' (in *FC*, 30). The receptive feminine aspect of Mercurius, also known as argent vive, is symbolized by the virgin. The *Aurelia occulta* calls Mercurius the 'most chaste virgin' (in *AS*, 226) (see **unicorn**). The cold, white, moist feminine nature which must be united with the hot, red, dry masculine nature (*sulphur) to form the *philosopher's stone, is frequently referred to as *Diana, the virgin huntress. Diana is also a symbol of the *white stone and the *albedo. The crowned virgin symbolizes purity, and is associated with Sapientia (wisdom) and salt. In her role as Sapientia, the virgin is identical with the philosopher's stone which, arising from the reconciliation of opposites (female mercury and male sulphur), results in divine knowledge or wisdom. Robert Fludd wrote of the cosmic virgin Sapientia in 'Integrae naturae speculum artisque imago': 'On her breast is the true Sun, on her belly the moon. Her heart gives light to the stars and planets, whose influence infused in her womb by the mercurial spirit ... is sent to the very centre of the Earth. Her right foot stands on earth, her left in water, signifying the conjunction of sulphur and mercury, without which nothing can be created' (in Godwin, *Robert Fludd*, 22–3). In Andreae's *The Chymical Wedding* 'our Virgin' acts as Christian Rosencreutz's mercurial psychopomp, guiding him through the trials and triumphs of the alchemical opus.

virgin's milk   the transforming mercurial waters, the white mercury of the philosophers. Thomas Aquinas said that the virgin's milk is obtained by dissolving litharge in vinegar and in treating the solution by alkaline salt (acetate of lead) (van Lennep, *Alchimie*, 62). Synesius equated virgin's milk with *Mercurius as *prima materia, describing it as 'the blessed Water, the Water of the Wise, the venomous Water, the most sharp Vinegar, the Mineral Water, the Water of Celestial grace ... For this alone perfects both stones, the *White* and the *Red*' (*The True Book*, 169). In the process of the opus, two crucial spirits or mercuries are said to be extracted from the *green lion ore. The first mercury is white and opaque and is called virgin's milk. The second is red, and is known as the blood of the green lion. According to both the 'Treatise' of St Dunstan (f. 3) and Artephius's *Secret Book* (44), virgin's milk is the name given to the pure, spiritual, white fume which ascends to the top of the vessel at the first distillation, clouding the receiver with a milkish shadow and moisture. Colson's *Philosophia maturata* refers to 'our white water, which we call our white tincture, our Eagle, our white *Mercury*, and Virgin's milk' (38). The mercurial medium of conjunction, the third principle needed for the union of *Sol and *Luna at the *chemical wedding, is also known as the virgin's milk. At the point of conjunction the virgin's milk becomes one with Sol and Luna and is therefore no longer known under this name. During a later stage in the opus known as the *cibation, the *philosopher's child (or stone) born of the union of Sol and Luna, is nourished with 'Mylke and Mete' (Ripley, in *TCB*, 169). This milk or virgin's milk is a name for the mercurial water which is used to feed the infant Stone so that it may grow to maturity. In *Symbola aureae mensae*, Michael Maier wrote that 'The Stone should be fed, just as a child, with the milk of a Virgin' (in *AF*, 98). Virgin's milk is also a name for the white elixir which can tinge base metal to silver (see **queen (white)**). Surly in Jonson's *The Alchemist* taunts Subtle about the ambiguity of alchemical terminology: 'What else are all your terms / Whereon no one o' your writers 'gree with other? / Of your *elixir*, your *lac virginis*' (2.3.182–4).

vitrification   the conversion of matter into glass or a glassy substance through the action of heat. Martin Ruland defines vitrification as 'the Burning of Lime and Cinders into Transparent Glass' (*Lexicon*, 323). The alchemists used the image to refer to the final *fixation of the matter in the alembic into the *philosopher's stone. *The Rosary of the Philosophers* equates the fixation of the Stone with the crystallization of glass (McLean, *Rosary*, 96). Philalethes wrote of the action of the Stone on base metal: 'it would tinge it into silver pure, / Yea perfect gold by fire it entred in, / And to a white glasse turn'd it, which t' endure / All trials would teach other metals base' (*Marrow*, bk. 2, 23–4). Vitrification is used in an alchemical context in John Donne's 'Epitaph on Himself': 'till us death lay / To ripe and mellow here, we are stubborn clay. / Parents make us earth, and souls dignify / Us to be glass; here to grow gold we lie' (lines 11–14).

vitriol a shining crystalline body, such as zinc or copper sulphate. The supplement to Ruland's *A Lexicon of Alchemy* states that green vitriol is a symbol of the philosopher's crude matter, while red vitriol is the perfect *sulphur at the red stage of the opus (437). An emblem in Basil Valentine's *Azoth* (reproduced in van Lennep, p. 202) is encircled with the words 'Visita Interiora Terrae Rectificando Invenies Occultum Lapidem' (Visit the interior of the earth and by rectifying find the hidden Stone), making an acrostic which spells 'Vitriol'. This acrostic was often cited in alchemical treatises, including Isaac Newton's 'Praxis' (Dobbs, *Janus*, 305). Chaucer's Canon's Yeoman lists vitriol among other essential alchemical ingredients: 'Poudres diverse, asshes, dong, pisse, and cley, / Cered pokets, sal peter, vitriole' (*Canon's Yeoman's Tale*, lines 807–8).

volatile the epithet given to a substance with a tendency to vaporize and rise upward when heat is applied to the vessel, usually depicted as winged *dragons, *birds, *angels or *lions. In alchemy the volatile substance or 'spirit' has to be captured or fixed, and the fixed substance, the 'body', must be dissolved or made fluid during the process of *solve et coagula. Calid wrote: 'We have taught how a Body is to be changed into a Spirit; and again how the Spirit is to be turned into a Body, *viz.* how the fixed is made volatile, and the volatile fixed again' (*Booke of the Secrets*, 121). Mercurius or the mercurial water consists of two aspects, one which can fix or coagulate and the other which dissolves. St Dunstan said of the mercurial *green lion that it has the 'power to reduce Bodies into their first matter, and to fix volatile and spiritual things, and [is] therefore not unfitly called a Lyon' (in FC, 9). In Ben Jonson's *Mercurie Vindicated from the Alchemists at Court*, Vulcan tries to capture and fix volatile mercury to make the Stone: 'Deare *Mercury*! Help. He flies. He is scap'd. Precious golden *Mercury*, be fixt; be not so volatile' (lines 23–5). The term volatile is used in a metaphorical sense in Balzac's *Quest of the Absolute*, where the alchemist Balthazar Claes is described as 'young, and as handsome as Helvetius, and Lavoisier was not his only instructor. Under the tuition of women in Paris he soon learned to distil the more volatile elixirs of wit and gallantry' (24).

Vulcan the lame husband of Venus and goldsmith to the gods, who, according to Paracelsus, symbolized the archetypal alchemist and founder of alchemy (*PS*, 93). 'Vulcan' is the name Ben Jonson gave his alchemist in the masque *Mercurie Vindicated from the Alchemists at Court* (*c*. 1615). Vulcan is also the secret *fire of the opus, the midwife for the birth of the *philosopher's stone. Arthur Dee wrote mysteriously of himself as the Stone in his 'Arca arcanorum': 'Hungary engendered me, Heaven and the stars watch over me and earth nourishes me, and Though I am constrained to die and be buried nevertheless Vulcan carefully gives me birth' (Observation 31). In *The Advancement of Learning* Francis Bacon wrote of the alchemists, 'quitting and forsaking Minerva and the Muses as barren virgins, and relying upon Vulcan' (63).

vulture   one of the names of the *Bird of Hermes or philosophical *mercury. In Hermes Trismegistus's *Tractatus aureus* the vulture which stands on the mountain utters the enigmatic cry: 'I am the white of the black, and the red of the white and the yellow of the red, and I am very truthful. And may you know that the most important thing of the Art is the raven which flies without wings in the dark of night and in bright daylight' (in Salmon, *Medicina Practica*, 180). The four colours represent the principal stages of the opus alchymicum – the black (*nigredo), white (*albedo), yellow (*citrinitas), and red (*rubedo) – making the vulture a symbol for the whole work. Michael Maier's *Atalanta fugiens* makes the vulture the subject of the forty-third emblem, whose motto reads: 'Listen to the garrulous vulture, which does not deceive you at all' (*AF*, 268). Heleen de Jong comments that 'The vulture and raven symbolize the circular motion of the alchemical process; the black raven represents the putrefactio; the vulture is the completion of it' (*AF*, 272).

W

washing   see **ablution**.

washerwomen   see **laundering**.

water   one of the four elements, the mastery of which brings peace. Michael Sendivogius wrote of the water element: 'Water is the heaviest Element, full of unctuous flegme . . . without, volatile, but within fixed, it is cold and moist, and tempered with aire: it is the sperme of the world, in which the seed of all things is kept' (*New Light of Alchymie*, 85). 'Water' is also the name for *philosophical mercury or the matter of the sages when it is dissolved. The mercurial water is known as the water of life (aqua vitae) which first kills the metal or matter for the Stone, and then revives and regenerates it. Other names for this arcanum are the water which does not wet the hands, the fiery water, blessed water, water of the wise, permanent water, the *fountain, water of grace, *stream, *river

*Nile, stinking water, *poison, *urine, *vinegar, *gum, *sea-water, precious water, divine water, celestial water, *serpent, *dragon, *Bird of Hermes, *vulture and *eagle. See **aqua permanens**, **elements**, **fire**, **fountain**, **Mercurius**, **opus circulatorium**.

watering   the *imbibation of the body of the Stone (the 'earth') with its own *mercurial water during *distillation. This process is sometimes represented by the image of the adept watering the philosophical plant, the *tree of sun and moon (see **philosophical tree**). An emblem celebrating the alchemist Michael Sendivogius in Michael Maier's *Symbola aureae mensae* shows Saturn watering the trees whose fruits are the sun and moon (Stolcius, *Viridarium*, 164). Avicenna wrote: 'Beat the Earth oftentimes, and by little and little imbibe it from eight days to eight days ... and let it not weary thee to reiterate the Work oftentimes, for the Earth bears not fruit without often watering' (in *FC*, 100).

weaponry   a symbol for the action of the philosophical *fire, especially at the initial stage of the opus known as the black *nigredo, when the old metal or matter for the Stone is killed and dissolved into its *prima materia. The fire is variously symbolized by axe, sword, scissors, knives, the scythe of *Saturn, and by the teeth of such wild animals as the lion and the wolf. The *beheading of the bird, or the king and queen, indicates that the heating and digestion of the matter in the alembic should be continued until the blackened body is purified to whiteness at the *albedo. The motto of the eighth emblem of Maier's *Atalanta fugiens* – 'Take the egg and pierce it with a fiery sword' – indicates that the alchemist must use the secret fire to assist in the birth of the *philosophical bird or stone from its vessel (*AF*, 95) (see **egg**).

wedding, wedded lovers, wedlock   see **chemical wedding**.

well   a name for the alchemical vessel in which the various dissolutions and purifications of the matter of the Stone by the *mercurial waters take place; the mercurial water itself. It is synonymous with the alchemical *bath. In an anonymous poem collected in Ashmole's *Theatrum chemicum Britannicum*, the leprous *dragon (the unclean matter at the beginning of the opus) lies putrefying 'in the bottome of his Well' until by bathing and cleansing 'he altereth cleane / Into a pure substance' (*TCB*, 354) (see **ablution**). In a pseudo-Lullian manuscript 'Opera chemica' (*c.* 1470–5), the alchemical twins are shown burning in a well, symbolizing the putrefaction of the matter of the Stone at the *nigredo (van Lennep, *Alchimie*, 83). Johann Mylius's *Philosophia reformata* (emblem 16) depicts the *philosopher's stone in its gold and silver splendour, rising out of the alchemical well where it has been redissolved in its own mercurial *blood and augmented in power at the *multiplicatio (fig. 48). See **alembic**. Paradoxically, the well can signify not only the container for the mercurial waters of life and death, but also the mercurial waters which are its own contents. Abraham Eleazar wrote of 'Python'

48 The well

(Mercurius) in *Uraltes Chymisches Werck*: 'it is the *primum ens metallorum* [the first essence of the metals], that is, the well of the ancients, the flower which is covered and guarded by the griffins and poisonous dragons' (JA, 246).

West see **East and West.**

wheel see **opus circulatorium.**

white see **albedo, Luna, white foliated earth, white stone.**

white eagle see **eagle.**

white earth see **white foliated earth.**

white elixir a subtle, penetrating medicine with the power to transmute base metal into pure silver. The white elixir is attained at the lunar stage known as the *albedo and is synonymous with the *white stone. Roger Bacon wrote: 'the white Elixir doth infinitely whiten, and bringeth everie mettal to a perfect whitenesse' (*Mirror*, 14). Benjamin Lock wrote of 'the perfecte Elixir whyte: able to turne arg: vive into medicine and all imperfect bodys of the myne into most fine silver' ('Picklock', f. 21). It is symbolized by the *moon, *Luna, the *virgin, *Diana, the *swan, dove, white *rose, white *lily, snow, the silver sea. Henry Vaughan wrote of the elixir in 'H. Scriptures': 'In thee the hidden stone, the Manna lies, / Thou art the great *Elixir*, rare and choice' (*Works*, 2:441).

white foliated earth the alchemical *ash which is also called the *snow or *Luna of the *albedo, the sublimated earth, the purified body of the Stone which

EMBLEMA VI. *De secretis Naturæ.* 33

Seminate aurum vestrum in terram albam foliatam.

EPIGRAMMA VI.

R Uricolæ pingui mandant sua semina terræ,
  Cùm fuerit rastris hæc foliata suis.
Philosophi niveos aurum docuère per agros
  Spargere, qui folii se levis instar habent:
Hoc ut agas, illud bene respice, namque quod aurum
  Germinet, ex tritico videris, ut speculo.
              E   PLATO

49 The white foliated earth

awaits re-animation by the return of its previously separated soul (or the now united soul and spirit) (see **chemical wedding**). The motto to the sixth emblem of Maier's *Atalanta fugiens* says: 'Sow your gold in the white foliated earth' (AF, 81) (fig. 49). The *Clangor Buccinae* also states: 'Hermes said, sow your gold in the white, foliated earth, which means: sow the vapour and the colour giving force in the white earth, which should be made white and pure by preparation, and in which no dirt is present' (AA, 1: 550). This is the process whereby the soul/spirit represented by *Sol (gold) is sown into and united with the purified, whitened body of the Stone in the chemical wedding. During this stage Sol imprints the pure but amorphous matter with new form. From this union the *philosopher's stone is born. Martin Ruland's definition of the white foliated earth seems to differ marginally from the opinion of most of the alchemical texts. He wrote that the white foliated earth is the mercurial or spiritual water extracted from the ashes in which the gold is sown (*Lexicon*, 314).

white fume   see **green lion**.

white lily   see **lily** (white).

white queen   see **queen**.

white rose	see **rose** (white).
white smoke	see **green lion**.
white stage	see **albedo**.
white stone	the stone which has the power to transmute base metal into pure silver. This Stone is attained at the white stage of the opus known as the *albedo. Trithemius wrote: 'when thou seest the Matter white as Snow, and shining like orientall gemms, The white Stone is then perfect' (in ZC, 80). At the beginning of the opus the alchemist takes the *prima materia which contains the seeds of metals, philosophical *sulphur (male, hot, dry, active) and philosophical *argent vive (female, cold, moist, receptive) and unites them in a coniunctio or *chemical wedding. The united bodies of sulphur and argent vive, usually symbolized by a pair of lovers, are killed, dissolved and laid in a grave to putrefy during the stage known as the *nigredo. Their souls fly to the top of the alembic while the blackened *hermaphroditic body is sublimed, distilled and purified. When the body is cleansed to perfect whiteness it is then reunited with the soul (or united soul and spirit). At this point the spirit is materialized and the body spiritualized. Artephius referred to the newly whitened spiritualized 'body' as 'the white stone, the white sulphur, not inflammable, the paradisiacal stone, viz. the stone transmuting imperfect metals into white silver'. (SB, 17). The white stone is symbolized by *alabaster, *marble, the white *rose, white *lily, white *queen, *Luna, Lunaria, the lunar plant, the swan, dove, and other white things. See **philosopher's stone**.
white water	mercury; see **Mercurius**.
white woman	see **red man and white woman**.
wind	the mercurial vapour during the process of sublimation. Benjamin Lock wrote: 'By softe fyer there doth ascende from the matter a certaine fume and winde, which the philosophers call sublimation, and when the same matter is descended down and turned into water they call that solution and distillation' ('Picklock', f. 36v). The fourth law of the *Emerald Table says of the Stone that 'The wind carried it in its womb, the Earth is the nurse thereof'. Michael Maier decoded this law as meaning that philosophical *sulphur (the male seed of metals) is carried within female *Mercurius as *prima materia (AF, 55). In Zoroaster's Cave, argent vive (aereal Mercurius) is identified with 'wind': 'Argent Vive is called Wind, that is, Aereal Argent Vive' (64). During the process of sublimation and distillation *Mercurius is said to fly through the air like the wind itself. Zoroaster's Cave, citing Vobicum, associates wind with the (subtle) element air at the second stage in the opus: 'Our Stone in the beginning is called water; when the body is dissolved, Ayre or Wind; when it tends to consolidation, then it is named earth, and when it is perfect and fixt it is called Fire' (ZC, 64). See **zephyr**.

wine   see grapes.

winnow   to separate the pure from the impure, the subtle from the gross during the process of the opus. An anonymous treatise, *The Philosopher's Stone*, referred to the separation of 'a matter in itself as much extraneous to the seed of metals as the chaff to the wheat' (CC, 103). Psychologically, the winnowing refers to the act of discriminating between the true and the false which the adept learns on his labyrinthine pathway to wisdom. Andrew Marvell's '*easie Philosopher*' in 'Upon Appleton House' thanks the wind for assisting him in this process, after which he is able to emerge from the labyrinth of the wood unscathed: 'And unto you cool *Zephyr's* thanks, / Who, as my Hair, my Thoughts too shed, / And winnow from the Chaff my Head' (lines 598–600) (see also **harvest, grain**).

wisdom   see **sapientia**.

wolf   antimony, known to the alchemists as lupus metallorum, the wolf of metals, because of the ferocity with which it devours the matter of the Stone (fig. 50). Basil Valentine wrote that the body of the *king (the matter of the Stone) was cast to the wolf (antimony) which devoured it and purified it in the fire so that it could then rise again, resurrected (HM, 1:325). The twenty-fourth emblem in Michael Maier's *Atalanta fugiens* uses Valentine's text as its source. The motto of the emblem reads: 'The wolf devoured the king and after the wolf has been burnt, it returned the king to life' (AF, 186). In this context the wolf is synonymous with the *mercurial waters of life and death, the universal solvent

50 The wolf

which dissolves metals, then cleanses, purifies and regenerates them. See **antimony**.

womb   a symbol for the alembic or vessel. The generation of the *philosopher's stone from the *chemical wedding of *Sol and *Luna (form and matter) is frequently compared to the birth of a child. Thus the alembic in which the Stone is conceived, generated and born became known as the womb. Dorn's *Congeries Paracelsicae* spoke of 'the spagyric uterus' (PW, 285). In 'Love's Alchemy' John Donne referred to the alchemical vessel as the 'pregnant pot' (line 8) and in 'The Comparison' he wrote of 'the limbeck's warm womb' (line 36). Face, in Ben Jonson's *The Alchemist*, compares the alembic containing the growing Stone to 'a wench with child' (2.2.8–9). Mehung (pseudo-Jean de Meun) observed that the alembic needs a gentle fire 'just as an infant in the womb is cherished by natural heat' (HM, 1:136). The alchemical womb is synonymous with the *nest or *egg in which the alchemical 'chick' is incubated and hatched. The esoteric philosophers who regard the *mercurial water as their secret vessel have also compared it to the womb. Artephius wrote that mercury as the *bath of *aqua vitae and *dew which cleanses the blackened bodies of *Sol and *Luna, is called 'the *vas naturae*, the belly, the womb … It is the royal fountain in which the king and queen bathe themselves' (SB, 15). Geber wrote of a 'womb' of earth in which the *seeds of metals needed to generate: 'The thing that works perfection in metalls is the substance of Argent vive and Sulphur proportionally mixt, by long and temperate Decoction inspissate and fixt in a Wombe of clean earth' (in ZC, 59).

   The twenty-second emblem of Maier's *Atalanta fugiens* shows a pregnant woman attending the alembic on the fire. The verse accompanying the emblem indicates that after the whitening of the blackened matter of the Stone 'only women's work remains, / Then you should cook, like a woman, who puts pans on the fire' (AF, 177). The pregnant woman in this emblem is a personification of the pure white matter, the *white foliated earth attained at the albedo, into which the seed of gold has been sown. The *Semita semitae* says: 'The Water approaching, that is Argent vive in the Earth, encreaseth, and is augmented because the Earth is whitened, and then it is called impregnation, then the Ferment is coagulated, *viz.* joined with the imperfect Body' (FC, 66–7). This impregnation of the white matter (body) with the seed (soul) brings about the final stage of the opus, known as the *rubedo, when the philosopher's stone matures.

women's work   the work of cleansing and purifying the matter of the Stone; the second stage of the opus. The operation of purifying and refining the matter is accomplished through the *solve et coagula process known as *cooking, and through the *ablution or washing (see fig. 37, and **laundering**). In *Atalanta fugiens*, Michael Maier described the 'cooking' of the matter (refinement through heat) as women's work: 'When you have obtained the white lead, then do women's work, that is to say: COOK' (AF, 176). The motto of emblem 3 in the same treatise says of the ablution or washing process: 'Go to the woman who washes the sheets and do as she does' (AF, 66). In *Fasciculus chemicus* Arthur Dee cites and argues with

Attaman, who believes that the work in the early stage of the opus is too sordid for men and only suitable for women: 'And this Preparation, a first work he [Attaman] calleth a Sordid labour and adjudges it not worthy a learned man, therefore not unfitly said to be the work of Women'. Dee objects to the idea of relegating the 'sordid' aspect of the work to women, saying that the alchemist must be prepared to do such work himself: 'he deserves not Sweets, that will not tast of Bitters' (FC, 38). In other contexts the accomplishment of the second (and final) stage of the opus alchymicum is sometimes said to be so easy that women or children could do it. Artephius wrote: 'It is indeed a work so short and easy that it may well be called a womans work and the play of children' (SB, 32). The work of women and the play of children are also equated because they both represent the purifying process of the solve et coagula. See **ludus puerorum.**

worm   the *mercurial waters of life and death, the transforming arcanum, the secret *fire. In the sixteenth and seventeenth centuries 'worm', 'serpent' and 'dragon' were interchangeable terms, and so in alchemical texts 'serpent' and 'worm' are synonymous. The mercurial worm devours the old corrupt body of the metal or matter of the Stone in the vessel as coffin, and reduces it to its *prima materia. The worm is the secret fire which reduces the 'body' of the Stone into dust or ashes. In Michael Maier's *Atalanta fugiens,* the solvent devouring the corrupt matter in the vessel is referred to as 'worms' in the belly of the 'cormorant' (i.e. the alembic) (96). Basil Valentine wrote that the 'putrefactio imparts life to many worms' (HM, 1:340). The mercurial worm, like the serpent, is both the devouring worm of death consuming all corruption and the nourishing worm of life which feeds the alchemical chick, the infant Stone with its nourishing substance (see **cibation**). Johann Andreae's emblem of the worms in the alchemical vessel (BL Sloane 2560) is accompanied by a verse from Arnold of Villanova stating the familiar alchemical dictum that the worm of corruption leads to generation (in Klossowski de Rola, *Alchemy,* 118–19).

Y

yellow, yellow stage   see **citrinitas**

Z

zaibar   *mercury of the philosophers.

zephyr the mercurial vapour which rises in the alembic during the process of distillation and sublimation. It sometimes symbolizes the *white stone attained at the *albedo. In Ben Jonson's *The Alchemist* Sir Epicure Mammon uses the term to refer to Subtle's puffer, Face, who blows on the alchemical fire to keep it going: 'That's his fire-drake, / His lungs, his *Zephyrus*, he that puffes his coales' (2.1.26–7). See **wind, winnow**.

Bibliography

Abraham Eleazar, 'Abraham Juif Prince . . . Livre des figures hiero-
    glyphiques avec l'explanation des fables des Poetes, des misteres
    du christianisme; de la chimie, et de la Pharmacie suivant les
    nombres', University of Glasgow Library Ferguson MS 17
    Uraltes Chymisches Werck, Erfurt: Augustinus Crusius, 1735
Abraham, Lyndy, 'Alchemical reference in *Antony and Cleopatra*', *Sydney
    Studies in English* 8 (1982–3), 100–4
    'The Alchemical Republic: a reading of "An Horatian Ode"' (with
    Michael Wilding), in *Marvell and Liberty*, edited by Warren
    Chernaik and Martin Dzelzainius, London: Macmillan, 1998
    'The Australian crucible: alchemy in Marcus Clarke's *His Natural
    Life*', *Australian Literary Studies* 15 (1991–2), 38–55
    Harriot's Gift to Arthur Dee: Literary Images from an Alchemical Manuscript,
    The Thomas Harriot Society, no. 10, Cambridge and Durham, 1993
    '"The lovers and the tomb": alchemical emblems in Shakespeare,
    Donne and Marvell', *Emblematica; An Interdisciplinary Journal for
    Emblem Studies* 5 (1991), 301–20
    Marvell and Alchemy, Aldershot: Scolar Press, 1990
    'Milton's *Paradise Lost* and "the sounding alchymie"', *Renaissance
    Studies* 12 (1998), 261–76
    'Nabokov's alchemical *Pale Fire*', *Dutch Quarterly Review* 20 (1990–2),
    102–20
    'Weddings, funerals, and incest: alchemical emblems and
    Shakespeare's *Pericles, Prince of Tyre*', *Journal of English and Germanic
    Philology* (forthcoming)
    (ed.), Arthur Dee, *Fasciculus chemicus* (1631), translated by Elias
    Ashmole (1650), New York: Garland, 1997
Abu'L-Qasim Muhammad Ibn Ahmad Al-Iraqi, *Book of Knowledge
    Acquired concerning the Cultivation of Gold*, translated from the Arabic
    and edited by E. J. Holmyard, Paris: Paul Geuthner, 1923
Ackroyd, Peter, *The House of Dr Dee*, London: Hamish Hamilton, 1993
Adams, Alison (ed.), *Emblems in Glasgow: A Collection of Essays drawing on
    the Stirling Maxwell collection in the Glasgow University Library*,
    Glasgow: University of Glasgow French and German Publications,
    1992
Agnelli, Giovanni Baptista, *A Revelation of the Secret Spirit declaring the
    most concealed secret of Alchymie*, translated by R. N. E., London:
    Henrie Skelton, 1623
Altus, *Mutus Liber* (1677), introduction and commentary by Jean Laplace
    (Bibliotheca Hermetica – XVI), Milan: Archè, 1979
Amis, Kingsley, *Stanley and the Women*, London: Hutchinson, 1984
Andreae, Johann Valentin, *Chymische Hochzeit*, Strasbourg: Lazarus
    Zetzner, 1616
    The Hermetick Romance or the Chymical Wedding written in high Dutch by

Christian Rosencreutz (a translation by E. Foxcroft of *Chymische Hochzeit*), London: A. Sowle, 1690 (commonly known as *The Chymical Wedding*; all page references in the text are to this edition)

Andrewes, Abraham, *The Hunting of the Greene Lyon*, in Elias Ashmole (ed.), *Theatrum chemicum Britannicum*, 278–90

Aquinas, Saint Thomas (attributed), *Aurora consurgens*, edited by Marie-Louise von Franz, London: Routledge and Kegan Paul, 1966

Arcanum (by Jean d'Espagnet), in Arthur Dee, *Fasciculus chemicus*, 155–268

Archelaos, 'Poem of the Philosopher Archelaos upon the Sacred Art' (AD 715–17), cited in C. A. Browne, 'Rhetorical and religious aspects of Greek alchemy', 134

Aristeus Pater, 'The Words of Father Aristeus to his Son, done out of the Scythian Character or Language into Latin Rhyme', British Library MS Sloane 3641, ff. 61v–63v; MS Sloane 2567, ff. 63r–68r, *c.* 1600 (printed in Schuler, *Alchemical Poetry 1575-1700*, 472–6)

Ars chemica quod sit licita exercentibus, probationes doctissimorum iurisconsultorum . . ., Strasbourg: Samuel Emmel, 1566

Artephius, *The Secret Book of Artephius* (1612), facsimile reprint, Largs: Banton, 1991

Artis auriferae quam chemiam vocant, 2 vols., Basel: Conrad Waldkirch, 1593

Ashmole, Elias, 'To my worthily honour'd William Backhouse Esquire Upon his adopting of me to be his Son' (1651), Bodleian Library MS Ashmole 36–7, ff. 241v–242r

——— (ed.), *Theatrum chemicum Britannicum* (1652), facsimile reprint, New York and London: Johnson Reprint Corporation, 1967

——— (ed. and trans.), Arthur Dee, *Fasciculus chemicus* (1631), London: Richard Mynne, 1650 (see Lyndy Abraham)

Ashmole MS 1420, Bodleian Library, Oxford

Ashmole MS 1788, Bodleian Library, Oxford

Atalanta fugiens, see Michael Maier

Aubrey, John, *Brief Lives*, edited by A. Clarke, 2 vols., Oxford: Clarendon Press, 1898

Aurifontina chymica, see John Frederick Houpreght

Aurora consurgens, see Aquinas, Saint Thomas

Backhouse, William, 'The Magistery', in *Theatrum chemicum Britannicum*, edited by Elias Ashmole, 342–3

Backhouse, William (trans.), 'The Pleasant Founteine of Knowledge', by Jean de la Fontaine, Bodleian Library MS Ashmole 58, 1r–23r (in Robert Schuler, *Alchemical Poetry 1575-1700*, 66–122)

Bacon, Francis, *The Advancement of Learning* (1605), edited by Arthur J. Johnston, Oxford: Clarendon Press, 1974

——— *Apophthegms*, in *The Works of Francis Bacon*, edited by Basil Montague, 3 vols. London, 1823

Bacon, Roger, *The mirror of alchimy, composed by the thrice-famous and learned fryer, . . . Also a most excellent and learned discourse of the admirable force and efficacie of Art and Nature written by the same author. With certain other worthie treatises of the like argument*, London: Richard Olive, 1597

The Mirror of Alchimy Composed by the Thrice-famous and Learned Fryer, Roger Bachon (1597), edited by Stanton J. Linden, New York: Garland, 1992 (all page references in the text are to this edition)

Balzac, Honoré de, *The Quest of the Absolute* (1834), translated by Ellen Marriage, London: Macmillan, 1896

Bartas, Guillaume du, *The Divine Weeks and Works of Guillaume de Salustre Sieur du Bartas*, translated by Josuah Sylvester, edited by Susan Snyder, 2 vols., Oxford: Clarendon Press, 1979

Bath, Michael, *Speaking Pictures: English Emblem Books and Renaissance Culture*, Medieval and Renaissance Library, London: Longman, 1994

'Benjamin Lock, His Picklock to Riply his Castle', Wellcome MS 436, Wellcome Institute for the History of Medicine

Benlowes, Edward, *Theophila or Loves' Sacrifice. A Divine Poem*, London: Henry Seile and Humphrey Moseley, 1652

Binns, J. W., *Intellectual Culture in Elizabethan and Jacobean England: The Latin Writings of the Age*, University of Leeds: Francis Cairns, 1990

Bonus of Ferrara, Petrus, *The New Pearl of Great Price* (1546), translated by A. E. Waite, London: Vincent Stuart, 1963

Brooks-Davies, Douglas, *The Mercurian Monarch*, Manchester University Press, 1983

Brown, Norman O., *Hermes the Thief*, New York: Vintage Books, 1969

Browne, C. A. 'Rhetorical and religious aspects of Greek alchemy', *Ambix* 2 (1946), 129–37

Browne, Sir Thomas, *Religio Medici and other Works*, edited by L. C. Martin, Oxford: Clarendon Press, 1964

'Buch von Vunderverken' (Buch der Heiligen Dreifaltigkeit) (seventeenth century), University of Glasgow Library, Ferguson MS 4

Bulman-May, James, 'Patrick White and Alchemy', unpublished Ph. D. thesis, University of Sydney, 1995

Burckhardt, Titus, *Alchemy*, Baltimore, Maryland: Penguin, 1971

Butler, Samuel, *Hudibras*, edited by John Wilders, Oxford: Clarendon Press, 1967

Calid, *The Booke of the Secrets of Alchimie, composed by Galid the sonne of Jazich*, in Roger Bacon, *The Mirror of Alchimy*, edited by Stanton J. Linden, 28–48

Canseliet, Eugene, *L'alchimie expliquée sur ses textes classiques*, Paris: Jean-Jacques Pauvert, 1972

Casaubon, Meric (ed.), *A True and Faithful Relation of what passed for many yeers Between Dr John Dee (A Mathematician of Great Fame in Q. Elizabeth and King James their Reignes) and Some Spirits*, London: T. Garthwait, 1659

Chalmers, Alexander, *English Poets*, see William Warner

Chambers, Sir E. K., *William Shakespeare: A Study of Facts and Problems*, 2 vols., Oxford: Clarendon Press, 1930

Charnock, Thomas, 'The Breviary of Naturall Philosophy', in *Theatrum chemicum Britannicum*, edited by Elias Ashmole, 291–303

Chaucer, Geoffrey, *The Canon's Yeoman's Tale*, in *The Complete Works of Geoffrey Chaucer*, edited by Walter W. Skeat, 6 vols., 1894, vol. 4, Oxford: Clarendon Press, 1940

Chou, Shu-Hua, 'Alchemical Explication of Three Renaissance Poetic Texts: Edmund Spenser's *The Faerie Queene* Book I; Sir Walter Raleigh's *The Ocean to Scinthia*; and Michael Drayton's *Endimion and Phoebe*', unpublished Ph. D. thesis, University of Manchester, 1996

A Chymicall Dictionary explaining Hard Places and Words met withall in the Writings of Paracelsus, and other obscure Authors, in Michael Sendivogius, *A new Light of Alchymy*, translated by J. F. M. D., London: Thomas Williams, 1650

Cirlot, Juan Eduardo, *A Dictionary of Symbols*, London: Routledge and Kegan Paul, 1962

Clarke, Lindsay, *The Chymical Wedding: A Romance*, London: Pan Books, 1990

Clarke, Marcus, *His Natural Life* (the serialized version), edited by Stephen Murray Smith, Harmondsworth: Penguin Books, 1970

Cleveland, John, *The Poems of John Cleveland*, edited by Brian Morris and Eleanor Withington, Oxford: Clarendon Press, 1967

Clucas, Stephen, 'Poetic atomism in seventeenth-century England: Henry More, Thomas Traherne and "scientific imagination"', *Renaissance Studies* 5 (1991), 327–40.

Thomas Harriot and the Field of Knowledge in the English Renaissance, The Thomas Harriot Society, Oxford and Durham, 1994

Collectanea chymica, London: William Cooper, 1684

Collop, John, M. D., *Poesis Rediviva: or Poesie Reviv'd* (1656), facsimile reprint, Menston: Scolar Press, 1972

Colson, Lancelot, see *Philosophia maturata*

Cooper, J. C., *Chinese Alchemy*, Wellingborough: Aquarian Press, Northamptonshire, 1984

Cooper, William, *William Cooper's Catalogue of Chymicall Books,* see Stanton J. Linden

'Coronatio naturae', University of Glasgow, Ferguson MS 208

'Coronatio naturae', University of Glasgow, Ferguson MS 230

Cowley, Abraham, *Poems*, London: Humphrey Moseley, 1656

Cradock, Edward, 'A Treatise Touching the Philosopher's Stone', Bodleian Library MS Ashmole 1445, item 6, 1–25, *c.* 1575 (collated with Bodleian MS Rawl. poet. 182 and printed in Robert Schuler, *Alchemical Poetry 1575–1700*, 3–48)

Crashaw, Richard, *The Poems of Richard Crashaw*, edited by L. C. Martin, Oxford: Clarendon Press, 1951

Crosland, Maurice, P., *Historical Studies in the Language of Chemistry*, Cambridge, Massachusetts: Harvard University Press, 1962

The Crowning of Nature, see Adam McLean

The Cultivation of Gold, see Abu'L-Qasim

Davenant, Sir William, *The Shorter Poems, and Songs from the Plays and Masques*, edited by A. M. Gibbs, Oxford: Clarendon Press, 1972

Davies, H. Neville (ed.), *At Vacant Hours: Poems by Thomas St Nicholas and his Family*, Reading: Whiteknights Press (forthcoming)

Debus, Allen G., *The Chemical Philosophy. Paracelsian Science and Medicine in the Sixteenth and Seventeenth Centuries*, 2 vols., New York: Science History Publications, 1977

Chemistry, Alchemy and the New Philosophy, 1550–1700, London: Variorum Reprints, 1987

The English Paracelsians, London: Oldbourne, 1965

Robert Fludd and his Philosophical Key, New York: Science History Publications, 1979

Science, Medicine and Society in the Renaissance, New York: Science History Publications, 1972

Debus, Allen G., and Ingrid Merkel (eds.), *Hermeticism and the Renaissance. Intellectual History and the Occult in Early Modern Europe*, Washington D.C.: The Folger Shakespeare Library, 1988

Dee, Arthur, 'Arca arcanorum', British Library Sloane MS 1876, ff. 1–83

Fasciculus chemicus, Paris: Nicolas de la Vigne, 1631

Fasciculus chemicus and the *Arcanum* (anon.), trans. James Hasolle (Elias Ashmole), London: Richard Mynne, 1650

Fasciculus chemicus, see Lyndy Abraham

Dee, John, *Monas hieroglyphica*, Antwerp: Guilielmus Silvius, 1564 (see also C. H. Josten)

The Private Diary of Dr John Dee and the Catalogue of his Library of Manuscripts, edited by James Orchard Halliwell, London: The Camden Society, 1842

Dee, John, see Roberts, Julian, and Andrew G. Watson

Dee, John, see also Casaubon, Meric

Dixon, Laurinda (ed.), *Nicolas Flamel: His Exposition of the Hieroglyphicall Figures* (1624), New York: Garland, 1996

Dobbs, Betty Jo Teeter, *The Foundations of Newton's Alchemy or The Hunting of the Greene Lyon*, Cambridge University Press, 1975

The Janus Faces of Genius: The Role of Alchemy in Newton's Thought, Cambridge: Cambridge University Press, 1991

'Newton's "Clavis": new evidence on its dating and significance', *Ambix* 29 (1982), 198–202

'Newton's copy of *Secrets Reveal'd* and the regimen of the work', *Ambix* 26 (1979), 145–69

Donne, John, *The Complete English Poems*, edited by A. J. Smith, Harmondsworth: Penguin Books, 1971

The Sermons of John Donne, edited by George R. Potter and Evelyn M. Simpson, 10 vols., Berkeley and Los Angeles: University of California Press, 1953–62

Dorn, Gerhard, *Dictionarium Theophrasti Paracelsi*, Frankfurt: Christoff Rab, 1584

Drayton, Michael, *The Works of Michael Drayton*, edited by J. W. Hebel, Kathleen Tillotson and B. H. Newdigate, 5 vols., Oxford: Basil Blackwell, 1930–41

Dryden, John, *The Poems of John Dryden*, edited by James Kinsley, 4 vols., Oxford: Clarendon Press, 1958

Duncan, Edgar H., 'The alchemy in Jonson's *Mercury Vindicated*', *Studies in Philology* 39 (1942), 625–37

'Donne's Alchemical Figures', *ELH* 9 (1942), 257–85

'The literature of alchemy and Chaucer's "Canon's Yeoman's Tale": framework, theme and characters', *Speculum* 43 (1968), 633–56

Dunstan, St, see St Dunstan

Durrell, Lawrence, *The Alexandria Quartet*, London: Faber, 1962

Eamon, William, *Science and the Secrets of Nature,* Princeton University Press, 1994

Eglinus, Raphael Iconius, *An easie Introduction to the Philosophers Magical Gold; To which is added Zoroasters Cave; as also John Pontanus, Epistle upon the Mineral Fire; otherwise called, The Philosophers Stone*, edited by George Thor, London: Matthew Smelt, 1667

Eleazar, Abraham, see Abraham Eleazar

Emerald Table, in Roger Bacon, *Mirror of Alchemy*, 16

Espagnet, Jean d', see *Arcanum*

Evans, R. J. W., *Rudolf II and His World: A Study in Intellectual History 1576–1612*, Oxford: Clarendon Press, 1973

Fabricius, Johannes, *Alchemy: The Medieval Alchemists and their Royal Art*, Copenhagen: Rosenkilde and Bagger, 1976

Ferguson, J., *Bibliotheca Chemica: A Catalogue of the Alchemical, Chemical and Pharmaceutical Books in the Collection of the late James Young of Kelley and Durris*, Glasgow, 1906

Ferguson MS 6 (untitled, sixteenth century), University of Glasgow Library

Ferguson MS 31 (untitled, eighteenth century), University of Glasgow Library

Ferguson MS 238 (untitled, seventeenth century), University of Glasgow Library

Ferguson MS 271 (untitled, eighteenth century), University of Glasgow

Ferne, Sir John, *The Blazon of Gentrie: Devided into two parts. The first named The Glorie of Generositie. The Lacyes Nobilitie*, London: Toby Cooke, 1586

Fevre, Nicaise Le, *A Discourse upon Sir Walter Rawleigh's Great Cordial*, trans. Peter Belon, London: Octavian Pulleyn, 1664

Five Treatises of the Philosophers' Stone ... By the paines and care of H. P., London: John Collins, 1652

Flamel, Nicolas, *His Exposition of the Hieroglyphicall Figures which he caused to bee painted upon the Arch in St Innocents Church-yard in Paris*, London: Thomas Walkley, 1624

    Philosophical Summary, in *Hermetic Museum*, 141–7

Flamel, Nicolas, see Abraham Eleazar and Laurinda Dixon

Fludd, Robert, *Mosaicall Philosophy*, London: Humphrey Moseley, 1659

    'Truth's Golden Harrow', see C. H. Josten

Fludd, Robert, see also Allen G. Debus

Fontaine, Jean de la, *La fontaine des amoureux de science* (1413), translated by William Backhouse (1644), Bodleian Library MS Ashmole 58, 1r–23r (printed in Robert Schuler, *Alchemical poetry 1575–1700*, 83–122)

Forman, Simon, 'Compositor huius libri ad lectorem', Bodleian Library MS Ashmole 1472, 6r–6v, 1597 (printed in Schuler, *Alchemical Poetry 1575–1700*, 66–70)

    'Of the Division of Chaos', Bodleian Library MS Ashmole 240, 33r–35v, c. 1595 (printed in Robert Schuler, *Alchemical Poetry 1575–1700*, 56–60)

Fowler, Alastair, see John Milton

Franz, Marie-Louise von, see St Thomas Aquinas

French, Peter J., *John Dee: The World of an Elizabethan Magus*, London: Routledge and Kegan Paul, 1972

The Fugger News-Letters (second series) Being a further selection from the Fugger papers specially referring to Queen Elizabeth and matters relating to England during the years 1586–1605, ed. V. von Klarwill, trans. L. R. R. Byrne, London: John Lane, the Bodley Head, 1926

Gautier, Théophile, *Romans et Contes*, in *Oeuvres de Théophile Gautier*, Paris: Alphonse Lemerre, 1897

Geber, *Liber fornacum*, in *Artis chemicae principes, Avicenna atque Geber*, Basel: Petrus Perna, 1572

Geber, *The Summa Perfectionis of pseudo-Geber*, edited and translated by William R. Newman, Collection des travaux de l'Academie internationale d'histoires des sciences, vol. 35, Leiden: E. J. Brill, 1991

Godwin, Joscelyn, *Robert Fludd*, London: Thames and Hudson, 1977

'The Golden Rotation', British Library, Sloane MS 1881

Gray, Ronald, *Goethe the Alchemist*, Cambridge University Press, 1952

Greer, Germaine, Susan Hastings, Jeslyn Medoff, Melinda Sansone (eds.), *Kissing the Rod: An Anthology of Seventeenth-Century Women's Verse*, London: Virago, 1988

Grossinger, Richard (ed.), *Alchemy: Pre-Egyptian Legacy, Millennial Promise*, Richmond, California: North Atlantic Books, 1979

Gunther, R. T., *Early Science in Oxford*, 13 vols., printed for the subscribers, Oxford, 1923

Hall, Joseph, *Virgidemiarum, Sixe Bookes. First three Bookes, of Toothlesss Satyrs. The three last Bookes, Of byting Satyrs*, London: Robert Dexter, 1597

Hartlib, Samuel, *Chymical, Medicinal and Chyrurgical Addresses, made to Samuel Hartlib, Esquire*, London: Giles Calvert, 1655

Harvey, Gabriel, *The Works of Gabriel Harvey*, edited by Alexander B. Grosart, 3 vols., London: The Huth Library, 1884

Herbert, George, *The Works of George Herbert*, edited by F. E. Hutchinson, Oxford: Clarendon Press, 1941

Hermes Trismegistus, *The Divine Pymander of Hermes Mercurius Trismegistus in XVII Books. Translated formerly out of the Arabick into Greek, and thence into Latin, and Dutch, and now out of the original into English; by that learned Divine Doctor Everard* (with a preface signed J. F.), London: T. Brewster and G. Moule, 1650

Hermes Trismegisti, Tractatus Aureus, in Salmon, *Medicina Practica*, 177–283

Thrice Great Hermes: Studies in Hellenistic Theosophy and Gnosis, the extant sermons and fragments of the Trismegistic literature translated by G. R. S. Mead (1906), York Beach, Maine: Samuel Weiser, 1992

Hermetic Museum (1678) edited by A. E. Waite (1893), York Beach, Maine: Samuel Weiser, 1991

'Hermetick Raptures', British Library MS Sloane 3632, ff. 148–87v, *c*. 1700 (printed in Schuler, *Alchemical Poetry 1575–1700*, 564–603)

Herrick, Robert, *The Poetical Works of Robert Herrick*, edited by L. C. Martin, Oxford: Clarendon Press, 1956

Hodgson, Joan, *Astrology, the Sacred Science*, Liss, Hampshire: White Eagle
  Publishing Trust, 1978
Holmyard, E. J., *Alchemy*, Harmondsworth: Penguin Books, 1957
Hortulanus, *A Briefe Commentarie of Hortulanus the Philosopher, upon the
  Smaragdine Table of Hermes of Alchemy*, in Roger Bacon, *The Mirror of
  Alchimy*, 16–27
Houpreght, John Frederick, *Aurifontina chymica, or a Collection of Fourteen
  small Treatises Concerning the First matter of Philosophers, for the discov-
  ery of their (hitherto so much concealed) Mercury*, London: William
  Cooper, 1680
Hughes, Ted, *Selected Poems 1957–1981*, London: Faber, 1982
The Hunting of the Greene Lyon, in Elias Ashmole (ed.), *Theatrum chemicum
  Britannicum*, 278–90
Hugo, Victor, *Notre-Dame de Paris* (1831) (trans. Boston: Estes and Lauriat,
  1833), reprinted as *The Hunchback of Notre Dame*, Philadelphia:
  Running Press, 1995
Hutchinson, Lucy, *Memoirs of the Life of Colonel Hutchinson*, edited by N.
  H. Keeble, Everyman's Library, London: Dent, 1995
'Incipit tractatulus de phenice siue de Lapide philosophico', British
  Library Additional MS 11,388, Collection of Francis Thynne,
  Lancaster Herald 1564–1606 (also known as Sir George Ripley's
  'Cantilena de lapide philosophico')
Johnson, Samuel, *The Rambler*, 16 July 1751
Johnson, William, *Lexicon Chymicum cum Obscuriorum Verborum et Rerum
  Hermeticum*, London: Guilielmus Nealand, 1652
Jones, Bassett, 'Lithochymicus, or a Discourse of a Chymic Stone prae-
  sented to the University of Oxford', British Library Sloane MS 315,
  ff. 1r–91v, *c.* 1650 (printed in Robert Schuler, *Alchemical Poetry
  1575–1700*, 227–358)
Jong, Heleen de, 'The Chymical Wedding in the tradition of alchemy',
  in *Das Erbe des Christian Rosenkreutz: Vorträge gehalten anläßlich des
  Amsterdamen Symposiums 18–20 November, 1968*, Amsterdam, 1988
Jong, Heleen de, see Michael Maier
Jonson, Ben, *The Alchemist*, in *Ben Jonson*, edited by C. H. Herford and
  Percy Simpson, 11 vols., Oxford: Clarendon Press, 1937, 5: 273–408
Mercurie Vindicated from the Alchemists at Court, in *Ben Jonson*, edited by
  C. H. Herford and Percy Simpson, 11 vols., Oxford: Clarendon
  Press, 1937, 7: 407–18
Josten, C. H., *Elias Ashmole 1617–1692: His Autobiographical and Historical
  Notes, his Correspondence, and other Contemporary Sources Relating to his
  Life and Work*, Oxford: Clarendon Press, 1966
'A translation of John Dee's *Monas hieroglyphica* (Antwerp, 1564), with
  an Introduction and Annotations', *Ambix* 12 (1964), 84–219
'Truth's Golden Harrow: an unpublished alchemical treatise of
  Robert Fludd in the Bodleian Library', *Ambix* 3 (1949), 91–150
Jung, C. G., *Alchemical Studies*, (1942–57), trans. R. F. C. Hull, Princeton
  University Press, 1967, 1983
Mysterium Coniunctionis, (1955–6), trans. R. F. C. Hull, London:
  Routledge and Kegan Paul, 1963

Psychology and Alchemy, (1944), trans. R. F. C. Hull, London: Routledge
and Kegan Paul, 1953, 1989

Karpenko, Vladimir, 'Christoph Bergner: the last Prague alchemist',
Ambix 37 (1990), 116–20

Kelly, Edward, 'Exposition of Ripley's *Compound*', British Library MS
Sloane 3631, ff. 51–63

*Tractatus Duo egregii, de Lapide Philosophorum, una cum Theatro
Astronomiae Terrestri*, Hamburg: Gothofredus Schultz, 1676

*Two excellent Treatises on the Philosophers Stone together with the Theatre of
Terrestrial Astronomy* (1676), edited and translated by A. E. Waite
(1893), Largs: Banton Press, 1991

Kelly, L. G., see Basil Valentine

Khalid, see Calid

King, Henry, *The Poems of Henry King*, ed. Margaret Crum, Oxford:
Clarendon Press, 1965

Klossowski de Rola, Stanislas, *Alchemy: The Secret Art*, London: Thames
and Hudson, 1973

The Golden Game: Alchemical Engravings of the Seventeenth Century,
London: Thames and Hudson, 1988

*Lachrymae Musarum: The Tears of the Muses; Written by divers persons of
Nobility and Worth, Upon the Death of the most hopefull, Henry Lord
Hastings*, London: Thomas Newcomb, 1649

Lambye, Baptista, see Giovanni Baptista Agnelli

Le Fevre, Nicaise, see Fevre

Lennep, Jacques van, *Alchimie: Contribution à l'histoire de l'art alchimique*,
Brussels: Crédit Communal de Belgique, 1985

'Liber patris sapientiae', in Elias Ashmole (ed.), *Theatrum chemicum
Britannicum*, 194–209

Linden, Stanton J., 'Alchemy and eschatology in seventeenth century
poetry', *Ambix* 31 (1984), 102–24

*Darke Hieroglyphicks: Alchemy in English Literature from Chaucer to the
Restoration*, Lexington: University of Kentucky Press, 1996

(ed.), *William Cooper's Catalogue of Chymicall Books (London 1673, 1675,
1688): A Verified Edition*, New York: Garland, 1987

Linden, Stanton J., see also Roger Bacon

Lindsay, Jack, *The Origins of Alchemy in Graeco-Roman Egypt*, London:
Frederick Muller, 1970

Lock, Benjamin, see 'Benjamin Lock His Picklock to Riply his Castle'

Lock, Humphrey, 'Treatise on alchemy', Ferguson MS 216, Glasgow
University Library

Lodge, Thomas, *The Complete Works of Thomas Lodge*, edited by Sir
Edmund Gosse, 4 vols., Glasgow: The Hunterian Club, 1883

Luther, Martin, *The Table Talk of Martin Luther*, trans. William Hazlitt,
London: Bell, 1902

Lydgate, John, 'Translation of the second Epistle that King Alexander
sent to his Master Aristotle' or 'Secreta Secretorum', in Elias
Ashmole (ed.), *Theatrum chemicum Britannicum*, 397–403

Lyly, John, *The Complete Works of John Lyly*, edited by R. Warwick Bond, 3
vols., Oxford: Clarendon Press, 1967

McLean, Adam, *The Alchemical Mandala*, Hermetic Research Series no. 3, Grand Rapids: Phanes Press, 1989

McLean, Adam (ed.), *The Alchemical Engravings of Mylius*, translated by Patricia Tahil, Edinburgh: Magnum Opus Hermetic Sourceworks, 1984

(ed.) *The Crowning of Nature: The Doctrine of the Chief Medicine Explained in Sixty Seven Hieroglyphicks*, Tysoe, Warwickshire: Magnum Opus Hermetic Sourceworks, 1980

(ed.) *The Rosary of the Philosophers* (1550), Edinburgh: Magnum Opus Hermetic Sourceworks, 1980

Maier, Michael, *Atalanta fugiens* (1617), edited by H. M. E. de Jong, Leiden: E. J. Brill, 1969

Lusus Serius: or Serious Passe-time, A Philosophical Discourse concerning the Superiority of Creatures under Man, London: Humphrey Moseley and Thomas Heath, 1654

Symbola aureae mensae, Frankfurt: Lucas Jennis, 1617

Maria Prophetissa, 'Excerpts from the dialogue of Maria the Prophetess, the sister of Moses and Aron ... with a certain philosopher named Aros', trans. Raphael Patai, 'Maria the Jewess – founding mother of alchemy', *Ambix* 29 (1982), 192

Marlowe, Christopher, *The Complete Plays*, edited by J. B. Steane (1969), Harmondsworth: Penguin Books, 1986

The Marrow of Alchemy, see Philalethes

Martels, Z. R. W. M. von (ed.), *Alchemy Revisited: Proceedings of the International Conference on the History of Alchemy at the University of Groningen 17–19 April, 1989*, Leiden: E. J. Brill, 1990

Marvell, Andrew, *Miscellaneous Poems* (1681), facsimile reprint, Menston: Scolar Press, 1969

The Poems and Letters of Andrew Marvell, edited by H. M. Margoliouth, third edition, revised by Pierre Legouis with the collaboration of E. E. Duncan-Jones, 2 vols., Oxford: Clarendon Press, 1971

The Works of Andrew Marvell, edited by Thomas Cooke, London: E. Curll, 1726

Mazzeo, J. A., 'Notes on John Donne's alchemical imagery', in Mazzeo, *Renaissance and Seventeenth Century Studies*, 60–8

Renaissance and Seventeenth Century Studies, New York: Columbia University Press, 1964

Mead, G. R. S., see Hermes Trismegistus

Medicina practica, see William Salmon

Mendelsohn, J. Andrew, 'Alchemy and politics in England 1649–1665', *Past and Present* 135 (May 1992), 30–78

Merkel, Ingrid, see Allen G, Debus

Meun, Jean de (pseud.), 'The Alchimyst's Answere to Nature', translated by William Backhouse (1644), Bodleian Library MS Ashmole 58, ff. 50r–67r, *c*. 1500 (printed in Robert Schuler, *Alchemical Poetry 1575–1700*, 171–93)

'Planctus Naturae: The Complaint of Nature against the Erronious Alchymist', translated by William Backhouse (1644) Bodleian Library MS Ashmole 58, ff. 27r–48v, *c*. 1500 (printed in Robert

Schuler, *Alchemical Poetry 1575–1700*, 133–59)

Milton, John, *John Milton: Complete Poems, Of Education, Areopagitica*, edited by Gordon Campbell, Everyman, London and New York: Dent, 1993

Paradise Lost, edited by Alastair Fowler (1971), London and New York: Longman, 1991

Mödersheim, Sabine, 'Mater et Matrix. Michael Maiers alchimistische Sinnbilder der Mutter', in *Mutter und Mütterlichkeit. Wandel und Wirksamkeit einer Phantasie in der deutschen Literatur*. Festschrift für Verena Ehrich-Haefeli, herausgegeben von Irmgard Roebling und Wolfram Mauser, Würzburg: Verlag Koenigshausen und Neumann, 1996

Moran, Bruce, *The Alchemical World of the German Court: Occult Philosophy and Chemical Medicine in the Circle of Moritz of Hessen*, Stuttgart: Franz Steiner, 1991

More, Henry, *The Second Lash of Alazonomastix*, Cambridge, 1651

Morienus, *A Testament of Alchemy*, edited and translated by Lee Stavenhagen, Hanover, New Hampshire: University Press of New England, 1974

Musgrove, S., 'Herrick's alchemical vocabulary', *Aumla* 46 (1976), 240–65

Mylius, Johann, *Basilica philosophica*, in *Opus medico-chymicium: continens tres tractatus, sive basilicas: quorum prior inscribitur Basilica medica. Secundus Basilica chymica. Tertius Basilica philosophica*, Frankfurt: Lucas Jennis, 1618–20

Philosophia reformata, Frankfurt: Lucas Jennis, 1622

Mylius, Johann, see Adam McLean

Nabokov, Vladimir, *Pale Fire*, New York: Putnam, 1962

Nashe, Thomas, *Strange Newes, Of the intercepting certaine Letters, and a Convoy of Verses, as they were going Privilie to Victuall the Low Countries* (1592), in *The Works of Thomas Nashe*, edited by Ronald B. Mc Kerrow, 5 vols., London, 1904, vol. I

Newman, William R., *Gehennical Fire: The Lives of George Starkey, an American Alchemist in the Scientific Revolution*, Cambridge, Massachusetts: Harvard University Press, 1994

'Prophecy and alchemy: the origin of Eirenaeus Philaethes', *Ambix* 37 (1990), 97–115

Newman, William, see Geber

Newton, Isaac, '*Commentarium* on the *Emerald Tablet*', Keynes MS 28, King's College, Cambridge, see Betty Jo Teeter Dobbs, *The Janus Faces of Genius*, 275–7

'Out of La Lumière sortant des Tenebres', Yahuda MS Var. 1, Newton MS 30, Jewish National and University Library Jerusalem, and Babson MS 414B, The Sir Isaac Newton Collection, Babson College Archives, Babson Park, Massachusetts, see Betty Jo Teeter Dobbs, *The Janus Faces of Genius*, 280–7

'Praxis', Babson MS 420, part, The Isaac Newton Collection, Babson College Archives, Babson Park, Massachusetts, see Betty Jo Teeter Dobbs, *The Janus Faces of Genius*, 296–305

'Sententiae notabilis' see F. Sherwood Taylor, 'An alchemical work by Sir Isaac Newton'

Nicholl, Charles, *The Chemical Theatre*, London: Routledge and Kegan Paul, 1980

The Creature in the Map: A Journey to Eldorado, New York: William Morrow, 1995

Norton, Samuel, *Alchymiae Complementum et perfectio*, Casparius Rotelius, Frankfurt: Guilielmus Fitzerius, 1630

Norton, Thomas, *Ordinal of Alchemy*, edited by John Reidy, Early English Text Society, London: Oxford University Press, 1975

The Ordinall of Alchimy, in Elias Ashmole (ed.), *Theatrum chemicum Britannicum*, 2–106

Ovid (Publius Ovidius Naso), *Metamorphoses*, translated by Frank Justus Miller, 2 vols., Loeb Classical Library, London: William Heinemann, 1977

Paracelsus (Theophrastus Bombastus von Hohenheim), *His Aurora and Treasure of the Philosophers*, London: Giles Calvert, 1659

The Hermetic and Alchemical writings of Aureolus Philippus Theophrastus Bombast of Hohenheim, called Paracelsus the Great, translated by A. E. Waite (1894), 2 vols., London: Watkins, 1924

Nine Books of the Nature of Things, see Michael Sendivogius, *A New Light of Alchymie*, 1–145

Paracelsus his Archidoxis: comprised in ten books, translated by J. H. Oxon, London: printed for W. S. 1661

Paracelsus: Selected Writings, edited by Jolande Jacobi, translated by Norbert Guterman, Bollingen Series XXVIII, Princeton, New Jersey, 1951

Patai, Raphael, *The Jewish Alchemists: A History and Source Book*, Princeton University Press, 1994

'Maria the Jewess – founding mother of alchemy', *Ambix* 29 (1982), 177–97

Pearce the Black Monke upon the Elixir, in Elias Ashmole (ed.), *Theatrum chemicum Britannicum*, 269–74

Pernety, A. J., *Dictionnaire Mytho-Hermetique* (1758), facsimile reprint, Milan: Arché, 1971

Les Fables Egyptiennes et Grecques (1758), 2 vols., facsimile reprint, Milan: Arché, 1971

Philalethes, Eirenaeus, *Ripley Reviv'd: or an Exposition upon Sir George Ripley's Hermetico-Poetical Works*, London: William Cooper, 1678

The Three Treatises: The metamorphosis of Metals; A Short Vade Mecum to the Celestial Ruby; The Fount of Chemical Truth, in *Hermetic Museum*, 227–69

Cosmopolita, *Secrets Reveal'd: or an Open Entrance to the Shut-Palace of the King*, London: William Cooper, 1669

Philoponos, *The Marrow of Alchemy, Being an Experimental Treatise discovering the secret and most hidden Mystery of the Philosophers Elixir*, London: Edward Brewster, 1654

Philalethes, Eugenius (pseudonym), see Thomas Vaughan

Phillips, Edward, *The New World of English Words*, London: Nathaniel Brooke, 1658

The Philosopher's Stone in *Collectanea Chymica*, 90–110

Philosophia maturata: an Exact Piece of Philosophy containing the Practick and Operatives part thereof in gaining the Philosophers Stone, published by Lancelot Colson, London: G. Sawbridge, 1662

Piccolini, Sabina and Rosario, *La Biblioteca degli Alchimisti*, Padua: Franco Muzzio Editore, 1996

Pontanus, John, *The Epistle of John Pontanus*, in Nicolas Flamel, *His Exposition of the Hieroglyphicall Figures*, 237–47

Epistle upon the Mineral Fire; otherwise called, The Philosophers Stone, in Raphael Iconius Eglinus, *An Easie Introduction to the Philosophers Magical Gold*, 92–6

Pope, Alexander, *Alexander Pope*, edited by Pat Rogers, Oxford University Press, 1993

Porta, Giovanni Baptista della, *De distillatione Lib IX*, Rome: Rev. Camera Apostolica, 1608

Powell, Anthony, *Temporary Kings*, London: Heinemann, 1973

'Praetiosum Donum Dei' (sixteenth century), University of Glasgow Library, Ferguson MS 148

Pritchard, Alan, *Alchemy: A Bibliography of English-Language Writings*, London: Routledge and Kegan Paul, 1980

Rabelais, François, *Gargantua and Pantagruel* (1532), translated by J. M. Cohen, Harmondsworth: Penguin Books, 1995

Raleigh, Sir Walter, *The History of the World* (1614), in *The Works of Sir Walter Ralegh*, edited by William Oldys, 8 vols., Oxford University Press, 1829

Rattansi, P. M., 'Alchemy and natural magic in Raleigh's *History of the World*', *Ambix* 13 (1965), 122–38

'The Helmontian–Galenist controversy in Restoration England', *Ambix* 12 (1964), 1–23

'Paracelsus and the puritan revolution', *Ambix* 11 (1963), 24–32

Read, John, *The Alchemist in Life, Literature and Art*, London: Nelson, 1947

Prelude to Chemistry, London: Bell, 1936

Through Alchemy to Chemistry, London: Bell, 1957

Regardie, Israel, *The Philosopher's Stone*, St Paul, Minnesota: Llewellyn Publications, 1970

Ripley, Sir George, *The Bosome Book of Sir George Ripley*, in *Collectanea chymica*, 101–24

'Cantilena', see 'Incipit tractatulus de phenice sive de Lapide philosophico', and F. Sherwood Taylor, 'George Ripley's Song'

The Compound of Alchymie (1591) in Elias Ashmole (ed.), *Theatrum chemicum Britannicum*, 107–93

'Emblematicall Scrowle', Ashm. Rolls 53 A. 1530 and 52. A. 1535, Bodleian Library

'Emblematicall Scrowle', British Library, Additional MS 5025

Verses belonging to an Emblematicall Scrowle, in Elias Ashmole (ed.), *Theatrum chemicum Britannicum*, 375–9

'The Vision of Sr: George Ripley', in Elias Ashmole (ed.), *Theatrum chemicum Britannicum*, 374

Ripley, Sir George, see Eirenaeus Philalethes, *Ripley Reviv'd*

Roberts, Julian, and Andrew G. Watson (eds.), *John Dee's Library Catalogue*, London: The Bibliographical Society, 1990

Roberts, Gareth, *The Mirror of Alchemy: Alchemical Ideas and Images in Manuscripts and Books from Antiquity to the Seventeenth Century*, London: The British Library, 1994

Rosarium philosophorum, in *De Alchimia opuscula complura veterum philosophorum … Rosarium philosophorum Secunda pars alchimiae de lapide philosophico vero modo praeparando*, Frankfurt: Cyriacus Jacobus, 1550

The Rosary of the Philosophers, see Adam McLean

Rosenberg, Bruce A., '*Annus Mirabilis* distilled', *PMLA* 79 (1964), 254–8

Rosencreutz, Christian (pseudonym), see Johann Valentin Andreae

Rousseau, Jean-Jacques, *The Confessions* (1781), translated by J. M. Cohen, Harmondsworth: Penguin Books, 1953

Rudrum, Alan, see Thomas Vaughan

Ruland, Martin, *Lexicon alchemiae, sive Dictionarium alchemisticum*, Frankfurt: Palthenus, 1612

A Lexicon of Alchemy (1612), translated by A. E. Waite (1893), London: John Watkins, 1964 (all page references in the text are to this edition)

St Dunstan, *Dunstan of the Stone of the Philosophers; with the Experiments of Rumelius of New-Market*, in *Philosophia maturata*, 82–92

'A Treatise of the most great Lord and Philosoph: Dunstan, Bishop of Canterbury: Concerning the Philosopher's Stone', University of Glasgow, Ferguson MS 9

St Nicholas, Thomas, see H. Neville Davies

Salmon, Guillaume, *Dictionaire Hermetique* (1695), facsimile reprint, Paris: Gutenberg Reprints, 1979

Salmon, William, *Medicina Practica with the Clavis Alchymiae*, London: John Harris and Thomas Howkins, 1692

Sandys, George, *A Relation of a Iourney begun An: Dom: 1610. Foure Books. Containing a description of the Turkish Empire, of Aegypt, of the Holy Land, of the Remote parts of Italy, and Ilands adioyning* (1615), facsimile reprint, Amsterdam: Theatrum Orbis Terrarum, 1973

Sawtre, John, *The booke … concerning the Philosophers Stone*, in *Five Treatises of the Philosopher's Stone .., By the paines and care of H. P.*, London: John Collins, 1652, 17–46

Schuler, Robert M., 'Some spiritual alchemies of seventeenth century England', *Journal of the History of Ideas* 41 (1980), 293–318

'William Blomfild, Elizabethan alchemist', *Ambix* 20 (1973), 75–87

Schuler, Robert M. (ed.), *Alchemical Poetry 1575–1700 from Previously Unpublished Manuscripts*, New York: Garland, 1995

Three Renaissance Scientific Poems, Texts and Studies, *Studies in Philology* 75 (1978)

'Secrets Disclosed', University of Glasgow, Ferguson MS 238

Sendivogius, Michael, 'A Dialogue of the Allchymist and Sulphur', British Library MS Sloane 3637, ff. 81r–93v, *c*. 1610 (printed in Robert Schuler, *Alchemical Poetry 1575–1700*, 514–31)

A New Light of Alchymie (including Paracelsus, *Nine Books of the Nature of Things*, 1–145), translated by J. F. M. D., London: Thomas Williams, 1650

'The Philosophicall Aenigma', British Library MS Sloane 3637, ff. 71r–80r, *c*. 1610 (printed in Robert Schuler, *Alchemical Poetry 1575–1700*, 496–507)

Shakespeare, William, *Shakespeare's Sonnets*, edited by Stephen Booth, New Haven: Yale University Press, 1977

William Shakespeare: The Complete Works, edited by Stanley Wells and Gary Taylor, Oxford: Clarendon Press, 1988

Shirley, John W., 'The scientific experiments of Sir Walter Ralegh, the Wizard Earl, and the Three Magi in the Tower 1603–17', *Ambix* 4 (1949–51), 52–66

Shumaker, Wayne, *Natural Magic and Modern Science: Four Treatises 1590–1657*, Medieval and Renaissance Texts and Studies, vol. 63, New York, Binghamton: MRTS, 1989

The Occult Sciences in the Renaissance: A Study in Intellectual Patterns, Berkeley: University of California Press, 1972

Sidney, Sir Philip, *Selected Poems*, edited by Katharine Duncan-Jones, Oxford: Clarendon Press, 1973

Singer, Dorothy Waley, *Catalogue of Latin and Vernacular Manuscripts in Great Britain and Ireland dating from before the XVI Century*, 3 vols., Brussels: Union Académique Internationale, 1928–31

Sirc, Susan, 'Emblematic and alchemical imagery in Goethe's poems "Auf dem See" and "Herbstgefühl"', in Alison Adams (ed.), *Emblems in Glasgow*, 134–61

The Six Keys of Eudoxus, in Israel Regardie, *The Philosopher's Stone*

Skea, Ann, *Ted Hughes: The Poetic Quest*, Armidale: University of New England Press, 1994

Sloane MS 3631, British Library (an anonymous treatise beginning, 'I have in my two preceding tracts so manifestly declared that art which was kept to secret by the ancient philosophers')

Smith, Charlotte Fell, *John Dee (1527–1608)*, London: Constable, 1909

Smith, Pamela H., *The Business of Alchemy*, Princeton University Press, 1994

Spenser, Edmund, *The Works of Edmund Spenser: A Variorum Edition*, edited by Edwin Greenlaw, F. M. Padelford, C. G. Osgood *et al*., 10 vols., Baltimore: Johns Hopkins University Press, 1932–57

Srigley, Michael, *Images of Regeneration: A Study of Shakespeare's 'The Tempest' and its Cultural Background*, Acta Universitatis Upsaliensis, Uppsala: Studia Anglistica Upsaliensia 58, 1985

Stolcius, Daniel, *Viridarium chimicum* (1624), translated into French with a commentary by Bernard Husson, Paris: Librairie de Médicis, 1975

Synesius, *The true book of the Learned Synesius a Greek Abbot taken out of the Emperour's Library, concerning the Philosopher's Stone*, in Basil Valentine, *His Triumphant chariot of antimony*, 161–76

Taylor, F. Sherwood, 'An alchemical work of Sir Isaac Newton', *Ambix* 5 (1956), 59–84

The Alchemists: Founders of Modern Chemistry (1951), St Albans: Paladin, 1976

'George Ripley's Song', *Ambix* 2 (3–4), 1946, 177–81 (see Sir George Ripley, 'Cantilena')

Theatrum chemicum, Strasbourg: Lazarus Zetzner, vols. 1–4, 1659, vol. 5, 1660; vol. 6, 1661

Theatrum chemicum Britannicum, see Elias Ashmole

Thorndike, Lynn, *A History of Magic and Experimental Science*, 8 vols., New York: Columbia University Press, 1923–58

Thynne, Francis, see 'Incipit tractatulus de phenice sive de Lapide philosophico'

Topsell, Edward, *The Historie of Foure-Footed Beastes*, London: William Jaggard, 1607

Trevisan, Bernard, 'The Fourth Part of the Book of Bernard, Count of Marchia Trevisana, of the Practise of the Philosophick Stone', British Library MS Sloane 3641, ff. 29r–34r, ?fifteenth century (printed in Robert Schuler, *Alchemical Poetry 1575–1700*, 446–58)

A Singular Treatise of Bernard Count Trevisan concerning the Philosophers Stone, in *Collectanea chymica*

Trismosin, Salomon, *Aureum vellus oder Guldin Schatz und Kunstkammer*, Rorschach am Bodensee, 1598

Splendor Solis (1582), London: Kegan Paul, Trench and Trubner, 1920

The Turba Philosophorum or Assembly of the Sages (tenth-century Arabic), translated by A. E. Waite (1896), New York: Samuel Weiser, 1973

Turner, James, *The Politics of Landscape: Rural Scenery and Society in English Poetry 1630–1660*, Oxford: Basil Blackwell, 1979

Tymme, Thomas, *A Light in Darkness which illumineth for all the 'Monas hieroglyphica' of the famous and profound Dr John Dee, discovering Natures closet and revealing the true Christian secrets of Alchimy*, Oxford: New Bodleian Library, 1963

Valentine, Basil, *Azoth*, Paris, 1624

Practica, withe Twelve Keys, in *Hermetic Museum*, ed A. E. Waite, I, 316–57

His Triumphant Chariot of Antimony . . . with the true book of the learned Synesius, with Annotations of Theodore Kirkringius (1678), edited by L. G. Kelly, New York: Garland, 1991

Vaughan, Henry, *The Works of Henry Vaughan*, edited by L. C. Martin, 2 vols., Oxford: Clarendon Press, 1914

Vaughan, Thomas, *The Works of Thomas Vaughan*, edited by Alan Rudrum, Oxford: Clarendon Press, 1984

The Works of Thomas Vaughan, edited by A. E. Waite, New York: University Books, 1969

Ventura, Laurentius, *De ratione conficiendi lapidis*, in *Theatrum chemicum*, 2: 215–312

Vickers, Brian (ed.), *Occult and Scientific Mentalities in the Renaissance*, Cambridge University Press, 1984

'Visio Arislei', in *Artis auriferae*, 1: 146–54

Vitruvius, *Ten Books on Architecture*, translated by Morris Hicky Morgan (1914), New York: Dover, 1960

Vreeswijk, Goossen van, *De Goude Leeuw, of den Asijn der Wysen*, Amsterdam: printed for the author, 1675

De Goude Son, Amsterdam: printed for the author, 1675

Waite, A. E., see: *Hermetic Museum;* Edward Kelly, *Two excellent Treatises;* Martin Ruland, *A Lexicon of Alchemy;* Paracelsus, *The Hermetic and alchemical Writings of Paracelsus; Turba philosophorum;* Thomas Vaughan, *The Works of Thomas Vaughan*

Warner, William, *Albion's England*, in Alexander Chalmers (ed.), *The Works of the English Poets, from Chaucer to Cowper*, 21 vols., London: J. Johnson, 1810

Westfall, Richard S., 'Alchemy in Newton's library', *Ambix* 31 (1984), 97–101

'Isaac Newton's Index Chemicus', *Ambix* 22 (1975), 174–85

Never at Rest. A Biography of Isaac Newton, Cambridge University Press, 1980

White, David Gordon, *The Alchemical Body; Siddha Traditions in Medieval India*, Chicago: University of Chicago Press, 1996

Wilding, Michael, *Aspects of the Dying Process*, St Lucia: University of Queensland Press, 1972

This is for You, Sydney: Angus and Robertson, 1994

Willard, Thomas, 'Alchemy and the Bible', in *Centre and Labyrinth: Essays in Honour of Northrop Frye*, ed. Eleanor Cook *et al.*, Toronto: University of Toronto Press, 1983, 115–27

Wither, George, *A Sudden Flash* (London, 1657) (Hazlitt no. 63), in *Miscellaneous Works of George Wither*, Publications of the Spenser Society, Issue no. 13, vol. 2, printed for the Spenser Society, 1872

Wodehouse, P. G., *The Heart of a Goof* (1926), Harmondsworth: Penguin Books, 1988

Thank You, Jeeves!, London: Four Square, 1963

Yates, Frances, *Giordano Bruno and the Hermetic Tradition*, London: Routledge and Kegan Paul, 1964

The Occult Philosophy in the Elizabethan Age, London: Routledge and Kegan Paul, 1979

The Rosicrucian Enlightenment (1972), St Albans: Paladin, 1975

Yourcenar, Marguerite, *The Abyss*, New York: Farrar, Straus and Giroux, 1976

Zachaire, Denis, 'The third part of the Work of Dionysius Zacharias concerning the Practice of the Divine Work', British Library Sloane MS 3641, ff. 20r–23v, 1567 (printed in Robert Schuler, *Alchemical Poetry 1575–1700*, 435–42)

Zoroaster's Cave, in Raphael Iconius Eglinus, *An Easie Introduction to the Philosophers Magical Gold*, 57–91

Zosimos of Panopolis, 'On Divine Virtue', in *Alchemy: Pre-Egyptian Legacy, Millennial Promise*, edited by Richard Grossinger, 7–10

Index of alchemical and literary authors

Authors are indexed here under the head words of the articles in which they are cited. Books commonly known by a title rather than by an author's name are listed by title with a cross reference to the author or putative author.

A

Abraham Eleazar (n.d.): **cross; griffin; well**

Abu'L-Qasim, Muhammad Ibn Ahmad (thirteenth century): **east and west; inversion; mountains; prima materia; rock; tears**

Ackroyd, Peter (1949–): **homunculus**

Agli, Nicola d'Antonio degli (fifteenth century): **castle**

Agnelli, Giovanni Baptista: *see* Baptista Lambye

'Alchimistiche Manuskript' (1550): **flowers**

'The All-wise Doorkeeper' (in *HM*) (1678): **Moses**

Altus (seventeenth century): **radical humidity; sheets**

Amis, Kingsley (1922–95): **homunculus**

Andreae, Johann Valentin (1586–1654): **ash; bath; beheading; Bird of Hermes; chemical wedding; cibation; Cupid; education; egg; feathers; griffon; head; homunculus: imbibation; mould; nigredo; orphan; paste; philosophical child; ship; theatre; unicorn; virgin; worm**

Andrewes, Abraham (n.d.): see *The Hunting of the Green Lion*

Anthony, Francis (1550–1623): **aurum potabile**

The Arcanum (in *FC*) (1650) (by Jean d'Espagnet): **abyss; labyrinth**

Aristeus Pater (*c.* 1600): **boil; nest**

Arnold of Villanova (*c.* 1240–1311): **adrop; cucurbite; garden; nose; Saturn; worm**

Artephius (?twelfth century): **albedo; aqua vitae; ash; bath; black; boil; chemical wedding; colours; conversion; cream; decoction; dew; dross; dye; faeces; fire; flowers; gander; glass; incest; inversion; laton; lead; liquefaction; multiplication; projection; smell; snow; sol niger; solve et coagula; vinegar; virgin's milk; white stone; women's work; womb**

Artis auriferae quam chemiam vocant (1593): **art and nature**

Ashb. MS 1166, Bibliotheca Medicea-Laurenziana, Florence (fifteenth century): **tower**

Ashmole, Elias (1617–92): **Adam; chemist; grain; Hermes tree; labyrinth; limation; philosopher; projection; theatre; transmutation**

Astell, Mary (1666–1731): **conversion; red elixir**

Aubrey, John (1626–97): **still**

D

G

Geber (*fl.* Middle Ages): **calx; furnace; Geber's cooks; gold and silver; imbibation; prima materia; snow; sulphur; Venus; womb**

The Glory of the World (in HM) (1678): **children's piss; inverted tree; ludus puerorum; marble; mountains; philosophical child; pumpkin; rock**

Goethe, Johann Wolfgang von (1749–1832): **calcination; homunculus**

'The Golden Rotation', Sloane MS 1881, British Library (seventeenth century): **chemical wedding; liquefaction; magnesia; red elixir**

The Golden Tract (in HM) (1678) (by Hermes Trismegistus): **antimony; dew; flood; garden; incest; leprosy; ludus puerorum; melancholia; menstruum; Mercurius; philosopher's stone; red earth; red servant; rose (white); sand; salt, sulphur** and mercury; **solve et coagula; tower**

Gower, John (?1330–1408): **multipliers; rust**

Greverius, Jodovicus (n.d.) (in ZC, 1667): **cloud; oval; salamander**

H

Hall, John (1627–56): **fixation**

Hall, Joseph (1574–1656): **distillation and sublimation; dung; grain**

'Handbucht ... Universal Tinctur', Ferguson MS 64, University of Glasgow (seventeenth century): **Ethiopian; peacock's tail; red lion; swan**

Happelius, Nicolaus (Raphael Iconius Eglinus, 1559–1622): **glue**

Hartlib, Samuel (d. 1662): **black**

Harvey, Gabriel (*c.* 1550–1631): **eagle; iatrochemistry; toad**

Hastings, Lucy (seventeenth century): **crucible; rust**

Helvetius, John Frederick (1625–1709): **chariot of Phaethon; metamorphosis; volatile**

Herbert, George (1593–1633): **calcination**

Hermes Trismegistus (legendary Egyptian sage): **Apollo; colours; Emerald Table; Hermes Trismegistus; Moses; vulture** (see also *Hermetis Trismegisti tractatus aureus* and *The Golden Tract*)

'Hermetick Raptures' (*c.* 1700): **caduceus; Hermes Trismegistus; philosopher; Venus**

Hermetis Trismegisti tractatus aureus (in MP) (1692): **beheading; colours; crow; lute; stream; vulture**

Herrick, Robert (1591–1674): **bee; children's piss; congelation; cream; divorce; honey; incest; liquefaction; lute; oak; orphan; red elixir; stream; vial**

Hester, John (sixteenth century): **iatrochemistry**

Hoghelande, Theobald de (sixteenth century): **grapes; red powder**

Hortulanus (n.d.): **creation; Emerald Table; grain; Hermes Trismegistus; thick and thin**

Houpreght, John Frederick (*fl.* mid seventeenth century): **tears**

Hughes, Ted (1930–): **crucible**

cervus fugitivus; deer; philosopher's stone; phoenix; salamander; unicorn

Lambye, Baptista (Giovanni Baptista Agnelli) (sixteenth century):
cervus fugitivus; golden fleece

Le Fevre, Nicaise: *see* Fevre

Liber sapientiae (in *TCB*) (1652): nest

Lock, Benjamin (sixteenth century): albedo; bed; citrinitas; crystal;
fishes' eyes; green lion; opus circulatorium; peace and strife;
pearls; red elixir; rubedo; sperm; white elixir; wind

Lock, Humphrey (seventeenth century): rubedo

Lodge, Thomas (1558–1625): cervus fugitivus; crow; dragon; eagle

Lull, Ramon (*c.* 1235–1316) (*see also* 'Opera chemica'): alembic; aqua
ardens; ash; coal; faeces; ferment; menstruum; prima
materia; sulphur

Luther, Martin (1483–1546): decoction

Lyly, John (?1554–1606): angels; ash; crosslet; cucurbite; fire; lead;
multiplication: quicksilver; rubedo; sal ammoniac

M

Maier, Michael (1566 or 1568 – 1622): ablution; abortion; amber; art
and nature; Atalanta; beheading; bird; boil; cock and hen;
coral; dog and bitch; eagle; east and west; Emerald Table;
ferment; fruit; garden; gold and silver; green lion; house;
Jupiter; king; laton; laundering; Mars; Mercurius; metamorphosis; Naaman the leper; Nile; philosophical tree; sapientia;
Saturn; sheets; snow; sun and shadow; sweat; toad; virgin's
milk; vulture; watering; weaponry; white foliated earth;
wind; wolf; women's work; womb; worm

Maria Prophetissa (Mary the Jewess, ?second or third century AD):
bain-marie; furnace; gum; inversion; philosophical tree;
Solomon; solve et coagula

Marlowe, Christopher (1564–93): philosopher's stone

Marvell, Andrew (1621–78): bird; cervus fugitivus; chemic; congelation; dew; doctrine of signatures; dye; Elysian Fields; fifth
element; fixation; glass; glue; harvest; hermaphrodite;
house; iatrochemistry; inverted tree; Nile; prima materia;
return; rubedo; serpent; stream; theatre; transmutation;
winnow

Mayerne, Theodore Turquet de (1573–1655): iatrochemistry

Melchior Cibinensis (*fl.* 1490): Ethiopian

Melville, Elizabeth, Lady Culross (*fl.* early seventeenth century): dross

Meun, pseudo-Jean de (late sixteenth century): art and nature; womb

Milton, John (1608–74): amber; bind; boil; chemic; digestion; distillation and sublimation; gold and silver; Hermes
Trismegistus; Mercurius; mould; multiplication; philosopher's stone; prima materia; Proteus; red tincture; refine;
sun; tartarus; transubstantiate; vial

Moffet, Thomas (1553–1604): iatrochemistry

R

S

St Dunstan (tenth century): **aurum potabile; flowers; green lion; Hermes' seal; mountains; retort; rose (white); urine; virgin's milk; volatile**

St Nicholas, Thomas (1602–68): **separation**

Salmon, William (1644–1713): **abyss; autumn; colours; Jupiter; Venus; vulture**

Sandys, George (1578–1644): **purple tincture**

Sawtre, John (n.d.): **cucurbite**

'Scala philosophorum' (in *AA*) (1593): **eclipse**

Semita semtiae (in *AA*) (1593): **king; sperm; womb**

Sendivogius, Michael (1556 or 1566–1636 or 1646): **air; art and nature; Diana; distillation and sublimation; earth; Elysian Fields; fire; fruit; philosophical tree; rubedo; Saturn; sea; spots; stream; urine; water; watering**

Shakespeare, William (1564–1616): **alembic; bath; crocodile; eclipse; fragrance; grave; head; homunculus; king; laton; laundering; medicine; philosopher's stone; red tincture; return; ship; sun; sun and shadow; tincture**

Sidney, Sir Philip (1554–86): **beheading; furnace; lead**

Siebmacher, Johann Ambrosius (early seventeenth century): see *The Sophic Hydrolith*

Sloane MS 3631, British Library (n.d.): **chameleon; chaos; rarefaction; rock; spots; star**

The Sophic Hydrolith (in *HM*) (1678) (by Johann Siebmacher): **abortion; albedo; blood; eclipse; fishes' eyes: fountain; furnace; gum; Noah; philosopher's stone; phoenix; prima materia; raven; sea; tincture; venom**

Spenser, Edmund (*c.* 1552–99): **bellows; snow**

Starkey, George: (1628–65) *see* Eirenaeus Philalethes

Stolcius, Daniel (sixteenth–seventeenth century): **cibation; Diana; snow; watering**

Synesius (n.d.): **coral; distillation and sublimation; magnesia; night; red powder; red tincture; ruby; sable robe; spots; vinegar; virgin's milk**

T

Tauladanus, Robertus (?sixteenth century): **heaven**

Thornborough, John (1551–1641): **bellows**

The Tomb of Semiramis (in *CC*) (1684): **head; incest**

Topsell, Edward (1572–1625): **basilisk; bee**

Trevisan, Bernard (1406–90): **colours; dye; fountain; oak; Saturn**

Trismosin, Salomon (fifteenth–sixteenth century): **art and nature; black earth; children's piss; deer; dove; Ethiopian; golden fleece; head; inversion; jackdaw; king; laundering; ludus puerorum; nigredo; pearls; philosophical tree; sea; sheets; theatre; tree (truncated)**

Trithemius, Johann (1462–1519): **colours; fishes' eyes; pearls; theatre; white stone**

Turba philosophorum (tenth century): **Bird of Hermes; children's piss; dye; forty days; Moses; Red Sea**

Tymme, Thomas (d. 1620): **creation; leprosy**

V

Valentine, Basil (fifteenth century): **antimony; blood; cornerstone; fort; Mercurius; purple tincture; Saturn; swan; wolf; worm; vitriol**

Vaughan, Henry (1621–95): **white elixir**

Vaughan, Thomas (1621–65): **azure; beheading; crucible; eagle; Geber's cooks; generation; glue; green; Nile; pearls; sapientia; sperm; star; sweat; vial**

Ventura, Laurentius (?sixteenth century): **blood; crow's beak; inverted tree; Mercurius**

Visio Arislei (in *AA*) (1593): **king**

Vreeswijk, Goossen van (1626–post 1674): **ark; flood**

W

Warner, William (*c.* 1558–1609): **leprosy**

Wilding, Michael (1942–   ): **dross; twins**

Wither, George (1588–1667): **salt, sulphur and mercury**

Wodehouse, P. G. (1881–1975): **philosopher's stone**

Y

Yourcenar, Marguerite (1903–97): **abyss**

Z

Zachaire, Denis (b. 1510): **castle**

Zoroaster's Cave (in Eglinus, *An Easie Introduction*, 1667): **ablution; adrop; ash; azoth; chemical wedding; cibation; coal; colours; coral; crow; cucurbite; dew; flowers; grain; hell; Luna; magnesia; Mercurius; mortification; philosopher's stone; prima materia; putrefaction; salamander; Saturn; seed; Sol; solve et coagula; torture; wind**

Zosimos of Panopolis (third–fourth century): **furnace; philosopher's stone**